Tango and
the Political Economy
of Passion

Tango

and the
Political Economy
of Passion

Marta E. Savigliano

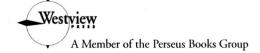

Westview
PRESS

A Member of the Perseus Books Group

Institutional Structures of Feeling

Copyright © 1995 by Marta E. Savigliano

Published in 1995 in the United States of America by Westview Press, Inc., 5500 Central Avenue, Boulder, Colorado 80301-2877, and in the United Kingdom by Westview Press, 36 Lonsdale Road, Summertown, Oxford OX2 7EW

Published by Westview Press, A Member of the Perseus Books Group

Library of Congress Cataloging-in-Publication Data
Savigliano, Marta.
    Tango and the political economy of passion / Marta E. Savigliano.
        p.   cm.—(Institutional structures of feeling)
    Includes bibliographical references and index.
    ISBN 0-8133-1637-5.—ISBN 0-8133-1638-3 (pbk.)
    1. Tango (Dance)—Social aspects.   2. Tango (Dance)—Social aspects—Argentina.   3. Sexuality in dance.   I. Title.   II. Series.
GV1796.T3S28   1995
784.18'885—dc20

94-32610
CIP

19 18 17 16 15 14 13 12 11

Printed and bound in the United States of America

 The paper used in this publication meets the requirements of the American National Standard for Permanence of Paper for Printed Library Materials z39.48-1984.

a mis abuelas
Angélica Martín de Savigliano y Etelvina Álvarez de Ahumada

Contents

Illustrations

Preface and Acknowledgments

Vuelvo al Sur
como se vuelve siempre al amor,
vuelvo a vos
con mi deseo, con mi temor.
Llevo el Sur
como un destino del corazón,
soy del Sur
como los aires del bandoneón.
Sueño el Sur,
inmensa luna, cielo al revés.
Busco al Sur,
el tiempo abierto y su después.
Quiero al Sur,
su buena gente, su dignidad;
siento el Sur
como tu cuerpo en la intimidad.

I return to the South
as one always returns to love,
I return to you
with my desire, with my fear.
I carry the South
as my heart's destiny,
I am of the South
like the moods of the *bandoneón.*
I dream the South,
immense moon, sky upside-down.
I search for the South,
the wide-open time and its afterwards.
I love the South,
her good people, their dignity;
I feel the South
like your body in intimacy.[1]

—*Vuelvo al Sur* (I Return to the South), 1988
Lyrics by Fernando E. Solanas
Music by Astor Piazzolla[2]

No *sudamericano*[3] would have asked me this question, but I am somewhere else. And precisely because today I am living somehow in some kind of exile—a transient's exile—the question came: "But, Marta, what is tango?"

I sat uncomfortably on that chair, in that office. Caught again. I had the distasteful hunch that I would do better talking about something else. How could I provide a brief yet nonenigmatic answer to this dance scholar's question? How could I respond in a simple and direct way without betraying the tango or trying her patience? I could give the "exotic" version of the tango. I know that one well. Perform exoticism. After being away from home for a while, I know how to do that. But would I please *decolonize* this self?

Tango and exile (in the sense of "being away from home" for whatever reason) are intimately associated.[4] On a personal level, it is more than common for any *argentino* living abroad to connect the experience of longing and nostalgia to the tango. It is a recurrent pattern, even for those of us who do not consider ourselves connoisseurs or fans of the tango, to be affected by the tango syndrome after being deprived for a while of our argentino "environment." The tango syndrome can affect one in various degrees: paying attention to the word "tango" whenever it is mentioned; reading whatever pops up about tango in newspapers and magazines or on posters; attending every tango performance we possibly can; recalling some fragments of lyrics in order to name puzzling situations we go through; viewing ourselves in the same shoes as some of the characters in old tango movies; and in some extreme cases, like my own, deciding to learn about it in a more or less systematic way. And we keep on telling ourselves, "I wouldn't be doing this if I were at home. ..."

Actually, when I left Argentina, friends and relatives warned me about this disease: "I hope the tango doesn't get you too soon ..."; "Don't even tell me when you catch the tango, I don't want to know about it. ..." And here I am, embarrassed, writing a whole book about the tango.

Tango is my womb and my tongue, a trench where I can shelter and resist the colonial invitations to "universalism," a warm, sad place in a "happy" space flooded by maniac denial, a stubborn fatalist mood when technocrats and theorists offer optimistic and seriously revised versions of "alternatives" for the Third World, an opportunistic metaphor to talk about myself and my stories as a "success" of the civilization-development-colonization of América Latina, and a strategy to figure out through the history of the tango a hooked-up story of people like myself. Tango is my changing, resourceful source of identity. And because I am where I am—outside—tango hurts and comforts me: "Tango is a sad thought that can be danced. ..."[5]

The history of tango is a history of exiles. The Sociedades de Negros, associated with the origins of the tango in the Río de la Plata region, re-created the rhythms and *ombligadas* of the African enslaved exiles; the *criollos* were moving out from the rural areas, holding a guitar in one hand and a knife in the other, to make space for themselves in the prosperous harbor city; the Spanish and Italian immigrants who populated the suburban slums of Buenos Aires, mostly economic exiles, danced in the streets to the precarious tango-times of the organ-grinder. Tango expressed exile, and it created it as well. The talented but poor tango musicians and dancers moved from Buenos Aires to Paris and New York, exiles in a reverse direction, in search of better luck; young French women followed argentino "dandies" and "beef barons" from Paris to Buenos Aires and ended up exiled, as professional *tangueras* and "hostesses" of the newly opened cabarets. The music, the lyrics, and the dance are witnesses to this process of simultaneous deterritorializations and have been strongly tinged with these intrusive and transgressive features. Race, class, ethnic, and erotic exiles cut the tango through and through from its very roots.

Tango crassly confirms the existence of the Other and the particulars of her Otherness. It expresses, performs, and produces exiles and alterity. Tango is simultaneously a ritual and a spectacle of traumatic encounters. Exile provokes both dramatic encounters and separations. Tango is more radically associated with the former. The history of the tango is a story of encounters between those who should never have met or between those who, having met, will remain forever disencountered. Brewing resentment, it is a stubborn story of impossible but fatal encounters, like the matching of pieces or mating of species that do not fit but will stick together. The tango is both a product and promoter of these hybrid events. Black and white, rich and poor, men and women, colonizer and colonized—each is brought much too close to the other; the tango embrace is dangerously tight. It proposes the violation of critical distances in such a way that the experience of tension and conflict becomes unavoidable.

Such is a story of tango. Such is my story—the story of this book: a stubborn story, to be sure, with many pieces that should not fit together but will not come apart. The experience has been fraught with tension. I have embraced conflicts even as I have avoided them; I have fled one conflict only to rush headlong into another. These pages are the result of my tangoing in and out of confrontations, widening and closing critical distances. Academic prose here, *ficciones femininas allí*. Too much rhyme and too many reasons. There are those whom I should never have encountered, but true to tango, I did. Some, *gracias a las diosas*, will be forever disencountered, and others, *ojalá*, will remain close, even over great distances. These are the *cariños entrañables* who made this experience of homelessness worthwhile to tango through.

My interest in tango was born out of disillusionment, pain, rage, and hunger to understand my role as a *latina* woman intellectual while studying for a doctoral degree in Hawai'i—a U.S. colony/state. Hawaiian politics gave me the opportunity to grasp the complexities of colonialism in an exploding, expansive way often blurred for me in the past by my entanglement in the everyday political strings of Argentina. Moreover, Hawai'i gave me the chance to meet Hawaiian women, local ("nonwhite") women, and Third World women with whom I shared colonized entanglements. Together we learned to rebel against nationalized identities, internationalized stereotyping (on the basis of race, ethnicity, religion, and all sorts of "mores and customs"), and universalized categorizations (of gender and class). What was agonistic and fatalistic for each of us individually turned out to be legitimate and promising when honestly shared. "Native" patriarchies have been our allies while facing "colonizers'" patriarchies and vice versa.

For creating a warm, receptive environment for what I had to say, I thank Ibrahim Aoudé, Aisha Ghaznavi, Susan Hippensteele, Adella Omori Islas, Masahide Kato, Saba Khattak, Pam Kido, Cindy Kobayashi, Gerry Kosasa-Terry, Maivan Clech Lam, David Liu, Sarita MacLeod, Ardalan Nikou, Raj Pandey, Nahua Patrinos, Berna-Lee Lehua Riveira, Salome Samou, Vidhu Singh, Teresia Teaiwa, and Hediana Utarti. Intellectual inspiration and personal, affective encouragement have gone hand in hand in the production of this book. Jeff Tobin instigated my intellectual boldness by following the writing process, word by word, along pages and shared dreams, with invaluable comments, delicious meals, passionate rewards, and witty celebrations; Farideh Farhi, my adviser and friend, provided me with innumerable insights, supported all my academic transgressions, and fed all my political dilemmas; Kathy Ferguson generously endured my intellectual questionings and challenged my views without imposing censorship; Bob Stauffer supported my unruly writing and questioned the politics of my intellectual "Third World" privileges from the beginning of this venture; Sankaran Krishna offered me all sorts of imaginative tips for sticking honestly to my project; Steve Goldberg engaged in such a profound reading of my drafts that I could never elude taking responsibility for each and every one of my statements. As outsiders from the field of political science, Steve Goldberg, Judy Van Zile, and Elisabeth Fowkes-Tobin helped tango images, dancing bodies, and lyrics speak politically to me.

I could not have tackled the case of tango in Japan without Joe Tobin's advice and assistance. He not only shared with me his knowledge of Japan but also accompanied me enthusiastically in the search for Japanese tangueros, acted as a translator, improvised tango steps in Japanese, and guided me, together with Janet Murakami, into tango clubs, music shops, and bookstores in Tokyo. I am deeply indebted to the following Japanese tango fans and artists for their attention, time, and thoughtful comments: Abo Ikuo, Eguchi Yuko, Higuchi Kazuko, Kanie Takeo, Kobayashi Taihei, Luis Komoriya, Kunieda Fukuko, Kyotani Koji, Kyotani Yuko, Nishimura Hideto, Oiwa Chizuko, Oiwa Isao, Oiwa Yoshihiro, Takahashi Masayoshi, Takahashi Teruko, Takashima Masako, Yamazaki Mieko, Yoneyama Eiko, and Yuzawa Sichi. I thank the Political Science Department at the University of Hawai'i-Mānoa for the Werner Levi Award for Doctoral Research, which allowed me to follow the tango to Japan.

For welcoming with enthusiasm and wise criticism my political introjections into the field of dance, I thank Susan Foster and Randy Martin. For sharing tango choreographic incursions with creativity, humor, and curiosity, I thank Susan Rose. I am grateful to my colleagues, the staff, and the students of the Department of Dance History and Theory at the University of California–Riverside, for giving me the opportunity to help launch a very special doctoral program. I thank as well the participants in the Choreographing History Seminar sponsored by the Humanities Research Institute, University of California–Irvine, for providing a stimulating and critical community. For warmly welcoming me back to anthropology (I never really left), I thank the faculty, staff, and students of the Anthropology Department at Rice University. A Rockefeller Fellowship for the Study of Culture at Rice allowed me to complete this book; I am *obrigada* to George Marcus for inviting me to apply and for urging me to call this book "done." I appreciate Steven Tyler's empathic and evocative reading of the last bits and pieces as the "whole" was freightfully taking shape. For their generous comments and warnings on an earlier version of the manuscript, I thank the readers for Westview Press, and I thank Gordon Massman, Connie Oehring, and Katherine Streckfus of Westview Press for their interest and expertise in turning my manuscript into this book. Christopher Coleman at UCLA University Research Library and Carlos Rivadulla at the Biblioteca del Congreso de la Nación lent me crucial assistance above and beyond the call of duty. *Mi agradecimiento* to Fred Ahrens, Soledad Kruger Gelles, Analía Vitale, Michelle Heffner, Cristina Bellelli, Arnold Tobin, Riselia Bezerra, Jamila Bargach, and Peter Adamczyk for following closely these last tango bookish steps, either e-mailistically or fully embodied.

For their generous advice and guidance, I appreciate the contributions of my *compatriotas* Bruno Cespi, Juan Carlos Copes, Eliseo Cutri, Jorge Dragone, Natalio Etchegaray, Horacio Ferrer, Aníbal Ford, Cayetano Francavilla, Natalia Gómez Hill, Nora Mazziotti, and Carlos Rivarola. *Mil gracias* to Mario R. Dos Santos, Jean B. Elshtain, Jeanne Laux, and Adriana Piscitelli for long-lasting intellectual dialogues and emotional empathy that reach far beyond the limits of this book. I also thank Glenda Avila, Rita Clasen, Sarita Torres, and Wolfgang Voss for exploring the tango bars in Buenos Aires with me. For their help and encouragement from a distance, including open arms for my eternal returns with Jeff to Argentina, I thank Luis Amaya, Jorge Azar, Cristina Bellelli, Noemí Castro, Mónica Francavilla, Ianina Grimblat, Elena Kujman, Graciela Maglie, Graciela Podestá, Sarita Torres, Analía Vitale, their *familias* and friends. For sharing my tango moods in foreign lands, I thank my brothers, Daniel and Eduardo Savigliano. And, for raising me up with a stubborn and defiant sense of dignity, I appreciate *desde lo más profundo* the painstaking endeavors of my parents, Martha Ahumada and Eduardo L. Savigliano.

Marta E. Savigliano

1
Introductions

(On the Micropolitics of Introducing)

I took some bad advice. I think I should blame my foot for it; for putting myself in this. (It is always the same big toe crawling imperceptibly into these holes without edges.) Anyway, now I'm stuck. Open the tango-box: "There is a story I want to tell but, every other instant, I'm overgrown by muteness. Because of sadness, because of love, because of powerlessness or absurd omnipotence, because of rage or solitude, because of so much pain, because of life itself and the death of others or even because of that in-between, when boredom tempts me like dryness in the mouth to stand in silence. Every other instant one feels like dying." Close the tango-box. I'll try to tell my story, scattered in pieces. Each piece is a tale with sketchy morals of its own. But there are some points in common, rather, some dots or, better said, some rebellious stains. Alright. Imprecise points of repetition. And every other instant the silence, overgrowing. Wind up the tango-box: "My foot, the wise one, this time said: 'Could you please try to *decolonize* yourself?'" The tango-box winds down. I wonder, why would you follow me through these pages? I know you did not expect me to address you like this. What kind of introduction is this? I can already sense some restlessness. I lower my voice and answer slowly: i'm ... trying ... to ... *decolonize* ... myself. I am tempted to apologize, to erase the whole thing and start all over again. Sorry for putting you in the spot, in my point, in the dot, in these stains.

An introduction should go like this:

Introduction

The purpose of this study is to contribute to the historical account of capitalism by adding a new dimension to the currently well-known Marxist and neo-Marxist depictions of its development. Through these pages I will entertain the thought qua hypothesis that a political economy of Passion has been occurring and that this economy has been juxtaposed and intertwined with the economies usually described on materialist and ideological grounds. A trackable trafficking in emotions and affects has paralleled the processes by which the core countries of the capitalist world system have extracted material goods and labor from, and

1

imposed colonial bureaucratic state apparatuses and ideological devices on, the Third World (periphery).

This imperialist circulation of feelings gave rise to an emotional capital—Passion—accumulated, recoded, and consumed in the form of Exotic Culture: "mysterious," "untamed," "wild," "primitive," "passionate." The emotional/expressive practices of the colonized have been isolated, categorized, and transformed into curious "cultural" patterns of behavior. The catalogue is vast and the specialties proliferate: Entries by "topic" (economy, kinship and marriage, religion, art, customs, etc.) and entries by "continent" (Southeast Asia, North Africa, Iberoamerica, the French Pacific, etc.) carefully follow a systematic logic of representation. Thus, "exotic" objects have been constituted by applying a homogenizing practice of exoticization, a system of exotic representation that commoditized the colonials in order to suit imperial consumption. In other words, peripheral-"exotic" Passion is molded in the shape of the world's core unfulfillable Desire. The colonizer constitutes his own "progressive" identity—Civilized, Enlightened, Democratic, Postmodern—on the basis of this confrontation with exotic, colonized (neo- and post- as well) Others. And the cycle of production, distribution, and consumption, including its "cyclic crises," continues: Exotic Passion, by (imperial) definition, is untamable and inexhaustible. Conversely, to the colonized-exotic-Other, this very allocation of passionateness provides both a locus of identity and a source of contestation vis-à-vis the colonizing-civilized-Desire—the Desire of and for the One.

The Exotic is not an item exclusively for the delight of the imperial West; it is in turn exported, in its new, colonized package—once modern, now postmodernized—to the Rest (including "Western" colonies such as Argentina, those from whom the "raw" emotionality was extracted in the first place). When exported to the (neo)colonies of "origin," practices of autoexoticism develop conflictively as a means of both adjusting to and confronting (neo)colonialism. Through these complex activities of autoexoticization carried out in the periphery's internal political settings, the exotic/exoticized representations end up becoming symbols of national identity. Such is the case of the *tango argentino*. Gender, class, race, religion, and sexuality as well as programmatic party politics are the main dimensions mobilized in the struggle to build independent yet colonized peripheral national identities: "exotic" in/dependent identities. The national-ness of the peripheral countries is simultaneously the product of the world's core demand for international, legitimate relations and the source of claims to substantive independence and self-determination. "Independent" nationalities are urged by the metropolitan powers when the need for an international market arises. International recognition is extended beyond statehood and bound territoriality to economic, political, and cultural independence. In terms of identity, the Passion of exotic others confirms the shape of the Imperialist One, but it overflows the borders of the one's Desire; conversely, Imperial Desire legitimates the passionateness of the other and naturalizes the Others' rebelliousness. Hence, in a neocolonial framing, the others are "primitive" and "barbarian," condemned to a second-class identity, an "uncivilized," incomplete identity in the process of "development" compared to the bold, superior, fully shaped Identity of the One. Note that the One is never an Other, even from the point of view of colonized others.

The capitalist production and consumption of the Exotic (exotic Passion) does not affect only those directly involved in hierarchical exchanges of cultural and emotional capital. Exoticism is an industry that requires distribution and marketing. Emotional capital must circulate, generating an ever-renewed anxiety over exclusion/inclusion. It survives by stirring the blood of up-until-then oblivious bodies, driving them into complicitous acknowledgments of each other. Thus, exoticism is also reproduced and amplified by the exotics among themselves as they practice exotic reciprocities looking through core/Western lenses: "Latinos," "orientals," "blacks," "tropical islanders," "Asians," and others relate to each other in already Western—even when decentered—exoticized terms. Exotic natives and exotic exiles/migrants/travelers meet in the West and at Westernized (neo- and post-) colonial settings, their representations already shaped by the mediation of a Western mirror. The imperialist West shapes the relations between the peripheral Rest into relationships among exotic Others, generating a new series of complex identity negotiations and struggles for relative positioning in the world vis-à-vis the core—now recognizable in its postmodern fragmentation.

The scandalous tour of the tango in the early twentieth century from Argentina and Uruguay to Paris, London, and New York, its final rage in Japan about the time of World War II, its blooming in Buenos Aires in the 1940s while secluded from the territories of the *aliados*, its sustained hold on followers in Medellín and on small clicks in Finland and Turkey, and its revival all over Europe via Broadway and South American exiles in the late 1970s and 1980s are examples of the complex occurrences giving life to the world economy of Passion. However, tango—like other popular music and dance forms—is not a mere mirror image of more relevant or decisive economic and political realities or just a reflection of necessary social functions. Tango has deflected its own incorporation into the world political economy of Passion as an exotic raw material and has simultaneously lured itself into co-option by conforming to various tastes regarding music and dance. These episodes, at different times and places, have involved the tango in the intricate process of constructing the *argentina* national identity—a process that should be traced within the musical/danceable dimension itself as well as at local and global levels of the world political economy. As Line Grenier and Jocelyne Guilbault observe, "The world political economy is not a force imposed from 'above' upon totally deprived individuals and groups. Rather, it is a complex set of institutions, social relationships and economic practices that are socially and historically mediated and that are the object of multiple differentiated actualizations by individuals and groups within their respective environment" (Grenier and Guilbault 1990: 389, paraphrasing Martín-Barbero). Mediating exclusion and inclusion, always attentive to the parameters of identity established by an imperial world political economy yet systematically giving contradictory results, tango seems to attempt an assimilation while fuming an ironic, underground, culturally specific resentment.

(On the Micropolitics of Reintroducing)

How am I doing? Now, that looks better, says my colonizer. My colonized self agrees with relief.

Note (and protest): Tango is not an example; it is the main ingredient in this exercise of decolonization. It is an inviting metaphor that asks theories to dance, corporealized in the specificity of sweaty, sensual, fully efforted bodies.

Reintroductions

In writing this book I have dealt with many conflicting voices: academized and poetic, orderly and chaotic, male-hegemonic and female-subversive, elitist and impoverished, collective and personal, totalizing and specific, deconstructed and reconstructive, white and mestizo, pragmatic and nostalgic, in English and in Spanish ... of the colonizer and of the colonized. These voices are my own internal dispute, but far from being a product of my delirious imagination, they speak to me impersonating different audiences of a mixed colonizer/colonized nature. I have not been able to avoid these conflicts by simply privileging one audience over another, by following my personal preferences, by pretending to address an outworldly homogeneous audience, or by bowing to some contesting power within the academic audience. Is this difficulty due to the nature of the topic I have chosen? Is it because of my positioning as a "Third World" female intellectual? Tango is a strong symbol of Argentinean national identity, a patriarchal and hegemonic representative of my country in that it privileges the popular culture of Buenos Aires over the rest of the provinces and the protagonist role of men over women. Class, racial, and generational issues intertwine with these aspects to further complicate tango's legitimacy to represent Argentina as a people. This controversy over national representation cannot be dealt with in the same ways "at home" and "abroad."

Although national identity is a historical matter of obsessive disputes among argentinos, the nature of the dispute changes dramatically when on non-argentino terrain. This shift is informed by a change of perspective that displaces internal, local contradictions in the presence of external, global threats to Argentinean identity as a whole/nation. Hence, argentinos situated in an international arena adopt tango as a shield against the dissolution of identity. Tango represents a particular sector of argentinos at home, but it assumes national representation abroad. Argentina becomes a nation and tango its symbol when the question of identity is at stake owing to international negotiations that involve issues of representation, legitimacy, and sovereignty (self-determination). Thus, tango shapes and mobilizes Argentine-ness when confronted with imperialist maneuvers and is activated as a national representation as it crosses over lines of identity formation. Tango as a symbol of nationality has no space of its own but holds an unbalanced, tense position teetering between independence and dependency, or—in the terms I use throughout these pages— between the colonized and the colonizer. This unsolved dispute is played out through tango, claimed by the colonized as "authentic," appropriated by the colonizer as "exotic."

Tango's suitability to these manipulative operations resides in its dual malleability as a "popular" and a "cultural" product. "Popular culture," as that which convokes and represents people collectively through commonality, as well as in whose interest these "people" and their "culture" are identified, is a fertile environment for highly politicized contestations. Authorship and ownership of popular culture are inherently hard to establish, and the content itself is incessantly re-created. Disputes over popular culture point precisely at what popular culture is all about: identity, the demarcation of differences carried out through struggles to establish for which "people" and in the name of what "culture" popular culture is practiced. Tango, as popular culture, is thus the battlefield/dancefloor and weapon/dance-step in and by which Argentinean identity is continuously redefined. Who the tango dancers are, where they dance, what tango style they perform in front of which tango audience: Such issues deal with gender, race, class, ethnicity, and imperialism, frequently in terms of sexuality, always in terms of power. It is in these dancing terms, tracing detailed specificities concerning the politics of tango moving bodies, that I have tried to understand the constitution of colonized and colonizer identities.

Through tango I have dealt with my own questionings as an Argentinean living transitorily abroad, exposed to an intellectual training that urged me to reshape my own identity. Tangoing to myself, I have tried to resist intellectual colonialism. Following tango's negotiations between the colonizer and the colonized, I recognized my own dealings. Reflecting on the disciplining/promotion to which I was subjecting myself in academia, I saw tango's process of disciplining/promotion in the hands of dance masters and spectacle entrepreneurs. Looking at tango's endless search for origins and authenticity, I came to understand the colonized nature of this attempt. Amazed at tango's colonizing appropriation through exoticism, I found myself transformed into an exotic object: colonized. Even more stunned by tango's achievements at home as a result of playing the exotic game, I put into question my own autoexoticism. And here I am, with the tango, attempting to decolonize myself.

This is the nature of this text—a text in the world, populated by so many audiences that my fear could only be overcome by my rush to finish: the argentino patriarchal audience, the one that knows and is emotionally invested in tango;

the North American academic audience worried about the scholarly relevance of my project; the Third World audience, hungry for anti-imperialist insights; the audiences whose fields and specialties I have transgressed; the audience made up of those who inspired me and whom I have since forgotten; and the factions within each of these audiences, more or less receptive to my concerns, more or less merciless and for contradictory reasons. I have not been able to choose one audience over another—despite all well-intentioned advice—in order to formulate in my mind a homogeneous audience-type to address. For this reason I speak in bursts, splashes, and puddles, opening windows to what I have expected to be major controversial knots engendered by the juxtaposition of tango and decolonization. The open web, that floor full of holes without edges, that underlies the whole "thing" is this controversy of putting together that which I cannot resolve, sunk, as I am, in the conflicts themselves.

In this chapter, the windows are responses to what I expect to be major disagreements regarding my method, my decolonization project, and, related to this, my identification/representation of Argentina as a colony.

In Chapter Two I try to disturb the stereotype of an exclusively sexual/eroticized image of tango by introducing class and race into the erotic game. The context is Argentina in the late nineteenth century, under rapid urbanization, massive migratory movements, and the incorporation into Western imperialism as a neocolony with a latino tinge.

Chapter Three is a depiction of the operation of colonialism through "exoticism," the exoticization of the Other, both Third Worlders and women. I attempt to historicize exoticism and thus to denaturalize the exotic identities attributed to peasants, the urban poor, and foreign Others. I see exoticism also as part of a display of imperial power among nationalities disputing hegemony at the core. The context is Europe, the main contenders France and England; the rise of the United States is merely insinuated since I concentrate on the period ending around World War I. The purpose is to situate tango among other exotic music and dance productions and to understand the specific ways in which the dance disciplining/promotion industry was operating.

Chapter Four is concerned with "autoexoticism." Tango's popularity in the main capitals of the world, and its acceptance, primarily by the foreign elites, as a modern "exotic" product, generated local scandals. I analyze the tango scandal in Argentina in terms of a complex dispute among local sectors over the legitimate representation of the nation. The participation of "respectable" women in an up-until-then immoral dance, due to the Parisian stylization of tango, was a turning point in tango's local history. The tangueros argentinos faced a paradox as they enjoyed the benefits of foreign and local exoticism while they resisted tango's appropriation and exotic disfigurations. Tango histories and studies emerge in this context, as attempts to recover origins and authenticity and thus to define Argentine-ness in anticolonial terms.

Chapter Five depicts the encounter of exotic Others, Japanese and argentinos, through the tango. I give a detailed account of the different currents—the already exoticized tango styles—through which tango arrived in Japan. I analyze the ways in which these competing French, English, and argentino tangos have been appropriated by the Japanese themselves as markers of internal social distinctions. Questions of identity are again at stake as I reflect on the presence of historically established Western parameters of exoticism always mediating between exoticized peripherals. The case of Japan is particularly controversial in this regard, given Japan's own history of imperialism and its current economic position at the core of world power.

Chapter Six is a series of tangos in prose—confessions, protests, laments, and desires—offered as concluding reflections. Third World women intellectuals and tango are drawn into mismatching analogies bridged by the presence of imperialism and patriarchy in both the academic and the popular dance and music spheres. Decolonization is depicted as a process of "unlearning" the exotic positions allocated to Third World women within recently developed intellectual practices. Tango, in this context, has proven to be a resourceful *compañero*, not in its patriarchal tone, but in its teachings on how to resist within the imperial dance. I conclude with a protesting hope. I question my responsibilities as an intellectual woman, appropriating the tools of the colonizer—in particular, what I call "postmodern" tools—to represent the colonized—the ones with whom I can identify and who might identify with me.

There is more than one thread to follow along this unstable web: colored threads caught in embroidery. Not one of these threads failed to slip through my fingers or lacks the vestiges of being cut by my teeth and, hesitantly, being inserted back through the needle's eye. There is no thread lacking that little knot that stubbornly reappears each time I forget that my grandmothers said the thread shouldn't be so long ... so ambitious. Perhaps I could have followed a rope more easily. But then I would have had to walk on it, suspended in mid-air, in the abstract. And I am not a good acrobat. So, tired of weaving and stitching, I imagined myself following tracks, closer to earth—on dusty feet, in sneakers, and in high heels, according to where they took me. I could say I encountered a labyrinth, but it wouldn't be true. A labyrinth has a monster, a god, or bait waiting for you somewhere. Sometimes I felt that colonialism plays all these parts. But labyrinths are too artificial. They are not part of the world. Either in a laboratory or on an mythical island, you know when you get into them and they are self-consciously sought to demonstrate courage, capacity, strength of will. Have I been lured like a mouse? No, I cannot claim such intrepid innocence. So, abandon the labyrinth idea. These are worldly roads, earthy paths, everyday walks of which I have become aware, by merely walking. But I did something else: snooping. This is what each chapter, and each section of each chapter, is about.

I have walked down the streets and peeked into the windows. I have crawled over the thresholds into the rooms and spotted the oddities in them. I was always driven to those boxes, drawers, and cases and opened them with different care: music boxes, glass jewelry boxes with precious lockets, jumping jacks, drawers full of treasured letters and exotic postcards, cases guarding photographs and diaries, retables, hidden altars, boxes with miniature dolls. ... They played and danced for me and I danced back, interrogating and interrogated. Exhausted, I turned around looking for fresh air, and driven by my snoopiness, instead of going back to the window through which I had entered, I was taken by the curtains. Over there. In pulling them, I found a scene opened up to me, like the world economy of Passion, and looking again, a puppet theater disclosed behind its tiny drapes, a sensual couple of ruffians dancing a tango. Suddenly, I could hear the roar, smell the bubbles behind my back, and turning around, I found myself in Paris, in a cabaret, in the middle of a midnight champagne-tango party. And once, I was asked by exotics to do my own exotic tango, in black and white, and I was an exotic among exotics, and it was Tokyo. Then, I knew it was time for me to leave and to write about all these adventures, but I rebelled against my writing. First, I couldn't grasp it all; second, my points just couldn't be made; and finally, how many secrets should I report?

Some could read this story as an epic. If so, I hope it is one with a series of inconclusive battles in which the "opponents" struggle to disentangle an all too compact ethical entanglement. From the awry, cross-eyed view of some "Third World" women intellectuals, is "evil" to be found in colonialism? Does it reside in patriarchy? Is it embedded in our "native" male-chauvinistic cultures, which, once colonized, were from then on determined to self-colonize and recolonize everybody else, joining capitalism and, paradoxically, rebelling against imperialism—but only when and where they did not enjoy the status of mastering it? And what about colonized procapitalist women who seek a better place in this patriarchially oriented world, betraying all other classes of men and women? And all of us who think so exhaustively about it all and do so little about it? Could any "good" be found, then, in decolonization? From what? From whom? Where are the colonizers specifically located, how are "they" positioned, how do they operate exactly and under which rules? Imperialism, neocolonialism, late capitalism, globalization, postcoloniality ... and if "we" miraculously manage to figure this out before "they" figure it out and disfigure us, an easy matter given their considerable experience in these colonial matters, what would decolonization entail? Is there any way to win without having to hide the dead bodies after the battle? Does "good" then reside in forgetting about the whole thing, including our own complicity, even when, as things are now, innumerable bodies are already paying for this messiness to continue?

In writing about colonialism, aiming at decolonization, the temptation is to point at the essence of the colonized; at what we were before colonialism or what we are in spite of colonialism. In Chapter Four I try to establish the colonized nature of this search for origins and authenticity that takes us into autoexoticism and further colonization. Our incompleteness, hybridity, and struggles to establish homogeneous national identities among internal factions come back, bouncing against the colonial encounter. I trace our complicity—the one of the colonized—with colonialism. Through this search for Identity, the colonized can only reflect an incomplete image of the colonizer, never finding an identity of their own. Decolonization means rejecting the search for the origins and authenticity of the colonized in order to concentrate on the specific, original, and authentic ways in which imperialism operates.

This search is what has led me to historicize exoticism (in Chapter Three). The "exoticism" maneuver is not unlike the "civilization-progress" maneuver, but it is more persuasive and pervasive. Civilization and progress can be reached through "development," the colonized are told. But "exoticism" is always there to remind us of the difference between the old, really "civilized" peoples and the ones only recently, incompletely brought into civilization—the colonized who can never fully overcome the fact of carrying "primitiveness" in their blood. Exoticism is the hook that cannot be unhooked. It is the key to the Western constitution of the Other—since the West has constituted the Other, with a capital "O," through worldwide imperialism. I am not saying that only the West has exoticized and configured Otherness. I am saying that only the West has had the power to make its discourse of the Other come true globally—that the West alone has been successful in imposing worldwide exoticization on its Others. Thus, Western imperialism is what I am interested in.

In Chapter Two I try to expose the actual meat (bodies, people) processed by the Western exoticism machinery, to describe the voraciousness imbedded in manufacturing the Exotic—all it goes over and through. My analysis is not to be read as a recommendation for a "return" to origins or to the "authentic" before it was commoditized/exoticized but as a reminder of the elements that were at stake—socioeconomically and ideologically—at the time when Western exoticism was refurbished through the tango. What I wish to convey is that there is no place to go back to in tango that is not already colonized. This does not mean cutting roots, or erasing home. It means understanding roots-and-home in its complex, painful constitution and distinguishing the differences among the colonized themselves; their interplays and struggles (micropolitics) as choreographed through tango. This process is of extreme importance because the Western discourse/machinery of exoticization did not pick the elite's Europeanized manners to set identity among the neocolonized; it chose the ways of the oppressed within the colonized and dressed them nicely in satin décolletage and frock coats. I see it as an imperialist maneuver to incorporate those sectors of the colonized less touched and culturally co-opted, but also as a way to keep the dominant among the colonized in their place—as subordinates to the Western empire, a role they were forgetting to acknowledge. I believe Third World women intellectuals are caught today in a similar paradoxical interstice.

CHOREOCRITICAL PREVIEW:

POLITICAL ECONOMY OF PASSION

Tango Ronda on a slippery stage.

Cast: Desire, Passion, and Fate—three dancers, hardly distinguishable from one another.

Desire, Passion, and Fate perform ronda variations on a slippery stage, chasing each other to the point of exhaustion, following the taped voice of the Choreocritic, who pronounces ruminations as if the steps are choreographed in her mind. The dancers giggle and address short phrases to each other while dancing, as in a childish ronda.

The Choreocritic's voice:

Desire generates Passion in a different space, the space of alterity, as it longs for it. In the desiring imagination—informed by a philosophy of conquest and consumption—Passion is a vital resource lost when, driven by the ambitions of civilization, Desire abandons the paradise of wildness. Hence, Desire stands restless at the threshold of the rational world, keeping the memory of and the connection to the magical world of Passion. Desire's memory, however, is fragile, and in allocating Passion always somewhere else (in the past, in remote places and cultures, in bodies marked by a different race, class, religion, sexuality, and/or gender), it forgets that Passion is a power of Desire's own creation. For free of its ontological ties to Desire, Passion becomes empowered, although this freedom, rather than precluding bondage, will justify innumerable violent episodes of conquest and articulation. Passion takes hold of those bodies, places, and times imputed as Others, who then, empowered, alternately resist and succumb to that extractive operation by which Desire nourishes itself while multiplying its bottomless dissatisfaction.

Passion and Desire do not move in plain opposition to each other. They circle one another in an ambivalent, unbalanced dualism in terms of power. Desire is invested with legitimacy, the authority enjoyed by those in power; Passion's power lies in its illegitimate nature precisely because it is imputed to nature, to the primitive, to the irrational. Hence, Passion's power resides in "empowerment," in seeking to partake (part-take) of some crumbs of the power held in legitimate hands. Passion's power is akin to a terrorist maneuver that asks for containment. It is wild, inhuman, beyond conquerable nature—that is, supernatural—and must be subjected to the workings of the civilizing/humanizing Desire. Passion's doings are outside the realm of History; they belong to the universe of Fate. Desire gives rise to subjectivity: desiring subjects who master Passion by making of Passion artifacts and objects of Desire, which is permanently displaced, disembodied, and reincorporated into someone/somewhere else—hence the Lacanian riddle "desire of Other's desire, desire for the desiring Other." Desire follows and replicates the avatars of conquest, civilization, and progress. Contrarily, Passion resides right by the dead end of survival. Passion mobilizes agents, not subjects but messengers inscribed with the indecipherable muteness of Fate.

Desire sets Passion into circulation and not itself, as we often hear. Desire moves like a hunter who creates his own prey. Passion, the hunted, shows itself and hides away, lures Desire into existence so that it can attain existence itself, so that it can be recognized, identified, if nothing else in the shape of the provoking Other, inhabiting the space of those anti-selves whose own mesmerized desires belong to the realm of Fate. Passion is created as that inexhaustible reservoir of deep, strong, irrational drives, a treasure that naturally fell into the hands of those Others awaiting the needy pirates' discovery and pillage. Passion: that immense wealth, so overwhelming that it seems to exceed all theories of value, that turns the powerful into have-nots, rearranging the world order so as to reverse the allocation of guilt at stake in every colonizing episode. Desire, Passion, and Fate repeat endlessly a narrative of inscrutable bondage, a tango *à trois*: immoral in its doings, prudish in its careful justifications, and unable to repent.

Dancers end by defiantly facing the audience. The Choreocritic mutters the tango La Mariposa:

No es que esté arrepentido	**It's not that I repent**
de haberte querido tanto,	**having loved you so much,**
lo que me apena es tu olvido	**what saddens me is your forgetfulness**
y tu traición,	**and your betrayal,**
me sume en amargo llanto.	**it immerses me in bitter tears.**

—*La Mariposa* (The Butterfly), 1926
Lyrics by Celedonio E. Flores
Music by Pedro Maffia

Blackout

Tango, My Tango

Tango is a dramatic expression (dance, music, lyrics, and performance) that originated in the Río de la Plata region of Argentina and Uruguay toward the end of the nineteenth century. The worldwide popularity of the tango has been associated with scandal: the public display of passion performed by a heterosexual couple, the symbol of which is a tight embrace and suggestive, intricate footwork. As a powerful representation of male/female courtship, stressing the tension involved in the process of seduction, the tango performance has gone through successive adjustments as it has been adopted and legitimized by the upper classes and by Western hegemonic cultures. Tango was "polished" and ac-

cepted by the wealthy and powerful as it made its way from the slums and brothels of the South American harbors to the cabarets and ballrooms of Paris, London, and New York. By the 1920s it had become clear that the sin of tango was
related to its racial/class origins rather than to its erotic content. When appropriated by "high society," especially that of Europe, dancing the scandalous
tango became an enjoyable, spicy entertainment. As a performance of exotic
passion, like many other exotic products tango was promptly packaged and distributed by the show business industry: records, dance handbooks, films, fashion, stars. ... Tango in its new bourgeois version was readdressed to the world
market, including, ironically, those Third World nations where it originated.
Tango emerged as a symbolic expression and ended up as a sign of status. It became an "exotic" good in the political economy of Passion: appropriation, accumulation, marketing, packaging, commercialization, distribution, and consumption of the wealth of exotic feelings, that is, of the Passion of the
Other/*Otra*.

The tango I invoke in these pages is nothing but my own version of tango. It is
an appropriated tango (to which I feel entitled) that disrespectfully challenges
many existing legitimate versions. The distance from home (Argentina)—not the
distance of objectivity or even of insightfulness but the distance that allows for
trickery and distortion—has given me the courage to borrow the tango without
permission from my patriarchal culture and to disfigure and misrepresent it
through my newly situated interpretations. This endeavor is as much a series of
tangos of my own as an exercise about tango. The power of patriarchy and the
power of colonialism are overwhelming and paralyzing when taken stripped of
their own contradictions. I have tried to tango them—exaggerating *bien
canyengue* their disencounters, shaking off my fears.

Tango is associated with a male-oriented (sub)culture in which women did
and still do actively participate. Tango has been an important locus of identification for me, as an Argentinean woman, ever since I moved outside my culture. It
would have probably never occurred to me to use tango as a tool for resistance
in my own country—not because of its macho connotations so much as because
of the generational distance. Tango's last popular boom was in the 1940s, and
more recently, it has survived and coexisted with North American popular music, *rock nacional,* and other argentino and latino musical genres (some folkloric and some "American" oriented) as a relatively more intellectualized, refined, and/or ghettoized musical taste. In the 1970s and 1980s, however, a
battered generation took hold of tango as an expression of the experiences of
political terror and exile lived during the most recent military government (1976–
1983). As a result, tango went through a revival in Europe and some sensitive
argentino artists and astute impresarios launched successful shows in the
United States, Japan, and Buenos Aires. In addition, several movies produced by
both argentino and foreign directors situated tango at the core of their symbolism.[1] These events brought the tango back to the attention of a generation (my

generation) for whom it had been not lost but dormant—living in the memories of our grandparents and parents (see Pintos 1990).

It is far from my intention to prescribe tango as a universal tool against colonialism and oppression, not only out of respect for cultural specificities and self-determination but also because it would be absurd to proclaim tango as essentially liberating even within the argentino context. Tangos do not fit squarely into the category of protest songs or revolutionary music.[2] The lyrics mostly expose and sometimes denounce the miseries of everyday life as encountered by a marginalized sector of argentinos and *uruguayos* in the course of this century; they seldom point out alternatives or take sides with particular political projects.[3] Nevertheless, analyses of tango politics have focused much more frequently on the lyrics, and to some extent on the music, than on the dance itself. I attempt to draw attention to the patterns of body movement because of the dance's defiance to intellectualization, the powerful messages of the bodies in motion, the scandals and attempts at domestication the dance provoked at home and abroad, and the dance's key role in contributing to the tango's popularity (see Salas 1986).

My interpretations of the tango dance are ambitious, controversial, and too far-reaching. It was precisely this vulnerability, this potential for interpretation, that seemed promising to me. Untamable interpretations (in the sense that they are hard to prove in a positivistic sense) of bodies performing excessive movement, despite all the efforts invested in domesticating them, are good signs for a decolonization project.

The intertextuality already present in the tango[4] provides a richness of resources for confrontation and insurgency. What is sung (said) in a tango is not necessarily what is danced (done), and the music can dispense with both. Submissiveness and confrontation, silence and noise, quiet torsos and relentlessly moving legs enact episodes of power, simultaneously, in displaced dimensions. In my tangoing interpretations (about tango and stemming from it), I intend to learn these resourceful strategies, which are suitable to the decolonization of those who are already colonized, like myself.

By decolonization, a concept I will recall again and again throughout this book, I mean more than one thing—I transform and expand the concept just as colonialism transformed and expanded its gripping ways through hectic, historically specific accommodations. Decolonization entails learning/unlearning the preeminence of abstract, totalizing Enlightenment logics over bodies and their often absurd techniques of survival. It means questioning the interpretative privileges of intellectual vanguards over "doers," their discourses and messy theories of how to go about seemingly insignificant lives in a world consistently ruled by power and its irrationality; questioning the privileges of historicity over history, of the real over the surreal. By decolonization I also mean a commitment to social change, a humble yet desperate call for a "politics without cliché" (Elshtain 1993), an urgent tangoesque manifesto—that is, a tense, melodramatic, simultaneously serious and cynical urge, one position never canceling the other—against privileged denial. "I want my voice to be harsh, I don't want it to be beautiful, I don't want it to be pure, I don't want it to have all dimensions. I want it to be torn through and through, I don't want it to be enticing, for I am speaking of man and his refusal, of the day-to-day rottenness of man, of his dreadful failure" (Fanon 1988: 49).

Tango, Method and Theory

In this research I have been more concerned about "political implications" than about methods or theories. I have had bad experiences with methods and theories. Simply stated, these so-called tools tend to alienate methodical workers from their work, from their creative pleasures, from their complex positions of race, gender, class, and culture, from their honesty, and from their power for insurgency. Intellectuals produce their own tools, as do other workers, and all workers, including intellectuals, become alienated from their tools. The fact is that these research tools, like most means of production in this capitalist world, do not belong to the researchers/workers but to those who control academic capital. Methods and theories are also enabling, and so are all production tools under ideal conditions. But the labor of free intellectuals is subject to the laws of supply and demand of the academic market, and their ideas are subject to speculations over credibility, as in the financial market. Methods and theories enable intellectual production but they also package it for a market; schools of thought are the brands. For an intellectual situated at the core of the world economy this arrangement might seem clean, fair, based on more or less polite competition. Third World intellectuals, as well as minority, marginalized intellectuals, tend to live this situation differently.

For a latina woman intellectual, methods and theories are a question of politics and not the other way around. Intellectual competition and access to the academic market soon turn out to be a trap. "To be civilized and destitute," says Branislaw Malinowski while pondering the problems of educated colonized people, "often means to be revolutionary and unreliable."

> He may go as far as a European or American university; receive such academic degrees as become a member of a highly skilled profession. But when he returns to his own country, he will have to go through a dramatic experience. He will discover that the status of equality, or even equivalence, in matters legal, economic, political, and social, is denied him. [...] We may call it the Line of Integral Rebuff from total assimilation. [...] If, from the outset, it were possible to make quite clear in preaching the gospel of civilization that no full identity can ever be reached; that what are being given to the Africans [and other colonized people] are new conditions of existence better adapted to their needs

but always in harmony with European requirements, the smaller would be the chances of a strong reaction (Malinowski 1945: 157–160).

Malinowski's astute observations went unheard, not because of bad will on the part of the colonial administrators but because of the unmanageability of the colonial contradictions. Decades later, the colonized "she"s joined the "he"s, and it became explosively clear that applied anthropology and other developmentalist theories and methods did not give us "new conditions of existence better adapted to our needs."

> To date, the theory of applied anthropology has been one of the items imported into the underdeveloped countries—an imported item, as many others. We receive from producing countries (such as the United States, England, France and other European nations) many well-elaborated theoretical postulates, some of them perfectly adjusted to our reality and our needs; but others are infused with a different spirit, foreign to our interest and on occasions, decidedly contrary to them (Bonfil Batalla 1966: 92).

When neo-Marxism, feminist theory, poststructuralism, deconstructive methods, world systemic theory, and postcolonial writing (all of which I use in my writing) demand consistency, exclusivity, and royalties, they stop serving me. Instead of being liberating, they become confining. Critical theories and methods promise "total assimilation" to the academic market, but the "Line of Integral Rebuff" is never crossed.

When a question cannot be asked, theories or methods are in the way, in my political way. They are the wrong strategy. My main question is the one asked by the tango-box: Would I please *decolonize* myself? I am talking about my intellectual colonization. It is personal and political. Not because anything that is personal is necessarily political but because of the politics in which I am personally involved. At the time I started this project on tango, I was trying to get a Ph.D. from a U.S. university and planning to go back to Argentina. My whole family shouted at me: It doesn't make sense! Everybody is dreaming of leaving before the ship hits bottom and I, the one who could easily be saved from the catastrophe, I am choosing to return? And I was scared, scared of my own fear, the fear of the colonized. Will I be able to get a job? What kind of upbringing will this be for my children? What if my friends have already left? What about the violence in the streets, the riots, the strikes, the food lootings, the anger, the frustration, the uncertainty, the betrayals, the cynicism, the decadence, the melancholy, the apathy, the stagnation, … the tango? Because I was fearfully and thoroughly colonized, I tangoed. And to make things even more tangoesque, I did go back home—where I could not find a job. I received, instead, an offer from the United States, where I was not applying for anything, to teach precisely about these tangos. Tangos repeatedly make reference to these paradoxical wounds of absurdity.

Because I have no answers to my questions, I tango. I tango because I have to move in the midst of these uncertainties. And because I need to show myself and others that I can still move. Tango is my absurd way of challenging a colonized paralysis,[5] a paralysis nowadays absurdly proclaimed as "the end of History," "the end of Ideologies," the end of hope.

Tango is the most solid tool in my project of decolonization. It is solid because it is the only place in which I feel comfortable—restless but at home, especially when not at home. My first steps in tango taught me about both overwhelming domination and stubborn resistance.

In previous paragraphs I wrote that the tango would be used as an example to describe the political economy of Passion. But I have also protested against giving this place to tango: "Tango is not an example; it is the main ingredient in this project." Tango moves me and keeps me on my toes; it is my changing, resourceful source of identity. Through the tango I weave methods and theories to perform an exercise of anger and hope with the purpose of decolonization. I am not invested in methodological consistency; quite to the contrary, I am convinced that a coherent method would only reproduce my colonization. There are no "methods" leading to decolonization, only successful or failed experiences, inconsistent strategies, movements that cannot be easily foreseen or predicted, improvisation, the power of the unexpected. Unexpected and outrageous even for our colonized selves. And this is not a Machiavellian type of formula prescribing the use of any means to achieve a desired end, because in the process of decolonization the end itself shifts unexpectedly as well. Decolonization is a purpose in process, a search for self-determination, a process of liberation. Decolonization is endless. Moreover, decolonization is not a question of ends, it is a question of loyalties. Loyalty toward those for whom your life makes a difference and whose lives make a difference for you.

Tango is the main ingredient in my project of decolonization because I have no choice. It is the stereotype of the culture to which I belong. If I reject my stereotype I fall, caught in nowhere. Caught in endless explanations of what I am not and justifications of what I am. Caught in comparisons with the colonizer. By assuming the tango attitude and taking it seriously, I can work at expanding its meaning and its power. My power, actively tango. Tango is my strategic language, a way of talking about, understanding, exercising decolonization.

Sometimes I talk about tango and, simultaneously, about my way of talking: the irony, the sensualness, the pessimism, the resentfulness, the nostalgia, the melodrama. Other times, I apply tango to the understanding of something else, such as postmodernism, feminism, "native patriarchy," colonialism, intellectuals. When I focus on tango itself, its process of exoticization and self-exoticization, I am attempting a genealogy of a cultural strategy of accommodation, resistance, and insurgency. Tango is a strategy with multiple faces: music, dance, lyrics, performance, philosophy. ... None of these aspects exactly reproduces or reinforces the others. The dance stops when the music pulls; the lyrics challenge the dance; the male and female of the couple follow and resist each other's movements; the music, syncopated, surprisingly halts. Starts again. Tango is recognizable in these contrasts and in the tension that they generate. And the tension itself is dramatized in a melodramatic way, a melodrama of stereotypes on the move, unstable stereotypes, stereotypes of the unpredictable.

Tango is a practice already ready for struggle. It knows about taking sides, positions, risks. It has the experience of domination/resistance from within. Tango, stretching the colonized stereotypes of the latino-macho-Catholic fatalism, is a language of decolonization. So, pick and choose. Improvise. Hide away. Run after them. Stay still. Move at an astonishing speed. Shut up. Scream a rumor. Turn around. Go back without returning. Upside down. Let your feet do the thinking. Be comfortable in your restlessness. Tango.

My tango method is an attempt to poke at scholarly exercises that alienate, immobilize, and justify nonsensical politics by logically, rationally, and academically making sense. And still I have to pick and choose to avoid getting caught; I have no other choice but to use the tools of the colonizer, which are already my own, and to stir them up with creativity and resolution.

El Tango del Che

As a latina trying to decolonize, I have found much inspiration in revolutionary struggles and in the writings of intellectual revolutionaries. I echo some tactics of my compatriot Che Guevara, for example, in my own tangoings over writing. Like Che, I attempt to avoid any consistent or generalizable approach. "Another fundamental characteristic of the guerrilla soldier is his flexibility, his ability to adapt himself to all circumstances, and to convert to his service all of the accidents of the action. Against the rigidity of classical methods of fighting, the guerrilla invents his own tactics at every minute of the fight and constantly surprises the enemy" (Guevara 1985: 60–61). My project follows the same course in that it is entirely situational. I try to address the specific problem at hand, changing tactics as often as necessary, so as to avoid the trappings created by "the rigidity of classical methods." I place myself under no compulsion to "stick to the subject," to be "consistent," or to "follow the argument to its logical conclusion." Rather, I cherish the ability to flee in the face of overwhelming force, to "trick-back" the colonizing discourse.

> The fundamental characteristic of a guerrilla band is mobility. This permits it in a few minutes to move far from a specific theater and in a few hours far even from the region, if that becomes necessary; permits it constantly to change front and avoid any type of encirclement. [...] Characteristic of this war of mobility is the so-called minuet, named from analogy with the dance: the guerrilla bands encircle an enemy position, an advancing column, for example; they encircle it completely from the four points of the compass, with five or six

men in each place, far enough away to avoid being encircled themselves; the fight is started at any one of the points, and the army moves toward it; the guerrilla band retreats, always maintaining visual contact, and initiates its attack from another point (Guevara 1985: 58–59).

This is my tactic, too: to "hit and run," avoiding the encirclement of theoretical commandments. "There is in all this, it would appear," continues Che, "a negative quality, an attitude of retreat, of avoiding frontal fights." I know that decolonization is no more "honorable" than it is "scholarly." But like Che, I avow that the purpose is to win, in my case by tangoing disruptive tunes, breaking the rhythm of academic silences.

Che used an analogy to dance (the minuet) to explain his decolonizing strategy, and I am borrowing some tactics from his *Guerrilla Warfare* to explain my tangos. But frankly, I can no more fight a war than Che could dance the tango.

There is a dance that night, and the friends decide to go. It's a bustling crowd, and the couples seem to multiply on the dance floor. Ernesto ["Che" Guevara] approaches his friend and tells him in a low voice, "Runt, listen well. I'm going to dance, but you know. ..." Alberto [Granados] doesn't need any kind of explanation to know that his friend is incapable of distinguishing a military march from a *milonga*. "When they play a tango," Ernesto requests, "kick me, then I'll know what it is. Agreed?"

More or less every other piece played by the improvised band is a tango, but for some reason they suddenly play a Brazilian *shoro* entitled "Delicado." Granados remembers the song was popular at the time his friend began to court Chichina, and wishing to remind him of that time, taps him with his foot.

Ernesto takes a young woman out to dance. The tempo of the *shoro* is quick, but he doesn't hear it. He dances to the beat of a tango, marking off his steps with mathematical precision.

Alberto watches him and can't hold back his laughter. [...] Ernesto doesn't worry about it: he himself laughs at his lack of talent as a dancer (Cabrera Alvarez 1987: 77).

The parallel is far from perfect. The lesson is to use what is available. Che's decolonization struggle inspires and informs my own, and if Che is not normally included in the pantheon of academic methodologists, I believe it to be a loss. The classification of "Guevara" as a "guerrilla" is just as delimiting as is the classification of "Foucault" as an "author." Doing and saying are thus neatly severed; the elements remain unmixed and inert. The romance of "El Che" ensures that he will be studied as an example but not as an authority. He is constituted as a doer, not as a sayer or writer, and anything he wrote is understood only in terms of what he did.

"*Guevarismo*" has become exactly what Guevara cautioned against: an -ism. And even (especially?) guerrillas succumb to the cult-phenomenon—to the codification of Che's teachings. For example, is Guevarismo essentially "*foquismo*," or is it equally essentially political vanguardism? Such have been the debates among the Guevarists (e.g., Hodges 1977). Even (especially?) Che seems to have fallen victim to Guevarismo. Was he reading/following his old revolution—enmeshed in the specificities of Cuba—instead of writing/leading a new one—in Bolivia? "Yes. One might say, if it were not so foolish to pass judgment at this point on a giant like Che, that to some extent Che suffered the consequences of his own experience, without intending to" (interview with a leader of Fuerzas Armadas Revolucionarias of Argentina [1970], quoted in Hodges 1977: 124).

Guevarismo can be fatal, and fatalistic for those who confound Guevara with Guevarismo and conclude that *it* does not work. Che is thereby reduced to the position of a "guerrilla" and excluded from the position of "author." His texts do not matter, but only that he ended in "failure." Yet I am mobilized by Che's campaigns and by his texts, which is not to say that I am determined to follow in his footsteps. My tango steps arise out of a different place and at a different time. This "method" is my own, and I would no more offer it as a rule book than Che offered his. "All these recommendations are flexible; they are based upon an experience in a certain place and are conditioned by its geography and history; they will be modified in different geographical, historical, and social situations" (Guevara 1985: 129). Thus he fought, and thus I tango. And thus neither one of us is prescriptive or methodical about our methods. The purpose is not to theorize, generalize, or totalize. The purpose is to decolonize.[6]

Argentina and "Decolonization"

Decolonization? Argentina? Why do I speak of decolonization, when Argentina won its independence 177 years ago? On the surface the term "decolonization" could be dismissed as imprecise. "Colonialism" and "decolonization" have been sloppily extended beyond their technical referents. I could explain that Argentina is not *really* still a colony, and that my project is not *really* decolonization. But I do not use these terms loosely, either. My intention is to unleash the instability arrested in the formal or "operative" definitions of these terms and to release them into circulation. Technical terms and rhetorical strategies are a substantive part of the politics of every intellectual. The naming of the problems that an intellectual is trying to address situates both the intellectual and the problem in an already politicized context. The text that comes out of the intellectual exercise talks to other texts; it is intertextual. More important, it talks in a political/politicized world where the intellectual and the text are already conditioned to play parts and fit into certain slots (Said 1983).

In the practice of writing, the arguments are conditioned by the naming of the problems addressed (as in my case, where I name the problem "colonialism").

This is an internal, textual, discursive happening; but in terms of the audience—
the worldliness in which the text speaks—the naming or labeling already sets a
tone and a position—a political position—predisposing the readers in various
locations to be supporters or critics of the politics of the text.

Writing in late capitalism—a society of massive, intensive, hyper-rapid consumerism—augments these features; the name of the problem has become a
crucial signifier for political identification. The proliferation of writing and the
superficiality of reading are escalating at a fast pace. Writing has always been a
seductive practice, but today it is more blatant, overt, scandalous. This is a time
of "stand-up" reading, like eating hors d'oeuvres. "One should wander through
the bookstore aimlessly; it's a matter of suddenly recognizing which book is
sending out a signal to you, and picking it up. [...] If you perceive that [signal]
and you get the book, then it's the same as already having read it. You don't have
to read the whole thing from cover to cover—I think it's all right just to put it by
your pillow" (Asada as read/consumed by Ivy 1988a: 429). This is a time when
Foucault's desire to slip imperceptibly into discourse (Foucault 1971) no longer
applies. The problem now is not how to slip in, but how to jump out. At least this
is my political concern. How do I get someone to listen to me? How can I draw
your attention? How can I make a point? How can I move you?

Colonialism. Yes, Argentina and colonialism. Almost two centuries of formal
independence, of statehood, and still colonialism. Third World, underdeveloped, dependent and unevenly developed, semi-periphery, south of the North.
... Sure, but still colonialism. A new stage of colonialism, neocolonial, of course.
But colonial nevertheless. Stubbornly colonial. Incomprehensible. I agree. And
this is one of the basic problems for us argentinos: We can't believe it ourselves.
The underdeveloping process, the experience of becoming less and less "developed," more dependent, increasingly poor, more harshly exploited, economically and politically more polarized, of losing dignity, of compromising
unnegotiable values, is hard to admit. It is not a crisis; it is not an obstacle on the
road to progress; it is not a temporary regression; it is not a break until we gather
new breath and start pushing ahead once again. For the vast majority of the people it resembles a bottomless bottom. It is colonialism. I need a stop word, a definite stand. A harsh concept that evokes a turning point. A reaction that can't be
calmed down by false promises. I talk about colonialism because I am already
setting up the context for a project of decolonization.

When I choose to name the latinoamericano "problem" as colonial, I am joining the decolonization struggle—decolonization authors, texts, attitudes, skills,
strategies, and decisions. I am attempting a decolonized understanding and a
decolonizing practice. Latino intellectuals have been too confused for too long.
We cannot afford it. We cannot enjoy the scientific, technocratic luxuries of the
imperially located academics anymore. It's over. Our protected niches within the
research centers have shrunk, the crumbs and leftovers are scarce. ... Some of us
latino intellectuals flee like rats toward the core of the empire. They call it "the

brain drain"; it reminds me of the colonial administrators hurrying back home in the midst of the anticolonial struggles. But we are not colonial administrators and for some of us this is not "home." Who are we that we should leave? Neocolonial administrators? Colonial subalterns? Postcolonial critics? Migrant workers? In this state of emergency we are forced to figure out who we are and where we belong.

Capital has no nationality anymore. This is the time of multinational corporations, of a process of transnationalization. ... Fine. But the headquarters move to the latinoamericano continent only to celebrate the *Carnaval*. Imperialism now carries a double life: Like a flashy exhibitionist, the current imperialist exposes his power in the safe dark alleys of the world and hurries back to his formal business suit, private airplane, and portable phone. A cross-national imperialist class maybe, but still imperialist. An imperial technology that hides its power from itself, disguises it in transnational cloaks and manners. Whom does the analytically precise fixation of the terms benefit?

For a latinoamericano intellectual aiming at decolonization, it is essential to produce counternarratives, rhetorical strategies resistant to colonial discourse, not solely anticolonial but also decolonizing. My decolonizing narrative begins with the assertion that colonialism did not end with our formal "independence." Furthermore, our colonization started before our incorporation into capitalism. Colonialism is neither a political nor an economic category *strictu sensu*. Colonialism is a set of practices, encompassing formalized institutions all the way through personalized attitudes, through which societies reproduce the domination, exploitation, and extermination of the many in the hands of a few. Racism, classism, and sexism are integral parts of the technology of colonialism. Colonialism operates through a careful detection and fixation of differences and inoculates the fear, guilt, and anger of not being one and the same—the same as the colonizer. Colonialism, moreover, writes epic narratives about these occurrences and praises itself for developing a precise, meticulous description. Whether theological, philosophical, or technological, these are narratives of self-justification.

A decolonizing project must state that colonization does not end with so-called "independence" and the point should be made obvious. The discourse of decolonization is a strategy of anti-imperialist, decentered mobilization.

Argentina and Colonialism

I am rushed by the present to try to explain the past. It is the traumatic and disconcerting recent history of Argentina that makes me search for explanations in the world entanglements of colonizers and colonized. Is it my ignorance, my lack of mastery in this field, a paranoid obsession or a tango mood stubbornly installed at the end of yet another century ... ? I see layers of colonialism: Spanish conquest and colonialism; independence from Spain and British neocolonialism; time for the empire to change hats, American imperialism; time for a re-alignment of the world, North-South imperialism; time for modernizing the obsolete international division of labor, multinational colonialism, transnational financial colonialism, cybernetic postcolonial colonialism. … Some of the waves of imperialism benefited América Latina more than others. True. Argentina in particular received a considerable share of wealth a couple of times during this century.

It is surprising to learn about these discontinuities: Between 1869 (the date of the first national population census) and 1914, the population of the country multiplied more than six times (from roughly 1,143,000 to 7,885,000 inhabitants) and more than 3 million immigrants, mostly from Italy and Spain, entered its borders. In half a century (1860–1910), the area under cultivation increased from 580,000 hectares to 24 million hectares and the railroad network grew from 10 kilometers to nearly 34,000 kilometers (Díaz Alejandro 1975). In addition, in those years Argentina was one of the world's main suppliers of corn, wheat, and wheat flour as well as the major exporter of flax, oats, and fresh, frozen, and preserved beef. Between 1880 and 1914, the value of Argentina's international trade rose from 50 million to 500 million gold pesos (Cortés Conde and Gallo 1967). Massive foreign investments in Argentina (33 percent of all foreign investment in América Latina), especially of British origin (42 percent of British investments in the region), entered the country to support transportation (railroads and harbors), urban services, and meat packers (Di Tella and Zymelman 1967; Ferrer 1968). In terms of income per capita, by the 1920s the country was positioned among the most privileged in the world, the state provided free education, and the population's social mobility was stunning. Argentina's government was democratically elected through universal suffrage and secret ballot in an admirable climate of civic liberty (Sábato 1988).

Although Argentina was perhaps the first of the NICs (Newly Industrialized Countries), we argentinos did not understand that this situation was ephemeral. We were inaugurating a new form of not being independent.

> Argentinean development, which during the fifty years prior to the First World War was one of the most rapid in the world's economic history, […] ultimately was the result of the symbiotic relationship, commercial as well as financial, with Great Britain. The (asymmetric) interdependency between both countries was such that not only was Great Britain Argentina's main buyer; in several years, Argentina was the main provider for Great Britain, excluding the United States, but including all the other members of the Empire (Escudé 1988: 3).

Argentina, independent from Spain, was enjoying a development "boom" due to neocolonial arrangements with Great Britain. This rapid growth gave rise to a period of strong accumulation. But who were the ones appropriating this surplus and how did they do it? Moreover, what did they do with all that wealth? The change of imperial hats was not so flourishing for all argentinos:

> The May revolution attempted to break the Spanish system according to which we could buy and sell only at the Cádiz harbor. With the years it seems as though Argentineans would want to impose on ourselves the obligation to buy and sell exclusively at the Liverpool harbor. [...] If this coloniality meant an emphasis on people's search to compensate for economic needs, we would oppose it on the grounds of the freedom principle, but we would see that tolerance in the struggle would be a necessity. However, since it brings attached to it hunger, decadence and exploitation for the masses, we feel that we must be unbending (Homero Manzi [1936], "¿Qué es FORJA?" quoted in Ford 1986: 16).[7]

Homero Manzi, a prominent tango lyricist and political activist, was clearly sensing in 1936 the traps of our British-dependent development and the puzzling desire "to impose on ourselves" this renewed coloniality.

In Roberto Fernández Retamar's words, "There was simply no way an eventual Argentine bourgeoisie could develop. Latin America was a late arrival to that fiesta" (Fernández Retamar 1989: 28). José Mariátegui had explained: "The era of free competition in the capitalist economy has finished in all areas and in all of its aspects. We live in the era of monopolies, or better yet, of empires. The Latin American countries came late to capitalist competition. The inside lanes had already been assigned. The destiny of these countries in the capitalist order is that of being simple colonies" (Mariátegui [1929] 1992: 38). Most colonized peoples know very well that they have arrived late to the capitalist fiesta. The dream of having arrived on time is a luxury that only the privileged among the colonized can afford to indulge. And their dream has oftentimes come true, provided the list of guests was kept sufficiently restricted. Argentinean elites, while proclaiming national interests and hopes in their political speeches, have usually been transnational in their private economic decisions. They have been convinced that "Argentina had material conditions superior to the United States of America, and would some day be greater than that nation" (Alois E. Flies's address to the Sociedad Rural Argentina [1889], quoted in Tulchin 1990: 17–18). And messages from abroad reinforced Argentina's hopes.

What began as a belief in the possibility of catching up ended in a detached defense of genocides, exploitation, and repression. All in the name of *Civilización y Progreso*! No. The process of colonization does not stop with formal independence. Colonization colonizes; colonization reproduces itself; a successful colonization is one that is internalized by the colonized (Deleuze and Guattari 1983). Juan Bautista Alberdi, in his pragmatic notes for a constitution for the recently unified nation, supplied an instructive example of the dangerous dilemmas faced by the colonized committed to the task of continuing colonization:

We need to replace our citizens with others who will be more able to profit from liberty. But we need to do this without giving up our racial character, or, much less, our political control. ... Should we, perhaps, bring in conquerors more enlightened than the Spaniards? [...] South America has an army for this purpose, its beautiful and amiable women of Andalusian origin who have been improved under the splendid sky of the New World. Remove the immoral impediments that sterilize the power of [South] America's fair sex and you will have effected the change in our race without losing our language or our racial character (Alberdi [1852] 1969: 406).

After Argentina gained independence from the illegitimate Spanish conquerors, the challenge was to purify the racially irrational and lazy criolla population of América Latina; Alberdi counted on the enticing charms of the not sufficiently exploited criolla females to attract European immigrants. Domingo F. Sarmiento, another argentino "development" fighter, interpreted Alberdi's message with these justificatory twists:

Many difficulties will be presented by the occupation of so extensive a country; but there will be no advantage comparable to that gained by the extinction of the savage tribes. [...] It may be very unjust to exterminate savages, suffocate rising civilizations, conquer peoples who are in possession of a privileged piece of land. But thanks to this injustice, America, instead of remaining abandoned to the savages, incapable of progress, is today occupied by the Caucasian race—the most perfect, the most intelligent, the most beautiful and most progressive of those that people the earth. Thanks to these injustices, Oceania is filled with civilized peoples, Asia begins to move under the European impulse, Africa sees the times of Carthage and the glorious days of Egypt reborn on her coast. Thus, the population of the world is subject to revolutions that recognize immutable laws; the strong races exterminate the weak ones and the civilized peoples supplant the savages in the possession of the earth (Sarmiento [1883], quoted in Fernández Retamar 1989: 23–24).

This is the language, the tongue of the colonizer spitting through the teeth of the colonized, ready to assume a recolonizing task. Alberdi was writing *Las Bases para la Organización Política de la República Argentina* (1852), and Sarmiento would soon become a *presidente*. ...[8] América Latina's history is the history of the gigantic costs of this entangled confusion; a confusion plagued by awareness, a tragedy in which colonialism is perpetrated by the colonized in an attempt to move beyond colonizing consequences.

Colombian novelist Gabriel García Márquez, in receiving the Nobel Prize in 1982, addressed América Latina's colonial damnation:

For our crucial problem has been a lack of conventional means to render our lives believable. This, my friends, is the crux of our solitude. ... The interpretation of our reality through patterns not our own serves only to make us ever more unknown, ever less free, ever more solitary. ... No: the immeasurable violence and pain of our history are the result of age-old inequities and untold bitterness, and not a conspiracy plotted three thousand leagues from our homes. But many European leaders and thinkers have thought so [...], as if it were impossible to find another destiny than to live at the mercy of the two great masters of the world. This, friends, is the very scale of our solitude (García Márquez [1988], quoted in Galeano 1988: 262–263).

García Márquez urged understanding América Latina by moving to a different dimension, where solitude adopts the scale and the weight of the loneliness of the ones who cannot and will not be left alone. He addressed the crux of our solitude, the longing for isolation and the fear of its occurrence. The paradox of a "culture of dependency" (Corradi 1979), invested in reproducing more of the same while attempting to create alterity, carried along in successive layers of colonialism: neo-, multi-, trans-, post-, as well as plain. A culture devastated by the experience of colonialism, not by Catholicism or Iberianism, although these might have helped to pave the way.[9] The "cultural bomb" of colonialism (Ngũgĩ 1986), which taught us how to hate ourselves, how to look at ourselves as if we were an Other, how to hope for ourselves the worst in order to attain the colonizer's best through a magical leap or a paradoxical slippage of appropriation. "It is the final triumph of a system of domination when the dominated start singing its virtues" (Ngũgĩ 1986: 20), believing colonialism will be exorcised when in the hands of the colonized.

Some authors blame the Argentinean oligarchy for not adopting a more aggressive expansionist policy—for not assuming a thorough colonialist position—at the turn of the century:

They chose consciously and deliberately to follow a line of policy that would keep Argentina at the margin of the international power struggle. [...] Argentines did not want the responsibilities of world power. They did not want to take up the white man's burden in Africa or Asia. Quite a few appeared willing to shoulder it in South America. [...] The oligarchy constructed the relations of dependency that would distort their nation's development for the next century (Tulchin 1990: 26–27).

Yes. Members of the Argentinean elite made political and economic decisions that distorted the nation's development, but not because they lacked grandiose ambition. Their ambitions were rather of such a proportion that they managed to juggle nationalist pride with sympathy for foreign interests and to close highly profitable commercial and financial deals while promoting political instability. Our oligarchies seem to have gained the most when the nation was at its worst in terms of economic autonomy and political stability (Sábato and Schvarzer 1988).

Still, many of them insisted, with Estanislao Zeballos, that Argentina was destined to be "the colossus of the Southern continent." The Argentinean elite was a profoundly colonized elite. Perhaps its members were cynical in promising national development while avoiding investments in domestically productive areas, keeping their capital as liquid as possible so as not to miss gains through speculation and even sending it abroad. Perhaps they astutely believed they could outdo the metropolitan imperialists at their own capitalist game by moving directly from colonialism to transnationalism, but as politicians they could not abandon the nationalist rhetoric. I cannot prove, expand, or, even less, settle any of these questions. My purpose is to present a rough picture of our complicated coloniality. For colonialism does not mean lack of agency or responsibility on the part of either the colonizer or the colonized; neither does it affect all the colonized in the same ways. These complexities, however, do not draw the fact of imperialism out of the picture, although complicity makes imperialism harder to grasp. In my opinion, members of the Argentinean elite—those with access to political and economic decisions of national import—were clearly invested in gaining and retaining as much wealth as possible, often regardless of the consequences for the rest of their nationals, *and* they were preoccupied with making Argentina one of the "civilized" nations in the world—in a world where trading in internationally valued goods meant "progress."

La Nación, a prominent argentino newspaper owned by an elite family, published an article on October 30, 1889, touting: "The Argentine Republic now has an established personality in the civilized world. From this moment forward one may say that Argentina will be highly esteemed because we have made known the rich products of our soil, of our industry and of our intelligence." These pathetic assertions show that Argentina's elite thought it necessary to prove its civilized status as it took on "the white man's burden." Argentina did not spare efforts in colonizing either its own territories or those of its neighbors—as in the tragic case of the Paraguay War—or in proclaiming itself as a civilizing leader on the "southern continent." Argentina's burden was not only the white man's but also the burden of "whitening" itself. Is this not the burden of colonialism? Layers of colonialism. A mixed-up series of colonial narratives where the aboriginal "savages" ended up lumped together with "immoral," "irrational" Spaniards, the "sweaty" African slaves, the "curiously brave" criollo knife-fighters of the pampas, the "miserable" Italian immigrants ... one by one entering into the category of the "native" or "latino" or "hispanic," one by one bearing the scars of the colonized. For argentinos the burden of colonialism has been translated in endless efforts to reaffirm our whiteness, our "europoid"—a rough draft of the European (Alejandro Lipschütz's term [Lipschütz 1963])—difference from the Rest and a mixture of melancholy and rage for not being able to fit into the West. Our colonization is complete when we forget that we *are* colonized.

Much has been written about the "miracle of Argentina's underdevelopment." None of the explanations are satisfactory (Larrain 1989; Escudé 1988; Sábato

1988; Sábato and Schvarzer 1988). Dependency theories cannot fully explain Argentina's successful development until the 1940s, and those focusing on the internal sociopolitical dynamics often distort Argentinean history through "culturalism" (the wrong Iberian-Catholic roots) or "personalism" (like the Perón-phobia). For those aiming at the salvation of the myth of development within world capitalism, the answer is that the timing of Argentina's insertion into the international market was wrong or that the speed was too overwhelming for any right political decisions to be made. More recently, scholars have been trying to understand the irrational behavior of the Argentinean elite and its stubborn resistance to U.S. imperialism. Some assert that the elite's lack of realism and failure to accept its position caused Argentina's self-destructiveness: Argentinos did not know how to change their imperial masters in time.

Argentina criticized the aggressive intervention of the United States in the Venezuelan boundary dispute (1895) and in Cuba (1895–1898). Argentina boycotted U.S. efforts to create a Pan-American Union (1882) aimed at ensuring U.S. hegemony over América Latina by securing the greatest portion of trade and a military alliance. It is worth quoting at length a 1947 document, released to the public in recent years, in which the British Foreign Office gives opinionated information about Argentina's reactions to the U.S. pressures.

> For forty years or more, Argentina has been a thorn in the flesh of the successive North American governments in that it has continuously offered to lead the Latin American resistance to United States hegemony in the Western hemisphere, a fact that almost all North American citizens consider a necessity as well as a right. [...] Argentine liberals, like Dr. Saavedra Lamas, to no less a degree than Argentine nationalists and militarists have exasperated the men of the North American state with their pretensions of being the voice of Latin America against "yankee" domination or "dollar diplomacy." In recent years their exasperation has been accompanied by the uncomfortable knowledge that Argentina represents more than a transient challenge, and that other Latin American countries, although prone to dislike Argentina because of its arrogant opportunism, nevertheless consider this nation a welcome spearhead against the penetration of the United States (Lord Iverchapel, February communication from Washington to the Foreign Office [1947], quoted in Escudé 1988: 29).

After succeeding in maintaining Argentina as a British neocolony up to World War II, Great Britain had given in to U.S. world leadership. Argentinos (governments and people) did not. Some persisted in the idea of a European-dependent development because they could not forget the glory days of the recent past. Others aimed at a national development that would keep Argentina as autonomous as possible. For Carlos Escudé, Argentina's resistance to U.S. imperialism was a sign of irrationality. "Argentina could not afford the luxury of irritating the

U.S. colossus, regardless of any ideas of justice and rights. Argentina fell into what could be called a 'syndrome of irrationality' in its political decision-making process" (Escudé 1988: 25). In Escudé's opinion, responsible peripheral nations should be able to realize that the favor or disfavor of the powerful affects their development possibilities; the "weakest part" should swallow its pride and move "with a more pragmatic consciousness of the cost-benefit calculations." He argued that national pride, in peripheral countries, is usually an excuse for self-destructive confrontations and is another manifestation of inequity within society. "National pride is an elitist product," and it often "feeds the egos of the elite" while sinking "the general population even further into poverty" (Escudé 1988: 27).

Although I fully agree with Escudé's analysis of the unequal distribution of the "benefits" and "costs" of ñational pride, I do not understand how the situation would change without national pride. If the "rational" road to development means opportunistic subserviency to the international powers-that-be (and he as well as others, I believe, have the past Brazilian and the more recent Chilean economic "booms" in mind), there is still a price to pay—beyond national pride—and the elite will certainly not pay that either. I gather that the same "general population" would pay it, and without the symbolic and emotional "benefits" of national pride. I do not think these are problems of political "culture" or "syndromes of irrationality." It seems as though "irrational" decisions oftentimes have provided the most beneficial results for some social sectors, at given moments. Political disorder and economic instability make a nation miserable but fill the pockets of efficient transnational speculators, including those who are residents of the nation undergoing miserable times, and despite their nationalist hurt feelings. These crazy, schizophrenic, no-win situations are a syndrome of colonialism—a colonialism in which we have been and are complicit in different ways and to different degrees, a colonialism that seems as painful to live with as it is impossible to live without, already invested as we are in ever stranger vertigos of recolonization.

In the midst of Argentina's celebrations of development glory, the centennial commemoration of independence from Spain (1910) was challenged by serious social disturbances ... followed by serious repression. Labor unions had been organizing for decades to protest the uneven distribution of prosperity. Low salaries, cyclic unemployment, unbearable working and housing conditions, and detentions and deportations of activists were all protested through sectorial and general strikes. Prosperity was there, but it was out of reach for the many. The Argentinean government did actively intervene in trying to create internal conditions for development;[10] however, the dynamic of an agro-export-dependent economy in the hands of a speculative transnational elite conditioned such efforts and multiplied the confrontations between the haves and have-nots.

Rather than taking the so-called "social question" for what it was, the political/economic elites engaged in developing repressive legislation and maneuvers. They passed a Social Defense Law (1910) aimed at detecting and deporting "deviant" and "perverse" individuals expelled from their own countries of origin, where "misery and alcoholism perturb the functions of the brain" (Meyer González [1910], quoted in Suriano 1988: 19). These were the recently arrived immigrants, regarded as socialist and anarchist "agitators." In addition, elite "nationalist" gangs would spend their leisure time setting fire to labor union buildings, popular libraries and social clubs, the print shops for *La Vanguardia* and *La Protesta,* and the Jewish and working-class neighborhoods. The social problems in Argentina would only be read, once again, in terms of race, class, and ideology—this time, pertaining to the immigrants. The dominant neocolonial discourse preached that all social inequalities would be eliminated through the workings of the marketplace; argentinos only needed to allow time for the marvelous healing process of growth to occur. The nation's golden future was guaranteed by the exports of meat, grains, and wool and by universal and free education. ... A traditional trickle-down theory of development.

Tango lyrics of the period confirm that the idea of "allowing time for the miracle to work" was not so easy to digest. They portray misery, prostitution, unemployment, unimaginable family dissolutions, unwelcomed relocalizations, unbearable promiscuity, and loneliness. They also show, in challenging sobs and alcoholic cynicism, the lack of faith in the development project as well as the lack of good faith of the Argentinean oligarchy. Although in Europe the cliché was "as rich as an Argentine"—in reference to the beef barons traveling abroad—tangos sang and danced the dark side of development. The ones in power were not ready to hear: The native oligarchy condemned the tango to the margins, where they enjoyed hunting the demimonde; the Europeans didn't understand the words and thought that these "natives" and their dances were charming.

2

Tango as a Spectacle of Sex, Race, and Class

SCENE ONE: THE TANGO EMBRACE

Multiple confrontational duets.

Cast: Choreocritic, Dancers, Mulattos, Soldaderas and Criollo Soldiers, Compadrito and Milonguita, Immigrants, Elite Men.

Choreocritic and Dancers (refrain): Tango started as a dance, a tense dance.

The dancers repeat the refrain while the Choreocritic recites the text. The Choreocritic is located at the left, centerstage. Each group of dancers initiates its steps as the Choreocritic makes reference to that group's intervention in the making of tango. They interrupt their movements each time the Choreocritic asks a question about the nature of the tango "embrace." As the recitation unfolds, the dancing couples move toward centerstage, closer to each other, interfering with each other's trajectories and exchanging partners, displaying confrontation. As the dancers accumulate centerstage, there are always more men than women. The dancers must compete to dance the tango.

Choreocritic's spoken text:

Tango started as a dance, a tense dance, in which a male/female embrace tried to heal the racial and class displacement provoked by urbanization and war.[1] But the seductive, sensual healing was never to be complete, and the tensions resurfaced and reproduced. Tango encounters were a catalyst for further racial and class tensions augmented by the European migration avalanche. Tango helped to provoke these encounters and, at the same time, expressed their occurrence.

Black men and women probably initiated the first tango steps in the Río de la Plata: flirtatious *ombligadas* and *culeadas,* bodies alternately coming close to each other and moving apart. Their displays of eroticism scandalized and created distance/difference, racial and class difference with their masters and exploiters (Assunção 1984; Natale 1984; Salas 1986), but they did not embrace. They did not need to hold tight; their color held them together.

The tango embrace was created, perhaps, in the midst of the internal wars that persisted for more than forty years following the independence from Spain: The tight and failed embraces of the prostitutes (*soldaderas* and *cuarteleras*) who followed the armies of poor *mestizos* and *pardos*.

After the unification of the country, which forced Argentina into a new national identity that focused on the interests of Buenos Aires—the harbor city, looking at Europe—tango's embrace became a must.[2] Racial and class displacements were intersected by rural-urban movements. The harbor city demanded new laboring flesh to get the beef ready for export.

Buenos Aires was changing from a big village into a city; the *criollos* and *mulatos* herding cattle to the city and working at the slaughterhouses and the *saladeros* were lonely, angry, and frustrated men. Their immediate world was changing at a pace for which their nomadism as former *gauchos* and soldiers was unsuited. They needed to embrace even tighter; no matter who or where. And they would fight for the opportunity.

This is the story of the *guapo* or *compadrito*, those men of different skin shades but the same dark fate who cultivated courage—courage as a skill and as a value. In Borges's words, these guapos were specialists in progressive intimidation, "veterans in winning without having to fight." With a few knife fights over questions of honor, few words but plenty of bad attitude, they established a reputation and territory for themselves on the outskirts of the city.

Guapos struggled for some maleness, fighting over women who were scarce in fact as well as in imagination.[3] Urbanization and industrialization had left their women behind, and these civilizing projects were being instigated by other men. Urbanization and industrialization wore a face, that of those wealthy men looking lasciviously at their poor women. These wealthy men paid to embrace poor women, being unable to touch the women of their own class without commitment.

Whether the guapos cared or not about their women it is hard to tell; they learned to look tough, to despise life, and to disdain women. Perhaps they disdained women defensively because women were unattainable or difficult to keep. Perhaps they came to despise life from fighting over women in order to keep on being men, despite their class. The macho identity was born out of this contradiction, and women's identities were born out of the competition among men: Macho men of different colors and classes pulling at women from different directions shaped women's nameless identities.

None of these tensions were resolved, and the European immigrants, a new army of laborers, had already arrived. No time for healing. More exiles, more distress, and again, few women. How tight could tango's embrace get? The stiff torsos of the black dances became stiffer; the swaying hips (*quebradas*) and the sharp interruptions of the dancing marches (*cortes*) lost their joyful fluidity and became grave, and so did the faces, concentrated in displaying filigrees of foot-

work (*figuras*) for an attentive audience of *pardas* and *chinas,* themselves escaped from domestic service to become near-prostitutes.

Whose embrace was the tango embrace? Tango's choreography emerged out
of mutual admiration and scornful disdain among the different races, classes,
and ethnicities lumped together in the city. The lighter-colored ones imitated
the skillful movements of the blacks and, self-conscious of their shortcomings,
ended up caricaturing them. The darker ones, in trying to rub on some fashionable white elegance but knowing that this would bring them no more respect, mocked the loose embrace of the quadrilles, mazurkas, habaneras, and
waltzes, tingeing it with bodily proximity and sweat.[4] The tango dance
emerged from these racial and class conflicts and competed for a place of its
own among the dances that were already being danced, pending, as always,
benediction in the cultural empires of the world. Men's and women's bodies
displayed tensions of the "correct" and the "incorrect," of the "civilized" and
the "primitive," of the "authentic" and the "parody," and all these tensions
were sexualized so as to render the conflicts natural, universal, and unavoidable.

Blackout

Rioplatense *Roots*

Digging into the "origins" of tango is perhaps the most popular and controversial topic among tangueros. It shares in the dangers and the fascination of most
archaeologies. In reconstructing roots, issues of inclusion and exclusion are at
stake: It is easy to forget one group's participation and to exaggerate the
protagonism of some others, and not always for innocent reasons. Rather than
fully engage these questions here, in the beginning of my excavations, I have dis-
persed them throughout the text. Excavating tango roots at different places and
times is a counterintuitive undertaking. It serves as a reminder that questions of
origins should not be gotten out of the way at the beginning so that the interpretation can proceed. Rather, problems of originating belong in the middle because they are central to the interpretation. Yet I do wish to address some
paradoxes from the very start so as to disturb the erotic stereotyping of tango,
which usually universalizes its appeal and banalizes its tragedy. Tango is rooted
in long-lasting conflicts over race, class, and gender supremacy. These conflicts
are locally performed but globally framed through judgments over sexuality,
that obscure question leading into—in Freud's words—a dark continent. Not
surprisingly, in tango's case this darkness is associated with its black *rioplatense*
roots.

Tango-eroticism-roots-sexuality-primitiveness-blacks is a chain of jumpy, imprecise associations that skip logical connections and yet make sense—a

rac(ial)ist sense hardly avoidable even in those well-intentioned antiracist attempts at understanding roots-tango-blacks-sexuality-and so on. ... So entrenched is the succession of these terms that the chain of thoughts is almost
impossible to hold back. The participation of the black population of the Río de
la Plata region in the making of the tango has been turned into the construction
of rioplatense blackness through the tango and its representations. In tango's
case, the recovery of black roots (initiated by Rossi [(1926) 1958] and heftily de-
bated ever since) has entailed difficult paradoxes. On the one hand, it has acknowledged the importance of black participation in the creation of rioplatense
popular culture—a fact that has frequently been neglected and even erased. On
the other hand, no matter how important black participation is considered to
be, positioning it at the "beginnings" of tango reproduces the racist association
between blacks and "primitiveness."

Figure 2.1 is an anonymous sketch of the *tango de negros* (blacks' tango), pre-
sumably drawn "at the time" (published in the periodical *La Ilustración Argentina* in 1882). The illustrator seems to be encouraging the viewers to associate the
black dancers of the primitive tango with a primitiveness attributed to
rioplatense blacks. Their postures emphasize ape-like, uncultivated movements:
The hands hang down clumsily from bent wrists; their prominent knuckles and
curved fingers are more reminiscent of paws and tractive abilities than of skillfully exercised "hands" (especially in the female figure). The heads are articulated to the spine at a sharp angle, stressing the effort involved in carrying its
weight upright (especially in the male figure), and the curve of the spine itself
seems to denote the recent acquisition of the erect position, the burden of evolution and, simultaneously, the brutification of black bodies through slavery. In
addition, the heads and bodies are disproportionately exaggerated, as in apes
and human infants; thus the artist associates the infancy of humankind and the
origins of tango with a stage of primitiveness and of experimentation rooted in
blackness. And in the middle there is also the shadow, that erotic darkness, embracing the dancers on the ground.

Figure 2.2 is Fernando Guibert's drawing entitled "Negros Milongueando 1"
(Blacks Dancing at a Milonga), from the 1970s. This drawing, produced many decades after the other, challenges the simian, experimental movements of the
previous depiction. Guibert's black dancers are humanized and adult, but in
compensation, they are loaded with lascivious sensuality—eyes hardly opened
to awareness, muscles bursting open trousers and stockings, trance, sweat, heat,
grounded and contorted movements. These dancers of the tango (which
Guibert associates with the *milonga*) are possessed, out of their minds and too
much into their bodies, and their bodies are so enlarged that they hardly fit together on the dance floor. Their shoulders in upheaval, the music snapping at
their feet, they tiptoe on high heels, carefully in balance, releasing fingers like
ribbons. The black bodies move in a languid frenzy, abandoned, trusting to be
held by the surrounding bodies of their "tribe," which are equally entranced,

FIGURE 2.1 *"El Tango," a sketch depicting the* tango de negros. Source: La Ilustración Argentina 33 *(November 30, 1882).*

FIGURE 2.2 *"Negros Milongueando 1" by Fernando Guibert (1972)*. Source: *Fernando Guibert,* Los Argentinos y el Tango *(Buenos Aires: Ediciones Culturales Argentinas, 1973).*

linked, performing the tango ritual of ... fertility? They are held down by the arches, through which the city is glimpsed. Thus, Guibert's portraits of early tango dancers (whether exclusively of blacks or, as in some of his other works, of a mixed, criollo protagonism) produce associations of blackness with "strong instincts," original primitive instincts that, although shared by all human adults, are untamable in blacks—and are contagious.

Lauro Ayestarán already pointed out in 1953 that the contribution of black African slaves to American culture was "one of the most profound and complex problems to be faced by American musicology." And he wisely noticed that there was a widespread confusion between African cultural developments (rhythm in music and dance) and black skin color.

> It is curious how spirits that are unprejudiced regarding the racial or social
> problems of blacks, become dangerously racist or utterly reactionary when it
> comes to music [and dance]. [...] The black brings to America a culture that
> crashes against the culture of the environment and, in many cases, is absorbed
> by it, since [unlike cross-cultural or cultural exchange phenomena] he [or she]
> does not come as dominator but as dominated (Ayerstarán [1953], quoted in
> Matamoro 1976: 75).

Contemporary, mainstream argentinos rarely speak about race and seldom address the issue of racism. We engage in racial politics, but only indirectly. Race is usually considered to be a supplemental or derivative element within Argentina's well-developed class politics. This is a self-image we argentinos actively cultivate. We tend to avoid racial politics much as *estadounidenses* avoid talking about their socially mobile society in terms of class. In Argentina, race and ethnicity are constantly invoked, but they are not analyzed. They are most often embedded in the Argentinean practice of nicknaming. For the most part, the names retain only a loose association with actual skin colors or ethnic backgrounds. For example, everyone of Middle Eastern ancestry (including Sephardic Jews and Syrio-Lebanese) is called *turco* or *turca*; Ashkenazic Jews (including those whose ancestors came from Germany) are called *rusos* or *rusas*; someone who shows criollo or mixed white and Amerindian ancestry or who is merely associated with customs of the "interior" of the country is called a *morocho* or *morocha*; and anyone who is especially loved or hated can be called *negro* or *negra*, regardless of skin color, complexion, or ancestry.

Thus, the stereotypes acquire the effect of excess, of being too obvious owing to the conspicuous artificiality of the linkage with the referent. Perhaps the stereotyping is a fraught attempt to create insurmountable distinctions in an environment in which class mobility and racial and ethnic hybridity are the rule. Or perhaps the nicknames are a lasting symptom, a domesticated ghost of Argentina's disappeared blacks and Amerindians. By the time the nation was constituted, most of the black and Amerindian populations had died in war or had been whitened through interracial marriage, but the widespread belief is that the blacks left (for Uruguay) and that there were never more than a scattering of Amerindians in our end of the continent. Then again, the ghost could be of European origin. Some of the immigrants to Argentina fled racial persecution in Europe only to find themselves unwelcome in their new land because the values they hoped to have left behind were held by criollos and other immigrants. Ours is a long history of forgotten Argentinean genocides inherited from abroad, a long succession of denials: dangerous denials that carry a poisonous seed and threaten to outgrow and overtake antiracist efforts with renewed proofs of racial difference.

For these dangerous reasons, unavoidable when one focuses on tango's "origins" and evolution—whether of a unilinear or multilinear type—I have chosen to join those who emphasize hybridization at the origins, and among those, the ones who, far from portraying easy blends or give-and-take, point to a kind of hybridization that retains the conflicts and tensions involved in the process—sexualized class, race, and gender conflicts, where global politics have had a definite impact on the local configurations. The eroticization of these complex social conflicts and their interpretation in terms of sexuality have rendered them opaquely natural, universal, and hence banal (as if nothing could be done to avoid them). And despite, or because of, these tensions, the tango embrace occurs. It is the embrace of dominators and dominated (class-, race-, and gender-wise) struggling with and clinging to each other; trying to hold each other in place while dancing displacements.

The rioplatense popular theater of the late nineteenth century portrayed the sexualized tensions that were present in the emerging tango. *Justicia Criolla* (Creole Justice), written by Ezequiel Soria with music by Antonio Reinoso, was first performed in 1897 by a Spanish troupe. The play presents a newly arrived Spanish immigrant who questions the black Benito (a doorman for the Congress building) about his relationship with Juanita, a beautiful white woman. "How is it possible that Juanita, who is a beautiful woman, white like a page of high quality paper [...] and eyes as black as the conscience of an attorney; how is it possible, I say, that such a woman could fall in love with a man of color, with a *moreno*?" (Scene 1) (Natale 1984: 164). Benito protests that black skin is a question of fate and that white faces frequently hide dark, sinful souls. After a chorus of women clothes-pressers invites him to a celebration in which a soft guitar will play quadrilles and tangos—leading dancers in quebradas (breaking the waist)—Benito narrates how he seduced the charming Juanita.

It was a *Carnaval* sunday
and I went dancing at the Pasatiempo.
I asked Juanita to dance a scottish
and I decided to draw out her love.
I poured laments into her ears,

I was so tender and talked so much
that she was moved
by my thousand promises of eternal love.
I told the broad about my courage [...]
She was silent and so I showed off prodigiously,
and then in a tango I was so skillful
that I seduced her with pure *cortes* (Scene 9) (Natale 1984: 166).

When interrogated about Juanita's qualities, Benito remembers his emotions
while dancing tango with her. "Hmm ... it was so good! (Closes his fist.) When
dancing a tango with her (mimics tango steps while he talks), I secure her on my
hip and I let the music's rhythm carry me away and I submerge myself in her
dark eyes and she bends her head into my chest and in making a turn the
quebrada comes ... oh, brother! It relieves, it relieves ... my bad mood" (Scene
14) (Natale 1984: 166–167). Juanita, the white beauty, rejects Benito in the end and
he immediately starts courting another woman. *Justicia Criolla* is the first record
of a staged performance of a tango *orillero* or *arrabalero*—a tango from the city's
slums. The tango sexually relieves, for a brief moment, the racial, class, and ethnic tensions.

In *Ensalada Criolla* (Creole Salad), written by Enrique de María with music by
Eduardo García Lallane, first performed in 1898 by an all-rioplatense troupe, the
social tensions are displayed even more conspicuously. In this piece, the tango
competes for a legitimate place among other popular "native" dances (*pericón,
zamba*, etc.). Interestingly, the plot includes a British character who has been assigned the task of "studying the national customs, types, and products, to assess
the feasibility of offering new loans" (Ferrer 1980b: 379). Three scenes subsequently develop in the presence of this "contract anthropologist" who represents the judgmental colonizing gaze. (I will readdress the centrality of such
"marginal" characters in the next chapter.) Three low-class men of different colors (the blond Pichinango, the dark Zipitría, and the black Pantaleón; see Figure
2.3) present themselves as famous knife-fighters who in addition have three impressive criollas (not immigrants) as sweethearts. They compete with each other
in cortes and quebradas, making fun of each others' skills, and in the end recognize the dancing superiority of the black. Their sweethearts arrive—Aniceta, the
blond, who "wants no acquaintance with blacks"; Tongorí, the parda; and María,
the morena. The men invite anyone to compete, blacks and whites, in dancing
and fighting, and the women fight among themselves over the exclusive possession of the men and end up shedding their tears in the arms of their appropriate
partners. All couples perform a tango with plenty of quebradas (Natale 1984: 168–
170). Here the tango is once again the occasion for displaying the racial and ethnic mixture (the salad) that never blends, but it provides a fair opportunity for
showing "real" values as well—courage and seduction as opposed to race/class
discrimination. Again, the social tensions are shown as embedded in gender re-

FIGURE 2.3　Ensalada Criolla. Source: *Cover of libretto written by Enrique De María with music by Eduardo García Lallane. Fourth edition (Buenos Aires, 1903).*

lationships. And they were. In the micropolitics of tango, all social tensions are simmered in the sexual cooking pot—a pot in which sexuality seems to be a male concern over questions of maleness.

Tango and the "Macho" Cult

When (male) rioplatense writers start reporting on the tango—its origins, its nature, its development—from the 1900s on, one senses a curious lamentation, an embedded allusion to decadence, to a loss. It is as if, over time, tango had witnessed the fall of a pristine and dignified male whose nature somehow became compromised by erotic, heterosexual concerns. Some, such as Vicente Rossi, whose *Cosas de Negros* (Things of Blacks) was first published in 1926, establish the tango de negros as an Ur-tango. Its originally most relevant choreographic and musical features (Rossi calls them *técnica milonguera*, or milonga technique) were ruined and disfigured when they were moved from the *academias* (dancing locales of the initiated) in Montevideo to the underworld of Buenos Aires—a city polluted by European immigrants and high-class adventurers. Others, such as Leopoldo Lugones ([1911] 1968) and Ezequiel Martínez Estrada ([1933] 1968a), wrote highly polemical anti-tango essays, bringing to their readers' attention the fall of the courageous *compadre*, now weakened and debunked, tamed and civilized into a bad copy or an apocryphal version of himself in the figure of *el compadrito*.

Rossi's black *milongueros*, masters of cortes and quebradas, had, once upon a time, applied their innovations to all social dances. This technique, which at some point gave rise to the tango, had the remarkable capacity to enact "true" maleness (*virilidad*); it allowed the milongueros to exhibit "self-control and reserved gracefulness." As the técnica milonguera was appropriated by the tango, it degenerated into a "superficial and showy" style contaminated by erotic preoccupations (Rossi [1926], quoted in Guibert 1973: 62). Romanticism and interest invested in women ruined the milonga style. Previously, "naturally" defiant blacks had danced a forceful tango, focusing their attention not on female partners but on outdoing other male dancers. In his praise of blackness and of tango's black roots, Rossi erases both sensuality and love from his choreographic construal of the rioplatense blacks. Black milongueros performed their mastery over rhythm and movement "taking advantage of the opportunities for 'sensualizing,' with the disinterest and sufficiency of the one who does not need them. [...] It was not sensual. [...] Not even romantic, because in the cruel, brutish Bajo [slums] there was no place for the idyllic" (Rossi [1926] 1968: 119). Thus, a brutish, primitive environment enabled a natural maleness to arise, powerfully, on its own. This maleness was invested in black bodies opening up a space for themselves in a decadent, white, male world. And it was danced.

According to Rossi, this is how milongueros danced in Montevideo, in the Academia San Felipe, in the 1890s:

The black and his *compañera* (never black herself because there were no black women in the Academia) tangled themselves into a braid following the most demanding ritual: He held her by the waist with his right arm, his open hand planted on her lower back; with the left hand, he held her right hand, dragging her against his left hip. The compañera threw her left arm over the black's right shoulder and rested her hand on his shoulder blade, holding a handkerchief to combat the sweat that smeared her white powders or else a cigarette that she smoked distractedly. The legs were apparently locked. The heads very close to each other, almost touching when not temple to temple. The couple evolved in a block of this sort, as if they were one piece, admirably obedient to the musical times; light, flexible, their trajectory hazarded by incisions and gyrations as much unexpected as appropriate; tramplings and conversions would at a whim interrupt any soft slipping (Rossi [1926] 1968: 117).

A serious and solemn attitude on the part of the dancers created the strange effect of a ritual, a "natural" ritual in that no evidence of effort was perceived as the *orilleros* (slum dwellers) followed the "insinuating anxieties of an irresistible cadence." Rossi explains that the notes "flew, soared and landed; started flying again, suddenly," never catching our dancers unaware. They traced with their feet an "invisible pentagram, graphing the musical language." Music and steps followed each other so closely that it was impossible to tell which one took place first, giving rise to the "suspicion" that "feet scribble" the music on the dance floor. This is how Rossi describes the milongueros' preparation for sketching through the technique of the corte:

The couple slid slowly, winding softly and correct. Every now and then, in a turn, the corte. Here the black would tear his foot from the floor with laziness, first the heel, describing a semicircle centered around his toes that have not yet left the floor; abandoning the leg as if it were heavy, until the thrust completed the turn (all this in a few seconds), the couple returning to glide like a reptile in slow and measured contractions (Rossi [1926] 1968: 117–118).

The corte interrupted the walk with a sudden crossing of the legs provoked by the male partner. This readiness for trampling was then "converted" through figures—the actual scribbling—that resembled geometric diagrams. These were the moments in which the milonguero would show off his acrobatic abilities: "Locked [...], ready to trample and fall, conjured easily by a conversion, showing off, provoking a *salida* (escape, exit) to the side, a *carrerita* (short run-away) and a *parada* (standstill) or a *quebrada* (displacement of the hips) with a stomping of the heels (*taconéo*) like a full stop at the end of a paragraph" (Rossi [1926] 1968: 118–119). This illiterate way of dealing with writing, mimicking with body movements the mastery over drafting scripts, was unsuccessfully imitated by both pardos and whites. As an eyewitness of these mutual attempts at appropriation,

Rossi concluded that "while the blacks created the feeling of dancing on the deck of a boat sailing in rough waters, pardos and whites balanced, instead, on an elastic floor" (Rossi [1926] 1968: 118). I believe this difference in overall effect is relevant to the way males related to their female partners in the course of the dance.

Early tango *bailarinas*, Rossi instructs us, were pardas and whites. He gives us no hints or possible reasons for this fact, but his remark situates the terrain of contestation—between skillful black male milongueros, on the one hand, and pardo and white male dancers, on the other—in the racial identification of these women (who, being of lighter skin, were a step closer than the dark-skinned men to the locus of literacy and power). The men were all competing for the favors of lighter-skinned women. In this context the blacks were the intruders; at the same time, they mastered the dancing skills that all the others were attempting to imitate in order to gain the bailarinas' favors. These "favors," however, were carefully distinguished from possible associations with sexuality or erotically in-vested seduction. Bailarinas, writes Rossi, "were not required to exhibit any trace of beauty, only good dancing." He is also quick to clarify that "dancing was not performed for the sake of a momentary [bodily] contact with the woman but for the dance itself." These professional bailarinas, who worked in the academias from dusk to dawn, enduring tremendous fatigue under the effects of alcohol and tobacco, "were 'masculinized' in that the natural shyness and delicacy of their sex was subtracted, robbing them of any remaining means of attraction that could have saved them from a failed life." The presence of these unfeminine women, "masculinized" by the early tango world in the hands of their male part-ners, proved Rossi's point (shared by most tangueros to the present day) that in authentic tangos, "it was only the cult of a new art of emotions and dancy acro-batics that was pursued [...] exempt from any traces of sensuality for our crio-llos, under the tin roofs of their academias" (Rossi [1926] 1968: 110–111).

How is it then that tango is so frequently associated with machismo, that ma-chismo is almost synonymous with the practice of womanizing, that womaniz-ing is so entangled with sexuality and sexual politics, and that sexuality is almost impossible to tear apart from eroticism, seduction, and sensuality? Is this puz-zling (male) "cult of a new art of emotions," then, what *machismo rioplatense* is all about? Which emotions were those that were subjected to a new crafting? How was that new art performed? Serene, grounded, dragging his steps, shoulders raised as in falling upon himself from above, crooked, never perpen-dicular to the floor, distracted yet fully in control of each move, now and then giving a hint, a flash, a spectacular sample of all the emotional ammunition he carried, restrainedly, inside, leaving spectators in the dark, puzzled, trapped in an enigma exuding a strong stigmatic odor.

Rendered in such choreographically lush terms as those of Rossi's depic-tions—and of mine, mimicking his—the wholesome potency of the male milonguero, rather than generating uproar, could possibly congregate endless queues of wallflowers of all sorts of genders/sexes, rushing from every latitude, waiting for a chance to fall, enraptured, into such macho arms. Rossi warns, however, that there is no outside to this ritual: All traces of femininity and of heterosexual attraction become perverted so as to fuel further machismo and macho pride. A telling reminder of a different sort is also at play here, given that Rossi was producing these depictions in an exalted tone of lamentation. Of all this practice there was little left; only a faded copy ruined by romanticism and heterosexual eroticism. Any interest in either love or sex (with a woman) would corrupt the macho picture.

Machismo is a cult of "authentic virility" fed by a sense of loss ... brought about by Civilization. Its pious followers have been as much the tango defenders, like Rossi, as its most obstinate detractors. As an example of the latter, Ezequiel Martínez Estrada may have no rivals. In 1933, Martínez Estrada published an essay, "El Tango" (included in his *Radiografía de la Pampa*), in which he addressed the erotic malaise that had taken hold of the tango. His is also a critique based on choreographic and musical elements, but, instead of dwelling on the male prowess of the past, he focuses (not without cynicism) on the weaknesses observed in his day. The result is, again, a lamentation over a tango in which gender and sexuality have gone down the wrong male road: "[Tango] has none of the exquisite elements implicit in the structure of other dances. It is not about a man and a woman [...] where each, him and her, maintain the peculiar specificity of their character, added to a certain elastic distance. In tango, it is the equality [sameness?] of sex [gender]; it is the already known without surprises." Martínez Estrada's anti-tango is explicitly informed by a Freudian reading of gendered body politics—he mentions that other dances can be sensual or exciting, as in a Freudian "transference." Tango, however, is the sexual act itself, "devoid of fiction, no innocence, without neurosis." He goes so far as to liken tango to a "solitary act" (of masturbation?). In Martínez Estrada's opinion, tango's shortcomings reside in its failure to build up eroticism through seduction: "[Tango] does not excite through the casual contact of the bodies. It is about bodies united, [...] fixed, attached. Thus coupled, the flesh's ardor becomes numb after a few musical times. [...] No arousal, none of the unexpected in the contact. It is a settled contact, a preestablished pact, the contract of the tango" (Martínez Estrada [1933] 1968a: 129). Slow, tired, dragging feet, movements restricted to a dance from the waist to the feet, rigid torsos, legs awakened only from time to time, simulating a failed step, back and forth, as in doubting its own capacity to develop a walk. ... All these characteristics (Martínez Estrada's phrases and images) are symptoms of a "sensuality" that has exhausted the potential eroticism of dance. The tango movements, devoid of gracefulness, retain merely "the seriousness of the human being when procreating" (Martínez Estrada [1933] 1968a: 128). The dancers, possessed by the music, perform a mechanical act requiring no effort of thought, will, or desire. They face no risks or surprises.

Addressing, on the one hand, the national and international bourgeoisies (who had adopted the tango, turning it into a sentimental exercise) and, on the other, the tangueros, who had carelessly engaged as accomplices in this decadent, disempowering exploitation of the tango, Martínez Estrada attacks where it hurts the most: women and homosexuality. "Vaguely, the woman follows the male dancer sliding almost disarticulated. [...] Flesh hardly alive, not feeling or fearing anything. Safe, submissive, heavy [...], compliant." Her body, "anastomosized" to that of her partner, provokes no desire in the male viewers. Moreover, "in taking her away from him, something of his would remain in her, as in kidnapping someone's wife" (Martínez Estrada [1933] 1968a: 130). And in order to further discourage women from engaging in such a choreographic practice, he adds: "It is a humiliating dance for women, having given themselves to a man who does not lead them, who does not require them to keep alert to his whims nor to give up her will. It is humiliating in that the man is as passive as she is" (Martínez Estrada [1933] 1968a: 129). Swirling and twisting multiple arguments, tangoing an essay of de-tangoization, snapping at gender identities, biting the macho pride, poking at sensitive issues of sexuality, Martínez Estrada dwells on the loss of a once clandestine, infamous dance that "lived its natural life in all the glory of its filigrees" (Martínez Estrada [1933] 1968a: 128). This was the "wild" tango of the slums and brothels as performed by a formerly brave and dignified compadre.

Blatant statements of machismo surround endless tango debates on the question of maleness. Take, for example, Tulio Carella, writing in 1956, trying once more to solve the dilemma of macho pride that haunts the tango. He was one of those stung by Martínez Estrada's arguments about the humiliation to which women were subjected in dancing tango with men as passive as themselves. In order to "verify exactly the opposite," Carella returns to Rossi (Carella 1956: 40), that magnanimous eyewitness of the early tangos, who said that, as a matter of fact,

> in this agitated dance, women were led by their partner's whim and the impulse of the figures that he provoked. Hence, it was easy for them to lose track of the rhythm [...] and they had to cultivate the faculty of divination in order to follow such fidgeting about. Added to [tango's] aforementioned stress on [the women's] imagination, the strong shaking to which they were subjected should be taken into account; they were led backwards, pushed back and forth, sometimes led to sit on the thigh of their partner, sometimes led to bend and lean back (Rossi [1926], quoted in Carella 1956: 40).

How much more speculation over female bodies' strenuous manipulations and over female eroticism can be shamelessly piled up in order to assess tango's alignment with the macho cult? Regrettably, I can give you more, this time related to the lyrics, which, although apparently emerging at a later stage, sustained the same preoccupations: obsessions about virility. Two well-known contemporary argentino writers offer stunning examples: "Commenting on the decadence of tango lyrics, which even then went in for 'loud self-pity' among sentimental compadritos betrayed by their wenches, Paredes remarked dryly, 'Any man who thinks five minutes straight about a woman is no man, he's a queer.' Love among such people was obviously ruled out; I knew that their real passion would be (male) friendship" (Borges 1970: 278). Paredes, Borges's tough key informant on *malevo* manners, draws the macho line in a telling riddle: More than five minutes devoted to a woman makes a man queer. Is it homosexuality then, and not woman herself, that haunts tango's maleness? How can men's interest in women, and not in other men—as one might presume nowadays— indicate queerness? Adding some more logs to the fiery question of tango's macho cult, Ernesto Sábato explains:

> It was not [sex] that the lonely man of Buenos Aires was worried about; nor what his nostalgic and even frequently cruel songs evoked. It was precisely the contrary: nostalgia for love and communion, the longing for a woman, and not the presence of an instrument of his lust: "In my life I had many, many *minas*, / but never a woman." Tango expresses an erotic resentment and a tortuous manifestation of the inferiority complex of the argentino, since sex is one of the primary shapes of power. Machismo is a very peculiar phenomenon of the *porteños*. [... The porteño] feels obliged to behave as a male to the second or third power. [...] The guy carefully observes his behavior in front of others and he feels judged and potentially ridiculed by his [male] peers (Sábato 1963: 14–15).

Tango is not about sex—at least not about heterosexuality—it is about love, but love and sensuality (according to our previous informants) are queer preoccupations. Hence, macho men only care about the true passion of male friendship (following Borges and his informant), and they are obsessed by the judgments of their male peers (following Sábato), which, in turn, frequently revolve around their ways of relating to women (following all of the above). Would it help at all to talk about male homosexuality, homosexual latency, or male homosociality regarding machos and tango? It has been done (and heavily resented by the tangueros).[5] Where do these arguments leave tango women, with their hetero- and gynosexual interests and practices and their possible gynosocial bondings? I cannot follow these thoughts here beyond mere speculative provocation or redundancy. The enhancement of male dominance is so crassly stated and obvious that any denouncing commentary sounds flat. Moreover, those interpretations of the male/female relationships in tango that insist on the centrality of male bonds or the existence of a male society (such as those discussed above) only add a new layer of credibility to the macho perspective. Are there any alternative ways to talk about machismo? Moreover, is it worth investing any effort in trying to do so?

Machismo is a cult of maleness and, as such, perhaps should be left in the hands of its devotees. This has been the position of most women interested in tango. And I see the point. There is so much macho pride (and so much macho history) invested in these misogynistic remarks that one is tempted to leave machismo to die on its own. The problem is that it might not do so. Do you follow my thoughts? There is something telling about machismo in Carella's debate with Martínez Estrada, in Rossi's comments, and in Borges's and Sábato's contrasting but complementary remarks. Although women are at the center of the polemics, they do not play a central role. Women are, so to speak, the exhibited signifiers. The misogynistic remarks are, in their uses of women, manipulations among men. Male bonding, male society—*maleness* is what is at stake. And it is a power play between men.

These men debating maleness in tango are not just men insecure in their maleness, as Sábato (1963: 15) and others seem to suggest. There is no such thing as pure, stable maleness that can be attained either through profound individual reflection or through exceptional childrearing conditions. Maleness and its counterpart, the unmale (*not* necessarily the feminine), are products and records of gendered and sexualized class and racial struggles and of the struggle over the ghostly question of national identity. And these uncanny struggles, needless to say, have severe consequences for heterosexual women and for all homosexuals. Machismo is not an essence; it is a practice and a product of history. It has an internal dynamic and a macropolitical dimension. At both of these levels of analysis, men and women play their asymmetric parts. They negotiate and struggle, but these negotiations and struggles are not restricted to questions of gender, although they have been rendered in gendered terms. On a micropolitical level, men of various racial/class ascriptions struggle over women of diverse classes and races. It is a struggle for male supremacy waged between men but carried out through women. Whoever gets to the top at a certain point gets to define what maleness is all about. Maleness will be the reason given for being at the top, and thus the victory will seem "natural" and incontestable. The victory is a victory of the men of one race and class over those of another race and class. This position of supreme maleness will be permanently contested and put in jeopardy by the men and women who are not beneficiaries of such a definition of maleness.

From a macropolitical perspective, maleness and national identity follow intertwined paths.[6] Machismo, in particular, is an outcome of international struggles over manliness. "Macho" is the Spanish word for "male," but it has been adopted by other languages/cultures to refer to a "wrong" kind of maleness—to unmanly maleness. Manliness is here contrasted with maleness. Macho men are not so much unmale as they are unmanly. Machismo is a synonym for the barbaric, uncivilized "virility" attributed to latinos. It is used not for the purpose of destabilizing the category of maleness as a whole but rather to contribute, by way of contrast, to the consolidation of manliness—a "civilized" bourgeois maleness that is universally supremacist over all other class, racial, and national gendered identities around the globe. Modern imperialist manliness is a new kind of maleness that, unlike the old-fashioned machismo, promises to distribute its privileges (mainly in the form of protective "rights") among the women of its own kind (with the right kind of womanliness). And this manliness foresaw the possibility of a trickle-down of such privileges to other more or less macho (uncivilized) cultures of the world, as soon as they became assimilated to this progressive and "respectable" brand of manly (Western) maleness. Bourgeois manliness and modern imperialism were one and the same ideology, one and the same practice. Colonialism, in its different stages—born of the competition with other races, classes, and nations of men—feminized and turned unmanly the peripheral world.

Tango is one among many expressions of this conflict over maleness and as such is caught up in both internal and international wars. Tango, as popular culture originated in the periphery, has been immersed in debates about correct/incorrect (i.e., "civilized"/"barbarian") kinds of male-female relationships and has responded to and challenged the modern bourgeois constructs of gender identity that were being imported from Europe. In early tango times, class and race conflicts were clearly displayed in a gendered code that dramatized complex social conflicts in sexual terms. Argentina's incorporation into global capitalism, with its promise of class mobility and erasure of racial conflicts, helped render tango a potent, quasi-universal expression of gender/sexual struggle/passion. The issues at stake were thus simplified. After all, gender conflicts were interpreted as given, universal, unavoidable dilemmas. The problem was reduced to mere sentimental banality and to the terrain of the apolitical.

Two tango styles took shape from approximately the 1880s to the 1930s. I refer to these as the ruffianesque and the romantic. Generally speaking, the ruffianesque was the earlier, old-time tango and the romantic was the later, modern tango, but mostly they overlapped, making them styles, not stages (see Romano 1983). Throughout this period, the ruffianesque tango underwent a process of romanticization, but this process was not altogether unidirectional. Even today, tango as it is danced in Buenos Aires offers solid glimpses of tango's ruffianesque past. Thus, tango allows for a fleeting grasp of a changing Argentine-ness in which past and future "ideals" have shaped each era.[7] These traces and retraces can be followed through the past century of Argentinean popular theater, choreography, music, and lyrics. The *compadrito* and the *milonguita*— the main characters of the passional tango plots—have performed gender stereotypes and heterosexual dynamics that have been disturbing and unsettling for the bourgeois patriarchy, given its fixation with stable gender roles and respectability. In tango lyrics and memoirs, la milonguita, characterized as a rebellious broad, and el compadrito, as a whiny ruffian, have transgressed these gender bourgeois constructs in their tragicomic quest for social mobility. This quest has often been rendered in romantic terms. Tango itself—as popular dance and music—and the tango characters—el compadrito and la milonguita—were strongly invested in this goal of "moving up," of becoming "popular" and widely accepted. In the following pages, I retain this intricacy as much as possible.

Positions for the Lady (La Milonguita, or the Rebellious Broad)

At first glance, tangos seem to offer women two positions:[8] They can be either the object of male disputes or the trigger of a man's reflections. In either case, it is hard for a woman to overcome her status as a piece of passional inventory. The difference is that in the first position, the woman is conceived as an inert object of passion, whereas in the second she is a living one.[9] The tango poet selects one position or the other by establishing his distance from the plot. Passional tango plots go like this:

Un patio de conventillo.	A patio in the slums.
[...]	[...]
Una percanta, un vivillo;	A chick, an abuser;
dos malevos de cuchillo,	two knife-wielding ruffians,
un chamuyo, una pasión,	seduction, passion,
choque, celos, discusión,	crash, jealousy, discussion,
desafíos, puñaladas,	challenges, stabs,
espamento, disparadas,	confusion, runaways,
auxilio, cana ... Telón!	help, cops ... Curtain!

—La Comparsa se Despide (The Comparsa Bids Farewell), 1932
Lyrics and music by Alberto Vacarezza (Gallo 1970: 267–268)

In Vacarezza's *sainete*, the character who presents these lines adopts the perspective of an outsider, a voyeur of a tangoesque dramatic ambiance.[10] The woman (a chick) is clearly depicted as an object of dispute between the men (the seducer and the ruffians). All the action is centered in the knife fight and a probable murder. The actual victim is unspecified. Tangoesque plots of the passional type present male characters who need to display anger, violence, and courage. The victim of such outbursts might be the rival man, the unfaithful woman, or both. In any case, the avenger ultimately has to deal with the police, either as a fugitive or in prison. The male bond is reinforced through the isolated, trapped image of the woman, constituted as his prey. From an outsider's point of view, the public world into which this woman dared to enter is violent and male.[11]

Another example:

No batió ni salute! como estaba	She didn't say a word! since she was angry
cabrera	

hizo un lío de pilchas, secóse un lagrimón,

se miró en el espejo, campaneó la catrera,

y taqueando apurada los patios pasó.

[...]

Cuando estuvo en la puerta dijo:
"De todos modos
donde quiera que vaya estaré mejor."

Llegó el coso cansado del laburo y haciendo

un esfuerzo inaudito en un papel leyó:

"Porque estoy hasta el tope de vivir padeciendo,

me decido dejarte. Perdonáme. Margo."

Fue tan seca la biaba que la mente turbada

como herido de muerte al momento quedó.

Reaccionó de repente, iba a ir a buscarla,

mas como era canchero, el impulso ahogo.

Es la historia de siempre: una mina perdida

y una pobre esperanza conservada en alcohol.

she bundled up her clothes, sobbed a big tear,

she looked in the mirror, glanced at the bed,

and hurried her steps across the patios.

[...]

When she was at the door she said:
"In any case
wherever I choose to go I'll be better off."

The guy arrived tired from his job and making

a tremendous effort, he read on the page:

"Because I've had it up to here with living in pain,

I decided to leave you. Forgive me. Margo."

The blow was so strong that his confused mind

stopped instantly, as if mortally wounded.

Suddenly he reacted, he was going to go after her,

but being a streetwise guy, he checked the impulse.

It's always the same story: a lost broad

and a poor hope preserved in alcohol.

—*La Historia de Siempre* (Always the Same Story), ca. 1925
Lyrics by Celedonio E. Flores
Music by Pacífico V. Lambertucci

I take Celedonio Flores's depiction in this tango as a close-up and an expansion of Vacarezza's single line on "seduction, passion." Flores's tango plot is focused on intimacy; it gives an insider's point of view. The relationship of the heterosexual couple is at the center, along with their power displays. The woman is able to plan an escape, choosing the right moment (when she can avoid facing the man) and even writing a letter where she states her reasons: "I've had it up to here with living in pain." When the guy is hit by the news ("as if mortally wounded"), he thinks of revenge but decides it is not worth it. She is a *mina*, after all. The end of this account is crucial for understanding the morals of tango. The male goes on to lead the life of an alcoholic (which he probably already was), hoping to forget her. And her practical hope is that "in any case / wherever I choose to go I'll be better off." However, the (male) author's premonitory conclusion is that she is a "lost broad." A woman lost in the male jungle. Where was she to go? Tango lyrics most frequently suggest that, once they have left their original maternal household, women could only go from one man to another in an ambitious, endless, and damaging search. From a distance, in Vacarezza's account—as well as in many feminist interpretations—the tango woman is a victim. Close up, in Flores's account, the tango woman rebels against her victimization, but ultimately (zooming back to the distance), she has no chance. The threat of prostitution and violence invades all her attempts at mobility.

For quite a while, tango went through a stage of being "forbidden music" (Tallón [1959] 1964). Tango dancing was restricted to low-class and red-light districts,[12] and to the *garçonniers*. The first lyrics were openly pornographic.[13] The "illnesses of development" had infested the city of Buenos Aires: too many men, fast and unstable moneymaking, and prostitution (Tallón [1959] 1964). "Former [municipal] regulations authorized the establishment of one brothel per block, and additionally, a tavern, inn, or hotel where prostitutes could live and ply their trade. [Those hotels] are the places where clandestine prostitution is fomented" (Manuel Gálvez, *White Slave Traffic*, doctoral thesis presented in 1905, quoted in Salas 1986: 46). In his study of white slave traffic, Albert Londres (1928) likens Buenos Aires to Babel—with its multiplicity of corruptions and languages.[14] He narrates how he was taken by the French pimps to the knot of their business— Buenos Aires—where they competed with Polish, Italian, and criollo pimps to keep hold of "their" women. These women, indistinctly prostitutes and tango dancers, mediated through their bodies the relationships between men of all classes, races, and ethnicities: Paulina *la tana* (Italian), *la china* Joaquina (creole), *la rubia* Mireya (blond *uruguaya*), *la parda* Flora (*uruguaya mulata*), María *la vasca* (Spanish Basque), and so on (Salas 1986). They were identified by their color and ethnicity. Many of these women have been immortalized in tangos through male evocations, but little is known about how they lived and about what their relationships with men were like.[15] Sebastián Tallón offers one of the few extensive portraits of one of these women who lived a tango life at the beginning of the twentieth century ([1959] 1964: 37–54). She was born Luciana Acosta but went by the name of *La Moreira* (The Moorish-like). She was best known for her relationship with *El Cívico* (The Henchman), her criollo pimp.

SCENE TWO: EL CÍVICO Y LA MOREIRA

Three tango tableaux vivants.
   Cast: Tango Historian, El Cívico and La Moreira (dancers), Choreocritic.
   Music: La Morocha (1905), played by an organ-grinder.[16]

Buenos Aires. A room in a tenement house, tidy and shiny "like a jewelry shop." Louis XIV furniture, dolls and bows, and cushions decorated by malevos at the prison. A bed with a knife under the pillow. A dresser on top of which there is a great collection of perfumes and make-up utensils, mostly for a man's hair and moustache.

El Cívico and La Moreira compose the first tableau vivant as the Tango Historian, standing downstage left, recites the text.

The Tango Historian's spoken text:

In the years (190)5, 6, 7, and 8, El Cívico, between twenty-five and twenty-eight years old, lived in room number 15 of El Sarandí, a tenement house located on the street of the same name. His profession was that of exploiting his woman, La Moreira. [...] He was of South Italian ancestry (Albanian); she was the daughter of Andalusian gypsies. It is unnecessary to depict El Cívico as an extremely good looking guy, because the key to his success, as we all know, lay in his seductive ways. [...] The second key was his acute cleverness, his hidden criminal coldness, his art with the dagger, his courage. The third key was his "congeniality," his wealthy manners, his refined sociability, his skill at dance and his verbal skill. [...]

At dusk, La Moreira would go with other women to the "bar" of La Pichona [...] where she "worked" as a prostitute, as a *lancera*, as a go-between for clients and other prostitutes, and as a dancer. As a lancera because she stole wallets from the drunk distracted clients and from the immigrants who had money; as a go-between because she was associated with her "husband" in that business of deceiving poor souls and selling them as "novelties"; as a dancer, because she was a great one and because La Pichona's "bar" was one of the places that helped to give the tango its fame and its association with prostitution. At night, she was a tango-woman. Brave gipsy blood ran through her veins, and, even though she was apparently very feminine and quite beautiful, in her dark endeavors she showed great "courage" in throwing the dagger, and that is where her name comes from. She usually carried a knife; but when she had to wander alone at night in the outskirts or in dealing with "difficult" business—just think of the resentment of the less successful ruffians, lazy and cowardly, but nonetheless dangerous, whose women she took away—she wore high boots, almost up to her knee, and in the right one she carried a dagger or saber. Do not forget that the outskirts of the city saw times of violent madness and lust. Her looks: Not too tall, perfect figure, sensuous voice, like her face; like her walking. [...] Blue or red silk blouse with white polka-dots. [...] She closed her blouse from the neck to the bosom with a silk ribbon. [...] The lace collar completely covered her neck. Her waist was held by a contoured corset, armed with whalebone. The skirt was pleated and of a grey or light green color, and its exaggerated width displayed the frou-frou of her starched petticoats. [...] Her hairdo, a roundlet at the nape of her neck, held by turtle-shell clips

and combs, big golden earrings—the size of a glass rim—and from the neck-
lace dangled a locket. Well, the locket carried a portrait of El Cívico. [...] And
he loved his woman. The most dreadful thing about this arrogant subject was
his love for his woman. That professional prostitute who every afternoon
kissed him good-bye on her way to the brothel. El Cívico loved her. La Moreira
was truly his beloved, his everlasting companion. [...] His political indiffer-
ence, among many other indifferences, gives evidence of that obsession. [...]
The endurance of their relationship was dependent in this case not on the
marriage contract but on his morbid loving, on his continuously renewed attractiveness, on his being a consecrated artist of sex. Free of bourgeois commitments, without distractions, without physical or mental absences, in private life all of him was a refined and continuous caress, attuned to the
sensitivity of his woman, and even asleep he knew how to be her sorcerer. [...]
When he hit her, she would let him do it, even though she was able to fight
back like a guapo, because he did not punish her with the brutality of those
who could not master their whores, but with the demands of a handsome
master or jealous lover. If she would have left him, he would have tracked her
down to kill her; or perhaps he would have sought forgetfulness in alcohol.
[...] Tango lyrics do not lie when they insist, since Contursi, on moving Argentinean people with the laments of the abandoned *canfinflero* (ruffian/pimp)
(Tallón [1959] 1964: 37–54).

El Cívico and La Moreira compose the second tableau vivant as the
Choreocritic recites the text, standing downstage right. They display discomfort
with the Choreocritic's analysis, turn their backs to the audience, and perform
grotesque movements. They challenge and question the Choreocritic's words
with gestures, comments, and hissing.
Choreocritic's spoken text:
Tangos frequently portray characters with complex gender identities that are
troublesome when seen under the scrutiny of bourgeois patriarchal eyes. This
perspective, in turn, opens up a space for the proliferation of worrisome "per-
versions." What could be expected of a couple such as the one made up of an
unmanly although very male (macho) man like El Cívico and a woman like La
Moreira, feminine in excess and yet aggressively masculine? Nothing but more
transgression. La Moreira seduces women, taking them away from other men,
competitors in the business of prostitution. She provides El Cívico with an income combining the gains of the women that she seduces with that earned
through her own sexual dealings with male clients. El Cívico lays around the
house or hangs out at the bar, drinking with his male friends, comfortable to
be provided for. He fights with other men when necessary, that is, when La
Moreira's dagger is not enough. What kind of heterosexual relationship is
this?—Tallón asks himself in providing this portrait to his readers in 1959, as an
eyewitness of troubling times past. El Cívico pathetically monogamous,
effeminately in love with La Moreira, "knowing how to be her sorcerer even

asleep." La Moreira more pragmatic in sexual matters, always threatening to leave him and still carrying his portrait in a locket. One a pimp/gigolo, the other a prostitute/entrepreneur; each performing excess and lack, both genderwise and in their fragile monogamous heterosexual duties. Their relationship entails a double masquerade in which each edge of the male-female compound is exploited and recombined, eclectically: He performs a dependent, sentimental ruffian, she a self-made, treacherous broad. They are locked in yet another parody: that of heterosexual bourgeois mores.[17]

Tallón's transgressive "great dancers" of the tango are threatening in their exuberantly shaped yet ambivalent, unstable genders and sexuality: El Cívico is a cruel, even violent ruffian, but he is sensual, loving, and coquettish, although exploitative and courageous, even when economically and emotionally dependent; La Moreira is an astute and merciless broad, ambitious and potentially treacherous but submissive and condemned. There is no doubt that he leads and she follows, but she can foresee his next move even before he thinks of it. This is the tension of the tango *malevo*, the dance of a whiny ruffian and a rebellious broad.

El Cívico and La Moreira compose the third tableau vivant, finally seduced by the Choreocritic's "theory," which offers a portrait of them as a "whiny ruffian" and a "rebellious broad."

Blackout

La Moreira and El Cívico impersonate the stereotypes of the Latin lover in its male and female versions: El Cívico, a charming, unproductive pimp/gigolo; La Moreira, a two-timer, aggressive and sexually demanding. Both ruffianesque characters are more threatening to the elite/bourgeois man than to the elite woman. For one thing: The elite man dealt with them, but the elite woman did not. Also, the elite man was the one who carried on a double life and provided for his family, just like La Moreira (although she was more than that, and it was precisely this difference that created her attractiveness: She was unfeminine and yet a sexually active woman). Passional relationships like the one between El Cívico and La Moreira were intrinsically unstable. (Tallón explains that there was no marriage contract, only constant seduction.) The ruffianesque tango lyrics exploit these relationships between characters of ambiguous genders, frequently through a dramatic, predictable rupture. She betrays him and he confesses his frailty.

Percanta que me amuraste	Broad, you who abandoned me
en lo mejor de mi vida	at the height of my life
dejándome el alma herida	leaving my soul wounded
y espina en el corazón.	and a thorn in my heart.

[...]
Para mi ya no hay consuelo
y por eso me encurdelo
pa' olvidarme de tu amor.

[...]
For me there is still no comfort
and so I get drunk
in order to forget your love.

—*Mi Noche Triste* (My Sad Night), 1917
Lyrics by Pascual Contursi
Music by Samuel Castriota

She betrays him because of her ambition, triggered directly or indirectly by the presence of richer men. (The frequent plot of the young woman who leaves her poor barrio to go to a better neighborhood would be an example of the indirect presence of rich men.) The wealthy man who takes La Moreira away from her compadrito is a "real" man: a provider and two-timer. His established manliness draws her into an acceptable femininity: La Moreira the mistress (economically dependent and faithful). In addition, her racial hybridity (gypsy, Moorish-like) will be stabilized by the whitening miracles of wealth.[18]

Pebeta de mi barrio, papa, papusa,
que andás paseando en auto con un bacán,
que te has cortado el pelo como se usa
y que te lo has teñido color champán.

Babe of my neighborhood, beautiful gal,
who drives by in a car with a big shot,
who has her hair fashionably cut
and who has it dyed the color of champagne.

Que en los peringundines de frac y fuelle
bailás luciendo cortes de cotillón.
[...]
Pensá pobre pebeta, papa, papusa,
que tu belleza un día se esfumará
[...]
y entonces como tantas flores de fango
irás por esas calles a mendigar.
Pensás en aristocracias!
Ya verás que tus locuras
fueron pompas de jabón!

Who dances flashy [tango] figures
in the elegant cabarets.
[...]
Think, poor babe, beautiful gal,
about how your beauty one day will fade
[...]
and then, like so many flowers that grow in mud
you will go begging in the streets.
You think of aristocrats!
Soon you'll see that your crazy dreams
were soap bubbles!

—*Pompas de Jabón* (Soap Bubbles), 1925
Lyrics by Enrique Cadícamo
Music by Roberto Emilio Goyeneche

La Moreira, now called *pebeta, papusa, flor de fango, mina, percanta, milonguita,* is inscribed into a broader narrative that can explain her behavior (gender/class displacements). She is looked at from a distance.

From a distance, the femme fatale of the ruffianesque tango lyrics is nothing but a poor, deceived young girl tempted by the "lights of the city" who is not wise or strong enough to resist the fall. She is Eve, she is Little Red Riding Hood, she is the *costurerita que dió el mal paso* (little seamstress who took a misstep) or the *musa de la mala pata* (bad luck muse) of whom Evaristo Carriego, a tango poet,[19] writes, and to whom so many tango lyrics make reference. And she will pay (either for her sin or for her naïveté), as soon as her beauty and sexual attractiveness disappear—and they will. Her years of pleasure and wealth (thanks to upward social mobility) will be no more than a dream, and she will age alone, remorseful, and declassé. From a distance, her rebellion—of class and gender—appears aimless and frustrated. This is what the tango poets say about her—in male confessions sung by both male and female singers for an equally mixed audience. La Moreira, in a chain of permutations through the *milonguita*, the *papusa*, and the *flor de fango*, has been softened, feminized, and stabilized in her femaleness. Her stage of gender displacement is a parenthesis between her female origins and her female fate. La Moreira does not have a voice.

The distance that I repeatedly evoke is the distance of the patriarchal, moralizing gaze of the ruffianesque tango. This is the gaze that controls the establishment of distance. Both men and women reproduce it. In taking a closer look (challenging that distance), I found that fewer than 2 percent of all tangos have been written by women and that fewer than 4 percent (including those written by men) put tango lyrics between female lips.[20] Tangos are male confessions that talk overwhelmingly about women. Teary-eyed men talk about how women (mis)treated them. Women's cynicism:

Pianta de aquí, no vuelvas en tu vida,	Get out of here, don't ever come back,
no puedo más pasarla sin comida	I can't miss anymore meals
[...]	*[...]*
ni oirte así decir tanta pavada.	nor listen to you say such stupid things.
[...]	*[...]*
Te crees que al mundo lo vas a arreglar vos?	Do you believe that you are going to fix the world?
Lo que hace falta es empacar mucha moneda,	What you need to do is gather all your pennies,
vender el alma, rifar el corazón,	sell your soul, raffle your heart
tirar la poca decencia que te queda.	throw away the scant decency you have left.
Plata, plata y plata ... plata otra vez.	Money, money, money ... money yet again.
[...]	*[...]*
El verdadero amor se ahogó en la sopa,	True love is drowning in the soup,

la panza es reina y el dinero Dios.   the belly is queen, and money God.
Pero no ves gilito embanderado,   But don't you see, you militant fool,
que la razón la tiene el de más guita?   that reason belongs to the one with the
                                                    most money?

Que a la honradez la venden al   That honesty is sold for cash
  contado
y a la moral la dan por moneditas?   and morality is given away for spare
                                                    change?

—*¿Qué Vachaché?* (Whatcha Gonna Do?), 1926
Lyrics and music by Enrique S. Discépolo

Women's trickery:

Tengo un coso al mercáo que me   I have a guy at the market who looks at
  mira,   me,
que es un tano engrupido e'crioyo;   who is an Italian pretending to be criollo;
yo le pongo lo' ojo p'arriba,   I bat my eyes at him,
y endemientra le pianto un repoyo.   and at the same time I steal a coal from
  ...   him. ...
Me llaman la Pipistrela, y yo me dejo   They call me "Pipistrela" [Goofy], and I
  llamar,   just let them call me so,
mas vale pasar por gila, si una es   it's worth more to pass for a goofy girl, if
  viva de verdad.   you're actually sharp.

—*Pipistrela* (Goofy Girl), 1933
Lyrics by Fernando Ochoa
Music by Juan Canaro

Women's class betrayal, plagiarized over and over again, from tango to tango:

Se acabaron esas minas   Gone are those broads
que siempre se conformaban. [...]   who always conformed. [...]
Hoy sólo quieren vestido   Today they only want dresses
y riquísimas alhajas,   and very expensive jewelry,
coche de capota baja   a convertible
pa' pasear por la ciudad.   for driving around the city.
Nadie quiere conventillo,   Nobody wants a slum,
ni ser pobre costurera.   nor to be a poor seamstress.
[...]   [...]
Ser amiga de fulano   [Rather] to be a friend of so-and-so
y que tenga mucho vento,   and for him to have big bucks
que alquile departamento   in order to rent her an apartment
y que la lleve al Pigalle.   and take her to the Pigalle.

—*Champán Tango* (Champagne Tango), 1914
Lyrics by Pascual Contursi
Music by Manuel Aróztegui

From an oblique, different angle, I see these women struggling to survive. I see them falling from the restricted space of their miserable class to the secluded space of the cabarets and the hands of other men—this time, wealthy men. The passage from one class of men to the other is always through the tango, *Maldito Tango* (Cursed Tango), which deprives them of their former class identity only to lure them into a false identification with a higher class.

La culpa fue de aquel maldito tango	Blame it on that cursed tango
que mi galán enseñóme a bailar	that my lover taught me to dance
y que después hundiéndome en el fango.	and that later mired me in the mud.

—*Maldito Tango* (Cursed Tango), ca. 1918
Lyrics by Luis Roldán
Music by Osmán Pérez Freyre

However, taking a closer look, cross-eyed—a look more challenging to the patriarchal discourse—I see that a whole array of manipulative stratagems, deceptive behaviors, and strategies for subversion are allocated in tango-women's hands. Some ruffianesque tangos even recognize the effectiveness of these practices, giving women credit for becoming stable mistresses, marrying, and even taking the money and running away from their rich catch. *Pero Yo Sé ...* (But I Know ...), written and composed by Azucena Maizani, calls attention to the fact that women were well aware of men's weak points and of the frailties men often tried to cover up, arrogantly pretending to be in control of their lives.

Llegando la noche	As night falls
recién te levantas. [...]	only then you rise. [...]
Lucís con orgullo	You wear with pride
tu estampa elegante. [...]	your elegant figure. [...]
Pero yo sé que metido	But I know that obsessed
vivís penando un querer. [...]	you live mourning a love. [...]
Yo sé que en las madrugadas	I know that at dawn
cuando las farras dejás	when you leave the parties
sentís el pulso oprimido	you feel your pulse oppressed
por un recuerdo querido	by a dear memory
y te ponés a llorar. [...]	and it makes you cry. [...]
Pensar que ese brillo	To think that the luster
que fácil ostentas	you so easily display
no sabe la gente	people don't know
que es puro disfraz.	that it is pure fakery.

—*Pero Yo Sé ...* (But I Know), 1928
Lyrics and music by Azucena Maizani

Rosita Quiroga composed the music to *Campaneando la Vejez* (Considering Old Age). Quiroga, like Azucena Maizani (who wrote the music and lyrics for *Pero Yo Sé* ... , quoted above), was an extremely popular female tango singer. *Campaneando la Vejez* asserts, in a somewhat celebratory mood, that the milonguita was "never blinded" by the lure of the tango world. Perhaps it is not a coincidence that the music for this defense of the tango was written by a woman, or that Eduardo Méndez (the man who wrote the lyrics) placed the words in female lips.

Las luces de la milonga	The lights of the dance hall
jamás mis ojos cerraron	never blinded me
y el tango, el bendito tango,	and the tango, that blessed tango,
a quien canté con amor	to whom I sang with love
en vez de ser mi desdicha,	instead of being my misfortune,
como muchas lo culparon,	as many have blamed him,
fue mi palabra de aliento	was my word of encouragement
para luchar con honor.	to struggle with honor.

—*Campaneando la Vejez* (Considering Old Age), ca. 1920
Lyrics by Eduardo Méndez
Music by Rosita Quiroga

The reference to tango as "encouragement to struggle" feeds my own perceptions of tango's capacity to evoke subversion in women. The reference to the "honor" involved in the struggle seems to mark a moral distinction, either about the behavior of the other milongueras or about other opinions of what "honor" means. The lyricist leaves us with ambiguity. What is certain is that tango provided a more or less honorable means of survival for Maizani, Quiroga, and many other working-class women at the time. For some it also meant a door to social mobility, which, although not a universal value, was a rather strong craving introduced with urbanization, industrialization, and Argentina's incorporation into the bourgeois civilized world.

In tango lyrics, women were the brokers between men—frequently, class brokers. Moving upwards in the social scale seemed more feasible for them than for their male partners in class. As erotic currency, tango women's circulation was quite restricted. They were secluded in brothels, cabarets, and dance "academies." Moreover, their erotic trafficking did not necessarily translate into social mobility. By offering erotic services to men of higher classes, they could move closer to wealth, but usually without moving up in social status. Their eroticism was more typically spent in an illegitimate transaction (unlike the marriage contract), and hence, their full integration into the upper class remained doubtful. Status and wealth, as components of class, played against each other, conditioning the milonguita's access to social mobility. Tangos' morals warned the milonguitas precisely about this fact: the precariousness of their social ascent.

Che, Madam que parlás en francés	You, Madam who parlays in French
y tirás ventolín a dos manos,	and throws around big bucks with both hands,
que cenás con champán bien frappé,	who dines with very bubbly champagne,
y en el tango enrredás tu ilusión.	and who entangles your illusion in the tango.
[...]	[...]
Sos del Trianón, del Trianón de Villa Crespo. [...]	You are from Trianón, Trianón of Villa Crespo. [...]
Che, vampiresa ... juguete de ocasión. [...]	You, vamp ... plaything of the moment. [...]
Muñeca brava,	Wild doll,
bien cotizada ...	very costly ...
Milonguerita. [...]	Milonga-girl. [...]
Tenes un camba que te hace gustos	You have a rich guy who spoils you
y veinte abriles que son diqueros,	and twenty Aprils during which you are in demand,
y muy repleto tu monedero	and your purse is overflowing
pa' patinarlo de Norte a Sud.	to go shopping all over town.
Te baten todos Muñeca Brava	Everybody has you pegged, Wild Doll,
porque a los giles mareás sin grupo.	because you beguile every fool.
Pa' mi sos siempre la que no supo	To me, you'll always be the one who didn't know
guardar un cacho de amor y juventud.	how to keep aside a bit of love and youth.
Campaneá que la vida se va	Beware of how life passes by
y enfundá tu silueta sin rango	and cover up your no-class figure
[...]	[...]
muñeca brava, flor de pecado. [...]	wild doll, flower of sin. [...]
Cuando llegués al final de tu carrera,	When you arrive at the end of your career,
tus primaveras verás languidecer.	you will see your springtimes languish.

—*Muñeca Brava* (Wild Doll), 1928
Lyrics by Enrique Cadícamo
Music by Luis Visca

From this point of view (yet another distance), the "wild doll" (the rebellious broad) is reminded of her low-class origins ("Villa Crespo") as a marker of the social status that no "'parlay[ing]' in French" or "overflowing purse" (education or wealth) could ever overcome. Her illusions of social mobility are "entangled in tango." She can beguile rich men for a while (trick them with refinement and whiteness, both provided by her *"champán frappé"*—bubbly champagne— manners), but as a "flower of sin" (of illegitimate erotic encounters), she inevitably will fade. No matter how close she gets to wealth, the milonguita carries a "no-class figure."

Translated into tango choreographic terms, these lyrics suggest that milonguitas could provoke the dance (call the attention of their target through their glances, figure, and dancing abilities) and tempt the class/race status quo into motion, but they would never lead or "mark" (*marcar*) in the moment at which the special steps were performed. Milonguitas could challenge their male partners with the thrust and energy invested in the walks; manipulate their axis of balance by changing the distance between the bodies, the points of contact, and the strength of the embrace; play with diverse qualities of groundness in their steps; modify the "front" given to their partners, choosing to "face" them in misaligned angles of torso and hips; disrupt the cadence sought by their partners by not converting their trampling cortes at the proper musical time (thus imposing a need for skillful syncopation in order to keep up with the music); and add unexpectedly fancy ornamentations (*adornos*) of their own to the figures "marked" by their partners (modifying the height to which a leg should be raised in order to complete a certain figure, adding small stompings in between each step, lacing one leg around the back or front of the other before engaging in a conversion), complicating the timing of the conversions, creating anxiety, and even causing their male partners to modify their plans for upcoming steps.[21] I am listing here only a few subtle and keen dancing tactics to which a skillful tango bailarina could resort. Overdoing these or engaging in other, more crass, moves, such as stepping on her partner's foot or refusing to read his "marks" or to perform the expected figuras, would leave her out of the tango-dancing game, making her a wallflower unless she had another dance partner waiting in the wings. If she foresaw that possibility, she could leave her dancing partner in the midst of a piece[22] (running away with a better catch), but a milonguita could not lead the tango or take control of the system.

Some exceptions come to mind here. Several women were known in the tango underworld for running brothels, academias, and other tango locales employing professional female dancers for their male clientele (Benarós 1977; Assunção 1984). These women were highly though scornfully respected by the tangueros. As great dames of the underworld, could they have wielded influence in the socioeconomic and political discussions of their upper-class clients? In addition, the tango literature includes some exceptional cases of women partnering with one another. If they were from respectable families, they were assumed to be "practicing" in the privacy of their homes because they were forbidden to attend the morally questionable tango clubs. If they were beneath moral exclusion, the assumption was that they were rehearsing privately in order to strengthen their skills before facing the competitive tango world (Carretero 1964). No interpretations entertain the idea that women took pleasure in dancing with one another. Instead, male authors have reasoned that woman-with-woman tangoing must be either a preparation or a poor substitute for tangoing with men. There are also records of a few early episodes of women dancing the tango with each other in public. These performances have been construed as acts presented for the pleasure of male spectators.[23] Again, the assumption has been that a woman's erotic interest was not in her female tango partner but in the men who gazed at the spectacle. Thus, women's eroticism is constituted as restricted to a heterosexual money economy. Eroticism, the currency that enabled a milonguera to subsist, also prevented her from attaining stability in a higher social position. The milonguera's eroticism circulated in a strictly limited way, confined to illegitimate encounters marked by heterosexism and class. In tango, women's subjection seemed to be more a question of gendered embodiment than of class, but it was the intricate combination of class, heterosexuality, and race that put tangueras where they were. Their position was not one of full subjection, nor was it one of stable upward mobility (though their mobility was admittedly glamorous). In ruffianesque tangos women were in a difficult position of struggle.

There are many women (perhaps a majority) who are missing from these tangos and from my accounts: the women of the middle and upper classes. In ruffianesque tangos, they are absent from the scene. I will search for their telling silence in the voice of the whining ruffians.

Positions for the Gentleman (El Compadrito, or the Whiny Ruffian)

Tangos are spectacular confessions. They are public displays of intimate miseries, shameful behaviors, and unjustifiable attitudes. In tango, intimate confessions are the occasion for a spectacle. Unlike private diaries, letters, or journals, tangos are attempts to make a popular hit out of privacy. Hence, tangos are expressions of the private, personal world, addressed to the public world. In tango, "the personal is political," but not in the sense of the radical feminist slogan. That slogan represents an attempt to transform the public sphere by gaining public recognition for women's private experiences of oppression. Tangos are, from the start, written with an eye on the public: the audience, the social system. Tango lyrics expose intimacy to gain a slot in the existing public space, but they do not put identities at risk or challenge the status quo. As public confessions, tangos turn intimacy into sentimental banality. How is this possible? It is because tangos adopt a male position (whether they are sung by men or by women).

As Waldo Frank's often repeated phrase goes: "Man is the creator of the tango dance because he conceives it on the woman's body" (Frank [1931] 1969: 350). Tangos are male because their intimate confessions are mediated through the exposure of female bodies and because they are overwhelmingly written by men. Tangos are male confessions, intimate but not private. The display of female eroticism helps to draw attention away from male intimacy.[24] The lyrics are both personal and detached; the voice of a whining ruffian. For example:

Si arrastré por este mundo	If I dragged through this world
la vergüenza de haber sido	the shame of having been
y el dolor de ya no ser.	and the pain of being no more.
Bajo el ala del sombrero	Beneath the rim of my hat
cuantas veces esbozada	how many times
una lágrima asomada	did a welling tear appear
ya no pude contener.	that I could no longer hold back.
Si crucé por los caminos	If I wandered the streets
como un paria que el destino	like a pariah that fate
se empeñó en deshacer.	was determined to destroy.
Si fui flojo, si fui ciego,	If I was weak, if I was blind,
sólo quiero que comprendas	I only want you to understand
el valor que representa	the value that is represented
el coraje de querer.	by the courage to love.
[...]	[...]
Por seguir tras de su huella	Following in her path
yo bebí incansablemente	I drank tirelessly
en mi copa de dolor.	from my glass of pain.
[...]	[...]
Ahora, triste en la pendiente,	Now, sad from tumbling,
solitario y ya vencido,	alone and already defeated,
yo me quiero confesar.	I want to confess.

—*Cuesta Abajo* (Downhill), 1933
Lyrics by Alfredo Le Pera
Music by Carlos Gardel

Tangos are male confessions of weakness in terms of sex and class; but the class issues are interpreted as a sex problem. So, despite their clear awareness of class inequalities, the tango authors choose to blame women for having unfaithful adventures with wealthy men. Women are accused of lacking class loyalty and are assured a decadent and lonely end. Sexual infidelity and class disloyalty are the meat of the ruffians' confessions. And these class/sex betrayals are so enmeshed that the confessions express dramatic impotence. Impotence filled with indignation and rage; impotence with (a claim to) power. The confessions sentence their sexual female partners to class exile. Thus, tangos, with few exceptions, show no mercy for milonguitas who are enticed by the wealth of more powerful men—men more powerful because of their class, more powerful because they are men with access to two classes of women. When the compadrito addresses wealthier males, he might mock their fancy looks and laugh at their naïveté, but he never dares to offer advice or to predict a blackened future for them. Such reproofs are reserved for the rebellious milonguitas of the tango. There is a certain respect to be maintained between males, especially when the male in question is more powerful. Rich and poor tango men are joined through erotic games with poor women,[25] but this closeness generates further class asymmetries.

The brothels and cabarets are at the center of the ruffianesque tango stories. They provided the out-worldly space where the ruffian/pimp made a living and the *niño bien* escaped the restrictions of his class. But the encounter between compadritos and niños bien is fleeting and conflictive. The fights that often ended the evening of pleasure exposed the markers of distinction: ruffians with knives, *niños bien* boxing with their fists. Actually, rather than putting an end to the pleasure, these confrontations—measurements of power—prolonged it. Tango and fights over milonguitas were one and the same. Dancing tango did not only mean enjoying female company; it also meant competing with other men over dancing skills—that is, capacity for seduction—although tangueros frequently deny both things and assert that dancing tango was and is about dancing, not about either sex or power. It was in this convoluted setting of competition that the men from higher social classes looked for further distinctions from lower-class men and where lower-class men would insist that seduction was not at stake in dancing tango. Compadritos changed the rules of the game or at least refused to play the one proposed by the rich intruders. Wealth was not enough to prove the niño bien's power; eroticism (the capacity to attract and seduce sexually) was the precise weak point of his class. Thus, the dominant-class male had to prove his sexual supremacy as well, and not just by having the means to buy women. The compadritos knew this and feared the consequences.

In the class/sex competition between tango men of different classes, sex was the unstable ingredient. Sexual prowess and class domination did not necessarily coincide. Purchased sex clearly went along with wealth and status (the components of class), but sex by seduction—"true" conquest sex—remained subject to dispute. The balance was in favor of the higher-class men, however: Seduction by status and wealth and seduction by sexual attractiveness were hard to distinguish. (And I believe this is precisely why tangueros refused so vehemently to equate tango dancing with eroticism, sensuality, and even interest in women.) The compadrito was losing terrain on all accounts ... and so he confessed. But he confessed his weakness, not his powerlessness.

Fue a conciencia pura	It was in full awareness
que perdí tu amor. ...	that I lost your love. ...
¡Nada mas que por salvarte! [...]	Only in order to save you! [...]
El recuerdo que tendrás de mi	The memory you have of me
será horroroso,	must be horrendous,
me verás golpeándote	you see me beating you
como un malvao. [...]	like a villain. [...]
Hoy después de un año	Today, after a year,
atroz, te vi pasar.	atrocious, I saw you walking by.
Me mordí pa' no yamarte! ...	I bit my lips to avoid calling you! ...

[...]   [...]
Se paraban pa' mirarte.   People stopped to take a look at you.
[...]   [...]
Sólo sé que la miseria cruel   I only know that the cruel misery
que te ofrecí   that I offered you
me justifica   justifies me
al verte hecha una reina.   seeing you turned into a queen.

—Confesión (Confession), 1930
Lyrics by Enrique S. Discépolo and Luis C. Amadori
Music by Enrique S. Discépolo

The ruffians of tango confessed strategically. By making a public display of their whining, they simultaneously admitted their defeats and justified their wrongdoings. They were entering the class/sex struggle from a perspective invested in pain, frustration, and anger. The audience of these ruffianesque confessions was made up of whoever could share the ruffian's pain, anger, and resentment. Wealthy men proved their access to two kinds of women: rich (wives) and poor (milongueras). Ruffians and pimps had access only to the women of their own class and were frequently dispossessed of even them. Wealthier women were beyond their reach. Those unattainable women were precisely the ones who could make a difference favorable to the compadritos in the class/sex competition of the tango world. The compadrito's confession was meant to elicit the sympathies of those wealthier women to whom he had no other access.

Through their tearful confessions (the truthfulness of which I do not doubt), the compadritos expressed their pain *and* exposed publicly the private undertakings of everybody else. The display of the ruffian's intimate feelings carried a vengeance. In order to explain his pain, he spread the rumor of the illicit adventures undertaken by rich men with the milonguitas. And once these were made public, the heterosexual class alliances were in jeopardy. It was not that the higher-class women ignored their men's infidelities ... but that the ruffians, through their confessions, exposed more than just transgressions. Their whining (which provoked the indignation of most "manly" males) gave proof of the sensitivity, the "humanness," the loving capacity of the ruffian/pimps. And by enlightening these other women, they moved them. The ruffians sought to demonstrate that the milonguitas were not merely the victims of sexual exploitation; they were also tricky wealth-mongers. In his confessions, the compadrito would never tire of listing the milonguita's strategies and manipulations or grow weary of whining about them. In addition, he revealed that the whole situation was at least as much a problem of double-standard morality as a problem of class inequality. The ruffianesque tango confessions were a whiny, loud claim to power: the power to become socially mobile.

Through these confessions the tango ruffian attempted to show that he had changed. The class and gender alliances of the higher-class women were challenged: True, they were abandoned by the men of their own class, just as the tangueros were abandoned by the women of theirs. According to the confessions, the milonguitas were not victims and did not deserve other women's pity. Thus, the ambiguous gender identities of the tango characters were set in motion; the class alliances were destabilized; the class inequity was questioned. The ruffian's social mobility was made possible through and in love. At this point, however, he was not a ruffian anymore. He was a symbol of the past and so was the ruffianesque tango.

Once confessed, the tanguero's weakness becomes his success. (How else could women forgive him for his past?) And, in confessing, he becomes romantic, justifying all his abuses, mistreatments, and excesses through love. Romanticized, tangos reached the middle classes, all kinds (classes) of women: It literally became "popular" ... and the tangueros made millions. A new kind of love conquered the women of formerly inaccessible classes, and it produced wealth. The ruffian, no longer a ruffian, attained social mobility. The tango produced new members for the middle class and in expressing their feelings it expressed the feelings of the old members, too.

Carlos Gardel, the "immortal" idol of tango, is a telling example (see Figures 2.4 and 2.5). His success at upward social mobility and the corresponding wide smile are venerated by all his followers. His bow ties and tuxedos, always present in his popular movies, stand out as signifiers of the new status and wealth he had attained (Ulla 1982). His lustrous hair, combed tightly backwards, suggests his readiness for a dive into the waters of glory and simultaneously shows a careful, oily preparation for a smooth slip, an inadvertent or welcomed penetration into a higher class. His social mobility is loaded with eroticism. Gardel is celebrated for singing *El Día Que Me Quieras* (The Day You Love Me), a romantic song (not a tango by any means, but "tangoized" because it was the tango idol who sang it). In the 1935 film of the same title, directed by John Reinhardt for Paramount Pictures, Gardel plays a wealthy young man, Julio Argüelles, who is madly in love with Margarita (played by the Mexican actress Rosita Moreno). She is a low-class woman—a professional dancer—who, although also in love with him, insists that class barriers stand between them. He proclaims that he is poor so long as he does not have her and promises that, despite the barriers, they will get married in the name of love. She cries, and with her, the audience. Love can (and should) overcome all social restrictions. Julio and Margarita (in a plot repeated innumerable times) become lost in each others' gazes—gazes as open to the future as they are closed to opposition from outsiders. Their intimacy is their power.

What is interesting to me about this Gardelian message is the operation of substitutions that it involves. Actually, Gardel was from the lower classes himself, and everybody was well aware of this. Thus, he was referred to as "*el Morocho del Abasto*" (the guy of a dark complexion from the Abasto—Buenos Aires's Central Market). He had fought his way up painfully, but in this film, Margarita, in a role

FIGURE 2.4   *Portrait of Carlos Gardel, c. 1930.*
Courtesy of the Archives of Bruno Cespi.

reversal, is the one waiting to be rescued by a rich and privileged Gardel in the role of Julio Argüelles. Gardel's actual past might have been displaced and hidden behind the female character's poverty, but I believe that Gardel's poor origins also played a part in the film. Gardel was undoubtedly a much more powerful "character" than any of the characters he played on the screen. Inevitably, there was slippage between the fictional character and the movie star. Thus, as "Julio Argüelles," Gardel performed the traditional romantic bourgeois role of a wealthy man saving a woman from poverty. But as "himself," Gardel demonstrated to his viewers that moving up was possible, since (through the tango) he had done it. And as both "Julio Argüelles" and "himself," Gardel communicated that once upward mobility was attained, men could pull lower-class women up with them. For the milonguitas the message was: "Wait until men of your own kind make it." For higher-class women the message was that Gardel's coarse, poor past was in the past, fully overcome, and that rather than being an impediment for love across class boundaries, a man's rise from poverty added spice to a romantic relationship. The ruffian never completely disappeared from the picture. The ruffian and his broad, the one whining and the other rebelling, persevered in the tangueros' romanticized confessions as milestones of an uncivilized past—a barbaric past, plagued by ruffianism—when Argentina was not yet as-

FIGURE 2.5   *Carlos Gardel and Rosita Moreno in* El Día Que Me Quieras, *1935, Paramount, directed by John Reinhardt. Source: Cover of sheet music for* Sus Ojos se Cerraron. *Lyrics by Alfredo Le Pera and music by Carlos Gardel. Southern Music International, Buenos Aires, n.d.*

similated to the Western modern project. Gardel's representations of a gaucho, poor and bent by fate, run parallel to his presentations of tuxedoed success. As such, this stubborn double presence was proof that social mobility was possible and that Argentina could actually develop. It was, after all, progressively—in both senses of "progress," as "advance" and as "ongoing"—being incorporated into the Western bourgeois world (a world of love as much as of money and politics).

From approximately 1918 to the 1930s, an important share of tango lyrics was devoted to this sentimental ruffianesque genre in which the compadrito laments the loss of his lover (who was often his provider, too).[26] Bourgeois manners were not settled in Argentinean society and the middle classes were in the making. When, through the acceptance of the Argentinean elite (facilitated by Parisian approval), tango and the middle classes got together, a new perspective on love was introduced into tango lyrics (Ulla 1982: 77). Vengeance and resentment were transformed into melodrama and nostalgia, and the ruffianesque characters blended into romantic heroes. Tango, in its lyrics and choreography, became more polished, and the musical time slowed down and became more sentimental.[27] However, this did not happen all at once. This vestigial ambivalence, the mixed nature of arrabalero and romantic, was the secret ingredient that made faith in social mobility and in national progress possible.

The ruffianesque/romantic lyrics were made popular through the *sainete* (popular theater). The compadritos performed ruffianism, either as low-class picaresque characters placed in tenement houses or dressed in tailcoats, drinking champagne in a cabaret. The first time one of these tangos was presented to the general public with great success was in the play *Los Dientes del Perro* (1918). In that show, the tango *Mi Noche Triste* (My Sad Night) was sung by a woman— Manolita Poli[28]—so as to buffer even further the potential shock of the ruffianesque lyrics (about a pimp abandoned by his prostitute/lover) (Salas 1986: 130). Obviously, the Parisian influence was already there; tango's boom in Paris had occurred before World War I. (Although tango's popularity in non-Spanish-speaking countries was more closely related to the dance and to the music than to the lyrics, the international acceptance of "tango" as a whole had a great impact on how lyrics of a dubious morality were received at home.) As a result, by the time the ruffianesque/romantic lyrics had proliferated in Argentina, the ruffians had already been sentimentalized and exoticized. Sentimentalization of the music (from a 2 x 4 to a 4 x 8 musical time, which made it slower and more languid) had been happening in parallel, especially at the behest of the argentino male elite, but also in response to the demands of the Parisian elite in general (and, as some authors also mention, at the request of the Italian and French female dancers of the Buenos Aires cabarets).[29] The purpose was to make tango a more "accessible" dance in sexual and class terms, but the transformation was not smooth. The sentimentalization of the tango was a struggle loaded with complex social tensions. As with the lyrics, the sentimentalized dance was at odds with an older style. The *canyengue* or arrabalero choreographic style (based on the milonguera technique) persisted on the stage as an exotic proof of the success of Civilization (see Rossi [1926] 1958; Martínez Estrada [1933] 1968a).

Docile Bodies in Rebellion

Women's participation in tango, whether as characters (representations of femaleness) or as audience members, presents a dilemma. Tango has avoided giving any straight answers about women, perhaps because they were/are seen as the pawns of the tangueros' male wars. However, tango's mixture of whiny male confessions about female trickeries and cruel admonitions for the female betrayers has led me to question the hegemony of the macho message. I read the whininess and the admonitions as evidence of women's rebellion. Without such perils, the whiny confessions would have no referents and the admonitions would have no purpose.

Estela dos Santos writes: "As a typical example of a macho society, the tango—created, administered and dominated by males—has had at its center a marginal zone inhabited by women who sang it and danced it" (Santos 1978: 2225).[30] In tango, the marginals are at the core. In the plots of tango lyrics, the presence of women is crucial. Women singers have been at least as famous as their male counterparts—with the exception of Carlos Gardel—and the female audience of tango has at times outnumbered its male counterpart (Santos 1978: 2226–2227).[31] Are these women simply the objects of male domination? I am reluctant to accept a thesis that would explain these facts by stressing men's ability to manipulate women, thus making tango just another example of the perpetuation of patriarchal power. I have, generally speaking, no doubts about men's intentions of manipulating women; my questions are rather about the echoed declaration of their complete success. Women have never been just "docile bodies" or "passive objects." Tango, both in its lyrics and choreographies, has recorded women's abilities to subvert and negotiate.

This is not to say that women succeeded either. What I wish to emphasize is that any approach that assigns winners and losers dismisses the relevance of the power struggle that pervades all tango stories. In taking the endings of the stories for the end of the struggle, such approaches neglect the actual operation of power in the heterosexual relationships. A reading of tango that is oblivious to the strategies of the weak—the active presence of women as resourceful subjects—rushes a continuing battle into frozen images. Women have been victimized by tango ruffians in the most cruel and patronizing ways, but they have given their men a hell of a lot of trouble. And I believe that despite the threatening outcomes of tango plots—overwhelmingly favorable to men—women followers of the tango cult were often heretics when it came to the macho cult, rejoicing over the female characters' abilities to make trouble.[32] Women were receiving useful knowledge.[33]

True, women in tango did not have a global, revolutionary project in mind; instead, they displayed a series of concrete subversive moves tempered by their interests in survival. In doing so, they reproduced the female stereotypes: prostitutes, mistresses, wives ... but, perhaps the copies were not perfect—subversive reproductions? The women aimed at improving their embodied lives, which in that context meant gaining a *more rewarding exploitation,* and this was not a minor endeavor. They discovered there was something they could do; they could move from the accepted poverty of one territory—the outskirts—to the questionable flashy lights of the downtown cabarets. *Move.* They were passionate objects, not passive ones. Objects that had, if not a say, at least a *move* to make in the power game. Women in tango are part object, part subject. To paraphrase Jean Baudrillard, the stratagems of the milonguita had the ironic thrust of a subjectivity in the process of being grasped (Baudrillard 1984: 134).

Power is thick, dense, heavy; its nature is viscous, ... it's sticky. The movements of resistance carry along old traces, recombine old stereotypes with new territories; rejected identities stick to new desires.[34] Are these stratagems, which only work imperfectly, so easily co-opted by the "macho" system? How can one define when the resistance ceases to play within the lax rules of the patriarchal game and actually starts to distort its very shape and limits? By lax rules I mean here the capacity of the ones in power to adjust and manipulate a challenging situation in order to preserve the status quo or the myth of a status quo. I believe that to address women's resistance merely as complicitist or as meek moves within the dictates of machismo is to reinforce the myth of a stable system and contribute to a politics of paralysis.

An account of the practices of victimization and subversion enlightens the actual dynamics of power in a way that the crystallized image of a victim cannot convey. A less powerful existence, even when the degree of inequality is dramatic, is quite different from a powerless one. This is not to minimize the abuses of male power to which women are submitted in tangos: Women are prostituted, exploited, and sexually abused by pimps and clients, beaten up, and even murdered. However, I insist on the importance of distinguishing between the experience of victimization and the attribution of an identity as a victim. The practice of victimization needs to be constantly reactualized in order to prevent insurgencies from becoming challenges to macho hegemonic power. Victims, as a fixed identity in the experience of powerlessness, are only those who have literally lost their lives. My mother says: "*No está muerta quien peléa*" (She who fights is not dead).

The operation of power—in its circularity of impositions, negotiations, and upheavals—permanently reproduces subjection and rebellion—at least as long as the subjected ones are present and alive. Is insurgency only another manipulation of the dominant "discourse"?[35] In Joan Cocks's (1989: 150) words, is it possible to "retain the notion of a phallocentric culture that is hegemonic but not totalitarian"? Or to put it in tango tongue, are these lively milonguitas just making fools of themselves when they try to cheat their pimps and ruffians? No doubt they are according to the tango authors' morals, but who believes that their morals are the actual end of the story?

At this point, I wish to invite the tango audience into the picture. If the female audience believed in the premonition of a bleak future for their "self-destructive heroines," they would be paralyzed. These women would never attempt any escape from their legitimate territory. If, in addition, their men and the whole "state apparatus," if you will, adhered to this belief, they/it would come to a restful status quo. The whole discipline and control apparatus would become unnecessary. Such a situation, besides leaving a lot of people jobless, would favor the reemergence of rebellion. Given the popularity of tango in Argentina, only a few must have believed in the tale's ominous ending. The popularity has to do not with the endings but with the depiction of the endless conflict between oppressors and oppressed: rich and poor, whitened and colored, "civilized" and "barbaric." The popularity, among women in particular, resides in the blatant exposure of strategies of insurgency on the part of the victimized heroines. The milonguitas were role models, even caricatures, but so were the bourgeois morals. And if the tango men and the bourgeois men and women believed in the defeated or self-destructive end of the milonguita, so much the better! (More room on the dance floor for her to perform challenging steps.)

SCENE THREE: TANGO ON POWER

Complete cast of characters, some reading, some listening, some reciting, some sleeping, most of them sitting on the floor, and a few walking. All of them deal, in some way, with the following text.

Chorus's spoken text:

Power is thick, dense, heavy; its nature is viscous … it's sticky. It hides from itself as if it would always be somewhere else and in someone else's hands, arrested, ready to be overtaken. It lures, it fascinates because of its absent presence. Permanently fretted, rubbed by/against it, unable to take it, a grasp.

Power melts when held in hands. It transports with its animal smell, promising to shape at last unspoken, unthought desires. Power is a movement, a displacement as such. When thought of as a thing, it can only be sensed by tracing its social life.

No clear point of departure, no clean line of trajectory, no constant thrust, no final aim except for the potentialization of itself. Its majestic, outworldly looks are tied to hypergrounded occurrences of struggle. Power moves in a dominion of pure specificity and total pragmatism.

Power seems to belong to a universe of full intentionality: It defies representation except for that of a "source" while endlessly pulling in resistant resources. Positionless and yet ubiquitous, power takes up faces and operates in a time and place it defines for itself. Cutting off patterns directly from embodied textures, stitching bureaucratically misfitting parts, one after another, with invisible thread, stepping relentlessly on the pedal like a mad, expert seamstress driven by ambitions of seamlessness, power *fabricates* nightmarish totalities. Fear.

Blackout

3
Tango and the Colonizing Gaze

SCENE FOUR: EROTICISM, EXOTICISM,
AND THE COLONIZING GAZE

Tango à trois.

Cast: Choreocritic/Milonguita, El General/Compadrito, Colonizer/Spectacle Impresario, Chorus.

The Choreocritic, a milonguita (centerstage left) sits at her desk writing. She pauses periodically to think or to browse through books, note cards, and the pages of a manuscript. As she writes, her tape-recorded voice "reads" the text; her voice adopts the fretful and detached tone of a milonguita. El General (an arrogant compadrito) and the Colonizer (a foreign spectacle impresario) repeatedly interrupt the Choreocritic's work. At first, they try to drag her onto the dance floor to dance a tango. She resists, and El General/Compadrito and the Colonizer/Impresario end up dancing with one another.

Meanwhile, as the tape recording of the Choreocritic's voice advances, the Chorus highlights some of her words by repetition and mockery.

Choreocritic's voice on tape, "reading" her text:

Tango expresses, performs, and produces Otherness erotically through exoticism, and in doing so, it plays seductively into the game of identification—an attempt at "selving" by creating anti-selves. Tango is simultaneously a ritual and a spectacle of traumatic encounters, and of course "it takes two": two parties to generate Otherness, two places to produce the exotic, two people to dance.

Chorus:

Of course it takes two ... *(nodding their heads).*

In thinking about two and tango it is the male/female couple who rush in, dancing Otherness and exoticism, but it actually takes three to tango: a male to master the dance and confess his sorrows; a female to seduce, resist seduction, and be seduced; and a gaze to watch these occurrences. The male/female couple performs the ritual, and the gaze constitutes the spectacle. Two performers, but three participants, make a tango. However, the gaze is not aloof and static; rather, it is expectant, engaged in that particular detachment that creators have toward the objects of their imagination. The gaze can substitute for the male dancer; the gaze can double itself and dance instead of the tango couple. The gaze and the tango performers can change places, but they cannot exchange roles. The tango couple, whether dancing or looking back at the gaze that usurps their steps, is fixed in a "down-up" relationship with the gaze, a position from which, in Eduardo Galeano's words, one can see only giants (1986: 117). Conversely, the gaze—a spectator by nature—will always be placed "up-down," a location from which everything is reduced to miniature dimensions.

When tango performers and spectators no longer shared a common race, class, and/or culture, tango became exotic for the ones "up" who were looking "down." When those situated "up" in the power hierarchy were drawn, for a variety of reasons, to perform the tango themselves, tango became exoticized; its choreography, lyrics, and music split and changed. Within the analytic (artificially drawn) boundaries of the national—as opposed to international—context, that is, within the domestic dynamics of the political economy of passion in Argentina, the gaze, the third participant in the tango, was mostly that of the male elite

Actually, it takes three ... *(consult with one another through the exchange of skeptical glances).*

The gaze can double itself ... but they cannot exchange roles *(shaking their heads strongly).*

"Down-up," all giants *(grave voices; bodies stretch, mimicking gigantic proportions).*

"Up-down," miniatures! *(giggles; bodies contract, mimicking miniaturesque proportions).*

intruding in and transforming the underworld of Buenos Aires. When the elite men,
fighting the *compadritos* for an active place
in the dance, started to tango with the
milonguitas, the tango saddened and
slowed down. When middle-class dancers
took the place of the ruffianesque ones, the
tango became so bland as to be hardly recognizable, but the lyrics, romanticized
ruffianesque stories, were there to remind
the new dancers that they could look "up-
down" at the barbaric past and "down-up"
at social mobility and civilization. These
elite and middle-class Argentinean gazes,
however, did not have the power to
exoticize on their own. They were dependent looks, and they carried dependent
hopes and desires. The gaze with the power
to exoticize is the colonial gaze, and this is
the lens through which local admirers
would see the tango.

When the elite ... *(Chorus anticipates tape; they adopt rigid,
snobbish postures).*

When middle-class dancers ...
*(Chorus anticipates tape; they
perform bland tango steps).*
But, but ... *(enjoying the sound
of the word).*

Dependent looks ... *(looking at
each other, puzzled).*

Exoticism and autoexoticism are interre-
lated outcomes of the colonial encounter,
an encounter that is asymmetric in terms of
power. And they contribute to the further
establishment of imperialism. Perhaps exoticism is one of the most pervasive imperialist maneuvers. The promises of incorporation into Civilization through Progress
can produce a stumbling development
filled with economic fits and starts. Previously nonexistent middle classes can
emerge from massive pits of poverty and
enjoy, now and then, crumbs of wealth. The
promise of development is a bourgeois,
modern, imperialist drug. But without exoticism, the hooking up would not be complete. Exoticism creates the need for Identity and assures that it cannot be attained:
It is the imperialist hook that cannot be unhooked. Exoticism creates the abstract,
unfulfillable desire for completeness in the
colonized while extracting his or her bodily

Exoticism! *(First, fascinated,
and then, following the text
word-by-word with extreme at-
tentiveness).*

Unfulfillable ... *(shaking their
heads in despair, sighing, and fi-*

passion. Exoticism is a colonial erotic game played between unequal partners.

In tango, the latina or latina-like couple dances for the bourgeois colonizing gaze. French, British, U.S. colonizers and their local allies have been key in shaping the scandalous meaning of the tango steps. Fascinated with what he interprets as the "erotic" male/female plays of compadritos and milonguitas, the colonizer sees a spectacle in miniature of his own plays with the colonized: the colonized female dancing in cooperative/resistant movements with the colonizing male, held tightly in his imperial arms, following his lead. The reverse, however, is probably even more true. The colonizer dumps on the tango his own representation of the imperial erotic relationship with the colonized. In addition, the colonizing gaze extracts tango's passion to nurture its bourgeois, respectable, but voracious desire—the colonizer's male, insatiable desire for conquest and domination. The colonizer dominates with desire; the colonized resist with passion. Furthermore, this subversive, struggling condition is not a choice; throughout history the colonized have been driven to resist by the imposition of imperial fate and its fatalist rulings. Tango scandalously fits the secret, dark, exploitative side of the imperial promises of civility and civilization.

Tango's erotic and exotic steps are hard to distinguish in this colonial context. For the purpose of drawing a parallel between the role of the colonized in the imperial dance and the female role in tango, I will briefly isolate the erotic component of the tango steps. It should be clearly understood, however, that the erotic and the exotic moves are performed at the same time and in unison and that the exotic component ultimately gives full meaning to the erotic.

nally, chatting distractedly in low voices until their next intervention).

The colonizer and the colonized … extract. *(At first, the reference to "the colonizer and the colonized" recaptures the Chorus's attention. They are soon taken, however, by the sound of the word "extract." They repeat "ct" and play with the making of the sounds in their mouths.)*

Dark, dark *(repeating and playing with the sound of the "k").*

Hard, hard, hard *(repeating and playing with the sound of the "d" until the Choreocritic's voice on tape pronounces "however" in a warning tone).*

However … *(looking at each other meekly; they remain silent and still until their next intervention).*

As the tape continues with "The Erotic Step," the Choreocritic/Milonguita and the Chorus pay attention to the movements performed by El General/Compadrito and the Colonizer/Impresario, which follow the rhythm of a languid tango.

The Erotic Step: Just walk. Walk together. Walk as close as necessary. So close that, at a certain point, the differences between the two of you will become essential. The need to master the other is irresistible. The resistance to being engulfed is hysterical. Keep on walking. You cannot give up. It is beyond your control. Just try to make it beautiful. Perform. Do not hide your fear, just give it some style. Move together but split. Split your roles. Split them once and for all. One should master, the other should resist. And forget that you know what the other is going through.

No matter how hard I try to isolate the tango couple from the gaze, the colonizer's viewpoint (either performed by himself or by his admirers) slips into the dancers' intimate scene. The sexual politics of tango cannot be split from the presence of the spectator, a male/colonizing spectator (even when the audience is a mixed male/female one), but I will try again.

Hard, hard *(dragging the sounds of the letters).*

Intimate ... hmmm *(extremely interested).*

In the tango-dancing couple, the role of the Other is performed by *la Otra* (the female Other). This Otra is guilty of Otherness or, to put it differently, is accused of being an Otra in that she lacks and exceeds in "something" compared to the male. Her excessive passion and her lack of control over it beg for the male's embrace and leadership.

La Otra! *(joyfully clapping and cheering at the mentioning of their heroine).*

The Choreocritic/Milonguita, unsatisfied with the Colonizer/Impresario's performance, takes his place in the dancing couple. The Chorus and the Colonizer/ Impresario now watch attentively as the Choreocritic/Milonguita dances with El General/Compadrito. The tango music accelerates as they perform complex footwork and figures.

She will be dragged into the dance, be led through it, and be held while performing unstable/excessive footwork. Her "instinctive" passion can never be totally subdued, and she passionately resists and is comforted by the male embrace/control. But her passion is aroused by the male desire. He instigates her passionate outbursts by that thigh of his, insistently seeking to slip it between her legs throughout the whole musical piece. She resists with her hips, disjointedly moving them back and forth, her smooth satiny skirt easing both his way in and her way out. Her high heels unbalance her own resistance; or it could be—and usually is—interpreted the other way around: It is precisely her suggestive hips and footwork that provoke his desire for sexual conquest. The dancing couple will not clarify the issue. Ambiguity in these erotic matters is the key to perpetuating the ritual. Their torsos show agreement, their faces, fatalism, tied up in their tightly held hair. But from their waists down, struggle. The erotic step is developed in this context, heavily focused in the presence—the body—of la Otra. The male imposes his reassurance, confirming his Identity by seating her, albeit briefly, on his lap (*la sentada* is the name given to this figure). She, la Otra, has helped him to define his masculine self: The movements of la Otra, her display of resistance/difference, provoke and constantly reshape his Identity. Her own identity, as she falls back on her feet, remains unsettled, incomplete, on the move in those transitions between accepting and resisting subordination to his Identity. Hers is a colonized identity born to be unfulfilled. Although this is the knot in which she is caught, it is not a problem rooted in her "essence" or in female "nature." Her incompleteness is rooted in the erotic power

Ambivalence in these matters … *(resigned at first and then enacting "torsos show agreement," "faces, fatalism," and so on, as in following choreographic instructions).*

Yes! *La sentada! (performing grotesque sentada figures).*

Knot … caught *(playing with the sounds of the words).*

FIGURE 3.1   *Dancers Carlos and María Rivarola perform a tango "sentada" figure.* Source: *Promotional poster for* Tango Bar, *1987, Castle Hill, directed by Marcos Zurinaga.*

game that establishes as a rule the search
for a stable, totalizing Identity.

In the intimacy of tango's erotic step the
male dancer and the colonizing spectator
become allies, almost O/one and the same,
hiding from each other their asymmetries
in power and hiding their power over her

altogether. La Otra should repeatedly resist, give in and resist, confirming simultaneously his Identity and the colonizer's supremacy. The female dancer's role is one of legitimizing the need for external intervention and leadership.[1] A phrase to keep in mind: "One's sense of self is always mediated by the image one has of the other. (I have asked myself at times whether a superficial knowledge of the other, in terms of some stereotype, is not a way of preserving a superficial image of oneself)" (Vincent Crapanzano [1985], quoted in Trinh 1989b: 144).

Keep in mind … *(wondering where "the mind" is: they look into each others' pockets, ears, shoes, buttons).*

The Exotic Step: In the exotic component of the tango dance, the latina couple, as a heterosexual couple, is the focus of Otherness (difference, distance, and inequality). The male/female erotic tensions (their intimate sexual politics) are consumed by the expectant desire of the colonizer's gaze. The couple, not the female anymore, is the passionate source for the reassurance of the colonizer's Identity. The latina "nature," primitive and close to human instincts, demands a civilized control while providing passionate defiance. The gaze of the colonizing spectator is now the single interpreter of the scene. The struggle between femaleness and maleness has moved a step down on the social evolutionary scale on which bourgeois imperial civilization reigns at the top. The latina couple has been exoticized. It stands there, before the colonizer's eyes, as a symbol of a primitive past. And the distance, the difference attained, is pleasurable.

Latina couple! *(celebrating at first and then confused as they try to "establish distance" and "consume" each other).*

Latina "nature"… *(Thrilled at first and then worried about the latina couple as they learn that the struggle "has moved a step down on the social evolutionary scale." They take measuring tapes and rulers, notepads, and pencils out of their clothes. They record each other's measurements and attempt to figure out a scale. They discuss their resulting positions on the scale until the Choreocritic's voice on the tape pronounces the word "excess.")*

In the performance of the exotic step, another dimension of Otherness is exploited: the ambivalent attraction and repulsion that the Other provokes in the One. Fascination. The exotic threatens the colonizer (the One) through her displays of excess. The exotic is the passionate haunting past at the margins of the imperial civilized world. For the Other to become an Exotic, this threat needs to be tamed, tilted toward the side of the pleasurable, the disturbingly enjoyable: the erotic. The dangerousness, however, should be retained, evoked again and again, as proof of the necessity of colonial civilized domination.[2] Exotic places, persons, and things often display the amiable side of the Other: plants, perfumes, clothing, jewelry, food and spices, art, courtship, songs and dances. The threatening side, equally exoticized, remains in the background, a haunting violence: dictators, volcanos, diseases, polygamy, poverty. The femaleness of the exotic is identified precisely in this ambivalence. The exuberance, sumptuousness, danger, and sensuality of the exotic are, again, a result of measuring the Other (as she is constituted) with the imperial bourgeois morality of the colonizer's stick. The exotic Other always comes out of this operation as an oddity lacking something—rationality, control, decorum, propriety—and exceeding in something else—violence, sensuality, passion.

Excess ... hmmm *(relieved).*

Exotic Other ... *(exuberantly seducing one another).*

The exotic tango steps are yet the immoral steps of a latina couple as seen by the colonizer's gaze on the stages or the screens of the theater of Civilization. Western imperial stages and screens are set up to pass judgment, to frame, and to present the exotic as such. These imperial bourgeois settings constitute the exotic. "Civilized" theaters (Western and bourgeois in their moral standards), whether actually located in the West or in the Rest of the World, stage and project exoticism as the return of the colonially repressed.

Exotic tango ... *(improvising "exotic" tango steps).*

The latina couple of the exotic tango performs passion in the imperial or

imperialized courts of the world without
compassion, compatibility, empathy, or any
other sort of reciprocal passionate response
on the part of the colonizing gaze. The
tango couple falls into the abyss of the col-
onizer's Desire. Exotic Otherness is precisely | Exotic Otherness is precisely
this condition of incompatibility (no shared | this condition of incompatibil-
pathos, no passion in common, no feeling | ity (no shared pathos, no pas-
together) that opens the necessary space | sion in common, no feeling to-
for exploitation to develop. | gether) that opens the
necessary space for exploitation
*(in unison with the voice on
tape).*
Turn, turn, turn *(gyrating dizzi-
ly).*

At the turn of the century, tango brought
a novelty into the exotic genre; it performed
a "distinguished" and demimonde, urbane
exoticism from the already in/dependent
colonial world. Tango was an Exotic suited
to the complex modern imperial bourgeois
ordering of the world. Tangueros were offered the most "distinguished" positions
among the exotics of the time, and performing tango was one of the few sources of
income available to them. In this triangular
paradox, autoexoticism was probably a (colonially) loaded choice.

The Chorus exits in disarray as the voice on tape ends. El General/Com-
padrito, the Colonizer/Impresario, and the Choreocritic/Milonguita bow for the
audience, proud, arrogant, "distinguished."

Blackout

In the following sections I address the specific ways in which tango was incorporated into the world economy of passion as one among many exotic dances.
Tango appears as an episode in the long history of colonial manufacturing of the
exotic. My own sketchy version of the process stretches from the late seventeenth to the early twentieth centuries. I focus on some events that pertain to
current practices of exoticism and to changes in the subjects/objects of exoticism. The goal is to understand the ways in which tango already "fit" and was
colonially tailored to fit into the colonizer's desire to consume passion. Thus, as
the narrative comes closer to the time of the tango rage in Paris (1900s), details

increase, offering a fuller picture of the social ambiance that was so receptive to this new exotic dance. Some reflections on the manufacturing of exoticism foreground the analysis of the tango craze in the main capitals of the world.

Manufacturing Exoticism

Colonialism is not only economic expansion and domination, it is cultural domination and ethnocentrism as well. Colonialism believes in only *one* culture [...] although the imperial perspective is not a simple denial of the others. The diversity of the world is "charming," tasteful for the colonialism of 1900. [...] It is kept in an illusory and mythical way in the imperial consciousness. Such is the function of exoticism (Leclercq 1972: 44–45).

Tango entered the realm of the exotic at the beginning of the twentieth century. By that time, the rules of exoticism were fully defined and developed owing to several centuries of colonialism. The history of the hegemonic centers of exoticization loosely coincided with that of the centers of "style"; and these centers in turn followed the avatars of imperialism. Venice, regarded as the capital of "good taste" in the fifteenth and sixteenth centuries, was displaced by Spain—a sign of its political claw in the New World. And France seems to have finally reached the rank of expert in the production of exoticism during the seventeenth and eighteenth centuries (Braudel 1981). Although contested by other world powers at that time as well as in the following centuries, the French have not yet been displaced as the experts in taste (including intellectual taste).

The production of luxury and of "primitiveness" went hand in hand with the manufacturing of exoticism: Variety was precious and denoted mastery over the world. As Stuart Ewen observes, "By the sixteenth century, Western European markets were filled with refined and delicate goods: silk and woolen cloth, fine pottery, spices, rare woods for inlaying furniture. These and other items contributed to an increasingly affluent life-style for those capable of purchasing it" (1988: 31). Detailed inventories of exotic goods and the hierarchical ordering of their correct combination were established in categories from *cuisine* to *ballet-opéra*. For example:

Among the various parts which make up the dinner of a real gastronomer, the principal ones come from France, like butchers' meat, fowl, and fruits; some are imitated from the English, like beefsteak, welchrabbet, punch, and so on; others come from Germany, like sauerkraut, Hamburg chopped beef, Black Forest fillets; still others, like olla-podrida, garbanzo beans, dried Malaga grapes, pepper-cured Xerica hams, and liqueur wines, from Spain; others from Italy, like macaroni, and Parmesan cheese, and Bologna sausages and polenta and sherbets, and more liqueurs; still others, like dried meats and smoked eels and caviar, from Russia; and others from Holland, like salt cod, cheeses, pickled herring, curaçao, and anisette; and from Asia come Indian rice, sago, curry, soy, Schiraz wine, coffee; from Africa the Cape wines; and finally from America come things like potatoes, yams, pineapples, chocolate, vanilla, sugar, and so on: all of which is ample proof of our statement, already often made, that a meal such as can be ordered in Paris is a rare cosmopolitan whole in which every part of the world is represented by one or many of its products (Brillat-Savarin [1825] 1972: 317).

This appropriation of goods collected from the "four corners of the world" was only a starting point. It is worth noting the political implications of the successive hierarchies established among the countries that provided the "principal" parts (France), "imitated" parts (England), "other" parts (Germany), "still other" parts (Spain, Italy, Russia, Holland), and finally the ingredients provided by continents-colonies (Asia, Africa, America). The next necessary step consisted in reshaping all that was raw and primitive so as to make it fit for the imperial taste (rebaptized "international" and/or "cosmopolitan" after the French Revolution). Thus, Jean-François Revel argues that French haute cuisine is "international in the sense that it has the capacity to integrate, to adapt, to rethink, I will say almost to rewrite the recipes of all countries and all regions" (1982: 215). Moreover, Ewen notes that during the reign of Louis XIV, France managed to establish itself at the center of the market of style. Wisely advised by Jean-Baptiste Colbert, the king developed an ingenious strategy: "With our taste let us make war on Europe, and through fashion conquer the world" (Colbert, quoted in Ewen 1988: 30). French industries interested in manufacturing style, such as haute couture, were then promoted to construct and exploit an aristocratic veneer. The history of the spectacles of entertainment available to European elites follows the same path delineated for haute cuisine and haute couture. The exotics (among *les étrangers*) were almost de rigueur in the political opéra-ballets organized under the surveillance of Louis XIV. The foreigners, like the foreign foods, were carefully classified according to the roles they could fill in the plays. The modes of representation regarding their temperaments and clothing were rigidly prescribed.

> The Greeks wear a round cap with several feathers around its rim. The Persian coiffure is quite similar. The Moorish wear short, curly hair, black faces and hands, uncovered heads unless you use a string of pearls as a diadem. They should wear earrings; the Turks and the Saracens should be dressed with a *doliman*, their heads covered with a turban and a tuft of feathers. The Americans wear a bonnet of feathers of diverse colors, a skirt of the same kind covering up their nudity; they always wear a collar made of the same feathers from which they take out a bouquet for each hand when they dance. The Japanese wear a big tuft of hair on the back of their heads (Menestrier [1682], quoted in Paquot 1933: 192).

Hippolyte Jules Pilet de la Mesnardière, in his *Poétique*, published in 1639, gives detailed recommendations on the temperaments that representatives of different nations should exhibit in plays and explains that although the typology is not meant to be completely rigid, some situations should be strictly avoided: "Do not ever make a warrior out of an Asian, a faithful of an African, an impious of a Persian, a truthful of a Greek, a subtle of a German, a modest of a Spaniard, nor an uncivilized of a French" (La Mesnardière [1639], quoted in Paquot 1933: 195). The illustrious servants to the courts of the Louises were obviously not shy when it came to stereotyping exotics, neighbor rivals, or even themselves. The politics of representation were taken very seriously so that every exotic would confirm the right to the mastery of the most "civilized."

Orientalism, or in Marcel Paquot's words, the "revelation of the Orient" (to the West), seems to have set the stage for the machinery of exoticism to develop. The practices of appropriating and reshaping the Oriental for the consumption of Western European elites were further applied, with adjustments, to other candidates for the exotic condition. One particular aspect of this process is especially relevant to the tango: the production of passion.

For the purposes of the "world of spectacle," that is, of making a spectacle of the world, toward the beginning of the eighteenth century L'Académie de Musique recommended incorporating the "fabulous system of the Orient" into the French opéra so that the new characters would provide "the variety that has become very necessary." "The ardent sentiments and the extremely *amoureuse* passions, such as we conceive them in Asia, could become a suggestive theme in the modulations of the music. The Orient is *par excellence* a matter of the opera" (Pierre Martin [1774], quoted in Paquot 1933: 184). In this way, Paquot continues, Turks, Assyrians, Persians, Chinese, Indians, and Tartares started singing and dancing "*le ballet.*" And *les Américains* joined *les Asiatiques,* based on the chronicles that narrated their "complete and very free loving practices." The genre of the *Ballet Héroïque,* composed during the time of the French imperialist efforts in the Oriental Indies and represented by such pieces as "Indes Galantes" (1735) and "Sauvages" (1736), helped to create a strong association between Asia and America, based on commingled erotic fantasies.[3] The plots elaborated an exotic version of the impossible, contradicted, and/or betrayed love theme. A typical story line begins with some gentle character driven by the wars among the Europeans into the colonies in search of the pleasures to be found in the mild climates. Pirates and the Indian Ocean are usually present, and a love/rescue story touches a special slave. Suddenly the scene changes and a volcano and/or earthquake situates the audience in Perú, where some Inca princess falls in love with a Spanish conqueror. A group of Caribs, Amazonians, or Tupinambas witnesses and approves of the situation with their offerings and *bon sauvage* good spirits, and some odalisks perform an Oriental dance. At this point, an intrigue occurs and the story ends with some sort of forgiveness (Paquot 1933: 185–186).

The morals of these opera stories are quite clear: First, exotics can be piled up, mixed, and homogenized under a few traits; second, the pleasures and passions that they enjoy are closely related to their "natural" as opposed to "civilized" geographical and cultural environments; third, "nature" and the "savages" are loaded with both pleasant and threatening promises; fourth, the "civilized" European heroes are susceptible to the fascination provoked by the exuberance of the exotics (and especially the exotic women); and fifth, a strong piece of advice: Although the seduction of the exotic might be unavoidable, the passion is incompatible and sooner or later unresolvable conflicts will arise. The encounter with the exotic is impossible; it will remain forever a disencounter, unless—of course—the exotic becomes tamed by Civilization.

Spain aggressively displayed its control of the "world" before the noses of its imperial rivals beginning in the sixteenth century, when it was the utmost colonial power. Toward this end, the *españoles* had accumulated exotic "cultural diversity" as well as gold from their colonies. Along with other exotic goods, exotic music and dances from the exotic American lands were introduced into Europe. The *zarabanda* and the *chacona, fandangos, zambapalo* (or *samba*), and *kalinga* were some of the exotic genres performed by those exotic peoples who had an exotic mixture of indigenous, black slave, and criollo bloods (Carpentier 1981). Thus, when the imperial tables of world power turned, the Spanish exoticizers ended up exoticized, lumped together with their passionate colonial subjects as bearers of a common provocative, untamable sensualness (or, to put it in other words, they shared the lack of civilized bourgeois capitalism). Curt Sachs, in his classic *World History of the Dance* (1963), quotes an unidentified "outstanding authority on modern Spain" in order to distinguish the "Spanish dance" from what "we are accustomed to think of as dancing"—"we" meaning refined Europeans—and stresses the connections between Spanish movements and those practiced in other exotic places: "We are accustomed to think of dancing as a movement of the feet, but the Spanish dance is more than that. In Spain they dance with movements of the hands as in India, Java, and Japan, they dance with the hips, with movements of the body as in Africa and Arabia, and the feet serve less for the locomotion of the dancer than as the physical expression of his emotions" (Sachs 1963: 349). The scholar upon whose authority Sachs relies is also quick to point out the primordial relevance of the "emotions" (as opposed to "locomotion") in the Spanish dance. The expression of ardent Spanish emotions produces an arrested dance with few displacements (that is, little locomotion), reflecting perhaps Spain's difficulties in adjusting functionally to the rational "locomotion" demanded by modern times.

Subsequently, Sachs's expert in Spanish matters offers some remarks about passion that are almost identical to those attributed later to the scandalous tango rioplatense:

> The Spanish dance is fundamentally different [from the European duet
> dances]. Its charm lies in the spectacle, not in the contact [of the bodies]. [...]

FIGURE 3.2   *Flamenco dancers. Courtesy of the Mansell Collection Limited.*

It symbolizes sensual receptivity and sensual power. Indeed, the most remarkable thing about it is the strongly marked symbolism of rejection. It is much
oftener a dance of coldness than of ardor. In love as in the dance resistance
and coldness are the best means of enticing men and driving them to madness
(Sachs 1963: 349).

Again the fundamental difference is stated, now in terms of the "spectacle" of
"sensual power": a sensuality so powerful that it dismisses the actual contact of
the bodies; so powerful that it could not avoid making a spectacle of itself. This
expert, whose insights Sachs admires, resorts to the notion of a universal (imperialist) symbolism (a "symbolism of rejection") to read calculated, manipulative
strategies of seduction into the Spanish dance, which he then relates, without
mediation, to those strategies applied by women to "entice" men, "driving them
to madness." The Spanish dance is feminized in its excess of passion and in its
passionate manipulations. The spectacularization of the exotic is thus complete
for the benefit of Sachs's expert's exoticizing imagination. Tango, which came
straight from *Sudamérica* in the 1900s, fell into the same interpretive frame. Tango's embrace, the proximity between the dancers' bodies, the abrupt stops and
entanglements of legs, were added curiosities to the exotic spectacularization of
passion. As a result, the fascination of the colonizers was updated and the discourse of exoticism was refurbished. Associations between tango and flamenco
based on the manipulative effects of a restrained passion (a passion struggling
to explode and show itself) are recognizable even today when the world show
business industry chooses to offer a strong, passionate, dancy dish to its exotic-
hungry public.

Another parallel between the exotic dances of Spain and those coming from
the newly in/dependent Latin American nations can be traced through the eroticism ascribed to their exotic women. The scholar admired by Sachs explains:

But aside from its aim of exciting the onlooker, the Spanish dance has still another goal—and that is self-excitation. The dancer fascinates the spectators
and dances herself into a state of ecstasy. The motion of the hips, the *zarandéo*
[high flapping of the skirts], with which it is possible to express every degree
and shade of sensuality from lasciviousness to the magic flame of ecstasy, is of
incredible suggestive power. One might say that in this movement lies the
magic of sex (Sachs 1963: 349).

Expressing "every degree and shade of sensuality," from lasciviousness to ecstasy, the *bailaora* displays "the magic of sex." Fascinated and threatened by his
own male/exoticizing imagination, Sachs chooses to problematize "her" rather
than his naughty thoughts. And, in order to redeem this temptress (whom
Sachs's expert equates with Eve), he mentions the "natural decency of the Spaniard," by which he meant Catholic piety. Thus there was some potential for

(moral) improvement. Finally, he admits that, fortunately, "all unpleasant and repulsive qualities" of these "semi-exotic" Spanish dances have been "freed" as they were "adapted to the conventions of the bourgeois home" (Sachs 1963: 350). Although belatedly, Spain, its dances, and its women were under a process of appeasement thanks to the influence of bourgeois norms, which freed them from the burden of wild passion. The "semi-exotic" Spanish dances were to be rescued by those who were genuinely exotic. Obviously, there were hierarchies of exotics to be kept.

Sachs and Leonardo Acosta (a dance specialist and a musicologist, respectively) have both attempted to explain successive European waves of hunger for exotic cultural goods. Although they come from opposite ideological positions, both conclude that the European appetite for exoticism is based on the need for renovation, for spicy flavoring, for true undegenerate emotions: that is, for passion. The decadence, the exhaustion of the European "culture" is taken as a given. Stressing the analogy with an aging, sickly body, Sachs suggests that exoticism is a must for keeping European expressiveness in shape because Europeans have lost touch with their "natural" human souls through the hardships of capitalist life. The return to "primitive" emotions through the emotions of the "primitives" was always a solution. Acosta adopts a less naturalistic understanding. In his *Música y Descolonización*, published in Cuba in 1982, the appropriation of indigenous American and Afro rhythms by imperialism is paramount. Acosta argues that the imperial decadence brought about by capitalism's alienation and the need to bring new products to the musical market together explain the craving for the exotic. The difference between these two positions is that whereas Sachs believes in the "naturalness" of the need for "new blood" (cross-breeding), Acosta emphasizes the historical exploitative needs created by the capitalist market economy.[4]

But what makes these "new bloods" valuable? And what made these musical and danceable performances "goods" invested with exchange value conveniently disposable due to the parasitic demands of the musical market? Without the manufacturing of exoticism and the constitution of exotic subjects and cultures, the bourgeois consumerist societies—located either at the core or on the periphery of the empires—would not have had a sense of their own lacks or of their own "decadence." The contrast created with the passionate exotics made the need for strong "feelings," "emotions," and "body sensations" natural. The difference established between the "civilized" and the "primitives"—the lack of passion on the one side and the passionate excess on the other side—allowed consumerism to become a true fulfillment of "needs." Capitalism did in fact massively alienate the workers, but the existence of the sensual exotics (also turned into such by imperialism) "reminded" them of what they had lost and now could buy. Exotics—peoples not yet assimilated into bourgeois capitalism—were there for the civilized to consume and thus to overcome their afflicted "decadence." This disease of the civilized, respectable bodies would be permanently actualized and made into a chronic "desire." Desire for the "passion" of the Other, the exotic, uncivilized, and not yet contaminated barbarians. And the passion of the uncivilized, colonized peoples also proved to be "real" since those people resisted and/or performed exoticism, struggling for a better position as they were incorporated into the civilized, imperial world.

Europe's "Romantic" and convulsive epoch was a crisis of awareness of the evils of Civilization, and this awareness was brought about by the presence of the exotics. The happiness and fulfillment that Romantic colonizers attributed to less civilized peoples (peasants, marginals, and "primitives") were not there anymore for them to find. As the "primitives," "savages," and "barbarians" were being constituted into exotics (incorporated into the imperial capitalist world), they were losing precisely what the Romantics longed for. Colonized bodies and cultural expressions were being assimilated into the "world system" to play exotic "passion" while their anger, frustration, and shame were being neglected or mistaken for strong temperaments without palpable reasons or logical causes. The Desire of the colonizer could not be satiated by his own doings: His desire to dominate and master the Other's passion (self-determination) was incompatible with his desire to consume the Other's "passion" (as he had dreamed it in "exoticizing" undertakings). The civilized colonizer, however, sought to escape from his own trap by "discovering" new exotics, exotics of all kinds and with different angles of exoticism to them. Conclusion: The burden of the capitalist civilized disease would/should be carried by the colonized exotics.

Big changes occurred during these Romantic times at the "core" of the world: The French Revolution with its message of Universal freedom and equality; the American Revolution calling for the empire of Democracy; violence surrounding the Abolition of Slavery; the Industrial Revolution running at full steam. The bourgeoisie and Capitalism were now at the front. Accordingly, the sources of exoticism, the consumers of the exotic, and the techniques of exoticization went through a parallel process of "universalization," "popularization," and technological "modernization."

A Romantic period of ballet-mania took hold of the opera houses between the 1820s and the 1860s. Many of the so-called "classic" ballets still staged today—"Giselle" (1841), "La Sylphide" (1832)—were created during that time. Both the performers and the audiences of dance spectacles underwent major changes (Aschengreen 1974). Women, who had first appeared on European stages in the seventeenth century, now totally displaced male performers. Choreographers frequently promoted the parallel stardom of two talented danseuses who, through their contrasting styles, represented conflictive images of the feminine.[5] The ethereal, outworldly nymph or fairy danced on recently invented toe slippers, to emphasize spirituality; the earthy, voluptuous, gypsy-like temptress set the stage aflame, playing her castanets in "twisted, bewitching gestures." As the ballet spectacle projected more and more complex feminine/exotic images, the audience changed class and gender-wise. On the one hand, bourgeois prudery imposed on the ballerinas the use of longer skirts "so as not to inflame the male spectators." On the other hand, ballet devotees went to the performances to ogle and choose the most attractive danseuse for their next love affair (Anderson 1974). Thus, paraphrasing Susan Foster, the ballet offered both an idealized world of feminine threats and enchantments and the spectacle of scantily clad *damiselles* readily available for sensual fantasy and sexual action. Foster explains:

> Capitalist marketing strategies initiated by producers in the early 1830s supported and enhanced the objectified dancing body and the commodified female dancer. They pitted one ballerina against another in intensive, objectifying advertising campaigns and opened up backstage areas where wealthy patrons might enjoy the company of dancers before, during, and after the performance. Rather than evaluate a performance within the context of a given genre, or even character type, viewers were encouraged to focus on female stars with merciless comparative scrutiny. The progressive segmentation of the body occurring in physical education, anatomy and the new science of phrenology further supported the fascination with isolated parts of the female dancing body. Poorly paid dancers and insubstantial government support left the institution of dance vulnerable to exploitation, both sexual and specular (Foster n.d.: 9).

Although ballet as a spectacular genre started decaying in the 1850s, the Romantic image of woman (half melancholic virgin, half passionate temptress) survived for a long time, as did the stripping/fragmenting of the female body, which has been reproduced up to the present on stages and screens. As spectacles became more popular in terms of class, however, they simultaneously turned increasingly male-oriented. Class intermingling in public spaces produced gender segregation, especially in the middle and bourgeois classes, and the male audience demanded (female) "legs" and body exposure.[6] Toward the end of the century, music halls and cabarets were to replace this ballet-mania, but there were some exceptions.

A grand spectacle written and choreographed by Luigi Manzotti for La Scala Theatre of Milan in 1881 was soon transferred to Paris, where it ran with great success for a whole year. The masterpiece, called "Excelsior," celebrated the triumph of Civilization over the dark forces of Ignorance. In a story of relentless persecution, carried out through six acts and eleven scenes, the malign genius of obscurantism attempted to catch and imprison the Light (a beautiful woman). Civilization and Progress, however, were on the Light's side. Each part of the ballet staged a revolutionary scientific or technical achievement that dramatically caused the failure of the villain. The steamship, the telegraph, the Mont Cenis Tunnel (through the Alps), and even electricity came to the Light's rescue. Obscurantism attained victory only once, during the fourth act of the piece, when the Light lost herself in the exotic lands of the Simun Winds. In the middle of a desert, her caravan was assaulted by a sandstorm (the Simun) and attacked by a horde of bandits. Ready to die in the hands of darkmen, Light suddenly discovered a path for escape: the Suez Canal (Pasi 1987).

Figure 3.3 provides a lavish depiction of "Excelsior"'s final scene. Obscurantism has been defeated. Representatives of non-European peoples stand on the left, dressed in exotic garb, and European dignitaries (including military officers and priests) stand mostly on the right. They are joined in a celebration of Civilization as they witness the spectacle of the ballerinas dancing "an apotheosis of enlightenment and peace" (Fonteyn 1979: 84). According to this engraving, the finale was scenographically framed by numerous national banners and a scenic backdrop depicting fleets of trade and warships. Two colossal, Egyptian-like sphinxes were located as props on either side, downstage. Were the sphinxes intended to denote the appropriation of ancient technological advances as part of Western Civilization's genealogy? Were they part of a scenographic representation that located Ignorance downstage, as "the beginnings," and Civilization upstage (the diplomatic community, the fleets, trade) as "the goal" of humanity? The top half of the engraving (which appears to be the decoration of the proscenium arch) has Ignorance positioned below Civilization. The illuminated world emerges from dark clouds. Light, surrounded by the carefully chosen allegories of technological progress, raises her torch in triumph. This careful positioning in space of the world's forces in struggle, and the reiteration of the political message in several dimensions and through a diversity of media, assured "Excelsior"'s success. The piece was a monumental tribute to Western Progress. Knowing the weaknesses of his time, however, Manzotti was careful to include in his grand ballets some spectacular, semi-exotic, semi-"enlightened" costumes through which the prima ballerina could exhibit her pretty legs (see Figure 3.4).

The "general public" of the great European opera houses did not include the poor, of course. The lower classes, rather than contemplating breathtaking productions, worked hard in the factories of Civilization, both in the Old and New Worlds, and contributed to consolidating and entertaining the elites. In this case, class was the key to exoticism. The social practices of the poor—again food, fashion, music, and dance—were "borrowed" and "refined" for the pleasure of those who could afford them. Social dances can provide telling examples: After the abolition of the aristocratic minuet,[7] counterdances and the waltz inspired by "popular" dances—dances of the peasants and urban poor—entered into the ballrooms of the bourgeoisie (Franks 1963; Leppert 1988). Exotic, this time because of poverty and ruralness. Exoticized because of the Romantic quest for "authentic" national roots that would give the European nations under formation unified bases for struggling against each other over shares of power at the "core" of the imperial world.

This so-called Romantic period (roughly from the 1820s to the 1880s), in which the bourgeoisie was starting to enjoy its triumphs over the former ruling elite

FIGURE 3.3 *A depiction of the stage spectacle "Excelsior," produced by Luigi Manzotti in 1881. The scenery represented the rise of civilization. (top right) Steamship and iron bridge; (top left) the Suez Canal and the Mont Cenis Tunnel; (top center) discovery of electricity (the illumination of the world by a torch); (bottom left) the exotics; (bottom right) the priests and military officers; (center) the ballerinas. Courtesy of the Museo Teatrale alla Scala, Milan.*

FIGURE 3.4 *Virginia Zucchi in a Manzotti production, late 1800s. Courtesy of the Museo Teatrale alla Scala, Milan.*

and over the uncivilized at home and abroad, was not so pleasant for everyone. Urbanization and industrialization assembled a working class that soon realized it was paying for the bulk of bourgeois progress. Workers, peasants, students, and other marginals set up barricades to resist the barriers to their aspirations. Revolts led by socialists, anarchists, and other politically active groups challenged the European bourgeois by promoting the rights of the new (low- and middle-) classes to a share in power. The antibourgeois conservatives looked at these reactions sympathetically: They proved how unrealistic the bourgeois democratic dreams were and promised a strengthening of their own reactionary faction.[8]

Insurrections and suppressions had been alternating since the 1810s, the former conducted by secret organizations such as Young Italy and its counterpart Young Germany—groups of romantic young intellectuals and artists who opposed the bourgeois order from left and right (see Bronner and Kellner 1983). In 1848, the "Year of Revolutions," insurgencies swept all over Europe as a result of what some historians have called "the Hungry Forties": Berlin, Bavaria, Vienna, Paris.[9] But the new European elites had a strong card to play against the dangers that these internal insurrections represented for their respective hegemonies: nationalism. The nationalist spirit shifted the focus from internal sectorial disputes to an overriding major dispute regarding the redistribution of the world's former and new colonies.[10] The Romantic pursuit of "authentic" national roots in the customs of peasants and the poor at home and the pursuit for a cure to capitalist "decadence" in the foreign exotics of the colonies went hand in hand. The capitalist "division of labor" was being contested at all levels and everywhere: Workers challenged factory owners; weak nations resisted stronger ones; and colonials revolted against metropolitan powers. And all these confrontations fed each other. Britain (the "great") emerged as the "workshop of the world" and Paris as the world center of luxury and pleasure.[11] These nations displayed their respective masteries and mutual antagonisms through international fairs and exhibitions.

Dance Masters and Spectacle Entrepreneurs

International fairs such as the 1851 Great Exhibition in London and the 1889 Paris Exposition put the Exotic and the Modern on display. The technological treasures of the English colonial empire included Indian howdahs (complete with decorated elephants), Egyptian pyramids, Tunisian bazaars, and Canadian birch-bark canoes, whereas the pleasurable treasures of the French colonies included Oriental belly-dancers, gypsies, Loango villages and Kabyl tents, and Angkor pagodas (Burchell 1966; Rearick 1985). Edmond de Goncourt, a famous cultural critic of the time, wrote in his journal about some entertainments offered adjacent to the Paris Exposition. At the Rue de Caire he spotted some belly-dancers. Describing the most extraordinary of them, he wrote, "When people applauded her, with her body completely immobile, [she] seemed to make little salutations with her navel" (Goncourt 1956, 3:1027). He regretted not having the opportunity to observe one of them dancing naked, so as to analyze her muscular mastery (Goncourt 1956, 3:1000). Although some spectators found the *almeys* (belly-dancers) monotonous and coarse, most responded with fascination to the sensuality and exoticism of the movements. Belly-dancing became such a rage that Goncourt was "persuaded that at this point three-fourths of the women in Paris were secretly working on this dance" (Goncourt 1956, 3:1029).

In 1890 the Moulin Rouge, not yet a music hall but a dance hall with a pleasure garden, provided for the enjoyment of its fashionable international clientele by setting up a blue elephant (stuffed, of course) that contained a small stage where a belly-dancer performed, and next to it a pavilion in which ballerinas danced (Rearick 1985: 77, 121) (see Figure 3.5). The contrasting images of the two worlds (the one civilized and European, the other ignorant and colonized), put side by side, serve as a reminder of progress and of who should dominate/guide whom. The "elephant stage" presents the heavy, strong powers of the Orient that have nevertheless been conquered by the lace-like French stage, which is inhabited by ethereal ballerinas. These delicate, fairy-like women dance the triumph of bourgeois Western ways of dealing with both the world and the feminine: Civilization wins not because of strength or out of misleading seduction (represented by the belly-dancer), but because it is rational—the ideally proper, evolutionary thing to be. Female bodies in movement depicted the contrasts.

In the European cities of the time, dancing was in full swing: bourgeois social dancing in ballrooms and theaters, workers' rowdy dancing in taverns and low-class districts, mixed-class dancing celebrating national festivities. For the elites, dancing was a display of gaiety and renewed faith in progress. For the less privileged, it afforded an occasion to show aggressive cynicism toward bourgeois work ethics and prudery. National roots and the complementary masteries over the world were danced to, and so were frustrations (Laver 1966). Moreover, these dancing drives themselves became contested, co-opted, and promoted by two old rivals in the dancing business: the dance masters and the spectacle impresarios. The pleasure of dancing one's own body was being systematically segregated from the pleasure of watching dancing bodies on a stage.[12] The disciplinary machinery that presided over dancing bodies was defined and refined by the dangerous commingling of different classes and different national and exotic trends.

Orientalism and Hispanolism prepared the way for tango. So did the Romantic "rediscovery" of European nationalist roots through the exoticization of peasant dances (many of which were of Slavic origin). In addition, the rowdy dancing manners of the urban poor were staged as spectacles for the rich—exotic because of class. All these dances caused reactions of rage and indignation, including prohibitions. The music and choreography of practically every "new" dance—tinged at first by rural and later by urban low-class origins—as well as

FIGURE 3.5   Moulin Rouge summer garden, 1890. Source: L'Illustration, *June 15, 1889.*

the "truly" exotic ones provoked scandals and fascinations of wide proportions. The scandalized church dignitaries, government officers, and responsible citizens were not struck by the existence of poverty, barbarian indecency, or rural impropriety as such; the aberration resided in purposefully adopting traits and manners of the poor, of peasants, and of barbarians. The poor themselves, like the colonized, had no (public) word in these debates and eventually the market of leisure and distinction[13] used these scandals for its own benefit—as material for advertisements. Scandalous dances were staged in a further scandalized way and were simultaneously tamed of scandalous features for the purposes of social dancing. Exaggeration and taming were not restricted to choreography. Fashion—what the moving bodies wore—participated equally in the shaping of moral and immoral bodies. Some dances, however, resisted this twofold co-option and were usually left in the hands of one of the dance disciplining specialists (a spectacle entrepreneur or dance master) and the corresponding fashion designer. When the two-way system did work, the results helped to maintain bourgeois morality as paramount, but bourgeois capitalist gains were also at stake. Staged dances, and especially their scandalous connotations, remained in the spectators' fantasies. At least some of them felt compelled to revive those emotions by imitating the movements and costumes seen on stage.[14] Dance masters then instructed their clients on how to control the expression of their "bodily instincts" while keeping the scandalous staged version in mind. Both those who went and those who did not go to dance academies could purchase the allegoric costumes at fashion shops.

The system could also work the other way around. (New fashion inspired by dance spectacles sent some of its clients to the theaters and/or dance masters.) The spectators/pupils spent their leisure time and money enjoyably bouncing between dance halls, cabarets, music halls, and dance academies and demanded that the fashion industry dress them accordingly, whether they danced, enjoyed dance spectacles, or simply wanted to look fashionably "dancish." In late nineteenth-century capitalism, the dance complex disciplined the movements of bodies, the way the moving bodies looked and dressed, and how the money in the pockets of the clothes worn by the moving bodies was spent. Although this dancing business affected the whole class spectrum in various ways, it is worth noting that women's bodies were more directly implicated in these processes. Men participated widely, but mostly as spectators and partners or as framers of women's movements (spectacle impresarios, choreographers, and dance masters) and shapers of women's bodies (fashion designers).[15]

Waltz, polka, can-can, apache, and tango, to name just a few among many dance scandals, went through this disciplining process in which morality and profits were at stake. Through these dances, for over a century bodies in movement successively (and successfully) broke and made rules. The fascination with dancing resided in the belief that pure movements, without the interference of verbal expression, approached the "truth" (Ritter 1989: 41). It was said that dancing bodies could hardly lie. For this very reason, dancing was also dangerous. Dance masters and spectacle impresarios took advantage of these qualities of dancing, maneuvering within the restrictions demanded by bourgeois morality. Disciplining dancing was a challenge that promised high rewards. Rules of distinction (by class, race, gender, nationality, and degree of civilization) were permanently under menace in European and European-influenced cities at the end of the nineteenth century. These distinctions were kept in place, to a certain degree, by splitting social dancing off from staged dances. Scandalous dances were staged in produced, scandalous forms and framed clearly as spectacles. Thus, bourgeois moral bodies kept the protective distance of the gaze between the scandal and themselves. The body of the spectator remained unpolluted—disengaged and under control. The dance masters did their job scrupulously, starting from the point at which the promoter of a spectacle left the bodies inspired and loose, ready to be taught social dancing. Dance demonstrators played the articulation between the two as performers and teachers of the modestly proper yet glamorous. Dance masters and their widely read (by those who could read) manuals, some of them real treatises, had been ruling bodies for a long time.[16] Their favorite words were "decor," "good taste," and "education"; their favorite nasty words, "sloppiness" and "frivolity"; their main obsessions, the posture and the movements of every single part of the body in space and time; their purpose, to provide healthy and correct skills for sociability.

In the nineteenth century, an enhanced concern with "technicality" pervaded the teaching of both social and theatrical dance. Virtuosity was sought on stage and in the ballroom. Bodily strength, balance, and following more complicated rhythmic patterns were not easy to achieve, especially when partnering in public. Late nineteenth-century social dancing, in particular, generated the combined tension and anxiety of virtuosity, gracefulness, *and* sensuality. At the center of the problem was the basic question, "Who should be a mate for whom and how?" In public spaces, gender roles and relations were changing, being shaped and contained. Bodies were supposed to practice both morality and sensuality since respectful intimacy was a sign of bourgeois distinction. The bodies were intrinsically suspect—especially when they performed flirtatious, sexually charged movements. A new heterosexual amorous code was being shaped under the guidance of these defensive and scrupulous dance-masters (Franks 1963; Leppert 1988; Buckman 1978; Fonteyn 1979).

Dance masters and their manuals proliferated all over Europe, but the French were the greatest experts. France continued to concentrate cultural capital in this respect, and in ruling over the movements of the body and its social displays, France hegemonized the power of "expertise" in love, passion, and all sorts of erotic affairs.[17] The French became internationally famous for knowing all the secrets of *l'amour,* which they were actually creating, and French words for erotic matters were widely distributed to other languages.[18] Any popular dance (i.e., any dance not created by *les professeurs* or their disciples) obviously

(a)   (b)

trespassed the disciplinary codes. The posture, the holding or embracing attitude, the speed of the movements, the couples' mirroring or independent articulation of step patterns, and the stylization of the roles of leading and following
emphasized an erotic imagery of smoothness, harmony, compatibility, and fluid
complementarity among partners. These skillful performances of heterosexual
romanticism were widely classified as correct or incorrect, but some English
dance-masters qualified the rights and wrongs with a key word: class (see Figure
3.6). All these efforts at marking distinctions developed with the "democratiza-
tion" of leisure.

Montmartre, Fin de Siècle

At the heart of the already suspicious world capital of pleasure (Paris was the
center of unruly encounters between the elite members of different nations and
between these and the demimonde of irresistible cocottes) was Montmartre,
where the deepest, most underworldly, reprehensible—and glamorous—so-
cial/sexual encounters took place. Illegitimate relationships were concentrated
here in the transgressive encounters across class, race, sexuality, and nationality,
and they all had erotic connotations. It was the locus of transgressive pleasures

(c)

FIGURE 3.6   *High-class (a), low-class (b), and no-class (c) partnering styles.* Source: *Edward Scott,* Dancing as an Art and Pastime *(London: Bell & Sons, 1892).*

where a diversity of understandings of pleasure invaded everyone's class territorialities. At Montmartre, fin de siècle, marginals of all sorts and classes congregated to display antibourgeois sentiments. Satirists, singers, and dancers staged aggressive, coarse, defiant shows attacking members of the church, the government, and the military, but there was yet another audience that dropped in once in a while "to sample lowlife."[19] For these *mondains*—French and international elites—both the stage and the audience of rebellious *habitués* constituted the spectacle. The cafés and cabarets of Montmartre were the territory of artists, prostitutes, models, students, flaneurs, grisettes, lorettes, cocottes, homosexuals, dandies, radicals, rascals, the unemployed, gigolos, femmes fatales, lesbians, and combinations thereof.[20] In the eyes of the bourgeois elite they all amounted to a spectacle of the *mal de siècle*, a restless and hardly threatening marginality, a knowledge of which gave elite men an aura of distinction.

Montmartre was a place of combative enjoyment where pleasure was a weapon used against bourgeois order and morality.[21] Most performers (singers, satirists, dancers) were not engaged in any particular political organization, but they chose as their targets the privileged and the exploiters. Although not formally connected, artists, writers, and students shared a mix of disdain and rebellion against "the armies of Suffering." They demanded "the right to license and enjoyment" in response to the institutions and personalities that imposed an ethic of sacrifice and work (Paul Adam [1896], quoted in Rearick 1985: 47).[22] Bohemians such as Emile Goudeau, owner of the cabaret *Le Chat Noir*, offered their patrons an atmosphere of exciting abandonment, stirring up sensuality, metaphysical anxiety, and political posturing. Living in an era of strong national rivalries, they mixed their cries against "capitalistic feudality" and "cosmopolitan Jewry" with exaltations of gaiety—taken for a natural French mood inherited from the Gauls. The sought realm of liberated fantasy required them to expel foreign poisons—repressive Christian morality, German pessimism, Anglo-Saxon prudery—only to return to laughter, which was considered an endangered French trait (Rearick 1985; Siegel 1986).

The tango was first performed in this fin-de-siècle environment of the Montmartre cabarets, which were now fully devoted to providing an escapade—that is, an escape from the ordinary and the conventional. Bohemia exerted a perverse attraction in the bourgeoisie. Can-can (emphasizing the lifting of the skirts and the high-kicking of the legs) was a favorite spectacle of both bohemian and touristic Montmartre. Formerly performed in popular fests, at the end of the nineteenth century it was taken in by cafés and pleasure gardens (Beauroy et al. 1976). The can-can held a special place among the many provocative spectacles based on dramatizations of death, violence, debauchery, and sexuality, and it was the primary Parisian symbol of gaiety, of revolt, and of national character (see Figures 3.7 and 3.8). Identified with the lower classes since revolutionary times, can-can both attracted and disturbed other classes, and its irreverent kicks had been literally policed. Turned into acrobatic and highly strenuous performances, can-can and the *danse du ventre* (belly-dancing) frequently exploited magnificence along with vulgarity. In the 1890s, many famous dance halls became music halls where customers watched professionals such as La Goulue, Jean Avril, and Nini Patte en l'Air, whose skills inhibited untrained dancers' participation (Montorgueil 1898).

Gaiety and pessimism went hand in hand in *la belle époque*, and they were present in can-can. Bohemian revolutionaries shared "a lively feeling for the degradation of our era of transition," and for this reason artists chose to represent "the pleasures of decadence: balls, kick-choruses, circuses" (Paul Signac [1891], quoted in Bade 1985: 224). For art critics of a rival nationality, however, can-can was the last kick of a race (the "Latin race") in irreversible decadence: "France, the lovely, unlucky land, is today like a ruined ballroom in which the vilest crimes and the most heroic deeds are carried out side by side, by almost the same men. Already the ballroom burns on all sides and inside it, the muse of Lautrec dances with brilliant contortions, the last diabolical can-can" (Julius Meier-Graefe [1899], quoted in Bade 1985: 230). Racial interpretations that regarded national cultures as different species competing for the survival of the fittest were not rare in the Europe of the late nineteenth century. Gender representations also had a place in these social Darwinist interpretations. The French, being tinged by the Latin race, were said to show "sickly effeminacy" in their manners, arts, and customs compared to the "healthy virility" of their powerful German and English counterparts (Bade 1985). In their quest for unified and stable national identities, commentators drew on naturalized understandings of race and gender.

The different interpretations of the mal de siècle affecting Europe intersected in women, who were seen as having the power to bring about decadence or to provide the necessary pleasure to disrupt the system (see Birken 1988). Women were the stars of the French can-can and can-can denoted French gaiety; French gaiety was the last outburst of a decadent age. Decadence was a symptom of either the degeneration of the latina race or the defeat of the capitalist system. If the problem was the latina race, the name of the disease was effeminacy (produced by the feminine invasion of manliness) and the cure was more virility. If the problem was capitalism, the cause was overwork with no compensation (often interpreted as sexual repression) and the solution was more pleasure. Pleasure was thought of as unmanly by the promoters of virility (and hard work), but it was a man's undertaking for the "decadents" who enjoyed watching women do the can-can (see Mosse 1985). Thus, women were the objects of these male-centered speculations. The increasing obsession with women and the female body in the dance spectacles, visual arts, fashion, and literature of the time is notorious.[23] And so is the power attributed to women, although it is sometimes only traceable through the efforts invested in controlling women's looks, movements, instincts, and passions. It is difficult if not impossible to establish what this prevailing male-focus-on-women meant for those women in everyday life. I am thinking about these women who saw/lived themselves through the male gaze as powerful objects who were advised to accept and even seek male protection (from other men) and male control (of their own female powers).

In Parisian music halls at the turn of the century, women were the special feature, performing their enigmatic power while doing the can-can, belly-dancing, dancing a Victorian-like striptease (in which removing layer under layer of petticoats and lingerie exhausted the show before any nudity was revealed), and even engaging in boxing matches. This display of dancing temptresses inspired fear and adoration. Dancing was thought to reveal the instinctual nature of women, their truth communicated by physical means. In novels, operas, and pictorial works of the time, the Romantic *femme fragile* is replaced by the imagery of the femme fatale. One only needs to think of Carmen (Merimée's novel in 1846; Bizet's opera in 1875), Delilah (Saint-Saens's opera in 1877), Lulu (present in several of Widekind's works from 1892 to 1905), Salome (the subject of seventy oils by Moreau, Huysman's novel *A Rebours* in 1884, Bearsdley's illustrations, Wilde's play in 1893, and Strauss's opera in 1905), and Electra (Hofmannsthal's libretto and Strauss's opera in 1909) to trace the recurrence of women's enigmatic powers exposed through the dance (Ritter 1989; Allen 1983; Bade 1979; Meltzer 1987). The aerial, supernatural nymphs and sylphides—who were not totally innocent since they often drew their enraptured human lovers to their outworldly do-

FIGURE 3.7 (above) Can-can at a Parisian cafe-concert, late 1800s. Source: *Michelle Perrot, ed.,* A History of Private Life: Volume 4, From the Fires of Revolution to the Great War *(Cambridge: Belknap Press, 1990). FIGURE 3.8 (facing page) French can-can dancer "Saharet," late 1800s. Courtesy of The Raymond Mander and Joe Mitchenson Theatre Collection.*

mains—were being displaced by these mostly exotic counterparts, half human and half insect, reptile, or plant, long hair in disarray, sickly pale and slender, free and unrestrained by bourgeois mores. Deadly. Although it has often been said that the femme fatale can be identified by her irresistible attractiveness to men, I believe that her threatening powers resided in her awareness of a distinctively feminine eroticism. Her own body had become sensual and sexualized, and she knew it (see Allen 1983; Doane 1991). She was not the ethereal romantic sylphide who, through her purity and lack of erotic understanding, could drive her lover to suicide. She stood defiantly in opposition to the Victorian matron, who was burdened by family duties and reproductive demands. The femme fatale "discovered" female sexuality. She was passionate and displayed sensuality, she involved men erotically, both willingly and unwillingly, and she took pleasure in doing so.[24]

In can-can as well as in belly-dancing, which were both popular on late nineteenth- and early twentieth-century stages, women danced alone or in female choruses, provocatively displaying their own eroticism and power, and they seem to have enjoyed it. La Goulue ("the glutton" or "the greedy one"), for example, made her appearances at the Moulin Rouge escorted by Valentin. She kicked, gyrated, and strode around the dance floor as a can-can femme fatale. She gestured provocatively at the clients, got into fights with other dancers, and aimed her famous high kick at Valentin's hat. Thus, the mixed audiences witnessed the potency of the femme fatale's eroticism. They cheered and clapped at her powerful displays, including her symbolic decapitation of Valentin.[25] With tango, the focus of the next dance boom of the early twentieth century, the femme fatale would not disappear. But the rôle of the male partner framed her eroticism in a different way. The tango femme fatale faced a fatal man—a man as good as she was in playing wild eroticism to death.

I have not found any record of a famous can-can dancer also dancing tangos in the early twentieth century, but there were certainly spectators who attended performances of both genres. Mistinguett, a famous *revue danseuse* at Eldorado, the Moulin Rouge, and La Scala and probably the first star to perform a tango in Paris, recalled one of her distinguished followers (Edward VII) as an attentive spectator of both can-can and tango (Mistinguett 1954). Looking at Figure 3.8 (a can-can dancer), I kept wondering how it would have been for her to move from the world of the rowdy can-can to the world of the tango. The result is in Plumette's Diary.

SCENE FIVE: PLUMETTE'S DIARY—

FROM CAN-CAN TO TANGO

Solo.

  At centerstage: a big door, two steps at the threshold, white papers on a step. Plumette's Impersonator picks up the diary fragments and reads aloud. She is

dressed awkwardly as a can-can dancer and strips into a tight tango costume of
black satin as she advances through the text. She signals the parts of the body re-
ferred to in the diary entries, unable to perform the movements or to re-create
the ambiance.

Music: Can-can, tango, and ragtime played on "old" records.

Plumette's spoken text:

Montmartre. A knock on a door. On the steps, at the threshold, she left only
her whoosh and this:

August 1897: I woke up this morning knowing that I would kick high, higher
than ever, higher than anyone has ever kicked before. And then, every man will
hold his breath, and I will do the deep split. All hearts in Paris will pound to the
beat of my kicks. My rowdiness will nurture the revolt of pleasure. My skirts, up
and down, up and down, will cut the air and choke the audience. Everyone will
toast to the liberation of the senses. Wine and beer will spill on my ruffles attempting to wet me down, to soak my feathers, to prevent my flight. But no one
can stop my cascade of lace. *Mesdames et messieurs! Je suis Plumette!* Boots and
sticks cannot arrest the rising and falling of my long striped legs. I am the
queen of *Le Chahut.* Each kick of mine is a gust of encouragement and an inspiration to rebellion.

March 1898: I twisted my ankle, I tore my petticoat. This drunken painter is
making me sick, visiting every night with the same excuse. ... That roaring
bunch of bums is leaving me deaf. I wish I could stop playing the revolutionary
danseuse. ... My wings are aching!

July 1911: No obscene gestures, no scandalous remarks; no one was shouting
at me tonight. Perhaps my age is finally showing. Or maybe, this time, the audience could easily tell that I would not be listening. I would not even be looking at them, raptured, as I was, in following my partner's will. My soul, though,
was reaching at them with every step, asking for reassurance. Remember me,
Plumette? My kicks of freedom, my ruffles of provocation? My body is now confined to a tight satin dress, confined in a tarnished embrace, confined to a var-
nished stage. Everyone seems relieved after the kicking rowdiness of my former
can-can, myself included.

It must be this music. ... "It's good business," he said. "*Le tango* attracts our
best clients, those who can afford to drown their nights in champagne." And as if
by some magic trick, I was wrapped up in black; my rage, hopes, tenderness, all.
Wrapped up. My legs have been put back to earth. Trapped in his legs, they have
lost their flight. No more froufrous to play, display concealment. My legs, permanently denuded under the tight, slit skirt, and my power contained. But my
arrest seems to fuel silent, expectant passions. Deplumed *Plumette.* Nocturnal
shackles around my waist. Indecently following a man, in public. His presence
on stage is my embarrassment. He leads me. His steps prevent my kicks from
spreading in unfettered arousal. How could I have come to accept this? It must
be this dark music that promises bitterness and feeds on my surrender.

October 1915: They came to the club tonight, a whole bunch of them, their uniforms disheveled, drunken moustaches crawling out from under their forward-tilted caps. They want to believe that the splashing blood is a bad dream and that this scene is real. The fact is that the maps are changing and the world trembles with expansionist roars. Bodies are restless. They want to move to the rhythm of exotic music, they are ready to hear orders for advancing over foreign lands. Skirts will be short tonight. Our clients have no time to spend wondering about legs hidden in drapery. Animal dances, they call them. They are right for our times.

(It seems that soon after the last entry, Plumette gave up dancing and became a cook. In any case, the back of the last page of the diary contains a recipe for frog legs sauteed with garlic and peppercorns.)

Blackout

Through this story I have tried to show some of the changes that a dancing femme fatale might have experienced around the turn of the century.[26] The transformations I wish to point out are focused on her legs, the primary female erotogenic zone at that time.[27] Plumette of the can-can is a dancer who, although an object of male desire, was in control of her erotic powers. She had, literally in her hands, the capacity to show and conceal her arousing legs from beneath her petticoats. Plumette of the can-can was actually a Romantic-style femme fatale. She was childish and aerial, displaying the flights of her legs through the ruffles of her petticoats. When she chose to do a spectacular split, she suddenly became earthly, fallen down as deep as one can get to the ground. This fall—the sin—was self-induced. She mischievously combined her flight and sin and the exposure and concealment of her legs to arouse the male audience at *her* will, but Plumette of the can-can, in order to keep her power active, had to display herself in dancing motion beyond her own body's limits of exhaustion. She tires of symbolizing the revolutionary; she recognizes that she is a dancing token with little say.

This gay Paris of the bohemians, characterized by antibourgeois, anticapitalist philosophies expressed through such particular behaviors as unconventional dress, irregular employment, and a strong investment in festive nightlife, was a magic circle of male homosociality aimed at establishing a new model of masculinity. Women, like the can-can dancer, were subordinate to the bohemian artists as providers of inspiration. Bohemian men rejected bourgeois notions of proper female behavior. They favored and spectacularized what they considered the "freedom" of working class women: the liberty to work outside the household, to engage in extramarital sexual relations and enter into *unions-libres*. But these feminine muses (prostitutes, dancers, laundresses) are referred to as no more than *petite amie* or *femme galante* (see Wilson 1991).

Plumette of the tango is the image of a totally grounded femme fatale. She is attached to the earth through her gliding steps, caught in a tight skirt. She has no control over the exposure or concealment of her legs. Her hands are busy; she must firmly cling to her male partner. Her legs, permanently insinuated under her glossy, long, slit skirt, confront other legs: the legs of the fatal man who guides and traps her steps. This man, holding her tightly on stage, is far from playing childish games. His legs that lead and interfere are threatening. This is a different erotic game. It is seduction. The fatal man, half dandy and half ruffian, has learned how to play with her eroticism. He plays it back on her, the femme fatale, a disguised prostitute, after all. In the last entry of Plumette's diary, the stumbling femme fatale is faced with the fatality of war—a war among those fatal men who seek to reassert their power in showing total violence, open aggression toward each other. This ritual of virility has pushed the femme fatale backstage. Plumette helps to dress the girls for the clandestine shows.[28] (Dancing was officially forbidden during the war years by a police order [André Warnod (1922), quoted in Humbert 1988: 71–72].) The "girls" are hardly femmes fatales anymore. They are sensual, but more comforting than disturbing. Their legs under those short skirts are immediately available to the male gaze. Women's power has been minimized, trivialized through a settled exhibition. Seduction is a banal struggle, a hardly threatening game when confronted with the "real" battle: the cruel war between men where power is measured in terms of life and death.[29]

Tango in the World's Capital of Pleasure

Tango arrived in Paris in the early 1900s.[30] Argentino beef-barons, together with some adventurous tango musicians and dancers, introduced it into the elite circles, cabarets, and music halls of la belle époque.[31] The world's capital of pleasure, however, was not the exclusive hostess of tango in France; Marseille was another French port of entry for the tango. Marseille's world-wandering sailors and white-slave traffickers were tango's other—déclassé—introducers.[32] Tango arrived in Paris by way of both the top and the bottom of the social scale. This is perhaps one of the reasons why tango provoked such divisive responses in the social milieu of la belle époque. Tango was scandalous and fascinating, but the differences in opinion did not strictly follow a class division. Tango was resisted by bourgeois moralists and by a sector of Parisians who, far from being scandalized, were opposed to the distinguished, classy tinge of this sultry exotic dance (Assunção 1984). Perhaps the Parisian lower classes or those who identified with them ignored tango's own lower-class origins, or perhaps they were aware of these origins but resented the tangueros playing up to European aristocrats and bourgeoisies by practicing a pathetic autoexoticism for the benefit of the decadent market of pleasure. Moreover, perhaps the elite's warm reception of such exotics was a suggestive warning for the defiant Parisian working class. The message could have been: European labor is not altogether indispensable, not even as exoticizable objects of dissipation, given that there is a whole independent and neocolonized world out there, at the core's disposal, waiting enthusiastically to be incorporated.

For whatever reasons, and probably not simple ones, the tango, a hybrid in terms of race and class in its original setting, generated mixed feelings of acceptance and rejection at both extremes of the Parisian class structure. These mixed reactions at multiple class levels were signs of the simultaneous operation of class, race, and nationality markers in European society, markers that contradicted each other when facing exotics. The reactions to tango were showcases of these complex social tensions. In the early twentieth century, tango brought novelty into the exotic genre—a "distinguished" and demimonde, urbane exoticism from the already in/dependent colonial world. Tango was an exotic genre suited to the complex modern imperial bourgeois ordering of the world. All contradictory alignments were played out through tango in terms of the erotic.

The tango was originally poor but moving upwards, urban with some traces of ruralness, white with some traces of color, colonized with some traces of a native barbarian in the process of being civilized. It was a perfect candidate for the modern capitalist condition of the exotic. It was an exotic on the move, unlike previous versions of crystallized exoticism. It also displayed a new kind of eroticism, transgressing all socially established barriers. In tango, eroticism was controlled and suggestive. Tango did not perform "instinctive" sensuality (like the dances of the "primitives"), rowdy excitement (like the dances of the peasants), or overt impropriety, cynicism, or defiant aggression toward the upper classes (like the dances of the urban marginals). Nor did it focus solely on the erotic powers of the female body, like other "traditional" exotic dances. Tango's sexual politics were centered in the process of seduction. A fatal man and a femme fatale who, despite their proximity, kept their erotic impulses under control, measuring each other's powers. In its choreography, the tango resembled a game of chess where deadly contenders took turns moving invisible pieces with their dragging feet. Their mutual attraction and repulsion were prolonged into an unbearable, endless tension. And everything took place, apparently, under male control. Women's erotica, a threatening discovery for the nineteenth-century bourgeoisie, could not be tamed by male bourgeois manners. When faced, however, with a Latin-type male—the man of wild passionate nature, as untamed as the woman—heterosexual erotics seemed to fall back into a proper male-centered course.

In addition, the tango couple did not exhibit a clear-cut class or a clean race. At times, the fatal man resembled a distinguished dandy or suddenly behaved like a ruffian/pimp. The femme fatale would alternately seduce and reject her partner, and it was hard to tell whether she was a skillful prostitute or a sensual lady. Tango was a newly developed exotic/erotic hybrid. As such, it entrenched in itself the capacity to perform the major characteristics of the bourgeois colonizer's Desire. And this prolonged, unfulfillable, male-controlled Desire was performed passionately. Tango was a mirror representation of the bourgeois colonizer's Desire, performed with the passion of the neocolonized. In tango, the gaze of the colonizer could take a look at itself by looking at the tense, passionate, dramatic steps of the colonized molded into the shape of the colonizer's cast. Tango understood the colonizer's Desire from within. Tango could be clothed in tails and satins. But it could also be put in its place: the place of the colonized in the process of being civilized. Tango then put on its gaucho costumes: the robes of exotic passion, of freedom and loose wilderness of the *pampas*. Tango was a versatile, hybrid, new kind of exotic that could adopt the manners of the colonizer while retaining the passion of the colonized, both at heart and on the surface.

Tango opened a place for itself among *les dances brunnes*: the Afro-American cake-walk, the Brazilian maxixe, and the apache (see Figure 3.9). The exotic "nature" of the first two was related to their African slave origins in North and South America, respectively (although it is worth noticing that frequently these roots were stressed and even invented for the sake of exotic flair). The apache is another curious example in the making of exoticism. Apache was a dance performed by the French *canaille*—the ruffians of the Parisian prostitution underworld (some of Marseillaise origin) who adopted for themselves Apache pseudonyms after the names of publicized brave North American Native Indian chiefs (Salas 1986). A highly exaggerated form of the apache dance was brought into the cabarets, where a squalid-looking prostitute dressed in rags would fight for her life in the arms of a violent pimp/aggressor. In the end, he would throw her to the floor and attempt to kill her with his knife. At that very moment, the lights were turned down as the police were called and the spectacle came to an end (Francisco García Jiménez [1968], quoted in Assunção 1984: 245). The Parisian stage version of the tango adopted some of the striking moves of the apache (for example, the figure by which the women's legs were set in the air).

Searching for an explanation for tango's puzzling triumph in Europe, José María Salaverría writes for *Caras y Caretas* in 1914: "For the public of Paris or London, tango is no more than a vaguely sinful exotic dance, and they dance it because of its sensual, perverse elements and because it is somewhat barbaric." Fernando Assunção (1984) adds to Salaverría's insightful and cynical remarks some background on the Parisian social environment before World War I. After mentioning the major changes that were taking place in art and literature, which were causing a "subjective, tortured trend closer to the oneiric world than to the real," he refers to the crisis of individualism suffered by an agonizing generation "facing an increasing enmassment because of consumerist society." Tango fit this scenario because its embrace was a healing practice of intimacy and because "[tango] has a more than proletarian origin, an almost marginal, currish, base, linked to brothels, to the flesh; it is the product of the encounter and disencounter of the European culture itself, in the context of a new America, exotic, reiterative and unknown, but which, more than anything, is looked at as a

FIGURE 3.9 *Dancers performing the apache. Photos by Otto Sarony. Courtesy of the Dance Collection, The New York Public Library at Lincoln Center, Astor, Lenox and Tilden Foundations.*

land of hope" (Assunção 1984: 242–243). Tango, this exotic hybrid coming from the southern end of the neocolonial world, carried promises of both identification and rejection on the part of every social sector of European society. It was an exotic dance that could be easily stretched in various directions, and the spectacle impresarios, dance masters, and fashion designers did not waste any time stretching it.

Tango, World Scandal, and Fascination

Scandal and fascination are separated by a very thin line. Both attitudes are born out of the attention devoted to a common matter/event. Both point straight at the attraction exerted by a powerful object of dispute. Actually, in their confrontation, scandal and fascination create the power of the object. Exotics, dances, women's bodies, all have fallen into this objectifying and empowering trap. Usually transgressions are associated with the objects/occurrences in themselves, as if they were immoral per se. Actually what makes certain events unusually erotic is the debate. The tension created between scandalized and fascinated reactions eroticizes the object of dispute.[33] Scandal and fascination arise out of a struggle for power. Tango was an object of these power struggles from the very beginning, and it became erotically charged by them. In the Río de la Plata region, both reactions, scandal and fascination, were hardly more than low-key rumors until the dispute turned up in Europe. The debates over the tango in Europe immediately amplified tango's "erotic problem" at home. Thus, scandal and fascination were subject to colonial relationships within a global economy of passion.

If the interplay between imperialism and exoticism is not taken into account, the puzzle created by a class analysis of tango's acceptance is difficult to piece together. Tango specialists frequently point out that certain sectors of the Parisian elite—and of the European aristocracy in general—accepted the tango more readily than any other social class. The contrasting response on the part of the Argentinean elites is equally well known. Exoticism, as Salaverría and Assunção argue, is the clue. From a bourgeois imperialist point of view, exotics, whether of a low- or high-class origin, remain exotic; that is, they are easy to assimilate into an imperial hierarchization of the world within which class is a matter of further details. Imperialist exoticism allows for the indiscriminate discrimination of outsiders/colonized. Take, for example, the argentino Lucio V. Mansillas's comments about his visit to Paris in the 1850s, as related by Gabriel Montergous: "The Marquis de La Grange organized a party to exhibit him, as if he were '[a native American] Indian or the son of a nabob.' [...] The ladies said: '*comme il doit être beau avec ses plumes!*' [He must look beautiful with his feathers!]" (Montergous 1985: 45). At the time of the Parisian elite's fascination with tango, similar comments were made regarding other "native" aristocrats. Maharajas, Hungarian princesses, Russian dukes, "very wealthy" Syrians, millionaires of "different horizons," and first-class French cocottes joined the French elite in their private parties to "dance one tango after another until late into the night" (Irène Frain [1984], quoted in Humbert 1988: 8). It seems as though the Parisian aristocracy enjoyed exotic dances in the company of exotic aristocrats and their fancy lovers. How many more layers of spicy, innocuous amusement could they get?

Around 1910, the elites of the imperial colonial powers belonged to a class that no other class or classification in the world could threaten. Their position seemed so secure that they did not need to worry about the low-class associations of the exotic practices they enjoyed or even about the precise national origins of such practices.

Robert Cunninghame Graham published in 1914 a detailed description of the decadent, festive, elite environment in which tangos flourished. He starts with the arrival of the patrons to a Parisian hotel: "The ladies descended delicately from their cars, offering a fleeting view of their legs covered by transparent stockings, through the slits of their skirts. They knew that every man [...] would be excited by such a spectacle [...] and even the most virtuous sense pleasure at their capacity to disturb men's emotions. [...] This is how without a need for the vote, they demonstrate they are equal to men" (Cunninghame Graham [1914], quoted in Assunção 1984: 251). Once in the hotel, the traveler continues, "the atmosphere is charged by the emanations of flesh and the fumes of whisky." And back to women, "Lesbos had sent her legions, and women exchanged intelligent looks. [...] The color of their cheeks accentuated when their eyes met, unexpectedly, those of another priestess of the secret cult." North Americans, Hispanoamericans, and Jews met French and English, and all were united by "talking about nothing but money." After the tea, everyone moved to a great hall where a live band played. On their way, "Men approached women in an oppressive manner, murmuring into their ears anecdotes that made them laugh, embarrassed. Those were the days of the 'tango argentino.' [...] Women declared it enchanting. Men stated that it was the only dance worth dancing." A couple of professional dancers would then enter the dance floor: "A young man [...], straight black hair sticking to his head, immaculate trousers so pressed that they seemed made out of card-board, led a young woman fitted in such a tight skirt that she could not have moved if it would not have been slitted up to the knee." Subsequently, Cunninghame Graham describes the dancing itself:

> They were so close to each other that the leg of the carefully pressed trouser would disappear in the tight skirt, the man holding her in such a close embrace that the hand ended-up by the woman's face. They gyrated in a whirlwind, bending down to the floor, advancing the legs in front of each other while turning, all of this with a movement of the hips that seemed to fuse the impeccable trousers with the slitted skirt. The music continued more tumultuously, the musical times multiplied until, with a jump, the woman would throw herself in the arms of her partner, who would put her back on her feet

with great care. Immediately after, the couple bowed and disappeared
(Cunninghame Graham [1914], quoted in Assunção 1984: 252–253).

Robert Cunninghame Graham, who in these observations was mocking European decadence as well as stressing his knowledge of the real Argentinean
"thing," continues his list of crimes with references to the enthusiastic exclama-
tions of the tango audience: " 'Charming!' 'Marvelous!' 'How graceful!' '*Vivent les
espagnoles!*' [...] It is so Spanish, so free from conventions; it combines all the
aesthetic movements of those images that appear in Etrusque vases with the
strange grace of the Hungarian gypsies" (Cunninghame Graham [1914], quoted
in Assunção 1984: 253). The audience, notes Cunninghame Graham, had no rec-
ollection or interest in political matters such as Argentina gaining its independence and believed that Buenos Aires was a part of Spain. To them, Paris, London, and New York amounted to the "whole world." The ambiance of the *tango-
thé,* as described by the Scottish traveler, was indisputably decadent. For him
that meant: rotten rich, up to the point of uniting racial, ethnic, and national enemies; highly sexualized, when considering proper heterosexual manners; sexually deviant, in that women would show desire for each other; gender transgressive, in that women played seduction openly just as they craved for the vote; and
unpoliticized, in that everyone ignored the most basic world affairs. The tango
that was performed in such an environment was monstrous, a tango exoticized
by decadence. This was the context of the scandal.

Tango detractors largely relied on exotic analogies to denounce tango's dangers: "The tango is a pseudo-dance that should be censored! It is truly impossible to describe with precision what one is seeing in Paris. However it could be
said that the tango resembles a double belly-dance, where lasciviousness is ac-
cented through exaggerated contortions. One believes oneself to be watching a
Mahometan couple under the effects of opium" (Max Rivera [n.d.], quoted in
Humbert 1988: 74). The "diabolic" influence of the tango and the ways in which
it took hold of the naïve like an exotic drug were also emphasized: "Inconse-
quent young man, imprudent young woman, you should know that starting
from the very moment that you try the first of the six steps, by which the method
teaches us the principles of tango, right from that moment, your spirits will have
only one thought; to dance the tango, and the different evolutions of the tango
will be imposed on your limbs as if they were reflex movements" (Nohain 1913:
376).

The opposition to tango began in Paris around 1913. Articles, columns, and
enquêtes of several personalities were published in widely read newspapers and
magazines. And the church intervened through the Archbishop of Paris, whose
verdict was appealed to the Pope.[34] Reactions of high authorities appeared all
over Europe. Ludwig of Bavaria, in a personal letter addressed to the heads of his
army, wrote, "The tango dance is absurd, and moreover, unbecoming to those
who wear honorable military uniforms" (Sábato 1963: 91). In England, some aris-

tocrats strongly resisted the practice of the tango, but in Paris, 1913, the poet Jean Richepin chose tango as the topic of his presentation at the annual meeting of the French Academy of Arts:

> Tango has been strongly slandered. We have been told that this dance emerged from the Argentinean underworld and that it is improper for the practice of distinguished ladies and gentlemen. True; but is there a dance whose origins are not associated with the People? It has also been said that the tango is dishonest, that it takes indecent postures. ... The tango is honest or dishonest according to the one who dances it. I am not only bringing the tango to the Academy on the occasion of its annual opening, but also taking it to the theater in a play that I have written in collaboration with my wife (Jean Richepin [1913], quoted in Novati and Cuello 1980: 39).

In order to give further legitimacy to his defense, this member of L'Académie added to his presentation an interesting twist: He linked the origins of the tango to ancestral Hellenic dances. Richepin was joined in his defense of the tango by a myriad of passionate tango followers. They based their arguments on the lack of knowledge and the misrepresentations displayed by tango detractors. They tried to minimize the phenomenon, and they cried out for some joy and pleasure for the young in those years of despair. Perhaps the most remarkable defense was that launched by the poet Pierre Handrey under the title of "Le Médicine et le Tango" (1913). He argued that the School of Medicine should recommend the practice of *le tango* for health reasons. "Dance the tango, youngsters! [...] The progress of our race will be the work of the tango" (Handrey [1913], quoted in Humbert 1988: 82). And some astute dance *professeurs*, such as M. André de Fouquiéres, defended the practice of the tango among Parisians by emphasizing the healing, nurturing powers of the exotic.

> Tango is a subtle and voluptuous dance. It was born in the slums and it was refined in the *salons*. Tango is sad, caressing, suggestive. It gave us a lesson in musical psychology, and we have invented for this Argentinean dance a literary choreography. Our life is hectic, restless. ... Tango serves us as a relief and comfort for the spirit. It is like a discrete return to primitive instincts. [...] With tango, classic memories resuscitate. In some myrrhic vases, in the attitudes of some bacchanal dancers whose blue veils undulate with the wind, we find its rhythm (Fouquiéres, quoted in Rossi [1926] 1958: 164).

Scandal and fascination fed one another. Music-hall and cabaret owners, dance professeurs, and fashion designers joined efforts to further scandalize, tranquilize, and tailor the tango. The tango that Richepin and others defended was the tango introduced by professional "dance demonstrators" invited to present dance novelties at fashionable locales (see Figures 3.10 and 3.11). The detrac-

FIGURE 3.10 *Dance demonstrators exhibiting tango steps in Paris.* Source: *Alfredo G. Linares, "El Tango en Paris,"* Elegancias, *May 1913.*

FIGURE 3.11 Mistinguett, star of the Parisian revue, performing the tango with M. Robert.
Source: El Diario, *February 20, 1911.*

tors—although worried about the young and especially the women among the middle classes—had in mind the scandalous images of the tango as performed by the artists of the luxurious French revue: spectacular, extravagant, exotic. Defenders and detractors alike were referring to two different choreographic variations of tango that had been recently developed in Europe for stage and ballroom purposes. The original choreography had been stylized into glamorous, almost balletic, postures (extended arms, stretched torsos and necks, light feet) and rough apache-like figures (deep dips, backward bends, dizzying sways), with marching walks in between. In general, to dance in a tango style meant to combine in a piece both airy elegance and tumultuous earthiness, the result being an effect of sensuality and passion. The tension and contrasts observed in the Argentinean tango were overdone and misinterpreted, and the result was a grotesque mismatching of qualities. The choreographies developed for the *genre tableaux* followed either a ruffianesque, martial style or a Hispaniolized one, ardent with passion. Costumes and gestures were at least as central as the movements in these tangoesque styles. Thus, the basic continental tango was glamorized on the stages and tamed in the ballrooms. Although phonographic recordings and sheet music from Argentina were available, the music was especially composed so as to be exotically languid and retained only some of its rhythm.

Argentino dancers and musicians could not easily find jobs in the midst of the tango rage. When they did, they had to give in to autoexoticism and perform the

French version of the tango or wear gaucho costumes![35] (See Figure 3.12.) Tangueros had been traveling to Paris, London, New York, Venice, Nice, Madrid, and Barcelona probably since 1903. They followed the seasonal migrations of the gay transnational elite and sought to escape each war, working as dance exhibitors in hotels and dance halls, establishing dance academies, and performing at bars, cabarets, and music halls. Some of them were renowned in Argentina, and others were adventurers. Alfredo Gobbi (composer, singer, and actor) and Flora Rodríguez (singer) had traveled to Philadelphia in 1905 to record some of their pieces for the Victor Co. In 1907 Angel Villoldo (composer, instrumentalist, singer, and actor) joined them in a trip to Paris for the same purpose. They stayed for seven years working in several European capitals, composing and recording new pieces for the French Pathé Co. In 1912, Enrique Saborido (composer and dancer), owner of a dance academy in Buenos Aires, opened a tango school, first in France and then in London. His activities were interrupted by the war (see Gobello 1980).

More tangueros arrived in Paris in 1913. Casimiro Aín and his wife and partner Martina toured with several argentino musicians through Parisian cabarets, Biarritz, and New York in 1913 and 1914. Aín moved to the United States in 1916, where he stayed for three years running his own dance school. In 1920, he returned to Paris and, with Edith Peggy (a German dancer), performed all over Europe, including Scandinavia, Turkey, and the Soviet Union (Del Greco 1993). Bernabé Simarra moved to Paris in 1911 where he and Ideal Gloria (a famous Cuban dancer) won the tango contest for professeurs organized by *Fémina* at the theater Folie Magic in 1913. He taught tango in M. Camille de Rhynal's academy, worked as a dance demonstrator in the Hotel Excelsior, Venice, and finally moved to Barcelona where he established an academy devoted exclusively to the high society (Salas 1986; *Club de Tango* 2, 1992). Mariano Podestá, Juan Pasquariello Lastra, Francisco Ducasse, and Carlos Herrera (actors and dancers) were some of the others who sought to take advantage of the 1913 tango boom. Back from Paris that same year, Herrera reported on the labor situation to the daily *Crítica* of Buenos Aires. Asked about his prompt return from Paris, Herrera replied that the tango business was already saturated by dancers and teachers. He mentioned that there were more than one hundred argentinos trying to make a living on tango. As a result, it was impossible to survive even in the remotest corner of Montmartre. Even such a remarkable figure as Francisco Ducasse could not afford to stay for more than fourteen months. José Ovidio Bianquet, "*El Cachafaz*" (The Insolent), traveled to the United States in 1911 and, back in Buenos Aires, opened one of the most successful tango academies. In 1919 he worked for the "El Garrón" cabaret in Paris, becoming one of the last true tangueros of this first wave to "make it" in Europe (Salas 1986; Lara and Roncetti de Panti 1969; Gobello 1980).

These professional dancers, who often traveled without their regular female dancing partners, lacked an organization (such as L'Académie des Professeurs

FIGURE 3.12 *Bernabé Simarra and the Cuban dancer Ideal Gloria demonstrating tango in Paris, 1913.* Source: Fray Mocho, *March 28, 1913.*

de Danse de Paris) to back them up and market their unique tango product.[36] European impresarios and dance associations encouraged them to perform their admirable skills in order to promote their own tango businesses. Very soon, impresarios established a clear distinction between these polished tangueros argentinos and the European artists so as to avoid competition and enlarge the tango options available for consumption.

Paris, certainly the "manager" of the tango, reshaped its style and promoted it to the rest of the world as an exotic symbol of heterosexual courtship. The dramatically insinuating, languid tango was a Parisian product practiced mostly by the elites before World War I and further popularized after the war (Klein 1985: 179). Social dancers who performed a bland version of the glittering stage tango style (under the supervision of the dance professeurs) were reminded of its inspiring "naughty" connotations. "Primitiveness," in the tango form of instinctual passion, was a healing dance practice for the "decadent," "civilized" Europeans.

Although glamorized "instinct" was desirable on the stage in order to suit the colonizer's taste for the exotic, tango's wild passion required taming to fit the shy bodies of the bourgeois commoners. The dance masters simplified the improvised characteristics of the tango into a morally acceptable and physically affordable set sequence of steps. They wrote tango manuals and took the dance to their congresses to order and normalize the choreography (see Figures 3.13 and 3.14). Some of the dance experts identified seventy-two tango "attitudes," while others recommended eight to twelve set movements (Otterbach 1980: 278–279). M. André de Fouquiéres, in his "Les Danses Nouvelles: Le Tango," published in Paris in 1913, explains: "A dance of the famous *gauchos* [...], cattle herders of South America, [...] rough men who evidently cannot enjoy the precious manners of our salons—their temperament goes from brutal courtship to a body-to-body that resembles a fight—the tango [...] cannot be directly imported. It must be stopped at customs for a serious inspection and should be subjected to serious modifications" (Fouquiéres 1913: 58). Suggesting a choreographic transformation suited to French manners and good taste, Fouquiéres proposes to consolidate the otherwise untamable disarray of steps into eight main figures "characteristic of the tango dance." They were: "El Paseo," or *promenade*; "El Medio Corte," or *demi depart*; "El Corte," or *depart*; "La Media Luna," or *demi-lune*; "El Veteo," [sic] or *pas tourné*; "El Cruzado Cortado," or *croisé-coupé*; "El Cruzado por Ocho," or *croisé par huit*; and an eighth step that remained unnamed. The set continental tango figures retained some of the lure of the Spanish names but restricted the challenging duel of different yet articulated figures found in the original to a series of repetitive and expected mirrorings (Fouquiéres 1913: 58–61). Many other instructive articles establishing similar rules followed in 1913 and 1914.[37]

These attempts to domesticate the tango were for the most part favorably received. Sem (an influential columnist and satirist), for example, in an essay enti-

(a)

(b)

(c)

FIGURE 3.13 *Figures demonstrating (a)* La Promenade, *(b) The Dip, and (c)* Pas Oriental a la Gauche. Source: *Gladys Beattie Crozier's dance instruction manual,* The Tango and How to Dance It *(London: Melrose Ltd., 1913).*

FIGURE 3.14 *Diagram illustrating tango steps.* Source: *Franco Giovannini's manual* Balli d'Oggi, con 70 figuri demonstrativi, grafici e brani musicali e uno studio critico sulle danza nouvissime de Giovanni Francheschini *(Milan: Ulrico Hoepli, 1914).*

tled "Les Possedés" (The Possessed) writes: "It is a miracle to see how the French, with their exquisite sense of moderation, have transformed it, putting it *an point.* [...] A tango a bit caramelized, a bit *parigoté,* with a decent and light grace, an air of scarcely any touching, a bit of a better tone [...] where the good taste and tact of its followers is demonstrated, making of this dance of savages an elegant flirt of fine and modest legs" (Sem 1925: 45–46). All theories and technical courses stressed that, when dancing tango, attitudes, gestures, and proper conversation were far more important than the actual steps. In this manner, dance masters attempted to compensate for the actual difficulties of the dance, fearing the resistance of their potential students.

Both the ballroom and the music-hall tango versions were stylized, regimented, produced. And the different social spaces for which they were developed were enclosed, restricted, and in no way interchangeable. The fantastic exotic style of the stage could not be the same as that applied to the quotidian social dance, but the two styles certainly fed on each other. The fashion industry also joined in the tango business, shaping bodies and promoting a new morality while selling tango articles. A tango color was promoted in the red-orange spectrum, a color akin to sensual ignition. A variety of tango cocktail-dresses were especially designed for attending tango teas and midnight champagne tango encounters (see Figure 3.15). These evening gowns had slits in the front to facilitate the dance glides and usually included an Oriental item: the harem trouser-skirt (*jupe-culotte*) (García Jiménéz 1965). Another model included "*le ventre de couleur*" variation: a corsage and a skirt of the same color worn with a special (sometimes padded) piece of a contrasting shade wrapping the abdomen. The purpose of this attire was twofold: On the one hand, it enhanced the gracefulness of the tango contortions; on the other, it allowed the rapid detection of possible excesses, thus discouraging scandalous proximities among dancing partners (Bonafoux [1913] 1992). The special tango make-up had Oriental touches, such as kohl bordering the eye rims and dark red lipstick. Tango attitudes included the use of long, Oriental cigar holders, and walking *à la tango* implied tight, delicate steps, reminiscent of Salome's movements when constrained by jeweled anklets (Carter 1975). A new kind of footwear was designed, the tango slipper, with wide straps that wrapped around the ankles (see Figure 3.16). The slippers were a complement to the tango gown, since the gown was shorter than the usual length and allowed the feet to be exposed, particularly during the dance, but the most revolutionary and contested tango fashion innovation was probably the tango corset.

Perhaps more than any other single factor, the popularity of the tango and similar dances led many women to abandon orthodox corsetry in 1913 and 1914. Some corset advertisements complained that, "at balls one sees a number of women who affect an excessive lack of constraint [and] have abandoned all support; the bust undulates to the rhythm of the dance in a loose fashion."

FIGURE 3.15   *The tango skirt designed by Bakst and executed by Paquin in 1913. Courtesy of the Victoria and Albert Museum.*

FIGURE 3.16 The tango slipper.
Courtesy of the Victoria and Albert Museum.

Other advertisements—such as one on "Chiffons and Tango"—bowed to the
trend and promoted short elastic corsets, maintaining that they "prevent mus-
cle fatigue," so "dancers prefer them." Indeed, one "all elastic" model that
slipped on over the head was called "the tango" (Steele 1985: 229).

These notorious changes in fashion, together with the display of sensual
movements in the dance, led Béatrice Humbert to assert that the tango was a
true "detonator" of a new morality in France. She argues that, unlike tango in its
original *sudamericano* setting, tango in Europe in the first decades of the century promoted women's liberation (1988: 69). Tango opened a venue for women
to exhibit sensuality in public. This was perhaps a novelty for European women
of the middle classes and for some of the elite just as it was in Argentina. I am reluctant, however, to state that the tango brought any such "liberation" for
women anywhere. I rather think that tango showed and performed the strong
changes in gender roles that were under way at the time, conflictively joining
voting demands, dress reforms, and the recent scientific findings in birth control
as well as the psychoanalytic incursions in female sexuality. At times, the practice of the tango stirred up these questions in a favorable way for some women;
at other times, it banalized the most earnest feminist efforts. None of these results could be properly ascribed to the tango—except that they happened at the
same time.

In any event, tango's impact on rioplatense women can hardly be judged as either negative or positive. Tango happened *with* women and was entangled through racial, class, and sexual issues to men and other women; it affected different women in different ways in conjunction with many other things. And in Paris and everywhere else, women also affected the tango by introducing subversive skills or romanticizing the ruffianesque stories, by dancing something spicier or tamer than what other women were doing, and by participating in the formation of a national identity strongly tinged by bourgeois morals that would, among other things, generate differences among women. There was never just one tango; tangos took and gave—conflictively, ironically, pathetically, politically—an aestheticized melodrama of boiling social despair. I cannot forget that tangos and wars were born together.

In the 1910s tango shared staged exoticism with other musical genres: "tropical" and especially Cuban music, flamenco, Russian and Hawaiian dances, and, a little later, North American jazz. It was the time of World War I; the maps were changing and the world was expanding. People's bodies were uneasy; they wanted to move. Soldiers concentrated in the big cities, moving their bodies to the rhythms of exotic music, waiting to move on to a war over exotic lands/colonies.

In the production of exotic dances, France was hegemonic but not without contenders. France's struggles with English codes of social dancing are a well-documented skirmish in the long-lasting battle between the two economic, political, and cultural empires (Leppert 1988). This competition was clearly understood by the argentinos themselves, who attentively followed the French-English disputes to establish the steps and postures of the "authentic" tango. British impresarios organized "tango teas" (see Figure 3.17); dance masters established their schools; fashion designers produced tango evening-gowns; and an accomplished Englishwoman wrote the first full-length book ever devoted to a social dance. In London in 1913, Gladys Beattie Crozier published *The Tango and How to Do It*. The book included dance instructions, answers to the most frequent moral concerns, recommendations on manners, proper dress codes, and useful tips on how to organize a tango-tea event at a private residence. The hostess of such an event was to pay attention to lighting, flower arrangements, adequate furniture, floor polishing, and carpet removal as well as to the number of guests and the wording of the invitation cards (Franks 1963). From Paris and London, the tango made its way to New York and repeated the same, now familiar story: scandal, dance masters and manuals, and a version for the stage. In the United States, however, tango was awaited by two special hostesses: ragtime and the movie screen (Buckman 1978; Roberts 1979).

At some point during this period the competition over the tango carried out among the major world powers turned into a distribution of "specialties." London and Paris, for example, became rather complementary, promoting the tango as a social dance and a stage *diva*, respectively. Paris, the capital of pleasure, de-

FIGURE 3.17 *The tango tea—the latest fashion in London in 1913. The caption reads: "The novelty of the hour is the tango tea. It may be seen at the Queen's Theatre, London, with the stalls removed and replaced by tables and chairs for afternoon tea. The band is on the stage, where M. Clayton and Mlle. Marquis give us tango dances and this is supplemented by a dress parade of all the latest fashions." Source: From a drawing by F. Matania, 1913. Courtesy of The Raymond Mander and Joe Mitchenson Theatre Collection.*

veloped the spectacular scenarios of the revue and the music halls (Moulin Rouge, Folies Bergère, Olympia, Casino de Paris, etc.), where entertainers and dancers from every part of the world dreamed of having a consecratory debut. Mistinguett, the undisputed queen of the French music halls for about twenty years, introduced the tango into elaborate stage productions as a part of her *Vals Challoupée* (see Figure 3.18).

London, the creator of the music-hall genre, soon devoted its efforts to the social dance industry. Assuming England's role as the "workshop" of the world, English dance-masters not only codified dance styles in manuals but also aggressively promoted the sport of dancing; they even periodically organized dance matches—International Dance Competitions—where rules and regulations closely followed the model of quasi-Olympic games. Tango, after hard debates, was incorporated into the category of "modern" (as opposed to "latin") dancing. The United States, as I have already mentioned, participated enthusiastically in all branches of the business of disciplining and promoting dance. Vernon and Irene Castle, a famous professional "exhibition ballroom" dance couple (who demonstrated new fashionable dance trends), picked up the tango during their visits to Paris before World War I (see Figure 3.19). They developed their own manual, which described a variety of dances including some of their own creation, filmed short clips for teaching purposes, organized a number of dancing schools, and toured throughout the United States with great success.[38] But the "specialty" of the United States was the movie screen, which soon displaced, to some extent, all other dancing business branches.

After World War I, popular movie stars (like Rudolf Valentino) were exoticized with the help of tango and tango stars (like Carlos Gardel) were internationally promoted through the Paramount aura (see Figures 2.5 and 3.20). Valentino performed his celebrated tango (the one that would set the tango-style standard for Hollywood movies up to the present) with Beatrice Domínguez in the *Four Horsemen of the Apocalypse*, filmed in 1921. The scene is announced by a title that reads: "The famous Boca quarter of Buenos Aires was a port of last resort." The first shot shows Valentino, in full gaucho garb, smoking and staring at an attractive brunette: Domínguez. She is wrapped in a heavily embroidered Spanish *mantón* (a large mantilla) with long fringe and has a carnation in her hair. She is dancing with an unpleasant male partner. Valentino approaches the couple and gestures to the man, indicating that his turn is over. The man resists and Valentino bravely strikes the man across the face with a *rebenque* (riding crop) (Curubeto 1993). The orchestra starts playing a habanera (not a tango). Valentino and Domínguez enter the frame from opposite sides and begin to dance. After some individual gyrations, their hands join and they move around the dance floor performing smooth glides, controlled dips, and slow, sensuous swayings. Finally, they embrace too closely and she breaks into contortions attempting to avoid a kiss that he insistently seeks. Unable to satisfy his desire, Valentino pushes her away with violence. Domínguez lands on the floor and drags herself

FIGURE 3.18 *Mistinguett in her dance "Vals Challoupée," where she introjected the tango figures, c. 1920s.* Source: *Mistinguett,* Mistinguett: Queen of the Paris Night *(London: Elek Books, 1954).*

132

FIGURE 3.19   Steps for the "Tango Argentine," the "Innovation Tango," and the "Maxixe Brazillien." Source: *Vernon and Irene Castle,* Modern Dancing *(New York: Harper & Bros., 1914).*

FIGURE 3.20   Rudolf Valentino and Beatrice Domínguez performing their famous tango scene in The Four Horsemen of the Apocalypse, *a 1921 Hollywood silent movie directed by Rex Ingram and scripted by June Mathis. Mathis adapted Vicente Blasco Ibañez's novel of 1918 to make it a showcase for Valentino's Latin lover.*

to his feet in an ambivalent gesture of hatred and rapture. Then the sounds of a whip cut the air, bringing more tension into the scene. In the end, he resorts to a secret weapon, *las boleadoras*, which he kept hidden between the folds of his gaucho pants, and lassoes her. Like a Patagonian bird, she falls prey into his arms (Bates and Bates 1936; Richards 1992). The fatal Latin man carries the secret native weapons with which to, if not tame, at least handle the femme fatale.

In addition, the United States rejuvenated and popularized ballet by introducing modern dance choreographies. Perhaps the most famous American live performer of exotic dances was Ruth St. Denis (see Figure 3.21). She attained international fame by performing successfully in Parisian theaters. The major source of inspiration for the stunningly exotic choreographies that she developed with her partner, Ted Shawn, was the 1912 volume of *National Geographic Magazine* (Sherman 1979). The Denishawn "Gringo Tango" was choreographed by Shawn in 1924 and first performed that year at the Academy for Music in Newburgh, New York. The piece was subsequently presented on their tours of the Far East in 1925–1926 and of the United States in 1926–1927.

Shawn composed a trio with Anne Douglas and Ernestine Day. The scene took place in an imaginary saloon at the Texas-Mexico border. A Texan cowboy, a blond saloon hostess, and a brunette Mexican temptress develop a jealousy plot. The women, on opposite sides of the male border, attempt to seduce the cowboy through their dances. The hostess, dressed in pink and scarlet ruffles, performs a frantic can-can solo while he stamps and claps to the music. When the Mexican "girl" walks in, dressed in black with a red scarf, the rowdiness is over. It is time for the gringo tango. Unlike Valentino's tango, which was clearly Frenchified and smooth (despite its menacing ambiance), the gringo tango was closely related to the British version but with an Americanized twist: It was more energetic and included abrupt half-turns, deep dips and backbends, some bouncing and stamping of the feet, and finally, a cheek-to-cheek run-away, arms and eyes ahead … frustrated. The hostess comes back to claim the man. The cowboy cannot make up his mind, either about women or territories, and places his arms possessively around each woman's waist (see Figure 3.22).[39] "Gringo Tango" is a telling tango story of colonized women's bodies and feminized colonial lands. Passionately tangoized parodies of colonialism were set to travel all over the world. Exoticism and the newly industrialized dancing complex collaborated closely in the creation of new, passionate products and new markets ready to consume passion.

FIGURE 3.21 *Ruth St. Denis performing exotic dances (1914–1920s): "Egyptian," "Mexican,"*
and "Eastern" with Ted Shawn, "Japanese" with Charles Weidman. Source: *(top left) Photo*
Ira Hill; (bottom left) photo L. G. Bigelow; courtesy of the Dance Collection, The New York
Public Library at Lincoln Center, Astor, Lenox and Tilden Foundations; (top and bottom
right) courtesy of the Mansell Collection Limited.

FIGURE 3.22   Finale of Gringo Tango (1924), choreographed and performed by Ted Shawn with Ernestine Day and Anne Douglas. Photo by Nicholas Muray. Courtesy of Jane Sherman, from her personal collection.

4
Scandalizing National Identity

Tango Back Home

Although tango originated in the Río de la Plata region (ca. 1880), it was only after it achieved success in the main capitals of the world (ca. 1911–1913 and again after World War I) that it gained full popularity in its original setting. Local bodies practiced pleasure taking into account external judgments of taste. Local dancing styles proved to be dependent on those "civilized" judgments. Moreover, the very concepts of pleasure related to dancing—including the focus on sensuality—followed the dictates of those people recognized as culturally superior. When, where, what, how, and with whom to dance, as well as which feelings should be identified and developed while moving with the music, were as culturally dependent on the colonizer as the economic and political fates of the neocolonized nations were. This does not mean, however, that local developments were nonexistent or that resistive dancing moods were inexorably co-opted. In the Río de la Plata, tango followed its own conflictive paths linked to local political struggles, including those over the issues of dependency and colonialism. Locally established class distinctions (dependent on, but not fully determined by, relations with imperialist powers), translated into moral codes (again, subordinated to bourgeois imperialist codifications, but not without specific local contradictions), had prevented vast sectors of the local upper and middle classes from engaging in the tango. After all, it was the marginal, hybrid, and low working-class local sectors that had originally created and practiced the tango. Within the higher classes (which were generally more conforming to moral prohibitions than the lower classes) there were important exceptions following gender distinctions—a fact that turns any analysis based solely or primordially on class differences into a paradox. Elite and middle-class men frequently broke the rule of avoiding the tango environment. Their adventurous moves across class and moral boundaries did not, however, call into question the boundaries per se; rather, they made use of set distinctions for confirming class, ethnic, and gender superiority. The transgressions of wealthier, Europeanized males into the tango world entailed stepping over rigid boundaries—a challenging trespass—but did little to break up the moral and class divisions established in local society.

Women were constituted as the bourgeois bastions of morality and were segregated into one social space or the other to stand as markers of naturalized social boundaries and simultaneously as the draw for male comings and goings between the two worlds. As a result, males were lured by two classes of women displaying two complementary kinds of erotic power. The defiant eroticism of lower-class, racially impure tangueras tugged men into leaving their legitimate loci of class and morality, whereas the comforting eroticism of the non-tango women of their own kind drew them back into their legitimate social places. For this reason, tango could not be said to have actually crossed local social barriers until women located in opposite classes and moralities joined in the dancing practice of the tango. This cross-over hardly occurred before tango's popularization in Paris.

The acceptance of the tango in Europe affected the class and moral identification of the tango in its local setting. It affected the cultural codes of distinction among the men and women of the various local classes and generated new distinctions in the tango itself. The European acceptance affected the hegemonic power of national representation based in the economic, political, and moral superiority that local elites had enjoyed up until then. Foreign/superior recognition empowered the tango—which had been a locally denigrated cultural expression—and made it a competitive marker of national identity. This complex external intervention into Argentinean national politics through the tango was no more than an episode of cultural imperialism within a broader and long-standing struggle between formal independence and substantive self-determination.

Cultural, economic, and state/institutional politics do not necessarily follow the same roads, but they certainly intersect and affect each other in political ways. In addition, none of these dimensions exclusively determines, expresses, or exhausts the others. Tango, for example, stemmed from a particular social situation (within which economic, political, moral, class, racial, and gender dimensions can be specifically analyzed) and provoked events that affected this social situation, which in turn had not remained static (or congruent in all its dimensions). Tango adjusted to the newly developed local social situation (i.e., was changed by it), partly to express those changes and partly to challenge further realignments. What I believe to be of particular interest is the way in which external imperial interventions, through the process of exoticization, affected the local reception of tango and how tango intervened in the local and foreign debates concerning the shape of Argentina's national identity. To this end, I will analyze specific characteristics of tango's scandal/fascination dynamics, including references to the local strategies of disciplining and promoting the tango. In addition, I will discuss the emergence of lay and scholarly interests in producing a history of tango that establishes national roots and authentic features—interests arising out of the restless and contradictory quest for national identity in in/dependent settings.

As I deal with exoticism and national identity through the tango, a tension constantly reemerges in my written thoughts. That tension is between the empowering effects of the process of exoticization, which grant local recognition to certain social sectors and their practices, and the co-opting effects of the exotic manipulations by which the empowered practices remain entangled in new exoticisms (reifications/fetishism), which require continued strategic shifts on the part of the resistors. These complex issues are unevenly delineated and not nearly exhausted in these pages. I fully engage contradictory interpretations, tangoing too close to opposite positions, bouncing from one specific struggle to another, finding myself endangered—with no clear-cut answers—while searching for decolonizing moves. Resistance is so pragmatically specific, stubborn, and resilient in its powerlessness and is so cruel and wise in its lack of Reason but plagued by just justifications that I have often been tempted to step aside— theorize, ideologize—to find comfort beneath a colonizing/paralyzing shade. My resulting tango and my own identity remain incomplete and in struggle.

Local Scandals and Fascinations

> The controversy unleashed by the tango is actually one of the most remarkable issues ever discussed in mundane circles. It is an issue that agitates London, New York, Paris, Berlin, and Rome, all at the same time. The monarchs proscribe the tango, the priests disapprove of it, and, in the meantime, "tea-tangos," "tango-suppers," and "tango-contests" pop up everywhere (a British correspondent [1913], quoted in Rossi [1926] 1958: 165).

The "tango controversy" that engaged major world powers was equally remarkable among argentinos. As a matter of fact, much of the debate over the moral connotations of tango was fueled by the first reactions of some key argentino government officials living abroad. Enrique Rodríguez Larreta—minister in Paris—and other intellectuals and high-ranked members of Argentinean delegations publicly denounced the ill-famed origins and practice of the tango dance in their native land. The argentinos attempted to enlighten the "international elite," and especially the honorable ladies, about the "pornographic spectacle" that they were naïvely performing. Consider these warnings meant to inform Europeans about tango's true nature, circa 1913: "In Buenos Aires tango is a dance belonging distinctly to ill-famed clubs and to taverns of the worst repute. It is never danced in tasteful salons or among distinguished people" (Larreta [1914], quoted in Etchebarne 1955: 82). And: "The purpose of the tango is to describe the obscene. [...] It summarizes the choreography of the brothels, and its fundamental task is the pornographic spectacle. [...] When the ladies of the twentieth century dance tango, they know or they ought to know that they are behaving like prostitutes" (Leopoldo Lugones [1913], quoted in Ferrer 1980a: 126–128). Tango, they advised, will inadvertently contaminate noble reputations. Leopoldo Lugones[1] added the following: "The prohibition of this indecency is not only honest and distinguished but also, to a large degree, patriotic. Argentine men should not serve as a label for this practice of marginals. It is not dignified nor true to do so. Tango is not a national dance, nor is the prostitution that conceives it" (Lugones [1913], quoted in Ferrer 1980a: 126–128). Larreta, Lugones, and other Argentinean detractors of tango stated their accusations with noticeable indignation. Something extremely crucial was at stake in the tango controversy, something far beyond the decency of the foreign elites. The indignation of the Argentinean elite was the bitter reaction of a betrayed dignified class. Their problem was the banality and insensitivity of imperialism in dealing with class and national identities. In a special edition of the newspaper *El Diario* published in December 1912, a balance of what had disappeared and what had remained as a part of Argentine-ness was offered to the readers on the occasion of the Christmas and New Year's holidays. Tango was at the center of this exercise in Argentinean self-reflection.

> When we were all almost convinced that Europe was no longer considering us as "savage" and that in the old continent our wheat, corn, and the frozen meats were undisputed proofs and the best examples of our civilization and astonishing progress, we received—several years ago by now—the unexpected news that in Paris they were suddenly aware of our existence, not through the valuable products of our soil [...] but through the tango. [...] Moreover, it cannot be superfluous to make here an important remark: The tango, as it is danced in Paris has little to do with ours except for the name and the music (*El Diario*, December 1912, quoted in Novati and Cuello 1980: 37).

Tango, a practice close to the identity of a different/inferior class of argentinos, called into question the elite's legitimacy to represent the nation. In addition, *El Diario*'s journalist stated grudgingly that if tango—already a *poor* representation (in both senses of the term, as in low class and as in a bad copy) of the national being—was going to stand for Argentina, the Europeans could at least respect the authentic Argentinean practice.[2] Argentina, by way of the tango, was being doubly misrepresented. Argentinean identity was being manipulated first through the projection of a "popular" image of the national culture—an image that challenged the "civilized" image the Argentinean elite wished to project—and second by the simultaneous appropriation and distortion of the practice (through which the elite was being mistakenly represented). Hence, the elite's representativeness was being questioned and the popular culture was being misrepresented. Together, these strategies of rerepresentation undertaken by the main world powers affected Argentina's national identity. *El*

Diario's article suggests that two bourgeois/positivistic rules of representation had been transgressed. The first rule would establish that legitimate representatives of a nation can be distinguished from illegitimate ones and that the morally superior sectors should represent the morally inferior ones, usually meaning that the civilized, wealthier ones should represent the uncivilized, poor ones. The second bourgeois/positivistic rule would specify that representations should be accurate, that is, they should respect the shape of the original. Placed in an imperialist context, these rules of representation were not only transgressed, but the transgression itself was both necessary and legitimate. The colonizer has the power to reverse the "natural" hierarchy of representations by making legitimate representatives of those not recognized as legitimate in the colony itself. The imperial powers, a step above the colonized nations in the hierarchies of morality, civilization, and wealth, could choose to represent the colonial nations through whichever sector they wished, whether that sector was the most powerful or the most powerless among the colonized. The only accuracy that counts for the colonizer is the one that is faithful to the colonizer's own stereotyping of what colonies are like. It is for this very reason that the representatives of the colony should be the most "uncivilized," the most "primitive," the most distinguishable/different from the colonizer—and hence, the ones most easily manipulated into the image that the colonizer has already constructed of the colonized.

Moreover, in commenting on the European misrepresentation of the original tango, *El Diario*'s journalist misunderstood the intentions of the colonizer. The "cultures" of the colonized were a source of enjoyment, of pleasure, not a serious exercise in representation involving questions of legitimacy or truthfulness. In addition, the colonized should not pretend that the "civilized" colonizer will replicate their "barbarian" manners. As a matter of fact, the colonized should be grateful for both being chosen as a source of enjoyment—which implies recognition—and for being subjected to a civilized refinement—a benefit that the colonized could enjoy, thereby improving their resemblance to the civilized colonizer.

In developing representations, the colonizer follows a colonial purpose, colonizing understandings, and colonialist strategies. The colonizer identifies and represents the colony (Argentina, in this case) in order to reaffirm the relative positions of the colonizer and the colonized. In Argentina's case, the colonizer had no interest, to the bitter regret of Argentina's arrogant elite, in recognizing the legitimate identity of an independent nation in terms established by either colonized sector. In addition, the colonizer's distortion of the cultural practices of the colonized was, in the colonizer's view, positive and legitimate; the misrepresentations were naturally more "civilized" and hence cultivated the coarse culture of the colonized for the benefit of both colonizer and colonized. Exoticism was thereby rendered a desirable and legitimate civilizing practice undertaken by the colonizer and the colonized allies. The offended sector of the Argentinean elite was made a victim of those same practices that it had previously accepted and applied in order to keep other sectors of their own nation in subordinate positions. The fate of imperialist trickery had turned them unexpectedly into "natives" and thus had generated "nationalist" reactions.

The Western bourgeois colonizer's fascination with tango affected the internal struggles for national representation among the colonized. For the members of the conservative Argentinean elite, the problem was a class struggle over representations of national identity—representations that had been affected by the exoticizing interventions of the civilized imperialists. Through tango, the disputes over national identity had shifted from the domestic terrain controlled by the colonized elite to the international terrain controlled by imperial powers. The responses of the Argentinean elite, however, were not monolithic. There were those, the "liberals," who saw themselves positioned so close to the European elite that they claimed to share the joys of exoticism regardless of the nationality of the object. Tango was a part of the culture of their native land (the "popular" part), but their identity was not being threatened. They saw themselves as a part of a transnational elite. Actually, the members of this "open-minded" sector of the elite had been consuming the tango for a long time. They were frequent visitors to the brothels where women danced the tango in couples in order to create a stimulating environment for the clients.[3] They were the ones who actively participated in the street *carnavales,* mocking the tangos performed by the black *comparsas.* They were the members of the gangs that invaded the bars of the poor and marginals, looking for some spice and violence.[4] This part of the Argentinean elite was precisely the one that contributed to the promotion of the tango in Paris through frequent trips abroad. The opposing sector was made up of those who despised being thrown into the same bag together with blacks, pimps, prostitutes, dock workers, servants, and *orilleros.* They felt that the class boundaries so well known in their home territory were difficult to distinguish at a European distance and hence that their *argentino* identity was being threatened. On both accounts the Argentinean elite aspired to the rank of the "civilized"—that is, they strove to be peers and part of Western culture—but their strategies of representation and identification were different.[5]

The Argentinean elite, not unlike foreign elites, expressed opposing opinions of the tango that accorded with the positions they assumed within the world economy of passion. For members of the Argentinean elite this positioning was especially fragile given that they were a colonized elite (an elite susceptible to being exoticized together with the tango). To accept the tango as representative of Argentinean national identity potentially affected both their class identity and their power as legitimate representatives of Argentina. In Argentina's internal politics, tango had been representing the elite's antagonistic class for a long time. It had been precisely one of the markers of social distinction. The foreign exoticization of tango could (and would) affect the shape of Argentina's national identity by putting the arrogant elite sector of the neocolonized back into its place as "distinguished natives." The ambiguous message of the bourgeois neocolonizer was misleading: Although a fair amount of economic development, of whiteness, and of refinement (i.e., incorporation into the imperialist capitalist economy) should be praised and encouraged, this was not a sufficient motive for attaining a "civilized" Identity—and it would never be, precisely because Argentina's development and civilization were dependent on the colonizer's interests and judgments.

Other sectors of argentinos benefited from tango's acceptance abroad—namely, the sector that the worried faction of the elite feared to privilege through tango's association with national identity. The original tango fans and performers were empowered by the neocolonizer's exoticization of the tango. After the "international elite" acknowledged the tango (albeit as "exotic"), Argentina's national ("native") elite finally recognized the existence of the "popular" class from Buenos Aires (*porteños*). The tangueros responded ironically and pragmatically to this new opportunity. Whoever had the chance moved to Europe and, later, to the United States to search for jobs as dance professors, dance demonstrators, and musicians.

In the meantime, the national question was kept in mind. The Bates brothers (Héctor and Luis), writing in the 1930s, asked themselves: "Who is conquering whom? [...] Every exotic thing, anything extravagant and unknown, was adopted by the Parisian society, which sought new sensations in order to exhibit them before the astonished eyes of its tourists. [But] Paris was far from knowing that, instead of being the conqueror, it would end up conquered by our popular dance" (Bates and Bates 1936: 60). They addressed exoticism's negative connotations by reversing the usual terms of the colonizer/colonized power asymmetry. By acknowledging this result as unexpected and reminding their readers of the "pacific and unpretentious" nature of tango's "invasion," however, the Bates brothers were careful not to brag too much. After all, "in its own home [country] it [tango] had never achieved more than absolute prohibitions" (Bates and Bates 1936: 61).

Vicente Rossi, writing in 1926, poked fun at the elite for losing control of Argentina's representation in Europe. Moreover, he clearly connected these events with class competition for the legitimate representation of the nation. "It would be unfair to deny that tango, the great current delirium of all Europe, has had a remarkable educational influence; in the last six months the public has gotten to know the name and the geographical position of the *República Argentina* better than it had after years and years of information about railroads and crops" (British correspondent, quoted in Rossi [1926] 1958: 160). Argentina was finally becoming recognized as a place in the world, thanks to the tango. And although "tango's *argentinidad* [Argentine-ness] had its objectors," continues Rossi, "it had been logically established by the nationality of its introducers" (Rossi [1926] 1958: 160; 162). It was clear to the followers of the tango–national identity debate that the "objectors" were members of the Argentinean elite and the "introducers" were the musicians and dancers from Argentina's "popular" classes and that the elite wanted to deny the latter the legitimacy of representing the nation.

Nevertheless, thanks to the tango, and to the quasi-fortuitous fact of its having been "chosen" from among many other possible exotic dances, the popular sectors were representing the nation—despite the reactions of the elite. That tango, however—the world-seducing "peaceful conqueror"—had little to do with the tango practiced by the popular sectors in Argentina. Tango had been exoticized—identified *and* changed—by the enraptured neocolonizers. The dancers and musicians who were aggressively spreading the tango at the world's "core" were obliged to perform exotically so as to adjust to the colonizer's expectations. The tangueros, who had crashed a local class barrier thanks to the intervention of the colonizer, were now facing an international mark of distinction: exoticism, the mark of imperialism. With tango, sectors that had been marginalized gained the power to represent the nation, but this power had a price. Exoticism, an imperial manipulation, would also put them back with the rest of their conationals (both friends and foes) in the place of the colonized. Moreover, the very enthusiasm with which the colonizer associated tango and Argentinean national identity was suspicious. The colonizer, sharing the racist/classist prejudices of the colonized elite, used the "sensual primitiveness" associations of the tango to tinge Argentina's identity as a whole with uncivilized connotations—reminders of Argentina's colonized condition.

Exoticism is a potent tool when in the hands of imperialists. It allows the colonizer to handle paradoxical colonial situations, precisely the material out of which imperialist power reproduces and sustains itself. Exoticism seduces both the colonizer and the colonized, as the tangueros clearly foresaw. The counterpart to the colonizer's fascination is the taste of empowerment experienced by the colonized. For the colonized, exoticization often means being recognized, noticed, and identified, but this glamorous recognition is also objectifying and binding. In order to perpetuate the exotically attained identity, the colonized must permanently practice autoexoticism and must do so tastefully; if the colonized fail in this task, recognition/identity can be withdrawn. Exoticism's mutually seducing game implied an uneven distribution of risks between the colonizer and the colonized.

SCENE SIX: DOÑA DIVINA'S TANGO
(THE ONE SHE NEVER DANCED)

Screening.
  Movie screen replaces stage. Projection and sound effects.
  At 2:35, sharp, every afternoon, Doña Divina slips back into her dreams. It cannot wait. It happens right on time. It is about to start any minute now.

Clarita takes off her shoes and sits on the small rug by the big bed, ready to watch her grandmother's memories flicker against the window, like old movies on a yellow screen.

Doña Divina, young. (Were you about nineteen?) She walks down the steps holding her skirt. She sneaks out into the siesta heat. (Where is your hat?) He smiles, invitingly, all tailored in blue. The Model A Ford rumbles away from the family's summer residence. A cloud of dust.

The chauffeur follows short directions. The Lieutenant, impeccable, tries to place hands on his beloved, now kidnapped and transformed into a victim. The smell of betrayal widens her nostrils and brightens her eyes. (Love or lust, Grandma?) The car door swings open on her side. She rolls out. A cloud of dust.

Great Grandfather Raimundo paces up and down the corridor, knotting his hands. A lawyer must be hired to defend the family's honor. Newspaper headlines. At the courthouse, Horacio writes up the case while fighting unappeasable thoughts. (Mamá never tired of mentioning Divina's legs: so agile, hairless, colored by two drops of native blood.) A cloud of dust.

Horacio wins the case and petitions for Divina's hand. Family relief. Church. Divina in a cloud of lace. Beautiful. (My mother never tired of mentioning Divina's posture, like a gypsy, the pride in her spine.)

Dorita, Mamá, and Ramón: three children born in low, earthy clouds. Divina cooked soap and beer—stinky bitterness that kept the household fermenting, alive—except on national holidays. (Didn't your *pasteles* ever harmonize your home?) Mamá and Ramón played *casita* in the yard. Dorita was the fairest and prettiest, the favorite, but she was always ill. Mamá slurped angel-hair noodles wishing she would turn blond and pink like a cherub. Ramón was punished for walking to the dinner table on his hands, preparing to flee with the next visiting circus. The air in the house was stuffy, a dusty mixture of unfulfillment and anger.

One day they were off to Paris, Grandpa attempting a second rescue. He could not speak or play outside of politics. Divina saw the tango for the first time that summer, before the Big War, on board *La France*. That evening, the waves rocked her scandal from the past into the present. There he was, on the third deck, that degraded lieutenant rhythmically entangled in her life. He remained impeccable, holding a woman who looked just like herself. Divina stuck in her dusty cloud, which now clung, feignedly, from the rim of her hat. For once, her choked sensuality ran red down her throat.

"Child," says Doña Divina interrupting her own tango, "I feel so much like dying that I can hardly wait anymore."

"Are you afraid?" Clarita whispers.

"No. It's not fear, *querida*. It's madness. I've gone crazy with age."[6]

"Is madness hopeless, *abuela*?"

"Yes. I had three hopes in my life, and those same hopes were the three things that bring *bandidos* to their ruin; but I did not get to be a bandit, so my three hopes are still running around on their own."

"Should I go out there and look for them?" asks Clarita, excited.

"Be modest, Clarita. Just talk about yourself. That's the only thing we can honestly hope to know."[7]

Clarita notices that, when dreaming, Doña Divina's eyes never close. They show dry sadness or malicious joy through a dignified cloud of Córdoba dust.

Blackout

Reappropriating the Exotic

Once exoticized—that is, transformed into an enjoyable and exciting practice through a careful screening of "indecent" features as well as through the establishment of a distance/difference between the ways of the "primitive" and the ways in which "primitiveness" could be appropriated by the "civilized"—tango was accepted by the Argentinean elite as a legitimate practice. Although tango had been enjoyed by elite men before the Parisian verdict, dancing tango was a somewhat clandestine undertaking shared with lower-class women. After the Parisian tango boom, women of the elite class would do the tango in a "civilized," stylized fashion and in public.

In Argentina, tango was sinful not only because it was danced in clandestine sexual places but also because it was danced in the streets and in the *patios* of the miserable tenement houses. The public space of the *arrabales* (urban slums), especially those street corners where the few street lamps stood and where the sidewalks were illuminated by shop windows (see Figure 4.1) were the gathering places of the tango characters (García Jiménez 1965a). It was not unusual to see men dancing with each other, either in the streets or in rundown places by the harbor, and the police frequently intervened to break up the violent outcomes of these homosocial dance duels (Benarós 1977; Novati and Cuello 1980). Although marginal and working-class men (and wealthy men, too, of course) had quite a choice of places for dancing tango, drinking, gambling, and picking fights—bordellos, *carpas, bailetines, perigundines, academias,* and, later on, dance halls and cabarets—poor women who wished to maintain a decent reputation were rather constrained. Among the poor, no private space was large enough for dancing, except when the workers' associations or popular social clubs (associations of immigrants) organized dance festivals either in *prados* or *romerías* (marquees set up on holidays), and *salas* (theater halls rented for special events such as the *carnavales*). With the exception of the streets, however, the dancing of tango was strictly under surveillance in most social locales: *bastoneros* or *encargados* (personnel in charge of supervising the dance) would

FIGURE 4.1 *Men dancing tangos in the streets of Buenos Aires, early 1900s.* Source: *Francisco García Jiménez,* El Tango: Historia de Medio Siglo *(1880–1930) (Buenos Aires: Editorial Universitaria de Buenos Aires, 1965).*

watch how the couples behaved and call *"¡Que haya luz!"* ("Let there be light!"— that is, space between the bodies), and warnings were often displayed prohibiting cortes and quebradas (Bates and Bates 1936; Carretero 1964; see Figure 4.2). In addition, these public dances were open to people of all shades and colors. The street and patio tangos were synonymous with indecency, poverty, and promiscuity—a promiscuity that flooded the streets, trespassing the borders of the proper. The improper, incorrect street dancing challenged the propriety/property of public space by calling attention to the dancers' lack of property/propriety. These tangos amounted to a multiple sin. The scandalized responses to the tango were morally concerned with sex, race, and class. In order to overcome the scandalous tango connotations, Argentinean "society" women needed to have their own propriety reconfirmed by the cultured colonizer. One such woman, Elvira Aldao de Díaz, wrote, "I saw the famous tango [...] for the first time—precisely that summer before the Big War—on board of the magnificent transatlantic ship, *La France*. [...] I must confess that the tango danced on *La France*—undulating with the waves of the North Sea—scandalized me ... and afterwards, I loved it thanks to seeing it danced in Paris and everywhere else" (Elvira A. de Díaz [1931], quoted in Ulla 1982: 26).

Echoing the Parisian success and inaugurating a new political era of *acuerdo* ("accord") between the elites and the lower strata, a *tango liberal* (Matamoro's term, 1969) took shape. Tango historians recall Baron De Marchi's celebrations at

FIGURE 4.2 *Dancing in a patio or* romería *in Buenos Aires, ca. 1908. Courtesy of the Archives of León Benarós.*

the distinguished Palais de Glace in downtown Buenos Aires. The celebrations took place in 1912, the same year that the Saénz Peña Law was passed by parliament. This law established universal, secret, and compulsory suffrage for male citizens over the age of eighteen. Following passage of the law, the Radicales, a populist political party, for the first time won several governorships, and in 1916, they won the presidential elections. De Marchi—an Italian aristocrat who had made Argentina his home by marrying into the porteña elite—organized several aristocratic tango events (in private mansions, restaurants, and clubs) to openly bring his high-life acquaintances into contact with skillful tangueros (musicians and dancers). Porteña elite couples not only enjoyed the spectacular tango demonstrations but also practiced its steps. These events had tremendous local repercussions.

An article published in 1913 by *Crítica*, a Buenos Aires daily, included lavish references to the ambiance, the celebrated tango compositions, and the most applauded tango dancers. The dancers, the reporter wrote, were instructed by the organizer to perform "discreetly and with composure."

> As soon as *Karakul's* music started, the five couples were out on stage. Bianchetti [José Ovidio Bianquet] took the lead by delivering a genuine interpretation of the movements while the rest followed the Baron's instructions. In the third tango piece, *L'Ecuyère*, of pure French style, [Carlos] Herrera couldn't hold himself back and also started to *meter pierna* [advance his leg between those of his partner] [...] and that evolved into a high pressure tango. The audience [...] applauded when Bianchetti showed off with a *sentadita* or a *carrerita*, placing an accent on the tango flair of past times. [...] It was a shame

that [...] they were subjected to severe restrictions instead of leaving them free to dance the way the tango goes (*Viejo Tanguero* [1913], quoted in Salas 1986: 121–122).

The journalist, under the pseudonym "*Viejo Tanguero*" (Old Tanguero), went on to regret the European influence on the tango. "Having stayed for too long in the old continent, it has become foreign so that in coming back home, it brings those slippery 'r's that make it almost French." Regarding the dance, he noticed that the postures were merely "sketched" and that the dancers took "small steps to one side and, then, to the other," following a musical time reminiscent of the habanera (*Viejo Tanguero* [1913], quoted in Salas 1986: 121–122).

Manuals and professeurs from Europe or tinged by European experience started proliferating on Argentinean soil (Bates and Bates 1936; see Figures 4.3 and 4.4).[8] The disciplinary/promotive capitalist machinery that developed at the imperialist "core" in order to rule and profit over dancing bodies started operating successfully, with some necessary adjustments, at home. Elite women such as Doña Elvira, as well as middle-class women, had to overcome the Argentinean version of the tango scandal. Argentinos from the middle and upper classes demanded refined styles, not only different from the style of the rough ruffians but also distinguishable from the exoticized versions developed in Paris, London, and New York. Again, class identity and national identity were at stake.

The dancing silhouettes that illustrate the cover of the sheet music for "*Alma Porteña*" (1923; see Figure 4.5) show basic choreographic postures of local tango styles. Distinctions can be traced by the distance maintained between the bodies of the dancers, by the stretched or retracted disposition of the torsos, by the amplitude of the movements of the arms and legs, and by what the dancers wore. In general, the silhouettes on the right represent a more refined style (closer to *à la française*) than do the ones on the left. The refined postures entail wider distance between the dancers, more extended arm movements, and stretched legs that avoid knee and thigh entanglements between the partners. The silhouettes at the bottom correspond to two clearly contrasting styles. On the left is the *tango criollo*—the one that mimics the underworldly movements of ruffians and prostitutes. The bodies and heads are held close to each other, the arms and legs describe tight, locked movements, and the gentleman wears a short jacket and also wears his hat while dancing (a revealing detail—a clear sign of "bad" manners and a common compadrito challenge). On the right, the embrace is looser but the arms stretch out more rigidly, the torsos do not tend to lean toward each other, the legs are extended in opposite directions, the lady's head is facing backwards, and the gentleman wears a tailcoat.

Although these silhouettes do not show the complete evolution of dance postures, they do show some paradigmatic ones—those performed at the moment of the corte (when the displacement is abruptly stopped and a special figura

FIGURE 4.3   *Professor Carlos Herrera promoting tango lessons at his dance academy in Buenos Aires.* Source: Caras y Caretas, *Buenos Aires, August 9, 1913.*

FIGURE 4.4   *Francisco Ducasse and Angelina Pagano demonstrating tango figures.* Source: Fray Mocho, *February 13, 1914.*

FIGURE 4.5 *Cover of sheet music for* Alma Porteña *(Porteña* Soul*). Lyrics and music by Vicente Greco, 1923.*

takes place). At that moment, in tango criollo the bodies of the dancers generally balance toward each other, whereas in more "refined" (European-like) styles, the bodies are balanced away from each other.

Ruffianesque and refined tango styles were combined in the local *tango de salón* (social dance tango) and *tango de espectáculo* (stage tango). The accent on morally defiant or conforming movements depended on the social occasion and the locale where a tango was danced, but it also depended on the music. *Tango-milonga* (a fast, jumpy tango) begs for more challenging figures and displacements than the languid, "sensual" tango music developed after tango's popularization in Europe and at home. Tango-milongas, tangos in 2 x 4 and in 4 x 8, and waltzed or fox-trotted tangos enjoyed periods of greater or lesser popularity, but the newer versions never completely displaced the others from formal dances, familiar settings, and stages. The contrasts enriched the pleasure of dancing and of exhibiting mastery over the tango. The impact of exotic tango versions was thus mitigated by local practices of reappropriation, including two combined strategies of autoexoticism: the substitution of exaggerated European features for local, criollo features within each dancing piece and the symbolic maintenance of criollo, *canyengue* pieces within the repertory of tango styles that were a part of almost every tango dancing occasion. As a result, artists, elites, and members of the middle class engaged in both exoticization and national self-affirmation by way of autoexoticism: exoticism under local control.

Beyond all diversities in style, a formula was developed to assess the quality of a good Argentinean tango dancer: elegance, serenity, agility in the legs and accuracy in following the musical time (Benarós 1977). The uniquely local tango criollo consisted of a tight, stable embrace; firm but flexible torsos slightly tilted toward a central axis located between the dancers; independent upper and lower body parts articulated through torsion at the waist; a linear trajectory interrupted by abrupt angular shifts; virtuosity, especially in performing surprising geometric designs with the legs; and, in general, a tense, energetic, sinuous, and grounded quality, as if each step had to be "overcome" by the next one. This effect was created by a heaviness in the feet and a knee-to-knee friction that contrasted with the thrusting of the thighs and the rhythmic breaking of the hips (see Figure 4.6).

The tango de espectáculo combined the choreography of the tango criollo with some traces of the glittery sensuality of the Parisian revue. The latter gave preeminence to the arms and the upper torso, requiring the dancers to stretch their spines from waist to neck and lower their shoulders. The revue choreography followed curvilinear trajectories and included special figures such as backwards bends and pronounced dips. A general sense of flow was given to the movements. The tango de espectáculo differed from the exotic French stage version by arresting its airy flair.

Tango de salón followed a similar process of recombination and readaptation. The Argentinean academies and dance masters taught a "refined" and banalized

FIGURE 4.6   Cover of sheet music for El Maco, tango criollo. Music by M. J. Tornquist. Published by Medina. The male dancer illustrating tango criollo figures is Arturo de Nava.

tango, based on European codifications, that downplayed the improvisational quality of the original criollo style. The tango de salón, however, skipped the tiptoed steps and minuet-like arms and torsos encouraged in the French style as well as the rigid backs and the stiff, distant embraces proposed in the British ballroom dance codifications. The lower and middle classes, more "proper" than the marginals of the original tango criollo but with no access to formal training in tango de salón, developed a *tango liso* (plain, bland), which introduced a general quality of "fatigue" and more monotonous and previsible figures for the enjoyment of all the bodies who could not afford the more demanding forms.[9] True tangueros despised the tango liso, but some practitioners saw interesting features in this more democratic, local tango offspring. Lázaro Liacho, for example, in his *Nuevas Premisas Sobre el Tango* (New Premises on the Tango), observed in the late 1930s that "the slow quality of the steps shows that the dancer does not perform spontaneously. He meditates over his movements: each movement responds to a purpose." He insisted that this intentionality, a responsibility of the male dancer, was nevertheless shared by the couple and that it applied both to footwork and rhythm: "It should be recalled that it [tango] is a syncopated dance. Its mechanism is accidental, unexpected, surprising: man and woman play different games, disencounters, oppositions known somewhat *a priori*, and thus they are enabled to continue gliding together" (*Columna* 7 [December 1937], quoted in Benarós 1977: 271). In this way, at least after a while, the tango liso was rescued as a popular local form that was intellectually if not physically challenging for its dancers and different from the imported bland ballroom versions.

A variety of tango choreographic styles emerged for stages, ballrooms, and family settings; new kinds of locales were inaugurated for the purpose of performing these different styles; new jobs were created in order to service these locales and to promote the different choreographic industries; and new musical creations arose out of the demands of these different sectors. New technologies, such as recordings and the radio, aided in establishing the distance between the original tango underworldish performers and the new tango practitioners. And the resulting popularization/taming of tango generated both enthusiasm and defensiveness in the old tanguero milieu.

The promotion of tango through imperial exoticism and through "civilized" appropriations generated such a diversity of tango practices that the need to establish an "authentic" tango became a must. This endeavor was not an exercise in banality. It was a matter of recognition, legitimacy, representation, and identity. The popularity of tango, in Argentina as well as abroad, did not mean that the tango (which had turned into a powerful symbol precisely because of its massive reception) lacked specific roots and authorship linked to class and anticolonial struggles. The diversity of tango styles, appropriated by colonizers and by different sectors of the colonized, threatened to wash out the dark origins of the tango—origins of exploited people—and silence the history of race/class/colonial confrontation that had contributed to tango's multiple hybrid cultural expression. Tangueros who had known the old tango perceived this stage as the tango's death. Tango had been taken for a universal representation of melodramatic episodes of lost love and fatal seduction. Tango offered the erotic gender conflict as a vehicle for universal identification, but tango was much more complex than that. Perhaps tango, in its lyrics and choreography, exploited the gender conflict far more than any of its other disencounters.

Race, class, and imperialist tensions were somewhat lost in a sea of male/female presence to the point where other social tensions became gendered in themselves. True: Tango did not perform overtly black/white, rich/poor, French/argentino conflicts. It played, sang, and danced about mulatas and dandies; French prostitutes and criollo pimps; Malena from the suburbs and a sentimental ruffian; the nouveau riche lady in a fox coat, driving her limousine past her former lover, now a homeless street beggar ... that is, gendered class, gendered race, and gendered colonialism, asystematically combined. The gendering/eroticizing strategy had been central to tango; it offered, so to speak, a relieving consistency from the chaos of exploitation's multiplicity. The scandalous colonial, racial, and classist histories of tango had been pacified under the exaggeration of its erotic display. In tangos, gender and heterosexuality had been regarded, so to speak, as the "main contradiction," but this complex history was endangered by tango's popularization and diversification, each of which encouraged forgetfulness.

Many tangueros reacted to this threatening side of exoticism by ridiculing the recently emerged tango variations and recovering the origins—the history—of tango. They were interested in an "authentic" tango choreographic and musical style, different from its exotic and classist variations, and engaged in a search for identity based in resistance to imperialist and "liberal" nationalist colonizations. This search for tango origins and authenticity led to a different set of complex practices of internal discrimination that were related to the issue of national identity—an issue soaked in colonialism.

SCENE SEVEN:

TANGOLAND, TANGUAGE, AND TANGOMANNERS

Duet of an androgynous, declassé, dark solo dancer and his shadow.

Bare stage. Dancers anticipate the movement instructions and descriptions recited by the Choreocritic, who stands downstage (center). Two dancers are located centerstage, one on the left, the other (a shadow) on the right. There is a triangular illumination effect from downstage to upstage.

Choreocritic's spoken text:

South of the South of the world, always just about to fall off of it, there is a flat, flat land so evenly spread that its people inadvertently live in a latent state of *horizontal vertigo.*[10] This strange malaise only manifests itself in the presence of someone else, provoking an irresistible drive to firmly grab and stare at the other without a smile and step on his or her foot. These manners should not be confused with a greeting, although it is a practice of recognition, of acknowledgment of existence. A profound sense of vacuum takes hold of the left foot: too much air, not enough ground despite the immensity. Legs grow longer and stronger attempting to control gravity if not history. It is a game of minds or, to be more precise, of bodies pushing mind boundaries; a somewhat repressed desire that began circulating before the turn of the last century, where the *pampas* meet the wide brown river.

Once you feel that the horizon should be empty and open, at your total disposition; that nothing or no one should get in your way—not because you wish this but rather because this is the way things are—that no matter what, you are always in the wrong place doing the wrong thing because you cannot remember what you were supposed to do or where, and there is no sign erected against the flatness to remind you, you have fallen into horizontal vertigo. Too much air, not enough ground despite the immensity, because of the flatness. Lying down is not an option; you cannot afford to let anything drop. Your ears start buzzing and the whizzing in your hairs stretches your spine, tail heavily held down to the ground, weak knees but a strong pulling, curving your neck at the top, lifting your shoulders in upheaval. If this is the case, and you clearly feel that unless your feet start moving endlessly you have lost your balance, you are ready for it. Arrogant and defiant, burdened and ready to tango. Step after step, the outer edge of the ball of each foot sliding as close as possible to the ground, leaving clouds of dust behind you; knee against knee as in making fire; a slight torsion at the waist turning shoulders and hips into opposite alignments and a casual but definite grave thrust. Always that restless drive to grab, to stare shamelessly, and stumbling to step on someone. Effortless. Embracing yourself does not help. The encounter has to be dealt with. It is right in the middle.

Dancer and "shadow" face each other without moving toward each other.
The choreocritic sings the following text (falsetto, in lunfardo) while the dancers perform a frantic, fast-paced tango-milonga:

Qué saben los pitucos, lamidos y shushetas;	What do those classy, pretentious, highbrows know;
qué saben lo que es tango, qué saben de compás.	what do they know about tango, what do they know of rhythm.
Aquí está la elegancia. ¡Qué pinta! ¡Qué silueta!	Here is elegance. What a look! What a figure!
¡Qué porte, qué arrogancia, qué clase pa'bailar!	What posture, what arrogance, what classy dancing!

Así se corta el césped mientras dibujo el ocho,	This is how one mows the lawn while drawing the figure eight,
para estas filigranas yo soy como un pintor.	to make these filigrees I am like a painter.
Ahora una corrida, una vuelta, una sentada;	Now a run, a turn, a "sitting down" figure;
así se baila el tango ... ¡un tango de mi flor!	This is how one dances tango ... a tango worthy of me!

—*Así Se Baila el Tango* (This Is How One Dances Tango), 1942
Lyrics by Elizardo Martínez Vilas
Music by Elías Randal

Choreocritic's spoken text continues as the dancers anticipate the recited movements. They improvise on "sad thoughts" and "absent-mindedness":

Since its inception, tango has always played on rivalry in search for identification—a specific rivalry, arrogantly antagonizing the usurper. Out of this solid tension that pretends casualness a monster is created: no head, one torso, four legs. It moves rhythmically, with no hint of the grotesque, following the uneven times of fate. Nothing can describe it better than the tanguage that says: "Tango is a sad thought that can be danced."[11] And it should be performed absentmindedly.

Blackout

Originating Tango

A quarreling chorus of tango historians, critics, and essayists could be added to the previous scene. They would debate in these terms: "Tango was born in the dirt streets of the slums. ..." "No. Tango was a practice of the brothels. ..." "No. Tango is a stylization of the knife-fighters. ..." "No. The tango was performed by the blacks in their secret societies. ..." "How dare you! Tango obviously has its origins in Andalusia. ..." "Sure, but that tango was inspired by the Cuban habanera. ..." "And what about the milonga played by the lonesome inhabitants of our pampas? ..." "There is some of that, but the tango is undoubtedly urban and it resembles the arrogant walking of the compadritos (ruffians) who had some trouble coping with the uneven suburban streets on high-heeled boots. ..." "Let's be serious. The word tango comes from '*tambo,*' and the tambos were the places where the liberated blacks met in the Río de la Plata during the nineteenth century. Here is the evidence. ..." "Sorry. But that is not the real tango. The tango-tango is the one of the overpopulated tenement houses where the newly arrived immigrants met the criollos. ..."[12]

I have been struck by the very existence and magnitude of the controversy over the origins of tango. No other aspect of tango has received nearly as much local attention. The controversy goes on and on, escalating up to points of delirium. Delirium over "origins," delirium over "authenticity," over roots and belongings, over identity. And I am not the first one to be shocked. Blas Matamoro, for example, noticed that in the mid-1920s tango started to be manipulated as an historical object. He observed that tango becomes a reflexive exercise, a past aesthetic form to be known and pondered so that it survives as a specific work of art. "Knowledge about tango starts accumulating. The rules of its creation are collected, organized in a tango code/index" (1969: 94). In his opinion, the search for tango origins responds to an effort at justification, an attempt to stress the differences between, on the one hand, the middle and working classes and, on the other, the marginals and their shameful dance now pushed into the past.

Argentina's conservative elite had not had any investment in recognizing differences among the local lower strata until the Radical party (Unión Cívica Radical) empowered the middle and working classes, which included large numbers of immigrants. A liberal pact was thus sought and it required the marginalization of the "underclass" that was culturally associated with the tango. True to an ideology that proclaimed the feasibility of social mobility, this "underclass" was doubly marginalized: The orilleros were not only outside of the new society based on class accords; they were also a thing of the past. Tango came to represent this past marginality that for some argentinos was best forgotten and for others recovered very carefully. Among the "permissionists," or liberals—that is, those willing to acknowledge tango's input in rioplatense culture in one way or another—tango's historicization took different paths. Opinions regarding tango's origins became divided: Histories were written, literary studies were undertaken, steps and styles were established (see Matamoro 1969). Vicente Rossi wrote the first historical legend (*Cosas de Negros*, 1926); Jorge Luis Borges produced the first mythology (*El Idioma de los Argentinos* [1928] 1963). In the course of the following decade, Carlos Vega, the folklorist, attempted a systematic genealogy (*Danzas y Canciones Argentinas. Teorías e Investigaciones. Un Ensayo Sobre el Tango*, 1936) and Héctor and Luis Bates wrote the first "complete" social history (*La Historia del Tango*, 1936).

The "permissionist" debates over tango's origins (I will not address here those of the "prohibitionists") soon shaped into two positions: One side, following Rossi, stressed tango's African roots; the other, following Vega, insisted on the importance of tango's Spanish roots (Guibert 1973). Interesting ideological differences can be traced in these historicizing orientations. Rossi and the Bates brothers, for example, attempted to shape tango's history into a broader anticolonialist narrative. They portrayed tango as a practice of symbolic resistance to Spanish colonialism, British, French, and U.S. neocolonialism, and elitist Argentinean subimperialism. Their task was to recuperate the memory of these struggles and to place rioplatense popular culture at the center of these past episodes. These tango histories carried nationalistic political messages for the readers of the time. Soon the repetitious, precision-oriented, and never-ending searches and debates over tango's authentic origins and original authenticities switched the focus from memoirs and eyewitnesses' anecdotes to an enamouredness with scientificity. Carlos Vega and most of his followers were invested in the promises of scientific rationality and thus challenged the other group's interpretations on the basis of historical inaccuracy and lack of reliable sources.

Science, a close partner of exoticism in its tendency to objectify its chosen subjects, empowered popular musical genres such as the tango by accommodating them in the pantheon of objects that deserved careful analysis. As a backlash, rationality offered a mask to contesting ideological agendas as it "universalized" the tango, removing it and saving it from the locally immediate. In Matamoro's words, tango "becomes the universal music of Argentinean society and a particular species that can be conceived of with the universal Reason of the '*música culta*' [refined and legitimate music]" (Matamoro 1969: 94). As a result, the politics of music and dance were pushed to the side into the category of mere context.

Since the 1930s, musicologists and dance specialists have tried to put some systematic order into tango origins. The story goes like this: In Cuba the African slaves developed new music and dances intermingling their traditional rhythmic sounds with a variant of the French *contre-dances* already appropriated by the Spaniards; the resulting habanera (from Havana) made its way into Europe and simultaneously into other New World colonies where it intermingled with local styles. The *tango andaluz* (Andalusian tango), the Brazilian *maxixe,* and the tango rioplatense (from the Río de la Plata region in Argentina and Uruguay) were the offsprings of this process; the last in particular was nurtured by the milonga, a local product itself of a certain Spanish troubadour style. When the milonga, carried by the gauchos, moved to the developing urban harbors (Buenos Aires and Montevideo), it collided with the tangos de negros (tangos of the African slaves) and the tango andaluz that was performed by the Spanish theater companies touring South America (Novati and Cuello 1980).

This complex, exhaustive, and exhausting narrative of the tango's "origins" leads finally to a moment of apotheosis when The Tango, the "authentic" *tango argentino,* appears on the scene. Despite the confusing background narrative, at some point it happened. Just like tracing down the origins of fire. ... No matter how it came to be, eventually it started to burn.[13] After endless debates, connections have been established with every sector that, at one point or another, claimed authorship and legitimate input into the tango. No wonder the poor immigrants who arrived in the past century have been the last to be incorporated into the story. And no wonder no reference is made to the possible presence of indigenous South American music or themes, buried perhaps under the chords of the gauchos' criolla guitars.[14] Establishing origins has carried the risk of reproducing divisiveness and discrimination. Science is a timid tool, incapable of overcoming ideological mandates.

Musicologists and scholars of native dances have also faced the difficult task of grasping the essentials of the "authentic" tango. Again, this endeavor has yielded mixed results. Universalizing knowledge and investment in systematization often blur political implications. Scholars devoted to identifying an "authentic" tango have frequently intended to confirm the legitimacy of a popular production that is at risk because of multiple exoticizing appropriations. The risk, however, reemerges when the carefully distilled "authentic" version turns into a crystallized, opaque, dead object of reference that can be used in discriminating among its own popular offsprings. In their *Antología del Tango Rioplatense* (1980), Jorge Novati and Inés Cuello provide a sophisticated musicological reconstruction of the tango from its origins to the 1920s. They suggest that by 1903 an identification of tango and "tradition" was well established in Argentina and that the resulting genre became "a definite representative of our music" (Novati and Cuello 1980: 20). In order to distinguish the "authentic" tango from previous variants, they propose to isolate some "permanent and determinant features of the style." Moreover, "The essential element is the total rhythm, a result of the constant rhythmic interaction between melody and accompaniment." This total rhythm, however, does not amount to an incessant repetition. A series of small resources—the musicologists continue—such as silences, syncopes, displacements of accents, and acephalous phrases, intervene and transform the rhythm into a characteristic *ritmo quebrado* (broken rhythm). The way in which these resources intervene is unique: "They are used without ever becoming something permanent. Most of the time they constitute rhythmic 'unpredictabilities'" (Novati and Cuello 1980: 23). Thus, "The tango was a new outcome in terms of rhythm, structure, and melody" (Novati and Cuello 1980: 25).

Distinctive choreographic elements of the tango have been similarly identified based on comparisons with other dances: (1) *enlace agarrado* (clinching grip), the tight flexible embrace, (2) *quebrada* (cleave), the movement of the hips, (3) *corte* (coupe), a halt or interruption of the dancing trajectory, and (4) *figura* (figure), a relatively stable combination of movements led by the legs, recognizable by a name (eight, double-eight, short race, half-moon, hook, etc.). The combination of the tight embrace and the figuras generated choreographic novelties such as sudden changes in the steps and in the direction of the dancing trajectory. Frequently, each partner performed a different step challenging the couple's synchronization with the music. In addition, the sequence of *marcha* (walks) and figuras (figures) was left to improvisation and was adjusted by the dancing couple to the musical stimulus (Novati and Cuello 1980: 26).

Novati and Cuello observe that the essential features they isolate in their descriptions correspond to the tango criollo, "given that it is the most antique and the one that through subsequent transformations, gives birth to the rest." However, "the proposed tango model [...] is a product of the analysis of the *materials currently available*," and "the *reconstructive work* faces serious obstacles" (Novati and Cuello 1980: 94, my emphasis).

The risk of falling into unpoliticized deliriums over the tango's "origins" could be matched by the risk of rising into unpoliticized obsessions over "authenticity." The scholarly temptation to chase after tango's "origins" and to identify the "authentic" tango leads to frustration, delirium, and obsession. The reconstruction of the tango poses not only methodological questions but also political risks and ideological choices. Tango specialists are insistently assaulted by two kinds of questions: "Can an original, authentic tango be reconstructed?" and "Why, and in whose interest, should our original, unique tango be established?" Rather than canceling each other out, these questions (and their respective derivatives) challenge the reconstructive project in terms of both its feasibility and its purpose. The systematic search for knowledge is thus confronted with the murky quest for national identity. Will the tango speak one day to this issue, like an oracle? Reified, the tango will probably continue delivering riddles. The "obstacles" faced by the "reconstructive work" will not disappear with the emergence of unknown sources of information ... but will grow, fatten, burst.

Take for example the tango criollo, considered to be the most "antique" and closest to the original, the one that generated the rest. Criollo—taken for granted as "native," the one closest to the roots of the argentino "essence"—already contains in itself our history of *mestizaje*, cross-breeding, hybridity. "Criollo" in Argentina (the use of this term in other colonies has been different) meant both the offspring of old, conquistador-time Spanish born in the colony and mestizos (those with a mixture of Spanish and indigenous blood). Criollo was defined in opposition to the Spanishness in Spain; to the people, attitudes, beliefs, and cultural practices that were pro-Spanish and procolonial. Even a Spanish-born person was considered criollo (or criolla) if he (or she) sided with the colonized and shared their rejection, their perception of difference with the metropolitan center of the empire. Criollo, in addition, had connotations of parochiality, unsophistication, and ruralness. Criollos were closely associated with the "interior" of the country, that is, the whole territory except for the sophisticated harbor capital city.

In Argentina there is nothing more criollo than the gaucho. Tango, however, is clearly an urban phenomenon, a product of the harbor capital with a painfully parasitic history of rejecting the "uncivilized" inhabitants of the country's interior. Tango was related to the rapid emergence of a huge harbor-city after the British took over the Spanish empire through neocolonialism. The criollos were flooded by successive waves of European immigrants (mainly Italian and Spanish but also many others from both Western and Eastern Europe and the Middle

East, plus a few Asians).[15] It was in this newly rehybridized milieu of Buenos Aires and Montevideo that the tango emerged as a paramount popular practice. Under these circumstances (rapid urbanization and massive immigration), "criollo" began to take on a different meaning. The oligarchy of Buenos Aires started to redeem the despised gaucho and to practice "nativism" against the new *malón blanco* (white savage invaders) who were—in a racist slip of their minds— as threatening to those settled in power as the Indian *malón* attacking the criollo populations at the frontier. Criollo in this urban, identity-under-siege setting was a claim to authenticity—legitimacy in power—in the face of the immigrant hordes. Moreover, criollo was defensively applied by both the old-money landed oligarchy, whose white hegemony was threatened, and the old no-money landless poor whose labor and housing opportunities were being disputed.

Tango and National Identity

Buenos Aires, 1890, looked like this:

> High-class people sleep in two-or-three-story French palaces in the North barrio. [...] The top people decorate their lineage, or manufacture it, with torrents of pearls and initials engraved on silver tea sets, and show off Saxony or Sevres or Limoges porcelains, Waterford crystal, Lyons tapestries, and Brussels tablecloths. From the secluded life of the [colonial] Big Village they have moved on to the frenetic exhibitionism of the Paris of America.
>
> In the south [of the city] are huddled the beaten-down of the earth. In abandoned three-patioed colonial mansions, or in specially built tenements, the workers newly arrived from Naples or Vigo or Bessarabia sleep by turns. Never cold are the scarce beds in the nonspace invaded by braziers and wash basins and chests which serve as cradles. Fights are frequent in the long queues at the door to the only latrine, and silence is an impossible luxury. But sometimes, on party nights, the accordion or mandolin or bagpipes bring back lost voices to these washerwomen and dressmakers, servants of rich bosses and husbands, and ease the loneliness of these men who from sun to sun tan hides, pack meat, saw wood, sweep streets, tote loads, raise and paint walls, roll cigarettes, grind wheat, and bake bread while their children shine shoes and call out the crime of the day (Galeano 1987: 230).

I wonder why so many tango specialists have systematically forgotten to include these poor immigrants in their analyses. Wouldn't these Italians, second-hand Spanish, Polish, French, Russians, English, Armenians, and so on also contribute some rhythms and steps of their own ancestry to the over-encompassing tango? The reconstruction of the origins is certainly selective.[16] Regarding the aristocrats, how could any history of tango forget to mention their gang incursions into the Buenos Aires demimonde where they learned in a single stroke to "become men," to tango, and to do violence? Fernando Assunção (1984) clearly states that tango's origins cannot be circumscribed to a single class ... of men, though they are associated with low class/low morals women. Race, class, and sex played on women's bodies. Every kind of man tangoed, whether openly or in secret, over this kind of woman: immigrant, criolla—in the old (negative/non-white) sense—or mulata. A new identity was engendering.

Buenos Aires was perceived as a changing feminine landscape. Julián Martel sorrowfully states in his novel *La Bolsa*: "It is possible to observe how a variety of types, the product of an overriding cosmopolitanism, have spoiled the Argentinean woman, taking away from her that Andalusian and spicy mark that she used to hold as a precious heritage of her Spanish blood. There are as many blondes as brunettes" (Martel [1889], quoted in Rodríguez Molas 1988: 5). Why then a tango criollo? What is the tango reasserting and denying through this newly refurbished *criollismo*? Within the new international realignment of power, the ex-Spanish-colonized, "independent," and neocolonized settings such as Argentina, immersed in a new wave of dependency, were urged, provoked, into developing a national identity. Criollo was not enough—that was outdated. Although some, like Martel, believed that the answer was in the re-creation of the "good old times" of the hispano-criollo tradition (and blood), others adopted a modern nationalist solution that emphasized the white homogenization of the country or a more moderate assimilation under "whiteness." An example of the latter position is self-explanatory: "I will explain myself: the soil is rich, the climate is admirable, the people are not bad, the [genetic] selection is carried out pretty well; at least I see in the streets some mixed women that would drive crazy the most sensible man, brunettes with blue eyes and hair dark as ebony. Have you ever seen anything more stupendous?" (Lucio V. Mansilla [1888], quoted in Montergous 1985: 57). The aggressive racist nationalist type is well represented by Estanislao Zeballos:

> It is worth remembering the favorable circumstance that [in Argentina] the inferior races, Indians and Blacks, were practically extinguished during the first century [after the 1810 independence]; the homogeneousness of the White race is one of the reasons, joined to the character of the institutions and to the gifts of nature, for the extraordinary cultural transformation and prosperity of the República Argentina (Zeballos, Conference at Harvard University [1923], quoted in Rodríguez Molas 1988: 6).

Nationalism was boiling over in Argentina between the 1880s and the 1910s and so was the tango. A reaction was under way against the potential changes that the newly arrived immigrants ("degenerative elements") could bring about: changes in the established power and wealth arrangements. It was a reaction against the liberal internationalist policies of the 1850s, which were now showing their effects. The brand of racism promoted by Domingo F. Sarmiento and Juan

B. Alberdi since the 1840s, which put a blind faith in Argentina's integration with the greatest of the world through the cultivation of European-ness and white-ness, was now a nightmare come true. By 1878, the Campaign of the Desert, led by General Julio A. Roca, had finally integrated the last portion of significant "In-dian" territory; both Indians and criollos died in great numbers while fighting on opposite sides. They were all defeated by whiteness, a brand of nationalism that excluded many nationals. In addition, the white European immigrants were ar-riving in masses—although they were not of the Swiss and German quality that was expected. The racist nationalists reacted against this last failure of the na-tion's building plan with a more sophisticated racism capable of distinguishing between whites and white trash. The language was not ready for this class/race conundrum; racist discourse only offered shades of color. Following that dis-course, many in the dominant, established class looked darker than the poor who had newly arrived. Criollo nativism was the answer, but it was born to fail in the hands of the tango.[17]

Criollo identity was a product of the confrontation with the Spanish empire; it was obsolete.[18] Although strengthened during the war of independence against Spain, criollo identity was not suitable to the next layer of dependency on the British or to the subsequent imperialism of the United States. The identity of an "independent" country should be a "national" identity—in this case, an identity as argentino.[19]

And so—my story goes—the exotic tango was added to the exotic criollo. The gaucho of the pampas, under threat of extinction by British railroads and fences, turned out to be as suitable to "nativist" manipulations as the tango of the brothels and tenements was to "nationalist" manipulations. As with the "nativ-ists," who celebrated the slaughter of natives, the Buenos Aires–centered "na-tionalists" celebrated the birth of a dependent nation. Nationalism was coming from abroad (see Anderson 1983). Argentina: rich *in* dependency and *because* of dependency. Tango, not criollo, was to be the symbol of the nation regardless of the criollo people—who tangoed, did other native dances, and organized strikes against Buenos Aires's hegemonic "nationalists" and "liberals" (international-ists) alike.[20]

Identifying the Colonized

Argentinean national identity was identified by the neocolonizers. Britain de-ferred to Paris in this task, since Paris was the center of the empire of taste. Paris detected the tango within its own cabarets, which were frequented by "Argentine beef-barons" nostalgic for some porteño pleasures. The Parisians, the English, and to a lesser extent the North Americans got carried away. And the local elites became scandalized, scandalized at not being identified as a powerful and re-spectable nation, scandalized at being identified with the poor and the margin-als of their nation, the ones whose women tangoed shamefully with them. In the end, the elites opted for co-opting the tango, for dressing the tango in tuxedos and glittery evening gowns, for accepting and nurturing the Parisian exotic version of the tango, of Argentina, and of themselves. Highly Westernized and yet exotic-to-the-West, tango became the national symbol. The Argentinean neocolonial identity—"national" identity—was assigned by the neoempire: tango. Except for Buenos Aires, little else counted legitimately as the nation.

A hegemonic national identity was an imperialist requirement; "independent" nations were to replace the obsolete colonies. Colonies were less suitable to "free-market" manipulations; "independent" nations could be more easily played against one another in the competition for metropolitan favors, but for nations to come into existence a hegemonic national narrative had to be provided, exalted, enriched (Bhabha 1990a). And sound narratives need sound beginnings, origins. Hence, the roots had to be dug up. National narratives should be unique, original, authentic so as to trace difference, distance, and potential competition with other nations. Moreover, dependent nations, colonized nations, should cultivate a national narrative exuberant in cultural traits, in exoticism, perhaps to compensate for economic dependency and lack of self-determination. The colonized, not able to provide a sound account of their nationality/independence, are caught in an endless search for an identity of their own. The search for origins and authenticity within an in/dependent nation is a painful sequence of self-destructive episodes: the national politics of the in/dependent nations.

By situating tango at this time and place, I am not pretending to join the polemics on the origins, on authenticity, or even attempting to identify a moment of invention preceded by painful experimentation. Mine is a counternarrative, and hence also a story, but a story that disbelieves in the stories that tie up and down. I do not intend to fill in the gaps of a hegemonic nationalist narrative that makes sense to the colonizers. The Western obsession with origins and authenticity is a way of delegitimizing the Other, the colonized; the Other never is. ... The Other is always a reflection, an illusion, a deflection of the One, of the colonizer. In Gayatri Spivak's words: "No perspective critical of imperialism can turn the Other into a self, because the project of imperialism has always already historically refracted what might have been the absolutely Other into a domesticated Other that consolidates the imperialist self" (Spivak 1985: 253).

The colonizer is never an Other, especially not to the colonized. The colonizer asserts an Identity in confrontation with the colonized; the colonized can never attain an identity in this asymmetrical power relationship. At least not an Identity in the same terms of stability, of rootedness, of the solid state of control of the conqueror (the One). For this reason the colonized permanently tracks back her origins and obsessively describes coming into being only to find layer over layer of hybridization.[21] Since there is no clear-cut answer, no self to which to return, no pure nationality to discriminate ourselves from our neighbors, the colonized is condemned to a lack of Identity in her search for origins and authenticity. The identity of the colonized bounces against the event of the colonial encounter and deflects fragments, hybrids, Others. The colonized is "made to stand outside itself to look at itself," as if it were another self. The colonized is exposed to images of her world as mirrored in the discourse of the colonizer (Ngũgĩ 1986).

The national identity of the neo/postcolonials is that of a permanent search for Identity. The tango saga displays this process and its protagonists: *criollos, chinas, mulatos, pardos, mestizos, franchutas, gaitas, tanos, rusitas, turcos, polaquitas, cabecitas negras* ... immigrants, exiles ... a nation of hybrids and borderliners with an identity in permanent displacement, longing for the Identity—the right to dignity. My maternal grandmother, a *criolla* herself, would defiantly proclaim her *india* (Native *sudamericano*) roots in resistance to the "nativism" of the romanticizers of creolism, who had robbed and trivialized her provincial identity; my paternal grandmother mentioned her white immigrant ancestry only when asked and searched for identity in the Gath and Chavez British-style department store. Their husbands enjoyed politics and tango and disputed over the pro-European or populist nationalist developmental models; one was from the *interior*, the other from the capital. They tangoed in sinful places with suspect women, suspected because of class, color, and morals, until Paris (not the Pope) said it was alright to tango with their wives. They all lived in restless company with one another and with themselves. Argentinos have a colonized identity; a colonized identity in resistance, like tango's female docile bodies in rebellion. The in/dependent nations are the feminine—legitimate and illegitimate—partners in the imperial dance.

The tango story is an episode within a long history of exiled, illegitimate peoples in search of an identity, recognition, and dignity. Through imperialist exoticism, the tango, among many other cultural practices, was exiled from the possibility of attaining a full identity, an Identity in terms of the definition elaborated by the "civilized" bourgeois colonizer. Argentina's national identity, dependent on the identification, the recognition of the main world powers, is subjected to a permanent, unfulfillable search for confirmation from the "civilized," "developed" ones, the colonizers. It has pushed us into exoticizing ourselves, into establishing uniqueness and unity, into drawing distinctions among the colonized in order to attain a more "distinguished" exotic position in relation to less privileged, more "primitive" exotics—following the fickle judgments of the colonizer. Tango inherited a painful paradox: We strive through tango to assert our national identity while falling into the trap of establishing stable, full, homogeneous, "civilized" bourgeois identities—identities inundated with forgetfulness, ashamed of monumental treasons, justifying an endless chain of injustices due to a complex of scarcity (a complex of immigrants and exiles), fed by the hand of the colonizer's Desire.

As a result, the search for tango roots and for the authentic tango has consumed trusted loyalties, the source of creative passion. Some tangueros have turned themselves into exotics, lost in a romanticized past, debating what is and what is not tango. Meanwhile, the struggles for national identity, for resisting a totalitarian/totalizing Identity, undertaken by other argentinos excluded from the legitimate representation of our national identity, have passed tango by. Folkloric creations from the "interior" of our country, the "*rock nacional*" and Argentinean "women's music," Astor Piazzolla's sophisticated tango versions, Horacio Ferrer's ambitious tango incursions into opera, Fernando E. Solanas's revindications of the tangos of recently exiled argentinos, Juan Carlos Copes's *Pesada del Tango* (Heavy Tango) show and his promises to choreograph a tango-rap, among others, all amount to the multifaceted, unstructured identity of the argentinos. All these manifestations are a part of a single history, of which many of us have lost sight, immersed as we have been in self-destructive internal marginalizations.

Argentina's internal politics of bloody sectorial antagonisms, its "miraculous" economic undevelopment, and its cultural fascism are all part of a consistent denial of our colonized condition—an understandable but dangerous, fatalist acceptance of dependency on the colonizer, a bitter resignation and "naturalization" of (post)coloniality. We have been missing the imperialist point of our long-standing history. And we have come instead to accept our irrational, violent, macho, lazy, corrupt, latino stereotyping out of despair. Tango and all our other hybrid productions are attempts at dealing with the constitution of an identity that will not assume a capital "I," a restless joining into the movements of transculturalism, struggles to actively grasp at global Westernization by creating outbursts of an alternative West and new, unmapped alliances with the Rest.[22]

5

Exotic Encounters

Redistributing the Exotic

Exoticism is a way of establishing order in an unknown world through fantasy; a daydream guided by pleasurable self-reassurance and expansionism. It is the seemingly harmless side of exploitation, cloaked as it is in playfulness and delirium; a legitimate practice of discrimination, where otherwise secretive fantasies can be shared aloud. Exoticism is a practice of representation through which identities are frivolously allocated. It is also a will to power over the unknown, an act of indiscriminately combining fragments, crumbs of knowledge and fantasy, in disrespectful, sweeping gestures justified by harmless banality. Perhaps all peoples have practiced exoticism of one kind or another, but Western exoticism accompanied by worldwide imperialism has had the power to establish Eurocentric exoticism as a universally applicable paradigm. With these thoughts in mind, I will address issues of representation and identity among exotics— peoples exoticized by Eurocentric colonialist discourses and technologies who reproduce, subvert, and reappropriate Western stereotyping as they relate to one another. Exotics-to-the-West will be seen as consumers and re-creators of exoticism who communicate through a world-capitalist web of exoticizing representations. Exoticism fits each "uncivilized," non-Western, or Western-alternative being, however uncomfortably, into a pocket.

Passion plays a major role in the production of exoticism. Western cartographies of exoticism rely heavily on categories of passion in order to classify and map exotics. Exotics are identified in terms of the qualities of passion they offer to the agent of exoticism, but the passion of the exotics is molded by the exoticizer's Desire. It is neither an essence nor a drive; it is a stigma of the colonial condition. In dealing with each other, those identified as exotics refer to the very categorizations that keep them bound and struggle to expand their identities through exotic reappropriations. Exotics negotiate their status as passionate objects so as to gain agency over their passionateness. Passion is the currency through which exotics negotiate their identity with other exotics and with exoticizers. In this endeavor, qualities of passion are at stake. The dynamics of exoticism are historically determined; thus, exotics and exoticizers change in relative power positions and reshape the meanings of passionateness and of Desire.

Tango in Japan is a case of double exoticism. Argentino and Japanese tangueros have been equally involved in reproducing and reappropriating Western exotic practices of representation, but Japan has moved from the periphery of world economic and political influence to a position at the "core." Thus, I will address the question of how relative world power in terms of wealth corresponds—and does not correspond—with the path of "cultural" hegemony, as seen through a tango perspective.

Exotic Reciprocities[1]

Japanese-Argentinean relations are quite uneventful from the point of view of traditional political science: A checklist would show few treaties, little trade, no conflicts, limited immigration, and only sporadic exchanges of diplomatic courtesies, hardly worth mentioning.[2] There is, however, an interesting story of relations between these two distant countries, a story loaded with complex emotions and marked by surprising twists and turns—the story of the tango in Japan.

We argentinos tell a version of this story that is both grandiose and simplistic. In this narrative, for example, the popularity of the tango in Japan is exaggerated and decontextualized. No one mentions that the Japanese have an appetite not just for tango but for other foreign music as well—rock, jazz, salsa, country, flamenco, classical. This lack of perspective derives more from a desire for acknowledgment than from ignorance; argentinos need to be reassured that we occupy a special place on the globe and deserve recognition. The tango is our symbol of national identity. Japan's acceptance and valorization of the tango legitimates our existence as a nation, culture, and people. But it is more than that. Japan is, to argentinos, the Far East, far away, over there. The tango in Japan means that our tango is *even* there. It is thrilling, flattering—our farthest flung, least likely cultural conquest.

Argentinos tend to make an epic tale out of the tango's popularity in Japan. Writing in the 1930s, journalists reported on tango's reception in Japan using militaristic metaphors, such as "battle," "conquest," and "invasion." On the occasion of the first tango competition held in Japan, Argentinean newspaper and magazine headlines read: "In far away JAPAN our tango wins another battle" (Rivarola and Rivarola 1987: 135). Or, "His majesty 'The tango' has trespassed the walls of the impenetrable! Defeating the stubborn resistance of the Japanese spirit to all kinds of invasion, tango conquered with no other weapons than its music" (*Sintonía*, December 16, 1934; see Figure 5.1). In their articles, Argentinean reporters alluded to the fearless courage demonstrated by the Japanese as a model of "resistance to all kinds of foreign" penetration. They evoked the "stubborn *samurai* spirit" with admiration, exalting Japan's nationalism, all the while setting a dramatic scene for tango's harmless conquest of Japan.

FIGURE 5.1 *Newspaper clippings reporting the first tango contest in Tokyo. The winner was awarded a trophy carrying the inscription "Copa Argentina." Source: Sintonía, December 16, 1934.*

Argentina's pride was not based in winning a battle with Japan, as these headlines might suggest. Tango's battle was with jazz (the music that represented Argentina's "enemy to the North"), and Japan was just a battlefield. Thus, the above-mentioned newspaper article, after declaring tango's latest victory, announced that jazz had been "banished by the Japanese" (Rivarola and Rivarola 1987: 135). In a similar spirit, in the concluding chapter of their *Historia del Tango* (1936), under the heading of "Tango in the Orient," Héctor and Luis Bates set themselves to "complete the series of conquests [achieved] by our tango." They assured their readers that "no region on this planet has failed to feel its [tango's] triumphant presence" (Bates and Bates 1936: 73). After citing tango's seductive intrusions into the "depopulated harems" of Constantinople—facilitated by the governmental prohibition of "ancient Oriental dances"—and tango's incredible reception in Japan, the Bateses stressed the uneven conditions under which

tango had to compete with other rhythms. Backed by strong "capital investments and interests," they wrote, North Americans successfully introduced music such as the fox-trot "into their colonies." Tango, in the argentinos' opinion,
had never enjoyed such support. Thus, tango's "conquests" abroad were referred
to in terms of miracles. On the one hand, tango's "triumph" was inexplicable,
and on the other, this miraculous happening was a source of hope for Argentina's battered national pride.

Far from offering an explanation in terms of sheer luck, or one that would
stress the geopolitical circumstances of tango's popularity in the "Orient," the
Bates brothers (and many tangueros after them) relied on exotic *and* empowering representations to score points on behalf of tango—that is, of Argentina.

> What kind of suggestive power emanates from its [tango's] notes, its rhythm
> and melody, in order for it to have gained a diffusion not comparable to any
> other dance of its time? [...] What strange seduction [did tango exert] over
> those fragile wooden houses facing Mount Fujiyama? What kind of enchant-
> ment emerges from the melancholic notes of "*Milonguita*" played by the
> *semisen* [*sic*] in the delicious hands of the *geishas*? [...] Those ample kimonos
> cleaving as they perform a *cortada* figure; those high hairdresses held by enor-
> mous combs, dreamy yellow faces under the spell of "*El Entrerriano.*" [...] It
> seems impossible to believe! However, there, as well as here, a *harakiri* must
> have ended a tormented existence accompanied by the final notes of "*No Me
> Escribas*" (Bates and Bates 1936: 73).

The questions and answers of the Bates brothers followed exotic paths. They
represented Argentina as a nation where a powerful, irresistible tango emerged
that could seduce even such "enigmatic" peoples as the Japanese. Japan's exoticism was evoked through ambivalent imagery: geisha and samurai—fragility,
delicacy, and beauty along with the tragic but courageous practice of *harakiri*.
The final bonding between the nations was provided by the exotic passionate
practices of suicide ("There, as well as here, a *harakiri* must have ended a tor-
mented existence") provoked by the "notes of '*No Me Escribas*'"[Don't Write Me].
Lost love, betrayal, and issues of honor provided the final identification between
these exotic nations.

Think of it: our tango in exotic Japan. A conquest of charm and seduction.
Tango's seductive powers must be overwhelming since even the enigmatic Japanese fell under its spell. (We argentinos smile, puzzled, immersed in mixed
waves of guilt and gratefulness.) Following in the Bateses' steps, contemporary
Argentinean reports on the fate of the tango in Japan are similarly glowing: Tokyo has become the second capital of the tango (after Buenos Aires, of course).
Victor-Japan and Columbia-Japan produce and reissue recordings of famous Argentinean tango orchestras and singers; visiting Argentinean instrumentalists
and dancers perform on Japanese stages, and Japanese tango orchestras play in

large ballrooms. Each year a dozen or more books on various aspects of the tango are published in Japanese. *Latina* (formerly *Música Iberoamericana*), a monthly Japanese magazine that has featured tango since 1952, has a circulation of more than 11,000. Tango holds a prominent position in Japanese social dancing competitions.[3] These contemporary lists of tango successes in Japan downplay tango's doomed fate in the West. Having been all the rage in Europe before and after World War I, it slowly gave way to North American ragtime.[4] In contrast, tango in Japan shared the postwar Western music market with jazz and "tropical" sounds.

The story I will tell of the tango in Japan is more complex and ambivalent than the epic, unilinear accounts. The tango in Japan is not a miracle, nor is it the result of a heroic Argentinean cultural conquest. A variety of tangos have coexisted in Japan since the 1920s, and the "Argentine-ness" of these tangos has been compromised on two accounts: First, Europeans and North Americans have intervened as active translators and mediators in the circulation of tango around the world; and second, the Japanese have reappropriated these Frenchified and Anglicized tangos along with tangos imported directly from Argentina. In Japan, much as in Europe or in Argentina, different tango styles have served as markers of social distinction, and as the positions of Argentina and Japan shifted radically in terms of relative power within global politics, tango went through changing phases of exoticism in Japanese representations.

Argentinos usually refer to the history of the tango in Japan in bilateral, argentino-Japanese terms. In so doing, they minimize the influence of the international market of popular dance and music. By stressing the independent and direct musical connections between Japan and Argentina, they contest the hegemonic control of the "core" powers over the peripheral nations. Numerous specific episodes, anecdotes, and visits are recounted as testimonies of the linkages established directly between Japan and Argentina through tango. Thus, tango symbolizes successful subversion from the world musical order controlled by the capitalists at the Western core. However, in order to exalt their respective national characters and to demonstrate to the world their unmediated, subversive encounters, Japanese and Argentinean tangueros made a spectacle of themselves and of their contacts. Argentinos and Japanese have performed tangos for each other as exotics, in exoticized circumstances.

For example, in the 1950s, when the first Argentinean tango orchestras arrived in Japan, the musicians photographed themselves with their hostesses: The exotic geisha, small, shy, stood like delicate ornaments silently testifying to the argentinos' visit to the Far East (see Figure 5.2). Meanwhile, all-Japanese tango orchestras identified themselves with names such as "Orquesta Típica Porteña" (Typical Porteña Orchestra) and "Orquesta Típica San Telmo" (San Telmo is the old, colonial barrio of Buenos Aires) and appeared on Japanese stages frequently dressed in traditional gaucho argentino attire (see Figure 5.3). In 1953 Ranko

FIGURE 5.2 *Juan Canaro's orchestra at a dinner in Japan, 1954. Courtesy of the Archives of the Canaro Family.*

Fujisawa, the "queen of the tango" in Japan, faced Argentina's public for the first time in the Discépolo theater of Buenos Aires. A famous Argentinean musician and composer introduced her, saying, "With something of Malena and Estercita, she brings to Buenos Aires her oriental emotions so as to let us know that over there, far away, under the pagoda-clad moon of the Orient, our sweet thing is breathed" (Alposta 1987: 72). Similarly, the cover of Ranko Fujisawa's popular tango record shows her dressed in a kimono with the city of Buenos Aires in the background (see Figure 5.4). Do these mementos and courtesies simply testify to the uniqueness of argentino-Japanese cultural encounters? If so, could the uniqueness worth remembering be reduced to the geographical and cultural distances overcome in these events? Could it be that argentinos and Japanese were expressing the noticeable differences in their national characters by representing themselves, reciprocally, as exotics under exotic conditions of encounter?

Among exotics, exoticism is a way of representing not only cultural uniqueness but also respective exotic conditions. In addition, in marketing the tango, argentinos and Japanese situated each other within the "community of exotics"—in full awareness of the grotesque results. A parody of exoticism? Some drawings from early tango sheet music display the exotic Orient, Africa, and Japan in the figure of the Odalisk (see Figure 5.5), the Tribal King, and the Geisha

FIGURE 5.3   Ikeda Mitsuo's "Orquesta Típica San Telmo," 1950. Source: Asahi Graph, *June 1, 1987.*

(see Figure 5.6). The satirical tone of these depictions is related to the fact that the exotically dressed men were famous Argentinean politicians. To reinforce the sense of ridicule, transvestism was added to exoticism. The Japanese also recirculated tango's immersion among other world exotics. For example, at a 1935 concert organized by the Insurance Association of Tokyo, Japanese orchestras played Hawaiian music and tangos. The Honolulu Blue Hawaiians (an all-Japanese band) played Argentinean tangos such as *Don Juan, Poema-tango, Yira ... Yira ...* , and *Confesión* for a Japanese audience eager for multiple exotic mixtures (Alposta 1987: 57–58).

Argentina and Japan could not escape from framing their tango exchanges within a series of exotic reciprocities, immersed as they were in exotic parameters of representation imposed on the world through a hegemonic Western music and dance industry. According to the "civilized" mapping of the world, Argentina and Japan belonged to the exotic lands and were populated by exotic peoples carrying exotic manners. The popular music and dance industry followed and expanded this cartography by detecting new musical, danceable exotic commodities for a world market that was aggressively incorporating new exotic consumers. Western imperialist discourses and technologies of exoticism had already mapped the world so thoroughly that the very exotics themselves could hardly find ways to identify themselves or other exotics outside of that dis-

FIGURE 5.4   *Cover of Ranko Fujisawa and Ikuo Abo's album* Tango en Kimono, *RCA Victor Argentina, 1964. Courtesy of BMG Electrosonora Manufacturas Seavedra S.A.*

course and those practices. The Western parameters of exoticism had been imposed universally—over local discourses of exoticism and competing imperial practices—through worldwide imperialist hegemonic power. Exotics of different latitudes and statuses would relate to each other on terms guided, so to speak, by the same Western map of civilization and progress. A Western-centered compass of exoticism served to identify representations among exotics: Shades, sounds, odors, and gestures were all measured on "universalist" scales of passion. The presence of the manufacturers of the device was irrelevant. The owners of the device could change, as could those who applied the measurements of exoticism. The interpretations of the readings of the exoticism-detecting device could be contested, but they could not be ignored.

FIGURE 5.5   Orientalist imagery on the sheet-music covers for two tangos: Black Eyes, *1910, music by Vicente Greco, and* La Mariposa, *1926, lyrics by Celedonio E. Flores, music by Pedro Maffia.*

In the 1910s, when the tango appeared on the world scene, Japan was in the midst of a frenzied era of importing Western manners. The West appropriated Japanese practices as well. Self-Otherness tensions escalated in this context. Japan had long been an Oriental, Far East exotic to the West. Japanese prints had a tremendous impact on Parisian artists at the end of the nineteenth century (Rhys 1971; Oberthur 1984). Appropriations of Japanese traits by the Western/colonial performance industry emerged after Commodore Matthew Perry's incursion, which provoked Japan's opening to the "world" (1853). David Belasco's play *Madame Butterfly* was produced in 1900 with enormous success. Loie Fuller, the Chicago-born but Paris-acclaimed dancer, presented the Japanese actors and dancers of the Hanako company, headed by Sada Yacco, at the Paris Universal Exposition of 1900. The Hanako troupe, probably the first Noh-tradition performers to set foot in the West, inspired further exoticism. Ruth St. Denis and Ted Shawn, as well as some of their students, choreographed Japanese courtesans and goddesses (*O-Mika* and *Kwanon*, 1913), a Japanese spear dance, and their own version of a Kabuki play adapted to modern dance (*Momiji-Gari*). The Denishawns performed these and many other exotic dances—including tangos—for European, North American, and Asian audiences in the 1920s (Sherman 1979; Sorell 1981; Morini 1978; Hastings 1978). During this period Japan became increasingly self-conscious, aware of its "self," as its contact with the West grew

FIGURE 5.6 *Exotics in tango and Argentinean politics, early 1900s. Drawings by Navarrete imitating the styles used by illustrators of sheet music and publicity posters for major theatrical events. Among exotic operas and operettas, the* Tango del Cangrejo. *Courtesy of the Archives of Horacio Ferrer.*

incrementally in conjunction with its incorporation into the system of Western worldliness (Sakai 1988; Buruma 1984).

Japanese practices of autoexoticism—of looking for identity through the Western mirror—have been addressed by several authors who, like me, have been playfully and conflictively dragged by the currents of postmodernism (Ivy 1988a, 1988b; Kondo 1992; Asada 1988; Sakai 1988; Jeffrey Tobin 1992; Mitsuhiro 1989). I found myself puzzled, surprised, smiling as I read articles and books about the tango in Japan written by *argentinos* in a similar mood. Who was the eccentric who first brought the tango to Japan? Why do the Japanese dance, compose, write, and—unlike most Europeans and North Americans—even sing tangos in Spanish? And, most important, why are *argentinos* more puzzled by tango's popularity in Japan than they are by the tango rage in Paris or New York?

Japan and Argentina are Others to each other—exotics facing other exotics, fascinated by the processes of autoexoticism, carried away into re-exoticizing the already exotic Other. The tango in Japan is an exotic among exotics, but the key to mutual exoticism is kept in the West. Baudelaire reminds us: "The promise was formerly in the East; the light marched toward the South and now springs from the West. France, it is true, by her central location in the civilized world, seems to be called to gather all the notions and all the poetries from around her and to return them to other peoples marvelously worked and fashioned" (Charles Baudelaire, quoted in Miller 1985: 92). In Christopher Miller's words, "This is poetic mercantilism, if not colonialism." Japan is one of those "other peoples" to whom the West, and France in particular, has been delivering "marvelously fashioned" notions and poetries, such as the tango, gathered from all over the colonial world. But France's hegemonic role in the production of exotic dances was disputed by other Western nations that developed musical/danceable products in their particular styles, competitive marketing strategies, and new categories of consumers both at the "core" and in the world's "periphery." The story of tango in Japan reminds us of the impossibility of exotics reaching each other without the mediation of the West.

Tango A Lo Megata *and the* Shakō Dansu *Instructors*

In 1926, after spending several years at leisure in the main capitals of Europe, Baron Megata Tsunumi was called home by his ill father to take care of the family business. He carried back to Japan, among other things, a handful of tango records and a keen knowledge of the dance. In 1956, Megata wrote: "In those days, soon after the First World War, dancing the tango *argentino* was the rage in Paris. One afternoon a friend asked me to go to El Garrón [...] where for the first time I saw an authentic Argentinean band. I was captivated by the music and decided right then to learn the tango. For three years my professor was master Pradir, in those days the most famous on the European continent" (Megata [1956], quoted in Alposta 1987: 32). Megata later visited London, where he took lessons with Victor Silvester, but in his opinion, "The tango is danced in a much more beautiful way in Paris than in London."[5]

Back in Tokyo, Megata started a dance academy to teach his fellow Japanese aristocrats how to tango. His classes were free and addressed to friends and acquaintances, but he undertook his role as a dance master very seriously. He tutored his disciples not only in the nuances of the music and dance but also in how to dress, behave, and even eat properly (that is, *à la française*). "Among other things, he would advise his students to avoid eating Japanese sauces before dancing, since these would provoke an abundant and 'strong' perspiration not recommended for coming close to the ladies" (Alposta 1987: 37–38). Obviously, Megata had picked up not only the tango steps but also the disciplinary ways of the European dance-masters. In addition, he had adopted the necessary quota of exoticism, as practiced by the French: On the occasion of one of his birthday celebrations in the 1930s, Megata danced the tango *Sentimiento Gaucho* (Gaucho Feeling) in the Dancing Florida—a *tanguería* in Tokyo. Megata's tango celebrated the Western embellishment of "native" (gaucho) sensuality.

According to Megata's followers, the tango was not considered scandalous in Japan. The public was ready for it—the aristocratic public, that is. The Japanese aristocracy was working hard to acquire the Western social skills that would allow them to mingle comfortably with foreign diplomats both at home and abroad. They wished to participate without embarrassment in the parties and social dances of international high society (Yoneyama 1990). At any rate, Megata could get away with almost anything, including the tango, thanks to his charm and aristocratic status (Kobayashi 1990).

Megata introduced his exclusive circle to a particularly stylized tango: the tango *a lo Megata*. He taught his students this version of the tango and other social dances popular in Europe at that time. Eiko Yoneyama, who learned the tango from Megata in the early 1960s, explained Megata's method as well as the circumstances that accompanied his success in introducing the tango in Japan.

> Megata offered private dance classes to the young girls and boys of the aristocracy. Our parents thought that it was important for us to behave properly in Western high circles. There were some young British dance masters around, but our parents didn't trust them. They didn't know them and they were foreigners. Dancing could be tricky, especially for young girls. ... So Megata was a perfect choice. His hour-long coaching usually started with fox-trots, then moved on to the waltz, and finally came the tango. I wanted to dance only tangos, but he wouldn't let me. He would say that in order to perform the tango correctly our bodies had to be relaxed, soft, ready (Yoneyama 1990, interview).

Megata would whisper into his students' ears some basic instructions on what dancing—Western dancing—was all about: "Whenever you dance remember you should feel as though you are in love with your partner, even if you have just met him" (Yoneyama 1990, interview).

To dance the tango a lo Megata meant to display elegance and style. The steps were not too long (so that the ladies could wear fashionably tight cocktail dresses), and the male led the dance through chest-to-chest contact, his right hand gently holding his partner's back, without grabbing or pushing. The woman's left hand rested relaxed on the man's shoulder; their faces were close to each other to allow for eye contact and conversation. Megata's golden rule for the tango was to dance it beautifully. He instructed his male students to take care of the appearance of their partners. "The women should look beautiful, stylized, elegant." All abrupt movements had to be avoided so as not to "distort the female figure" (Yoneyama 1990, interview). With these instructions, Megata distinguished himself from his contenders: the British dance-masters. While living in Europe, Megata had been exposed to the French-English tango war and had taken a side; the tango a lo Megata was definitely a French-style tango—a tango preoccupied with elegance.

By the 1930s, British dance-masters were traveling to Japan to teach the large foreign community in Kobe. Japanese who were acquainted with the foreigners had access to these *shakō dansu* (social dance) classes, and many others got hold of manuals and handbooks. The British-style tango was taught as one of a series of "modern" ballroom dances presented as sportive, competitive activities. The tango of the British dance-masters was strictly codified into rigid movements: The faces of the partners pointed in clearly opposite directions or, when facing the same direction, were turned completely parallel to the right or left shoulder. The position of the hands helped to reaffirm distance and emotional disengagement between the partners: The lady's left hand, with the palm turned down, touched the gentleman's shoulder perpendicularly as if in a military salute to the flag (see Figures 5.7 and 5.8). Students followed a carefully developed sequence of figures such as "walks," "promenades," "sways," "swivels," "reverse turns," and "chases," paying attention to a rhythmic pattern of "slow, quick-quick, slow *and* slow *and* slow-slow." (The figures and pace were—and still are—referred to by their English names.)

This English version of the tango, which is also followed and popularized by North Americans, is currently the most widely practiced in Japan. Some Japanese shakō dansu teachers I interviewed credit the English influence—not Megata's high status—with helping the tango escape its scandalous roots. The straight and stiff tango encouraged by the British school imposed detachment. As one instructor commented, "It is a style suited to dance partners who do not know each other, or who behave that way ..." (Ogata 1990, interview). The U.S. occupation provided a context that helped to spread and legitimize the British-tamed tango. Another instructor explained to me that among the "Latin" dances taught in shakō dansu classes, the tango "comes closer to the Japanese spirit. Tango does not require a physical expression of passion. The passionate feelings

Tango

田中　忠・節子夫妻の
ドロップ・オーバースウェー

FIGURE 5.7　*A Japanese* shakō dansu *couple performing the tango "over-sway" figure.*
Source: *Dance instruction manual by Wakahayashi Masao,* Modenu Dansu Kyotei *(Tokyo: Kodansha Press, 1983).*

can be kept inside. Japanese people are not drawn to show affection like the latinos; we don't hug, kiss, and agitate like you guys" (Sugi 1990, interview). Shakō dansu teachers insist that Japanese people accepted the tango—one in a series of Western ballroom dances—with the purpose of practicing some innocuous form of "modern" exercise. This interpretation, however, is far from Megata's aesthetic preoccupations and his efforts to spread Western social skills among the Japanese aristocrats.

Mori Junzaburo, one of Megata's disciples, expressed his admiration toward his teacher in these terms: "Baron Megata is the only person who knows how to dance the tango in an *authentic* way since he studied it in Paris" (Mori [1933], quoted in Alposta 1987: 40, my emphasis). Mori, converted by Megata into a fanatic of the tango, was the author of the first books on tango published in Japan: *Tango* (1930) and *The Argentinean Dance: Tango Dance Method* (1933) (Alposta 1987: 45). In one of his many articles devoted to tango, he writes:

> The main reason for the popularization of Argentinean music has been the social dance craze, and especially the fact that in those days the tango enjoyed England's general acceptance. [...] Once [the tango] was accepted as a form of "standard dancing" in England, [Japanese] people started to dance it more and more, the result of which was an actual boom of the so called "*authentic English school.*" The general opinion was that since the dance method was an English one, the music should also be played the English way; *the Argentinean style was out of the question.* In 1932 when the Dancing Florida of Tokyo invited some French musicians to play [...], the taste for the *latino style* started to develop. [...] The French musicians opened up the path for those who could play the *bandoneón*, among them Mr. Kogure from Mitsukoshi, an authentic forerunner who had studied it in Paris. On the other hand, taking Baron Megata as the central figure, *the group of 'fans' of the French style, that is, the latin style*, grew both in quantity and quality. One of those was the young Tadao Takahashi, a genius who continues working whole heartedly for the *promotion of the tango argentino* (Mori [1936], quoted in Alposta 1987: 49–50, my emphasis).

In this paragraph, Mori reflects the complexity of the colonial project, in this case, musical colonialism. The "tango argentino" appeared to the Japanese to be a raw material and an exotic resource; the "French" or "French-latin style" tango and the "authentic English style" were competing exotic tango products. As a result, the "authentic" tangos were either the French or the English versions; the "argentino style" was raw and unfinished, "out of the question," not ready to be consumed until it had undergone the necessary processing in the colonial factories of exoticism. The "authentic" tango was not the one danced in tango's places of origin but the one developed as a commodity by the manufacturers of exoti-

FIGURE 5.8   *A sequence of tango steps. The legend reads: "Passionate Tango: The back-open promenade and the over-sway are well liked and used even by high-class people. Together they create a big movement" (translated by Raj Pandey).* Source: *Shinoda Manabu,* Dansu Insutorakushion *(Tokyo: Kabushiki Gaisha, 1989).*

●タンゴ

情熱的なタンゴ、その中でも、ダブルで使うバック・オープン・プロムナードやオーバースウェイは、上級者も好んで使うシャープで、大きな動きをつくりだすフィギャーです

まわりこんで「Q」

もう一度左足横に「&」

オーバースウェイに女性しっかりと頭を左にまわす「S・S」

cism. "Tango argentino" was a label, not a brand; exotics provide enticing, suggestive labels but they rarely are able to market their own brands.

As the Japanese imported tangos produced and exoticized in Europe they also imported European strategies for appropriating, categorizing, and marketing exotic goods. The authentic French and English versions of the tango targeted different sectors of the Japanese market for Western culture. The French tango— or tango a lo Megata—was a handcrafted luxury good suited to the Japanese aristocracy, whereas the British-style tango was a mass-produced, quality-controlled version aimed at the Japanese middle classes. Megata's dance lessons were highly personalized and sophisticated. He never charged for his classes and taught almost exclusively within his aristocratic circle. The British-style dance masters, in contrast, were launching a business—the social dance industry in Japan; they sold classes and manuals and arranged competitions aimed at opening up a new market. The two enterprises shared the common goal of Westernizing Japan, but the uses they made of the tango were very different. To Megata and his aristocratic followers, the tango *à la française* represented distinction and class. To the shakō dansu instructors who popularized the British style, the tango represented modernity.

Shakō dansu teachers make a distinction between the controlled, sophisticated European tango and rowdy Latin dances. According to their social dance codes, the tango is included in the category of modern dances (together with the waltz and fox-trot), while the mambo, rumba, cha-cha, and samba belong to a separate Latin cluster. This distinction shows how thoroughly successful the Europeans were at domesticating the once-wild tango and helps explain the tango's appeal for middle-class Japanese attempting to incorporate and domesticate the West.[6] In questioning the essentialist assumption that tango owes its popularity in Japan to its affinity with the "tragic Japanese spirit," one starts to wonder whether Japanese efforts to domesticate the West have been triggered by an overwhelming worldwide imposition of "Westernization."

Megata and the shakō dansu masters played out parallel processes of Westernization, each in a particular style, for a particular class, mirroring an international division of class by national/cultural identity. France represented to the Japanese the aristocratic center of the empire of taste; the British, and later the Americans (an ex-British colony), represented the core of the industrialized world—including the music and dance industry. Neither of those centers of world power ever completely succeeded in displacing the other; in Japan, as elsewhere, they have been conflictively negotiating for control of particular processes of production and specific markets for increasingly differentiated kinds of consumers. In addition, Megata and the shakō dansu masters were "Japanizing" Western practices of exoticism in that the tango trends they followed were Western, exoticized products—exotic latino passion successfully transformed into European pleasure.

Tango Argentino in Japan

Tangos imported directly from Argentina or by argentinos joined the others, complicating the story of the tango in Japan. Arturo Montenegro, an Argentinean diplomat in Tokyo, was one of those who helped to popularize this strand of tango. He imported records from Argentina (recorded by a subsidiary of the Victor Company), gave tango lessons, and, in 1934, organized Japan's first tango dancing contests (Ferrer 1980a). These contests were similar to the international ballroom dancing competitions promoted at that time by the British-style dance masters. The promotion of dance contests exclusively for tango and organized by an argentino, however, added a new dimension.

Argentinean tango music was available in Japan through recordings, and pretty soon Japanese musicians were playing the tunes. These Japanese instrumentalists and singers made clear distinctions between the "Continental" tango and the original tango argentino. The most prestigious Japanese tango interpreters were those able to attempt Argentinean tangos in Spanish, complete with lunfardo (the slang of Buenos Aires). The challenge was not only one of pronunciation but also of feeling. The first Japanese tango singers studied with tango fans who had a sensitive ear for the tango even if they could not sing themselves (Abo 1990).

Most of the Japanese tangueros whom I interviewed suggested that a major political decision helped to promote the tango argentino in Japan: With the outbreak of World War II, the Japanese government banned Western music, meaning primarily U.S. popular music, but allowed German and Italian classics and the tango.[7] Thus, during the war years, the tango provided a substitute for the banned modern West. At the same time, Argentina was clearly differentiated from Japan's Western enemies.

Montenegro, the argentino diplomat in Japan, recalled that the Japanese often employed the word *shibui* to describe the tango: "The word has no translation, but it means something like the bitter appearance of that which is positively beautiful" (Montenegro, quoted in Ferrer 1980a: 255). I am not qualified to discuss the accuracy of Montenegro's translation of the term into Spanish; my intention is to emphasize here how the Argentinean diplomat chose to characterize the Japanese perception of the tango. To most argentinos, Montenegro's explanation of shibui as applied to the tango confirms the exoticism of the Japanese people and hence the exotic distance between the Argentinean and Japanese cultures. Montenegro's account of the Japanese perception of the tango displays the enigmatic, inscrutable features attributed to the Japanese through the Eurocentric cartography of the exotic. His answer to the enigma of tango's popularity in Japan is conveyed through an exotic Japanese poetic puzzle.

Conversely, when asked why the Japanese like tangos, most Japanese tangueros I interviewed in Tokyo emphasized the compatibility of the two cultures rather than the attraction of the exotic or the radically different. Kyotani

Kohji, a remarkable bandoneón player and composer, told me: "Tangos are basically sentimental, as are we Japanese. When we play we try to communicate to our audience the similarity of our feelings [with those of the argentinos] rather than the contrasts between the latino and the Japanese; it is what we have in common that counts—sentimentality, sadness" (Kyotani 1990, interview). Yamazaki Mieko, a tango singer, explained: "The tango is attractive to me because of the contrast between the rhythm and the strongly sentimental melody. This is a challenging combination for a singer. The Japanese women who sing tango understand these complexities because we are real city-girls" (Yamazaki 1990, interview). Abo Ikuo, a tango singer who has recorded with both Argentinean and Japanese tango orchestras, sees a connection between the lyrics of tango and *enka* (Japanese popular song):

> *Enka* and tango share melodramatic themes, themes of love; especially "lost-love" [in English] and betrayals. Things that make people cry. There are important differences. In *enka* it is mostly women who moan the absence of their lovers, while in tangos, those betrayed are mostly men, but the emotions are similar. By listening to Hibari Misora [a renowned *enka* singer], Japanese tango singers learn how to express themselves singing tango. Although the rhythms are very different, the feelings of sadness, separation, and forlornness are shared (Abo 1990, interview).

Abo had recently attempted to express this deep affinity in a tango he composed entitled *El Zorzal y la Calandria* (The Thrush and the Lark). The lyrics (written by Héctor Negro) establish the common fate of the Japanese and Argentinean souls by pointing out that the most famous Argentinean tango singer, Carlos Gardel ("The Thrush"), and the most recognized enka singer, Hibari Misora ("The Lark"), were both known by birds' names and died on the same date.

Un zorzal	A thrush
en Buenos Aires se largó a cantar.	in Buenos Aires lets out a song.
Y su voz	And his voice
abrió las alas y se echó a volar.	filled his wings and set him aflight.
Fue Gardel. [...]	He was Gardel. [...]
Japón.	Japan.
Donde otro pájaro nació ... ,	Where another bird was born ...
creció.	reared.
Mujer. ...	A woman. ...
Y fue calandria que cantó. [...]	And she was a singing lark. [...]
El cielo abrazará	The sky will join
calandria con zorzal. [...]	lark with thrush. [...]
Del Plata hasta el Japón,	From the Plata to Japan,

el canto se alzará.	song will fill the air.
Ya no habrá muerte ni silencio	Then neither death nor silence
que podrá. ...	will be able [to keep them apart]. ...

—*El Zorzal y La Calandria* (The Thrush and the Lark), 1990
Music by Ikuo Abo
Lyrics by Héctor Negro

Negro adds a romantic touch by lyrically musing that, although Gardel and Hibari Misora never met in life, death has brought them together as a couple in heaven.

Luis Alposta, who, like me, was puzzled by the Japanese-argentino tango connection, received similar counterexotic answers from the Japanese tango artists he interviewed. In 1951 he interviewed Koga Masao, a Japanese tango composer in Argentina:

ALPOSTA: Why is Argentinean popular music so liked in Japan?
KOGA: Because our musical feelings are convergent and the topics are extraordinarily similar.
ALPOSTA: Do you also sing about love and betrayal?
KOGA: Yes. We like to whine over the women who have abandoned us, just like the old tangos. Twenty-three years ago, one of the first waltzes I wrote was called Rage or *Shitaite,* which means: "Longing for the one who left." Almost all the tangos that are popular in Argentina are sung in Japan (Alposta 1987: 101).

In 1978 he interviewed Kanematsu Yoji, then president of Tokyo's Society for the Study of Iberoamerican Music (Chunambei Ongaku Kenkyukai):

ALPOSTA: Why do the Japanese like tango so much?
KANEMATSU: Because your music reaches our hearts very easily (Alposta 1987: 89).

These opinions of Japanese tangueros committed to the tango argentino contradict those of the shakō dansu instructors, who stress tango argentino's exoticism. Shakō dansu teachers believe that Europeanized tango is marketable in Japan because the sensuality of the original tango argentino has been successfully subdued. In contrast, the Japanese followers of the tango argentino emphasize the sentimental affinities of Japanese and argentinos, the unique spiritual kinship between seemingly alien cultures. Likewise, they establish clear differences between the original tango argentino and Westernized, inauthentic tangos (Oiwa 1990).

This loyalty to the authentic tango argentino and the belief in the similarities between the Japanese and Argentinean sentimental cultures are shared by a small group of tango connoisseurs who seek to distinguish themselves from both the Frenchified Japanese aristocrats and from the unsophisticated masses who prefer shakō dansu. These erudites and collectors of the authentic tango argentino have been more interested in tango's musical and lyrical developments than in the dance. Tango argentino gained recognition as a distinctive form separate from the Europeanized and North Americanized tangos when Argentina adopted an independent position from that of the Western Allies during World War II.[8]

Japanese followers of tango argentino are not monolithic. In the 1980s, a version of the tango dance developed by Argentinean impresarios for the Broadway stage was introduced to Japan. The spectacular style of this *Tango Argentino*, created by Claudio Segovia and Héctor Orezzoli in 1983 and featuring professional Argentinean dancers, is stimulating a new wave of desire for the passionate tango in the contemporary capitals of the "developed" world—including Tokyo. As a result, a new generation of Japanese tango fans has emerged with a taste for exotic passion. This new wave of popularity is reminiscent of the days of la belle époque, when tango was featured in Parisian revues. The distance between the exotic argentinos and the exotic Japanese has widened as Japan has moved to the "core" of the world system, despite the fact that argentino-Japanese tango relations are now more direct. The asymmetric power positions of Argentina and Japan vis-à-vis the Western "core" have affected the exotic encounter. The Japanese public has become quite proficient at reproducing Western practices of consuming less-privileged exotics. The Argentinean cast members of *Tango Argentino* are consumed by their Japanese audiences as embodiments of passion who have already been given the seal of approval by the cultural capitals of the West.

The Erotic Incompatibilities of Some Exotics

"Anyone who has felt this passionate rhythm [of tango] running through her veins can never forget it," said Ranko Fujisawa, the Japanese "tango queen" (and first Japanese tango singer), to Luis Alposta (1987: 75). In the Japanese-Argentinean relations carried out through the tango, passion has produced complex debates. Far from being an instinct or drive displayed in the tango, this passionate "nature" attributed to the tango is a product of the history of exotic representations. The Japanese have related to tango's passion in different ways as the representations of the two countries have changed their positions within the world of the exotics. Shakō dansu instructors say that tango's passion has been effectively subdued in Japan, except, perhaps, in the realm of fantasy: "Couples may have in their minds the sensuality of a Rudolf Valentino movie when they dance the tango, but they don't show it in their movements in our dance classes" (Ogata 1990, interview). The Japanese social dance teachers I interviewed took pains to clarify that the tango argentino is never performed at their dance hall (the

Odeon of Kabuki-cho, Tokyo). By "tango argentino" they meant *ashi no karami* (legs intertwined), suggesting an inappropriate display of sensuality. One instructor told me that Japanese people know of this tango style from television shows but that most of them consider it a bit vulgar or embarrassing (Ogata 1990). The tango argentino these instructors have in mind is clearly the Broadway-style tango popularized in Japan by Segovia and Orezzoli's touring company in 1987. In the opinion of the shakō dansu instructors, this tango is so exotically erotic that, for the Japanese, it would only be proper to watch it from afar as a voyeuristic pleasure.

As in Europe, the United States, and even the Río de la Plata, the dancing industry in Japan disciplines the moving bodies by providing contrasting tango versions for the stage and for the ballroom. A sanitized tango protects the reputation of shakō dansu instructors and clients, given that most of the former are men and most of the latter are women. Yoneyama Eiko pointed out to me that in the early tango days in Japan, "dancing could be tricky, especially for young girls," since the ballroom teachers were not trusted by the students' parents (Yoneyama 1990, interview). In the 1930s, most social dance teachers were foreigners, a situation that has changed today, but contemporary shakō dansu instructors (especially when teaching the tango) still bear the suspect status attributed to those who make a living by teaching social dance. In Japan as well as in other countries, dance instructors are associated with seducers or even gigolos and are suspected of taking advantage of the potentially romantic dancing atmosphere. The students who attend shakō dansu classes at the dance halls, wearing glamorous evening gowns, are equally suspect. The Japanese shakō dansu teachers protect and promote their own business by establishing essential differences between argentinos (latinos) and Japanese in their performance and reception of erotically charged movements.

Passion seems to be the toughest hurdle in the effort to establish a connection between Japanese and latino souls. According to the Western continuum of world exoticism/eroticism, Japanese and latinos are polar opposites. Anyone (who has sufficiently internalized the logic of Western exoticism) can tell the difference: Japanese people are cold, detached, and controlled; latinos, including argentinos, are expressive, passionate, and sensual. Japanese and argentinos each use this Western map of passion to make sense of the strange case of the tango in Japan. Both use strategies of "familiarization" to justify connections and, at the same time, reproduce icons of exotic, irremediable distance. They (we) all wonder: How can such a famously passionate dance as the tango argentino be practiced and enjoyed by such famously repressed people as the Japanese?

Students I interviewed in a tango argentino class in Tokyo gave answers that challenge the assumptions behind this question and contradict the assertions of the shakō dansu instructors. Takahashi Masayoshi said, "The idea that Japanese people are cold is all *tatemae* [surface, public appearance]; Japanese people are plenty passionate" (1990, interview). Takahashi Teruko added that "Japanese people are very passionate, that is why all this emphasis on politeness, etiquette and control is necessary" (1990, interview). And Takashima Masako pointed out, "To me, tango is very much like the Noh dancing: It is stylized, but the same kind of feeling is very strong in both tango and Noh if you know where to look. I have never done any other Western-style dances. They don't appeal to me, but something about the tango is beautiful and passionate; as in *Noh*, you hold the back very stiff and the movements of the legs are controlled, yet exquisitely expressive in their gestures" (1990, interview). Eguchi Yuko, one of the few Japanese dancers who teaches and performs tango argentino (as opposed to British- or French-style tango) explained: "Japanese aren't scandalized or offended by males and females dancing together. The concern is rather with the young ones, doing *tatchi dansu* [touch dancing] or *bodii kontakutu* [body-contact] dancing. Japanese are not puritans; they don't have a church, like in the West, telling them that things are evil. It's a question of propriety, not morality. That is why young people dance disco but not the lambada" (1990, interview). The teachers of this studio class, Eguchi Yuko and Kobayashi Taihei, are the leading Japanese proponents of the tango argentino version of tango, which clearly displays passion and sensuality (see Figure 5.9). They have launched a tango argentino campaign through an association they organized to popularize the authentic and passionate Argentinean tango in Japan. Ironically, they were inspired to undertake this enterprise when they saw the Broadway show *Tango Argentino* on Japanese television. (This show, created and performed by argentinos, was not presented in Buenos Aires until 1992, nine years after it began its worldwide tour.) Captivated, they went to Argentina to train with Gloria and Eduardo Arquimbau, a famous professional tango couple who were members of the show's cast.

Kobayashi and Eguchi's Tango Argentino Dance Academy is challenging the notion of an intrinsically dispassionate Japanese-ness. Cultivating dance as an art form—and not as a social skill or frivolous entertainment, as their forerunners did—they are grappling in new ways with the hard core of exoticism—that is, eroticism. In their classes they deal simultaneously with the stereotypical representations of Japanese erotica—as perceived in the prints that fascinated Paris of la belle époque (Sorell 1981; Morini 1978)—and with the eroticism attributed to the "authentic" tango argentino—the eroticism that led Mistinguett's manager to advise the famous femme fatale to perform the tango "only when you have a bed near by ..." (Mistinguett 1954: 60). They teach their 300 students a striking form of tango based on the style produced by argentinos primarily for the stages of Europe and the United States. Still, to an outside observer, and I suspect to most Japanese, something does not quite work. When Japanese perform the tango argentino, incorporating all the techniques of passion they have learned from Argentinean artists, they still look "Japanese." This is attributable not to any lack of "feeling" or skill on the part of the Japanese dancers but to the power of exoticism. The Western mirror stubbornly reflects Otherness.[9]

FIGURE 5.9 *Promotional flyer for a performance by Kobayashi and Eguchi in 1990. The legend stresses that the dancers "learned directly in Argentina, the birthplace of tango, from Gloria and Eduardo" (translated by Raj Pandey).*

SCENE EIGHT: A JAPANESE LESSON ON

TANGO'S PASSION

Dialogue.

Tokyo 1987. After the television broadcast of Tango Argentino, *a Broadway show, Maeda Bibari (a professional dancer) and Itzuki Hiroiuki (a tango connoisseur) engage in a public dialogue. Their purpose is to educate the Japanese audience on how to appreciate, judge, and perform passionate "feelings" through the exotic tango. The characters face each other, seated on chairs. As the conversation evolves, Maeda (remaining seated) hesitantly tries some tango steps.*

Background music: A lo Megata, 1981, lyrics by Luis Alposta and music by Edmundo Rivero.

Maeda and Itzuki's text:[10]

ITZUKI: Japan since the Meiji period has been trying to make the culture of other places its own, but there is still a long way to go.

MAEDA: When I started dancing, I wanted to do tango but people would tell me that it was as ridiculous and silly as when foreigners try to perform *kabuki*.

I.: You said on television that finally the age of adulthood had come to Japan. Tango, you said, is the culture, the heart of adults. The Japanese world of culture is still extremely childish. For example, in tango, when a man tries to make a woman his dancing partner, unless he is a real adult male, it just will not do. ... It will not work in the full meaning of the term. It is not only a question of dancing technique, it is the solidity, even the thickness of the bodies that is important. Like the fact that the stomach should protrude a little like in an adult, established man.

M.: Yes, in tango you should show the age you carry on your back. I learned tango from an Argentinean teacher who said he had come to Japan to bring culture from his country. I thought at first that I could do a tango in my performances, but then I felt that it would not be appropriate.

I.: Yes, because Argentinean people are quite something. ...

M.: Yes, they are so passionate and serious about what they do.

I.: Yes, they are passionate and perhaps, should I say, patriotic? Or maybe I should say that they have this special love for their people, their folk.

M.: So I thought of going to Argentina for the summer. There I learned that tango was born out of the mixing of blood of different people. I realized that it was born out of pain, the pain of being away from your country and not being able to go back home. The ones who created the tango were inhabitants of port cities who in order to chase a woman for the night, in order to impress her and show what a special man he was, developed these steps.

I.: These stories stir one's blood, don't they? I come from a generation for whom tango is synonymous with dance. Tango is a dance in which when the man sticks his knee between the woman's legs it is not rude, although it is the opposite of refinement and courtesy. This dance, to put it in extreme words, is a combat in which the woman provokes the man's sword *[laughs]*. The man's kneecap intrudes between the woman's thighs.

M.: Tango is different from other dance forms because the feelings do not rise in the course of the dance. The dance begins from a high pitch, from the combat itself, from the moment of heightened passion.

I.: And it ends like a cut. It never slows down. That is what is so magnificent about it. The ending in tango is like the cut of a knife. Tango music is like a cut in early Spring and that is its fate. Classic Western music developed status, money, fame, but the tango, despite its great potential, lost its life by being cut in early Spring. People who lamented this fact continued singing this music, treasured it, and so the torch of tango was carried in their hearts. It never extinguished. Now tango has taken on new bodies. There is no other dance like tango for expressing yourself through the body. Tango is the dance in which men and women are locked together, intimately. In waltz there was still a separation that is overcome only in the tango. The warmth of the bodies, the exchange of breaths ... everything communicates. Bathed in sweat, you are caught together in this degree of contact. Under these circumstances the humanness of your partner cannot help but communicate itself to you. Leaving aside for a moment the skill of the dance, the warmth of the body makes you think that your partner is a magnificent person. As a dance, tango makes you feel things like this. When it ends, you separate and it is like fireworks. It was interesting to see those men and women looking heavy, not attractive or really beautiful, making beauty together as soon as they start dancing. [...]

M.: Tango is called the dance of the feet, but the facial expression is very important. You never face the public fully. Your feelings should show that you are the best woman in the world even if you have been born with a painful fate. That same thing happens with the man. Unless you can show dignity through your expressions, you cannot do the tango.

I.: You have got that, so I say you can dance the tango. [...] Tango in Japan is not a boom, should not be a fad. Japan has a special mission to accomplish. [...] Japan, in the Far East, is the country chosen by tango. Just like when those different strains of people met in Buenos Aires, coming from foreign countries, and tango came to be. Japan is the one country in the whole world which has continued preserving the light, the torch, of the tango. You have been chosen by tango.

Maeda, still sitting on her chair, finally succumbs to tango's passion in an episode of trance.

Blackout

Tango in Japan and the Aesthetics of Exoticism

The previous dialogue illustrates how tango's passion is interpreted, taught, and encouraged among the Japanese public (and potential tango dancers) by construing and appropriating the exotic. The Japanese lesson on tango's passion resorts to suggestive, provocative, quasi-ritualistic imagery. Tango is invoked as a mission, a pagan religion that, with a will of its own, signals its victims and initiates. Tango's erotic powers take hold of Japanese bodies, setting them in a trance of re-exoticization. Itzuki and Maeda discuss the latest version of the tango in Japan (with the exception of some "punk" Japanese tango creations). The boom they refer to—advising that it should not be taken for a mere fad—is that created by the *Tango Argentino* Broadway show broadcast on Japanese television (see Figure 5.10). Maeda and Itzuki's publicly released conversation on intimate, passionate matters is a modern Japanese take on the representation of Japanese and Argentinean national positions in the world's political economy. Contemporary Japan exoticizes other, less privileged exotics, appropriating passion, but it does it *à la Western*:

> THE TANGO FESTIVAL will perform for the 100th anniversary of Francisco Canaro with Orquesta Festival Canaro & Quarteto Pirincho. 10/10: 1:30 & 5pm, TKH. 11/4: 6:30pm, SWU. S¥5000, A¥4500, B¥4000. Kyodo Tokyo 407–8248. S,P. For those searching for something *more emotional and dramatic*, The Tango Festival, featuring top *dancers and musicians from South America*, is definitely not to be missed (*Japan Journal 8(7)* [October 1988]: 53, 55, my emphasis).

The same 1987 issue of *Asahi Graph* that published Maeda and Itzuki's dialogue—an issue devoted to the *Tango Argentino* show—included an illustration reading: "*Tango Argentino* Preview—The Fragrance of Eroticism. The musical '*Tango Argentino*' was an enormous success in Europe and America and led to a worldwide tango boom. On this stage you will get everything of the tango: men and women, the flavor of eroticism, and numerous famous songs with history" (translated by Raj Pandey; see Figure 5.11). The images and texts were designed to persuade Japanese readers and viewers to consume worldliness and exoticism through an escalation of erotic redundancies.

Japan bears the burden of (North) Western exoticism despite its current economic power. Japan has entered the world's core of wealth and power, but it has not completely replaced or displaced former hegemonic Western centers. As a relatively new contender, Japan tensely coexists with the United States, Germany, France, England, and other (North) Western powers. The tensions become clearer when one considers the control over different kinds of products and markets among countries at the core and the simultaneous circulation of different currencies—some of which are not strictly reducible to the monetary.

FIGURE 5.10   Asahi Graph's *special issue promoting the* Tango Argentino *show, a spectacle conceived and directed by Claudio Segovia and Héctor Orezzoli in 1983.* Source: Asahi Graph, *June 1, 1987, cover.*

FIGURE 5.11 *Illustration for* Todo Sobre Tango Argentino *(All About Tango Argentino).*
Left: *Dancers Gloria and Eduardo Arquimbau.* Source: *Asahi Graph, June 1, 1987.*

Continental tango, British-style tango, tango argentino, and Broadway-style
Tango Argentino are different versions of an exotic product as it has been
restylized and consumed by Japanese impresarios, performers, and audiences.
All of these consumers mark their social distinctions through diverse interpretations of passion. Japanese aristocrats socially distinguish themselves through
taste, and the world's legitimate center of the empire of taste is still in Paris, or,
more generally, France. Hence, tango a lo Megata is a Japanese domestication of
the French-style tango and its cultivated, subtle sensuality and beauty. The
shakō dansu participants carry the banner of the middle class and thus practice
the sanitized British and North American tango that is produced and consumed
by the masses. The core of the mass entertainment industry remains under the
legitimate control of the Anglos, even when their economic control has been
drastically challenged. Through their tangos, shakō dansu followers try to develop active, sportive bodies that hint at "modernity." Tango argentino, as a
marker of connoisseurship sought by those Japanese who view themselves as
different from both the aristocrats and the masses, is a phenomenon tinged by
nationalistic (anti-Western, anti–American Occupation) feelings.[11] Japanese
connoisseurs of tango argentino, devoted to the musical and lyrical forms, challenge previous Western mediations among exotics and rescue the authentic
tango from its original Argentinean setting while emphasizing the sentimental
kinship between argentinos and Japanese. The Japanese followers of *Tango
Argentino* (Broadway-style) cultivate a different relationship with argentinos.
Like the connoisseurs of tango argentino, they search for an affinity between the
two cultures, but this affinity is focused on passion and the emotional invest-

ments of the body in movement. They are artists interested in exploring and impersonating the tango's "essence." Defiant of Western exotic stereotyping, they wish to demonstrate the passionateness of the Japanese. In so doing, they work at developing passionate "skills" with the assistance of argentinos—the Western core's emblems of distinguished passionate exoticism.

Exoticism reproduces itself. When challenged on one end (the Japanese) it grows on the other (the argentino). And argentinos actively participate in the task. For argentinos, exoticism à la Broadway is nowadays a living. In dealing with the West, Japanese people have had to cope both with the Westernization imposed on them (and on others, such as the argentinos) and with the domestication of Western and Westernized products (like the stylized *Tango Argentino*). Japanizing the West, from the perspective of a world economy of passion, means facing the subtleties of exoticism imposed by Western imperialism on non-Western or peripheral Western Others.[12] In following the circulation of the exotic, encounters such as those of the Japanese and Argentinean tangueros amplify, convolute, and challenge unidirectional understandings of the dynamics of exoticism. Exotic reciprocities, re-exoticizations, and exotic appropriations of the already exoticized take place, creating curious compatibilities where the "incompatible"—that is, the lack of a common passion—was previously allocated. Exotic categorizations expand, producing further specificities and generating puzzling convergences. Class, status, prestige, and power start playing a part in the aesthetics of exoticism through erotic manipulations, creating distinctions among some exotics and conflations among others. Low, distasteful, grotesque exotics find a common ground in their shared opposition to more refined Europoid exotics. Uneven access to wealth, manners, and tastes explodes exotic differences. Exotics who respect and desire Western culture, and who have been relatively successful at Westernizing themselves, are still judged by the West in exotic terms: according to their management of the erotic. Japanese and argentinos are thus bonded in exotic kinship and distinguished from other exotics by their aesthetization of profound feelings, informed emotions, and elegantly exhibited passions—when judged under Western and Westernized exoticizing eyes.

Exoticism operates exotically, following a strange logic and curious aesthetic rules. Danger, violence, and the disruption of the truly Other are kept, titillating, at the fringes, held back and evoked in palatable ways. The aesthetics of exoticism capture and represent these oddities through sophisticated and yet coarse techniques, operating at the pleasurable verge of the grotesque: pastiche, juxtaposition, montage—inciting eroticism by enlivening exotic imagery. The *Tango Argentino* show staged in Tokyo in 1987 was publicized through brochures exuding exotic eroticism: The layout (see Figure 5.12) invites one to "peek" into the intimacy of the dancing couples, who are tightly framed, fragmented, and thus fetishized, exchanging enraptured looks and entangled in sexually evocative postures. Men and women caught in fatal encounters are set alongside the iso-

FIGURE 5.12 *From the publicity brochure for the touring company of* Tango Argentino, *1987.*

lated image of a thoughtful, intense, but contained latino ("native") musician, aloof and yet witnessing excess. How much of this tango imagery, combining the native's fate with heterosexual erotic fatality, conjures, decomposes, and re-exoticizes the once exotic and now familiar image of a Rudolf Valentino—whose exotic appeal became degraded and grotesque with the changing erotic times?

The cover of this brochure (Figure 5.13), portrays a paramount yet cut-off image of a *Tango Argentino* "she" bearing the shadowed eyelids and the "Oriental" tiara once worn by Valentino, that feminized exotic "he" who impersonated sheiks and sons of sheiks in breathtaking movies of the 1920s. Valentino, however, did not perform tangos in those films; his famous tango took place in *The Four Horsemen of the Apocalypse*, in which he displayed macho unease garbed in gaucho attire. Exoticism builds up grotesquely, stylizing the grotesque results. Fragments and crumbs of exotic difference are blended loosely into newly crafted exotic imagery, homogenizing exotic distinctions and differentiating exotic sameness. Exoticism pervasively sweeps the world like a powerful whirlwind, collecting mismatched oddities—oddities that nevertheless follow a logic: the aesthetic logic of exoticism. The Western core reflects exoticism in its eyes, but it does so deviantly, as a distorting but never blurred mirror of passion, that uncanny mirror through which the Others see each other and themselves.

FIGURE 5.13 *Cover of publicity brochure for the touring company of* Tango Argentino, *1987.*

Argentinos have also reciprocated exotic aesthetics when dealing with the Japanese appropriations of the tango. Luis Alposta chose for the cover of his book *El Tango en Japón* Japanese-like calligraphy and a painting of an Asian-Oriental male in traditional Japanese costume and coiffure (see Figure 5.14). Sigfredo Pastor (the artist) Japanized the tango and tango-ized the Japanese character by having him play the bandoneón—symbolic of tango music—half-squatting, his gaze lost on the horizon. The message seems to be: "Yes! Tango in JAPAN of all places! Isn't that amazing?" Grotesque pastiche, exotic collage, pointing at the unusual encounter: exotic parodies generating parodies of exoticism. Japanese tangueros, when shown this illustration, wince and smile at this Argentinean representation of themselves, much like Argentinean tangueros wince when asked to perform tango in a Valentinesque style. To the exotics, exoticism is also an uncomfortable laugh.

Oiwa Yoshihiro, journalist and president of Porteña Ongaku Dokokai (Association of Porteña Music) expressed an ironic dissatisfaction both with Japanese attempts at performing tango and with Argentine tango creations addressed to suit the Japanese: "I don't like to listen to Japanese tango singers or to watch Japanese *Tango Argentino* performers. We [Japanese] talk and move differently, no matter what. I don't enjoy the tangos written by argentinos inspired by Japanese themes either. They lose their original passion and become too mental, too intellectual" (interview, 1990). Most Japanese and argentinos, however, indulge in their exotic reciprocities, mimicking each other in parodic plays of authenticity and reappropriation of Western exoticism. The "authentic" tango argentino, as created and performed by Argentinean musicians, lyricists, singers, and dancers, retains the prestige of the original, but the original is permanently haunted by exoticism and becomes originally exoticized by the Western core. The Japanese consume and "Japanize" all of it; the Argentinean tangueros produce as much of it as they possibly can.

In 1932, Eduardo Castilla, an Argentine writer, explained the puzzling connections between the tango and Japan in much simpler although no less extravagant terms: "The word 'tango' *is* Japanese. A city and a region of the Empire of the Rising Sun are called like this. One of the five popular celebrations of this country takes this name. [...] But there were a lot of Japanese in Cuba since the mid-eighteenth century. And it was precisely in Cuba where the tango was danced for the first time" (Castilla [1932], quoted in Lara and Roncetti de Panti 1969: 294–295).

Tango's Exotic Travels in Raw Poetics

In this section I give a last overview of tango's adventures around the globe, inspired by the title of Roger Wallis and Krister Malm's book *Big Sounds from Small Peoples* (1984). The result is a bad parody of *Gulliver's Travels*.

FIGURE 5.14   Cover of Luis Alposta's El Tango en Japón *(Buenos Aires: Corregidor, 1987),* drawn by Sigfredo Pastor.

Tango, as a musical and danceable commodity, has been produced, distributed, and consumed within a capitalist market economy hegemonized by "core" powers. As tango manufacturers and investors proliferated at the "core," tango was packaged into various competitive styles and new markets for the consumption of those different tango products were opened both at the "core" and in the world's "periphery." Different tangos thus circulated among producers and consumers of popular music-and-dance located, on the one hand, in Europe and the United States, and, on the other, in peripheral nations such as Argentina and Uruguay. The latter provided not only the "original" tango rhythms and choreographies (that is, the raw material and the labor) but also sensitized consumers for the new, core-refined tango products. The increasing competitiveness of tango refinements and the ambition of the manufacturers soon demanded further market expansion. Thus, other peripheral nations were incorporated into the tango distribution circuit. Turkey, Japan, Finland, and Colombia are some examples of countries that used this marketing strategy successfully.[13]

From the point of view of a political economy of popular music-and-dance, the production and consumption of "noise"[14] and movement have followed the path of what Wallis and Malm (1984) call "big sounds" (to which I add "big steps") originated by "small peoples." Those sounds and steps, however, would not have been "big" without the intervention of "big peoples" who were interested in developing the popular music-and-dance industry of "small peoples." Tango was one of those rhythmic noises-and-movements of "small peoples" that was turned into "big sounds-and-steps" by the investments of "big peoples." Thus tango came to be consumed by the "small peoples" from whom the "big sounds-and-steps" originated, and by still other "small peoples" who were incorporated into the market of "big sounds-and-steps" originated by the labor of other "small peoples." "Small peoples" often became connected to each other through these marketing circuits established by "big peoples."

In previous chapters I have tried to analyze how tango, an originally "small sounds-and-steps" complex, turned "big" through the process of exoticism. Rather than focusing on the technological and marketing aspects of the music industry, I chose to look at the politics of representation involved in the process. I have been interested in understanding how the identities of the "small peoples" (identities of gender, race, class, nation) have been affected as "big peoples" incorporated the tango sounds-and-steps into the capitalist market economy. In so doing, I have tried to explain how, through imperialism, some peoples have come to be "small"; how their sounds-and-steps made it "big"; how this aggrandizing process of exoticism has affected "small peoples" attempting to negotiate their identity, who ask themselves at this point, "Are we small or big?"; and how the "big" among the "small" (the privileged among the colonized) resisted this reshaping of their national identity while the "small" among the "small" (the less privileged among the colonized) benefited from it. I have also tried to describe how "big peoples" who intervened in this process were far from homogeneous, having class, racial, gender, and nationalistic disputes among themselves that generated different receptions of the "small sounds-and-steps" coming from their own small peoples (peasants, urban marginals) as well as from foreign small peoples (the colonized).

This process of representation and rerepresentation undertaken by "big" and "small" peoples (with subsequent "big" and "small" internal confrontations) involved complex negotiations that are difficult to capture when viewed from the perspective of a dry market economy of music-and-dance—a perspective that fails to incorporate the dimension of pleasure (negotiations in terms of Desire and passion).[15] Shifting the focus to the analysis of a parallel (although not independent) world economy of passion has allowed me to move tentatively in this direction, where exoticism and the constitution of identities are paramount. I have been pushed into sketchily generating this alternative framework. Rather than following a "model," I have followed the tango avatars around the globe. Thus, I could see a constant remapping of the world taking place as imperceptible people tangoed from one continental mass to another; in the process they carelessly hummed and redrew the contours so painfully traced by earlier cartographers.

Mapping tango's travels has drawn me into associations with the routes of spices and other exotic goods and has made me realize that this traffic has never been interrupted. The geography of pleasure and the spatial economy of capitalist production and consumption are strongly intertwined. What was pleasurable and valuable, for whom, and how were my main questions as I saw the tango immersed into the traffic of the exotic. The manufacture of exotic sounds and steps and the promotion of markets receptive to these exoticized, pleasurable trends have been analyzed in the context of "core"/colonizer and "periphery"/colonized relationships—relationships in which the colonizer and the colonized (the providers of pleasurable experiences) negotiated issues of representation and identification within a "libidinal economy."[16] I have tried to show how Desire and Passion have been constructed, allocated, and qualified through the manufacturing of exoticism in different cultural spaces ruled by imperialist understandings of who should provide "raw," "primitive" emotionality (passion) for the enjoyment and satisfaction of "civilized" Desire. I have paid special attention to the choreographical labor involved in this process.

In comparing tango with other exotic music-and-dance products (for example, Oriental belly-dancing or French can-can), I have traced categorizations and hierarchizations of exotics suitable to the particular historical cravings of the colonizer. Tango was constituted as a sophisticated New World exotic that provided a particular kind of passion, one that was thrilling because it mirrored the process of "civilization" in its dance/struggle as revealed by the male impersonator of Desire and the female impersonator of Passion; the spectacle as a whole, however, was viewed from the distance of the colonizer's gaze.[17] Exotic products (goods from the colonies made valuable by capitalist interventions) have been marketed (and a "need" for them has been created) among the "civilized" and among the "barbarians" in various stages of "civilization." Exotic aesthetics are reproduced, reappropriated, and re-exoticized among "exotics." Exoticism generates exotic differences and reciprocities. It is inexhaustible in its parodic and mercantile uses of the erotic.

6

From Exoticism to Decolonization

(On the Micropolitics of Concluding)

This chapter contains a story, a counterspell, a protest, a parade, and a series of reflections on the intellectual practices of "Third World" women. As a whole, it is an exercise of active unwinding, a practice of "unlearning," an act of coming closer to the ground, to my language, and to my home. In these pages the colonizer in me will be concluding and my colonized "self" will gain decolonizing terrain.

"First Steps in Tango" is a story that can be read as a feminist, poststructuralist critique of the tango world; "Latest Tango Steps: Postmodern Uses of Passion" is a counterspell against poststructuralist, deconstructionist, and Lacanian psychoanalytic "phallologocentric"[1] occultisms cast in a melodramatic tango mood; "Feminist Uses of 'Third World' Women" is a voiced protest against imperialist deafness within feminism; "Scene Nine: The Postcolonial Encounter" is a choreocritical tango parade of postcolonials crossing postmodern borders; "Female Intellectual Cannibals" and "Female Intellectual Invaders" are reflections that encompass and expand the previous readings concerning some dilemmas faced by female intellectuals searching for decolonization.

First Steps in Tango[2]

Don Beto was a cheap womanizer (*chinitero*, as they used to say) and, eventually, my paternal grandfather. He taught me how to dance the tango. Twenty-five years later, twenty after his death, I came to realize what those gazes and complicitist smiles dazzled across the festive living-room meant. The women of my family shared a secret. Don Beto, now *"el abuelo* Alberto" to his grandchildren, was once *un arrabalero*: an expert in the Buenos Aires underworld. The tango as he danced it could only have been learned through systematic, night-long practicing at brothels and cabarets. I was benefiting from a skill my grandfather had acquired embracing prostitutes and milonguitas (cabaret tango dancers). El abuelo Alberto did not participate in the chuckling ambiance; when we danced tango, he was serious. So was I. Only now I understand that through our tango I was being initiated into the spectacle of sex, class, and power of everyday life.

Don Beto, my abuelo Alberto, was a trespasser, not a transgressor. Like many argentino men of his generation, his nomadic steps were drawn to the crossing of boundaries. He wandered from the protected walls of his family life to the excitement of the cabaret underworld.[3] The signal for his moves was natural: sunrise, sunset. He never questioned the boundaries themselves; household and cabaret were as natural as the paths of the sun. So was the existence of the women confined in both places. Mothers and wives were to be found over here, prostitutes and milonguitas over there. Two worlds inhabited by different social classes. He never needed to ask why. It was a fact.[4] Don Beto *tangueaba* (tangoed) in and out, crossing over, never overtly challenging territories, indirect, tense, comfortably uptight in his irony, like the tango. He had power. A viscous power nurtured by two races of women. A solid bridge of eroticism tailored to his desire. My grandmother, here, washing and perfuming the shirts he wore to the cabaret. Mireya or Margot, there, sending him back home, invigorated by skillful pleasures. For him all women were blank pages on which to write his story. He wrote his story on those feminine bodies: immobilized, restricted in space like pages, equally bound to a household or a cabaret.[5] Honorably privatized or publicly blamed, they were all owned by someone: the same men they were devoted to, the men they loved. The tangueros like Don Beto were invested with this viscous power: a power produced of simmered erotic passion. So what was he so serious about?

Si soy así, que voy a hacer,	If I'm like this, what am I to do,
nací buen mozo y embalao para el	I was born good looking and wound up
querer.	for love.
Si soy así, que voy a hacer,	If I'm like this, what am I to do,
con las mujeres no me puedo	with women I can't restrain myself.
contener.	
[...]	[...]
Si soy así, que voy a hacer,	If I'm like this, what am I to do,
es el destino que me lleva a serte	it is destiny that makes me be unfaithful
infiel.	to you.

—*Si Soy Así* (If I'm Like This), 1931
Lyrics by Antonio Botta
Music by Francisco Lomuto

Don Beto's tango was pure tension, cyclic struggle in its steps, frozen conflict at the moment of resolution. He led, I followed. My eyes on the floor, attentive to the intricacy of the footwork. Tight embrace, straight torsos, never leaning on each other. Our gazes never met, nor should they. A slow run, walking in between each other's feet, facing directly toward one angle of the room, stop. Abruptly. This was the moment of the fancy figures with no displacement: the "eight," "double eight," the "hooks," the "backwards crossings" ... a sharp turn. A tense stillness. A new diagonal runaway, another bundling of legs. Every movement was contrasting in itself and with the next. Carefully entangled and incommunicatively connected from the first to the last musical time. ...[6] Suddenly the singer was louder.[7]

Quién sos, que no puedo salvarme,	Who are you, that I can't protect myself,
muñeca maldita castigo de Dios. [...]	damned doll curse of God. [...]
Por vos se ha cambiado mi vida [...]	Because of you my life has turned [...]
en un bárbaro horror de problemas	into a barbarous problem-filled horror
que atora mis venas y enturbia mi	that clogs my veins and stains my honor.
honor.	
[...]	[...]
No puedo reaccionar,	I cannot react,
ni puedo comprender,	nor can I understand,
perdido en la tormenta	lost in the storm
de tu voz que me embrujó, ...	of your voice that bewitches me, ...
la seda de tu piel que me estremece	the silkiness of your skin that makes me shiver
y al latir florece, con mi perdición.	and that flourishes thanks to my throbbing, and my ruin.

—*Secreto* (Secret), 1932
Lyrics and music by Enrique S. Discépolo

No smiles. Tangos are male confessions of failure and defeat, a recognition that men's sources of empowerment are also the causes of their misery. Women, mysteriously, have the capacity to use the same things that imprison them—including men—to fight back.[8] Tangos report repeated female attempts at evasion, the permanent danger of betrayal. The strategy consists basically in seducing men, making them feel powerful and safe by acting as loyal subordinates, and in the midst of their enchantment of total control, the tamed female escapes. The viscous power crystallizes. The tanguero witnesses, horrified, how the blank, inert pages on which he was writing his story grow an irregular thickness of their own. Female bodies are, actually, docile bodies in rebellion.[9] This is the tension of the tango, the struggle condensed in the dance. Don Beto doesn't talk about it. If you are doing the tango properly, conversations are sacrilegious.[10] The lyrics say everything that needs to be said. So listen.

No te dejes engañar,	Heart,
corazón,	don't let yourself be fooled,
por su querer,	by her caring,

por su mentir.	by her lies.
No te vayas a olvidar	Don't you go and forget
que es mujer,	that she is a woman,
y que al nacer	and that from birth
del engaño hizo un sentir.	it was her nature to deceive.
[...]	[...]
Falsa pasión,	False passion,
¡No te engañes! ... Corazón.	Heart ... don't fool yourself!

—*No te Engañes Corazón* (Heart, Don't Fool Yourself), 1926
Lyrics and music by Rodolfo Sciamarella

The lyrics keep on repeating the same story; plagiarizing again and again the same plot:[11]

¡Decí, por Dios, que me has dao	Tell me, by God, what you've given me
que estoy tan cambiao ...	that I'm so changed ...
no sé más quien soy! ...	I no longer know who I am! ...
El malevaje extrañao	The puzzled gang
me mira sin comprender.	looks at me without understanding.
[...]	[...]
Te vi pasar tangueando altanera,	I saw you pass by, tangoing arrogantly,
con un compás tan hondo y sensual,	with a beat so deep and sensual,
que no fue más que verte y perder	that just one look at you and I lost
la fe, el coraje, el ansia e'guapear. ...	my faith, courage, and the eagerness to fight. ...
No me has dejao ni el pucho en la oreja	You haven't left me even the cigarette behind my ear
de aquel pasao malevo y feroz.	from that rough and ferocious past.
Ya no me falta pa' completar	Now I don't lack anything to complete the picture
mas que ir a misa e hincarme a	but to go to church and get down on my knees and pray.
rezar.	

—*Malevaje* (Gang of Ruffians), 1928
Lyrics by Enrique S. Discépolo
Music by Juan de D. Filiberto

The dance continues. No harmony between the bodies, just the rhythm holding us together; the rhythm of fate. He leads, I follow. Tight embrace; no leaning on each other.[12] Don Beto prepares the stand; we are at the critical angle. Torsos stiff, feet in vertigo. My legs cut the air in all directions. He leads, but no one follows him now.

The voices of my brothers around the dinner table are suddenly audible; so are the kitchen noises. The family party is at its peak. Don Beto starts muttering "*Yira, yira,*" the tango philosophy treatise. He picks up his hat and leaves.

Cuando la suerte que es grela,	When lady luck,
fayando y fayando,	failing and failing,
te largue parao. [...]	stands you up. [...]
¡La indiferencia del mundo	The indifference of the world
—que es sordo y es mudo—	—that is deaf and mute—
recién sentirás!	only then will you feel!
Verás que todo es mentira,	You'll see that everything is a lie,
verás que nada es amor,	you'll see that nothing is love,
que al mundo nada le importa. ...	that to the world nothing is important. ...
¡Yira! ... ¡Yira! ...	It turns! ... It turns! ...

—*Yira ... Yira* (It Turns ... It Turns), 1930
Lyrics and music by Enrique S. Discépolo

Don Beto is not worried. He knows this is what life is all about. Sooner or later, I would be caught in another tango. New embraces and infinite rebellions. He had done his job.

Latest Tango Steps: Postmodern Uses of Passion

I wish to slip into your thoughts,[13] into the music of your untamable reflections, with the broken noise of my tango: a repetitive, syncopated, wet lamentation over postmodernism's absurd wound. You see, "I come from a country / turned permanently gray by forgetfulness," where "small pieces of memory and displeasure / drip into a lazy, slow [but insidious] grumble" and where tears turn into curses, there, in the "deep underground / where the mud subverts."[14] In this tango-mood I offer some choreographed contours of postmodernism as perceived by *una Otra*—a female latina Other from the South of the world. *El Sur también existe.*[15]

This chapter is a twisted ethnography of postmodernism in which postmodernism stands for the culture of late, postindustrial capitalism and for the paradigmatic philosophy of influential intellectual inhabitants of the First World.[16] The bold anthropologist who performs this dizzy analysis attempts to resist, through her interpretation of postmodernism, the imperialist shadow of postcoloniality. Eager to subvert postmodern teachings that attempt to naturalize and universalize the hectic despair and desperation of capitalism's most recent crisis, I invoke my tangos. The result is a challenging moan over postmodernism, a melodramatic attack in which I appropriate postmodernist strategies (poststructuralism, deconstruction, Lacanian psychoanalysis, postfeminist and postcolonial writings) in order to trick back rather than to unmask postmodern-

ism. Since it responds to a provocation, this is a strongly prejudiced interpretation, a move to join in what Artaud called "the right to lie" (Antonin Artaud,
quoted in Escobar 1988: 133)—that is, to accept the risk of exaggerating.[17]
Tangoing a passionate counterspell I intend to reverse postmodernism's curse.[18]

Through these pages, I (*una Otra*) depict "postmodernism" as a culture of Desire: A desire obsessed with passion. This obsession leads "postmodernists" to
pursue consumption passionately and to consume passion conspicuously. Unlike natural resources, passion, when it is subjected to conspicuous consumption, is not necessarily exhausted or depleted. Desire is fueled by passion, but it
also generates more of it, provoking an oozing fermentation and scooping out
the most precious part, right at the bottom. Exotic others laboriously cultivate
passionate-ness in order to be desired, consumed, and thus recognized in a
world increasingly ruled by postmodern standards. Autoexoticism plays an essential part in this regenerative process of identification, performing that value
that exudes a surplus without which there is no survival.[19] Autoexotically I return to the tango. It is my only solid resource. Tango is my strategic language, a
way of talking about, understanding, and responding to postmodernism from
an absurd position. Tango is a practice already ready for struggle. It knows about
taking sides and risks. And it knows about accusing and whining, about making
intimate confessions in public. Tango knows how to make a spectacle of its cruel
destiny. So here I am, with a tango on postmodernism.

This tango, like most tangos, stages a first person,[20] a possessive account in a
highly personalized voice of an "I" struggling to stand on her feet, untrustfully
relying on the strength of intimacy. Rather than representing or standing for,
tango's "I" attempts to move, to create in its audience of readers, musicians, and
dancers a co-motion, an empathy that will permit overcoming the grotesque nature of the "I"—that pretentious "I" claiming to be something or someone. In
tango lyrics, the "I" dangerously curves around ridicule as it exposes the need to
be interpreted. So that it can actually speak, the tango language needs to constitute an equally imperfect and human, personalized receptor/interpreter. Tango's "I" is dialogical and "sings nostalgically the loss of itself as it becomes an
other" (Panesi 1990: 22). To write tangos, then, is to write in a first person that will
be inhabited by others. Those who listen, sing, dance, read, and play tangos are
expected to introject their identities into them in a dialogue that curiously retains the tango "I" (Kamenszain 1990).

This tango, like most tangos, should be murmured, restrained between the
lips with precise difficulty, neither active nor passive (García 1990). In tangos, the
(active) subject denounces impotence and the (passive) object reveals the vital
powers of fate. Tangos perform an almost perfect exhaustion in their sentimental accusations of betrayal, skirting banality—tango's closest foe.

This tango, like most tangos, asks to be heard in a state of ironic distance. Tangos tell impossible truths (Panesi 1990) and repeat them up to that point at
which truth becomes a farce. Tango-voices display gendered parodies of dis-

grace: These voices are feminized in falsettos and broken by sobs and alcohol when sung by rundown men; masculinized by deep, sarcastic, streetwise nuances when sung by fallen women. Tango-voices create a space for disbelief alongside the earnest words of tango lyrics. Tango-voices seem to mock what they are saying and to place a scornful doubt on the identity of those who are saying it. Who is this "I," this Otra, seriously yet ironically claiming alterity?[21]

Don Beto was a cheap womanizer (chinitero, as they used to say) and, eventually, my paternal grandfather. He taught me how to dance the tango. Only now I understand that through our tango I was being initiated into the spectacle of sex, class, and power of everyday life. Postmodernism asks us to dance, intensely, a fantastic choreography rendered in the genre of horror-fiction. I read challenge in the postmodern attitude: a passionless invitation to perform Otherness passionately. Like a milonguita, I follow the steps of my postmodern partner, and I resist.

Don Beto, my abuelo Alberto, was a trespasser, not a transgressor. Like many argentino men of his generation, his nomadic steps were drawn to the crossing of boundaries. He never questioned the boundaries themselves. Don Beto tangueaba (tangoed) in and out, crossing over, never overtly challenging territories, indirect, tense, comfortably uptight in his irony, like the tango. He had power. A viscous power nurtured by two races of women. A solid bridge of eroticism tailored to his desire. The tangueros like Don Beto were invested with this viscous power: a power produced of simmered erotic passion. One of postmodernism's most elaborated stratagems is that of intellectual seduction. This "fatal stratagem," to put it in Jean Baudrillard's words, seems to be the rule and the limit of the postmodern game. Passion is the necessary thrust of intellectual play. Illusory and embodied participants become interchangeable players. In the guts of a postmodern, outbursts of committed passion are futile; what counts is the tension involved in seducing.

Postmodernism is the delirious political enterprise of meticulous actors, both thinkers and unthinkers: busy burrowers attempting to reveal the simultaneity of all mysteries only to leave them half bitten, exposed to erosion. First, its members think of themselves as endangered, as survivors of the modern world driven into a chaotic vertigo provoked by their own intellectual arrogance. Second, postmoderns reproduce the cult of instrumentality and efficiency, indefatigably obsessed with the discovery-and-development of "strategies" even though they disbelieve in human agency and its outcomes faced with the powers of chance. Third, the inhabitants of postmodernism question the possibility of a true self and worship an Other within a fragmented oneness, establishing the fragmentation of that which *does not* exist. Fourth, in the eyes of a postmodernist, life is a perpetual homesickness in a disharmonious world where we happen to miss experiences that actually never occurred and where desire for that which is impossible maintains the necessary tension to keep on living. Fifth, the postmodern world is ruled by Discourse, a powerful divinity—although not supernatural—

that controls and normalizes humans by exerting untraceable bureaucratic violence on their/our bodies; the subjects of Discourse are accomplices in this process by way of practicing techniques of self-formation or "subjectification." Sixth, postmodernists are prone to look at the world as a text, to rewrite what has been written, practicing a meticulous unwriting process named deconstruction, and are haunted by an unwritten volume that nevertheless has a well-known title and author: *The History of Bodies* by Michel Foucault. Seventh, postmodern intellectuals apply a strenuous genealogical and archaeological method in order to make sense of their own history based on exploring silences, repetitions, and difference, but they mistrust their own interpretations of past events just as much as they disbelieve traditional master narratives and all story-telling.

Needless to say, the list could be expanded. But my intention is to point out the proliferation of unsettling paradoxes present in the postmodern "ethos." Paradoxes are dramatized through images and scenarios of black mysticism. Think of Georges Bataille's exhibition of curses, sacrifice, and the ecstasied vertigos of mysticism and eroticism;[22] Jean Baudrillard's panicked explorations of the seductive power of obscenely exuberant signs;[23] Jacques Derrida's frenzy for erosion, chasing difference and crypts;[24] Michel Foucault's invitations to ritualized transgressions and to the contemplation of bodily horrors;[25] Jacques Lacan's impossible discoveries of cosmic terror such as the constitutive wound/split of the self, the impossibility of communication and the nonexistence of women;[26] Jean-François Lyotard's inflammatory callings to accept, beyond rejection, that domination and exploitation are desired, enjoyed by the libidinal bodies of its victims, a phenomenon that his libidinal economists should not subject to interpretation but rather witness, read, and keep in writing.[27] How to survive these occultist postmodern enterprises and their persuasive findings? Could it be through passion and by trusting the power of passion?

Don Beto's tango was pure tension, cyclic struggle in its steps, frozen conflict at the moment of resolution. He led, I followed. Our gazes never met. Passion is one of those feelings of impossible conceptual definition but also strong experiential presence. Passion is a performance, more of an "enacting" than an "acting-out," in which both actors and spectators are staged spectacularizing each other as entangled objects/subjects. According to Baudrillard (1984: 105, 119), passion is a "desperate and beautiful *movement*" of which everything could be said and yet, we know not what to say. It seems an impossible task to engage passion discursively without performing passionateness, without folding into a tense, polarized, rhythmic movement involving some kind of excess.[28] What constitutes "passion" varies, of course, sociogeographically, socioeconomically, sociopolitically, and sociohistorically, and the particular configuration of a passional universe, to a certain extent, allows one to define cultural specificities. An emotion, a statement or behavior regarded as passionate in one context, can be interpreted as "normal" in another, and these judgments often depend on how and where the threshold demarcating surplus or excess is established within a specific scale of "sensitivity"—a moral and political reading of physiology. Eugenio Trías, in his *Tratado de la Pasión* (1991), provides one example of this mimesis. After allegedly resisting to define passion for more than one hundred pages (a fact to which he calls attention), he finally succumbs (in his own words), laying out "a sextuple, although hypothetical statement" (thereby delivering an excess in a defensive state of full awareness):

1) Passion is something that the soul suffers. [...]
2) Passion is something that takes possession of the soul/subject [...]
3) Passion is something that insists on the pure repetition of itself beyond the resistances and obstacles that it builds for itself. This dialectic of insistence and resistance is the foundation of what we here call the passional subject.
4) Passion is habit, *habitus*, in the literal sense of the term [...]: it is the memory that the subject has of itself [...]
5) Passion is that excess at the core that commits the subject to the sources of its being, alienating and foundational at the same time. It is the *essence* of the subject (unconscious alterity that lays the basis for the subject's identity and sameness, the root of its strength and of its nontransferable power).
6) Passion is that which can carry the subject to its ruin, the condition that enables its rescue and redemption: it is that which creates and recreates subjectivity through its own immolation and sacrifice. Hence, its trying places are those of death, madness, crime, and transgression (Trías 1991: 126–127).

Western ethics and epistemologies from the Greeks to the stoics, to Descartes, Spinoza, Kant, and German idealism, to cite but a few moments of stardom, have produced variations on the sole theme of establishing *logos* or reason as a premise for a free, potent, and lucid subjectivity by conquering the always-threatening passions (Trías 1991; Rouanet 1987; Lebrun 1987). The differences within and among these schools and authors are very important, but my wicked tango only pays attention to points of repetition. Body politics have been at stake all along, and more precisely, gendered body politics: the feminine passions seductively luring the masculine qua human Ethos, Reason, or Desire (the focus changed with the times), provoking the necessary conquest. Theories of passions, whether philosophical or psychological, adopt the form of taxonomies—classifying and hierarchizing passions—and operate through paradigmatic oppositional categories, linking passions not only to reason but also to actions, again of an active or passive, sacred or profane, moral or amoral, social or antisocial, life- or death-driven nature. The creation and conceptualization of the universe of passions and their dynamics, moralized by stoics and Christians, economized by the theoreticians of value and interest, or medicalized by scientific psychology, always engage in politics of exclusion and inclusion, contention, and some kind of social world Order(ing). The confrontation of "legitimate versus illegitimate passions," at some obscure point between romanticism[29] and postmodernism, becomes a globalized, fluid dance partnering Desire and Passion, each keeping the other alive. The question of who has the right to revolt now returns, repressed, as "Is it possible to revolt?" At some point, Western civilization's discontents have shifted from problematizing passions to apathy, from discussing domestication to questioning mobilization, where virulence is the everlasting symptom.

Passion and its lack, containment and its shadow-mirrors of propagation and intensification, run in circles, chasing the minds of traditional philosophical foes up to the point of creating unthinkable alliances. Hegel and Nietzsche, for example, shared a profound admiration for passion's capacity to actualize/actorialize excess.

> Here we use the term *pathos* at a higher level, without any hint of censorship or selfishness. Antigone's sacred love for her brother, for example, is such that it consists of a *pathos* in the greek sense of the word [...]. Orestes kills his mother not under the dominion of one of those internal compulsions of the soul that we would call passion; the *pathos* that leads him to this action is well thought out and reflected upon. [...] *Pathos* should be limited to those kinds of human actions and it must be thought of as the essential rational content present in the human "I", which takes hold of and penetrates the whole soul. Nothing truly great could be accomplished without passion (Hegel 1953: 314–315).

> [Passion ...] is the condition in which one is the least capable of being just; narrow-minded, ungrateful to the past, blind to dangers, deaf to warnings, one is a little vortex of life in a dead sea of darkness and oblivion; and yet this condition is the womb not only of the unjust but of every just deed too [...]. The greatest deeds take place in such a superabundance of love (Nietzsche 1983: 64).

"Greatness" bridges, somehow, the pits of violence (Hegel's hero's murder; Nietzsche's hero's injustice) when passion is equated with that "compulsion that takes hold of the soul" or to that "vortex of life" that makes humans human. What constitutes this "greatness," however, is not passion itself but rather who the hero/heroine was and on whose side was the one telling the story.

Agnes Heller, in *A Theory of Feelings*, states that the need for a "unified evaluation of passions [...] belongs to the realm of problems of bourgeois society" and that every passion comprises, at the same time, a "grandeur"—something significant—and a problematic aspect. The greatness dwells in the intensity of the involvement—commitment—provoked by passions; the danger, in pushing aside or extinguishing other emotions—the "wealth of feelings" (Heller 1979: 109–110). To which I would add the danger of pushing aside the emotions of diverse intensity of all those people whose passions have no space in the realms of either greatness or wealth.

Interestingly, rather than exploring these vast uncertainties, postmodern authors have chosen to scrutinize the wound of "nothingness": that state of exhaustion and perplexity in between one outburst of passion and the next, the indifferent soft stone out of which events are carved. The melancholic longing of Sartre has finally been resolved in the stubborn lack of Lacan.[30] Passion and excess are there, only to flush humans—whether in a state of ecstasy or bored to death—down the flowing abyss. This unavoidable postmodern drive is called Desire.

Having said this, I risk giving a name to the unnameable mythical postmodern object of Desire—the ungraspable desire that circulates, unqualified like the breath of a phantom, through every postmodern text, speech, and life ... desire for the desiring Other, desire for other's Desire.[31] This longing, this lack, this vacuum that keeps the world stumbling rather than illusively flowing is the fearful desire for passion.[32]

Translated into tango-tongue, the postmodern desire would be something like a fearful passion, and the postmodern attitude, a "sentimental education" in cultivating a passion for fear.[33]

> Fear of soft talk from the enemy, but even much more fear of the unexpected dagger jumping into the recently befriended hand, piercing our open breast or annihilating us from the back. And then, who knows, in that "fear that sterilizes embraces" we might discover that it is neither this nor that, something or someone that we fear, not even fear of our own shadow, only fear of fearfulness. Scare, dread, fright. Anguish, metaphysical fear without object, everything and nothing serves it to self-consummation until it reaches the apex: fear of fear. [...] The saddest among the sad passions. [...] Anyone who has felt it, knows (Chaui 1987: 39).

But the postmodern version of fear is anxiety.[34] Destruction, death, and betrayal are no surprise and pain is expected. God and Man are dead, but Evil is still alive and kicking.[35] Its doings are no longer the doings of a blasphemous creature but are human doings; the doings of Others, but the Other is now also within the self.[36] "The anonymous other that is always 'within' splits the subject, leaving it a bit 'cracked' " (Taylor 1987: 81, paraphrasing Maurice Merleau-Ponty). The paranoid delirium of the postmodern soul is nourished by this anxiety. How long will it take until the next stroke of panic occurs? Who will I be after my next transgression? From where will the next blow come? Postmodern words of wisdom respond: "It is all on the surface; watch the play of surfaces." Moreover, Bataille recommends adopting the laughter of the idiot and Foucault's advice is to culti-

vate stupidity (Foucault 1977a: 107–109). Irony and cynicism are *passé* since they
retain the conceit of a certain wisdom. The stupid either enjoys or gets in trouble
without knowing it; the idiot commits cruelties and heroic deeds irresponsibly.
Postmodern wisdom prescribes unawareness before and after the event/catas-
trophe: the outburst of passion. *No smiles. Tangos are male confessions of failure
and defeat, acts of recognition that men's sources of empowerment are also the
causes of their misery. The viscous power crystallizes. … Female bodies are, actually, docile bodies in rebellion. Don Beto doesn't talk about it.*

Postmodernism is neither an epoch nor an attitude.[37] It is a historically specific skill. Fear has become a passion; the anticipation of fear, an obsession; the
domestication of fear, passionlessness. In Todd Gitlin's words, postmodernism is
the passionate pursuit of passionlessness (Gitlin 1989: 347). Apathy does not
mean insensitivity; it is rather a biopsy of passion. But the postmodern version
of asceticism is a perverse skill: On the one hand, it is an intensified awareness of
the dangerousness of passion; on the other, it is the desperate amplification of
the search for passionate experiences. In short, postmoderns attempt to master
passion—to develop apathy—both through panic and obscenity: They engage
in the multiplication of passion to the limit of the impossible and the sacrifice,
the annihilation, of that which was purposefully multiplied.

The trick by which the postmodern "ascete" piles up the passionate material
to be burnt in sacrifice consists in another skill: the proliferation of Otherness.
"Passion is always provoked by the presence or image of something that leads us
to react, in general unexpectedly. It is a sign of one's permanent dependency on
the Other. An autocratic being would not have passions" (Lebrun 1987: 18). The
postmodernist nurtures his or her passion by the presence or image of Others—
others who define the self, reassuring identity. However, the postmodern identity does not rely on sameness; it is unstable, permanently reshaped by the proliferation of Otras/Others, an Other/Otra even within the self. "A passion. And, as
in 'jouissance,' where the object of desire, known as object 'a,' bursts with the
shattered mirror where the ego gives up its image in order to contemplate itself
in the Other, there is nothing either objective or objectal to the abject. It is simply a frontier, a repulsive gift that the Other […] drops so that the 'I' does not disappear in it but finds, in that sublime alienation, a forfeited existence" (Kristeva
1982: 9). La Otra/Other is a provocateur of the floating Self and a provider of passion. La Otra/Other must provide the necessary excitement for the postmodern
playing with the Self.

La Otra's voice is my mother tongue, a tango-tongue. I quote Elizam Escobar,
a postmodern artist, to explain what this means:

> For the so-called First World the art and culture of the so-called Third World is
> the art and culture of the exotic (in Nietzsche's words, not only those who are
> on the outside but, contrary to the esoterics, those who look from "down-up")
> and in the best cases, it is the object of the true fascination with the unknown

and the Other. The tango is one of such art forms, in it there is aggression and seduction, drama and form, passion and control. An image that may have seduced [...] as a symbolic link between the European predominantly logocentric mentality and the 'natural' surreality of Latin America (Escobar 1988: 125).

Tangueros (tango dancers, singers, composers, musicians, poets, and fans) are invited to perform on the postmodern stage on these terms: as passionate, "exotic" spectacles of themselves.

The passion of the Other is being permanently recycled: sacrificed and re-created through new real or imagined Others. The postmodernist, a critic of Enlightenment colonialism, who cannot help but pursue further colonialist rationalizations, is an incorrigible "voyeur," an untamed predator and a skillful ascete. Colonialists and postmodernists write the history of humankind and reserve for themselves the leading role, be it as winners or losers.

Postmodernism is a corroding skill, like that of a circus freak who learns to chew on blades, to swallow fire, and to sleep on beds of nails; it is an exploration in the realm of pain carried out by those who see pain from a distance, who find it uninteresting to admit the experience of pain as an unavoidable stroke on their lives. For those for whom both pain and feeling, in the sense of "getting involved in something,"[38] are a choice—a question of strategy, a spectacle.

A "true" postmodernist is a strategist; her or his passion is to feel above or below, beyond or before the miseries of the world (in postmodernistic jargon, the world is a text; imperialist strategists assume the world is a map; in the courts of Louis XIV, the world was a *ballet opéra*; in Disneyland, the world is a bunch of singing dolls ...) fueled by the passion for passionlessness: the sacrifice of imported passion. Las Otras/Others—any Otra detected as a potential provider of the "real" passion still available on the planet—are invoked and invited to participate in the postmodern duel. Fiesta, women, tango, tortures, lotus blossoms, guerrillas, palm trees and tropical beaches, *desaparecidos, vírgenes,* flamenco, more women, blacks, Noriega, more violence, Colombia, Oriental veils, some more dictators, drugs, colored women, and so on.

Others provide the passion of the "one [who], full of hopes, seeks / the road that dreams / promised in response to his [or her] yearnings. [...]"

Pero un frío cruel	But a cruel coldness
que es peor que el odio,	that is worse than hatred,
punto muerto de las almas,	dead end of the souls,
tumba horrenda de mi amor,	horrendous tomb for my love,
maldijo para siempre y me robó	cursed me forever and robbed me
toda ilusión.	of all illusion.

—Uno (One), 1943
Lyrics by Enrique S. Discépolo
Music by Mariano Mores

To which postmoderns respond, transposing existential terms:

> But there is something stronger than passion: illusion. Stronger than sex or
> happiness: the passion for illusion. Seducing, always seducing. Breaking the
> erotic power with the furious strength of gambling and stratagem—building
> some traps into the same vertigo, and continuing to endure mastery of the
> ironic paths of hell in the seventh heaven—this is seduction, the shape of the
> illusion, the malign genius of passion (Baudrillard 1984: 119).

While las Otras face the precariousness of passion, postmoderns playfully
thicken every wound. Postmodernism enters into politics unexpectedly, making
a spectacular use of Others' passion. Cultivating apathy, postmoderns join the
power game by coming out of the trapdoor. But tango taught me that in this
dance of life (whether colonial, neocolonial, imperialist, or postcolonial) there
are no winners; only final musical times with a couple, incommunicatively connected, exhibiting frozen conflict at the moment of the resolution. And there is
always another tango: new dangerous embraces and infinite rebellions.

Don Beto starts muttering "Yira, yira," the tango philosophy treatise. He picks
up his hat and leaves. Don Beto is not worried. He knows this is what life is all
about. Sooner or later, I would be caught in another tango. New embraces and in-
finite rebellions. He had done his job. Foucault does his[39] tangoing that: "There is
no prediscursive fate disposing the world in our favor."

Female Intellectual Cannibals

> Prospero invaded the islands, killed our ancestors, enslaved Caliban, and
> taught him his language to make himself understood. What else can Caliban
> do but use that same language—today he has no other—to curse him, to wish
> that the "red plague" would fall on him? (Fernández Retamar 1989: 14).

Caliban—that rude, savage figure of Shakespeare's *Tempest;* that condensa-
tion of alterity evoked through the exotic image of the cannibal; that displacement of barbarism and murder projected from the conqueror onto the enslaved—makes use of the language of the colonizer to deconstruct colonialism,
to chew it up cannibalistically and to transform it. Caliban, as interpreted by
Aimé Césaire, Edward Brathwaite, Roberto Fernández Retamar, and others un-
derstands his condition by misunderstanding (subverting colonizing intentions)
and positions himself through mis-takes (taking that which he is not supposed
to take). The resulting calibanesque vision implies rethinking imperialism from
the *other* side (not the outside).

What are the viewpoints, the tongues, the shapes, the steps, and the thrusts
mobilized by these *other* protagonists—those embodied inheritors of colonial-

ism, imperialism, postcolonial nationalisms, and globalization, now aware of their gendered differences, class alliances, racial, ethnic, and cultural hybridiy performing large-scale nomadism? In an attempt to disturb those speculations that assert the imprisonment of Calibans, Calibanas, their descendants, and their future within colonially/linguistically imposed limits, I enact minor insurgencies in these written explorations while struggling with the issues of autoexoticism and self-marginalization.

"First Steps in Tango" and "Latest Tango Steps: Postmodern Uses of Passion" are the marrow of this book, my "motives" all along. Both are autobiographical fictions in the sense that they offer a personal interpretation of certain events in my life that have become significant for contextual/political reasons. "Latest Tango Steps: Postmodern Uses of Passion" is actually a counterspell for my *latest* tango steps and the most recent event from which I look back at my *first* tango incursions. These are parodic reconstructions. I am not concerned about how "objectively" true or false these accounts are; rather, I am concerned about the points, political points, I am trying to make. I don't want my voice to have all dimensions. I want it to be harsh (Fanon 1988). My voice has been lost in a multiplicity of dimensions for too long. None of those dimensions proved to be mine. Thus, both the story and the counterspell have the purpose of advancing some insights within a project of decolonization, starting with the decolonization of myself. They are attempts at *unlearning*.

Both the First and the Latest Tango Steps share a common plot; they describe rituals of initiation and focus on the protagonist's (first person, myself) "passing" through these rituals. The First Steps depict my initiation into the male world (patriarchy); the Latest Steps, into a particular kind of academic discourse—poststructuralism, deconstruction, Lacanian psychoanalysis—that promised liberation but proved to be paralyzing (colonialist). The fact that I have isolated these particular moments as rituals of passage does not mean that "experiences" of patriarchy and/or colonialism are reduced to that first tango or to these latest academic teachings. The pinpointing is rather my reconstruction of episodes of awareness, of breaking through patriarchy and colonialism.

In addition, by labeling the tango as patriarchal and postmodernism as colonial I do not wish to imply that the tango lacks colonizing features or that postmodernism is free of patriarchal shades. Precisely for these reasons I attempt to analyze tango within a colonial process of exoticization and to immerse poststructuralism, et al., into a setting of passion—female passion in opposition to male desire.[40]

Since I have been patriarchially and colonially trained in tango and postmodernism, I have tried to reveal a sequence of reinforcement between the two as well as their rupture by using one against the other. On the one hand, the Latest Steps are a new round of the First Steps, a repetition of an episode of subjection that was foreshadowed in the First Steps. (*Always the same story. ... Don Beto was not worried. He knew that sooner or later I would fall into new embraces and end-*

less rebellions.) This repetition confirms the fatalism that I have internalized through both tango and postmodernism. On the other hand, the rupture of this repetition is performed by using one against the other: tango to jump on postmodernism and poststructuralist-deconstructive-feminist strategies to question the tango. For this purpose, I attempt to avoid following the political agendas of either one. I apply some of their strategies—tricks that, by the way, are extremely similar. Compare the following teachings:

> When lady luck,
> failing and failing,
> stands you up. [...]
> The indifference of the world
> —that is deaf and mute—
> only then will you feel!
> You'll see that everything is a lie,
> you'll see that nothing is love,
> that to the world nothing is important. ...
> It turns! ... It turns! ... (Discépolo 1930: *Yira ... Yira*).

We should not imagine that the world presents us with a legible face, leaving us merely to decipher it; it does not work hand in glove with what we already know; there is no prediscursive fate disposing the world in our favor (Foucault 1971: 22).

> It's the same
> to be straight or crooked ...
> ignorant, wise or a thief,
> generous or chiseling! ...
> All is equal!
> None is better!
> A donkey's the same as a chaired professor!
> There are no rankings
> nor losers,
> the immoral have made us all equal.
> [...]
> It's the same if you're a priest,
> mattress-stuffer, the king of clubs,
> poker-faced or a stow-away! (Discépolo 1935: *Cambalache*).

Stupidity says ... "Here or there, it's always the same thing. ... It's all so senseless—life, women, death! How ridiculous this stupidity!" But in concentrating on this boundless monotony, we find the sudden illumination of multiplicity itself—with nothing at its center, at its highest point, or beyond it (Foucault 1977c: 189).

In addition, the choreography of the tango emphasizes movements that resemble very closely the deconstructive/poststructuralist writing strategies: splitting, inversion, displacement, decentering, juxtaposition, transposition, silence ... (Derrida 1976). And in both cases, what gives particular character to them is the combination of the dancing and writing steps so as to generate tension, conflict, a play of domination and resistance that never ends. Tango and poststructuralism, et al., also share a focus on marginality, one coming from the fringes of society and the other looking at the margins of the text and the silences surrounding discourse (de Certeau 1986).

Poststructuralism refreshed my memories of tango and provided me with a scholarly discourse to write about it; at the same time, tango allowed me to perform poststructuralist strategies quite "comfortably"—with the sense of ownership, of dancing the tango—and it pushed me into a critique of the multivocal, multilayered game. "Latest Tango Steps: Postmodern Uses of Passion" is actually a tango about postmodernism—a tango in prose, melodramatic like the tango. It is a tango account of postmodernism, as the First Steps are a poststructuralist, feminist account of tango (caricatures, representations suited to what I wish to emphasize, both ways). Postmodernism is a universalizing, naturalizing, and totalizing version of the cynicism and fatalism displayed by the tango. This is what I have tried to express in the "Latest Tango Steps."

My "attack" on postmodernism is an attack on an imperial attitude. The questioning of enlightenment modernist thought is often mistaken for a promise of liberation and is an academic exercise practiced with scarce acknowledgment of Third World specificities. The allegories of writing and textuality, discourse and power as used by deconstructivists and poststructuralists are not just imperfect but are also misleading in that they focus on a particular kind of text and a particular kind of subject constitution. They dismiss the existence of a differently worlded world. The understanding of the Western worldling of the world and the commitment to a complex "Third World" beyond those master Western texts is thereby compromised.[41] *Don Beto* tangueba *(tangoed) ... indirect, tense, comfortably uptight in his irony. For him all women were blank pages on which to write his story.* The practice of deconstruction, with no recognized moorings and no explicit history, and the Eurocentric teachings of poststructuralism contribute to the reproduction of a discourse of scientificity where political interests, passions, and values seem to be absent, not because they are undeclared but rather because they are regarded as philosophically unconducive, incalculable, uninteresting, or beyond the scope of the academic. Since scholars are mainly recognized as interested in reproducing their own class, poststructuralists and deconstructionists focus, narcissistically, on their own strategic practices. Scholars are invited to reflect on their privilege while history continues its violent course apparently in a different domain without intellectual interference.[42] *Our gazes never met ... a sharp turn. A tense stillness. A new diagonal runaway, another bundling of legs. Every moment was contrasting in itself and with the next.*

Carefully entangled and incommunicatively connected. Postmodern U.S. academics frequently celebrate the free play of differences for the sake of exposing multiple voices on controversial issues ranging from sexual harassment to the U.S. invasion of Panama. Thus, they subsume the impossibility to establish "the truth" under the comfortable umbrella of relativism and unexamined democratic values. Voices, however, are opinionated and interested utterances, and multivocality operates in a compromised field of contestation.[43] This postmodern project of freedom does not offer anything different from the liberatory promises of the "free-market" development proposal. Technocratically speaking, a "free-market" economy should work fairly and for the mutual benefit of all participants; historically speaking, this is an impossibility. For some this might mean that the "model" has some problems; meanwhile they continue accumulating capital and power; for the others it means continued economic regression and dependency.

The poststructuralist "model" of power-in-continuous-flow that is disputed among controlling discourses, technologies, and pockets of resistance provokes a similar effect: a sense of total disempowerment for the ones in resistance.[44] Postmodern discourse cannot take sides, lost in its loyalty to the consistency of inconsistency, *différance,* multivocality, relativity. Postmodernism is a borderline discourse in that it destabilizes the authority and provokes the outrage of the rationalist conservatives. But to expose the instability is not the same as to destabilize. *Don Beto was a trespasser, not a transgressor. His nomadic steps were drawn to the crossing of boundaries. He never questioned the boundaries themselves ... crossing over, never overtly challenging territories.* The U.S. academic version of postmodernism is a discourse of liberal dissidents, of loosening up. But it is not a discourse of liberation. It does not take the necessary risks in favor of the ones in resistance, and it does not lead intellectuals into questioning their own privileges.[45] The problematic outcome of an exercise of unmasking power, of showing its weak points, without going any further—taking risks—is that it contributes to the awareness of the powerful, who are already in a position to strengthen their alliances. Radicalizing academia certainly has different meanings for U.S. intellectuals in the academy, for intellectuals from underrepresented communities in the United States, and for Third World scholars working at U.S. universities. In addition, the impact of intellectuals in the U.S. context is a debatable issue. Postmodernism has not helped to put intellectual skills to work purposefully for political intervention. And yet, no matter how protected they are in their privilege, U.S. intellectuals do have an impact in politics, at the very least by default.[46] Postmodernism is a crude description of late capitalism, an account of a capitalist crisis. As such, in Frederic Jameson's words (1984), postmodernism performs an "abolition of critical distance" where the culture and its criticism are one and the same.

Postmodernism is too caught up in the flow of power controlled by the ones in power. *The "tangueros" like Don Beto were invested with this viscous power.* Because they lack a political-economic charting of their ideological production, postmodern intellectuals fail to distinguish their position in the international division of labor and their specific complicity in the reproduction of imperialism. These disavowals lead to political abandon, a political position in itself. Radical postmodernists trust that somehow, resistance to power will emerge, that they will recognize its emergence, that the insurgents will be interested in their alliance, and that as intellectuals they will certainly have something revolutionary to offer.

Cultural critique is replaced with critical culture—hence postmodernism as the "cultural dominant" (Jameson 1984) or as an "intellectual fashion" (Mitsuhiro 1989). Those who would decenter authority instead recenter it in their own authorship.[47] When all is said and not done, postmodernism is a successful academic movement that discourages social intervention. As such, it reproduces and supports the politics of patriarchy and colonialism. Conflicts surrounding class, race, sexuality, and nationality are typically dismissed under the rubric of political correctness, whether as research concerns or as social issues to be accounted for in making institutional decisions. Postmodernists in the United States tend to adopt an anti-essentialist paradigm on the premise that such a radically liberal position, all by itself, undermines a fundamentally discriminating social order at work. The assumption that theories are practices allows postmoderns to pass by the consideration that the practical effect of a theoretical "practice" depends not so much on the theory but rather on its social ties to institutional support. Some postmodernists assert that it is not in their power (and others that it is not in their interest) to affect the sociopolitical domain. Here messianic and self-aggrandizing connotations are the issues at stake. Liberal, anti-essentialist positions then turn from concerned detachment in the name of a disinterested renunciation to politically paralyzing self-suspicion. Postmodern academics openly declare their own corporate interests as they silently follow protective scholarly rules that separate them from the rest of the world. As they complicitly enjoy privileges gained by laboring on harmless, untranscendental matters, postmoderns map the comfortable limits to their self-criticism.

To self-declared ineffectual and suspect postmoderns the only untrustworthy suspects are those who do not understand or adhere to their convoluted rules: women in general, U.S. women and men of classes, colors, and sexualities that only recently arrived at the academy, and men and women of all classes, colors, sexualities, and political allegiances who come from the so-called Third World. These Others are the ambitious newcomers who are under suspicion for challenging the academic agreement by forgetting to be grateful. After all, postmodernism opened the academic gates for them (us) by arguing anti-essentialism and multivocality.

For an Otra this scenario is puzzling, muscle-binding, paralyzing, and yet it generates constant movement. Recognizing the privilege of being a token, laboring to maintain that privilege while fighting tokenism, betraying both the tokenizers who reward our performances as tokens and those who question our tokenism in agreement with our own perceptions of the privileges we enjoy. Not marginals by any means but tempted to indulge in self-marginalization to avoid facing our privileges. Practicing autoexoticism and yet dreaming of revolutions. Moving from exoticism to decolonization, back and forth ... between spectacularization and utopianism? *He wrote his story on those feminine bodies: immobilized, restricted in space like pages, equally bound to a household or a cabaret.* For intellectual wanderers of the textual world, Foucault's account of the "heterotopia," the centerless universe, and the situation of "pure difference" is a radical proposal (see Foucault 1970: xv–xxiv; Foucault 1977b). For the rest, and especially the Third Worlders such as the tangueros of *Cambalache* (Discépolo 1977), it is no novelty. A sophisticated scholarly description of the mess and the mud they (we) are in does not provide them (us) with insights for liberation. It rather confirms our pessimism and cynicism by turning it into something universal and natural—discursively natural. *The signal for his moves was natural: sunrise, sunset. Household and cabaret were as natural as the paths of the sun. So was the existence of the women confined in both places. Two worlds inhabited by different social classes. He never needed to ask why. It was a fact.* Naturally colonial and patriarchal. (Lacan makes his contribution to the latter.)[48]

In the "free market" of textual politics an Otra is either ignored or invited to participate as an "exotic"—and usually "native"—scholar. Following Elizam Escobar (1988), exotics are "not only those who are on the outside but, contrary to the esoterics, those who look from 'down-up'"; the exotics are those who provide the feminine passion that keeps the imperial world going in spiralized waves of male desire. *He had power. A viscous power nurtured by two races of women. A solid bridge of eroticism tailored to his desire. A power produced of simmered erotic passion.* The free flow of power occurs in a patriarchal and imperialist world where the flow is rather arrested and quite clearly under male and Western control. Postmodernism has re-created the hopes in a "radical intellectualism," already questioned in latinoamericano forums in the 1960s (e.g., Gunder Frank 1968). The insightful outcomes of these debates on the social responsibilities of intellectuals were burnt up by the military juntas of the 1970s and forgotten or denied by the intellectuals of the "politics of fear and silence" (Corradi 1979). I have had access to these documents only in a U.S. university and in English. Is it enough to apply a postmodern reading of these events and conclude that the dominant discourse, the technology of power, has silenced these voices and that they operate on multiple levels, including self-subjectification? Elucidating the "mechanisms" through which this happened should not prevent us from remembering that the empire keeps our history, dictates our history, prevents or conditions our access to it, and threatens us if we remember. The feminine and feminized "exotics" perform on imperial stages. ...

Postmodernism reminds me of the tango, of my place in it as the heiress to the milonguita, this time as an exotic milonguita performing in an imperial academic cabaret. Now I rebel against the identity of a docile body dancing tangos on the imperial stages of the world. I rebel against my subordination both as a milonguita and as an "exotic" intellectual. I turn one against the other, I resist. *He leads, but no one follows him now.* I cannot follow through this unlearning any further either and still I refuse to stop performing my steps by assuming that there are no partners willing to share these protesting stompings.

My present is explained by my past, my past is read in my present. *The women of my family shared a secret. My grandmother, here, washing and perfuming the shirts he wore to the cabaret. Mireya or Margot, there, sending him back home, invigorated by skillful pleasures. I was benefiting from a skill my grandfather had acquired embracing prostitutes and milonguitas (cabaret tango dancers).* The milonguita is already a product of colonialism. No comforting nostalgia for lost origins can help me here. Even the most "authentic" milonguita is just like the tango that did not get to be thought of as "authentic" until Paris retrieved it from the brothels of the Río de la Plata. The colonization of the milonguita adopts the shape of patriarchal colonialism exerted by both colonized and colonial male partners. Tangoing through postmodernity I perform my awkward decolonizing kicks in the midst of that patriarchal and colonial dance. There are no other dances available for me.[49] *Women, mysteriously, have the capacity to use the same things that imprison them—including men—to fight back. Tangos report repeated female attempts at evasion. The viscous power crystallizes. … The blank, inert pages on which he was writing his story grow an irregular thickness of their own. My legs cut the air in all directions.*

Otras are both the "exotics" of the colonial discourse—including academia and its new postmodern offsprings—and the milonguitas of the tangos. I have learned both languages, and using them—I have no others—I curse them back. Just like Caliban. … No. Like the women of his tribe, those cannibal females that Shakespeare and Fernández Retamar forgot to identify, I am decolonizing myself by biting my own head.

Feminist Uses of Third World Women[50]

Every feminist who deserves the title has gone through the ritual of watching at least one documentary on Third World women's subordination to some kind of native patriarchy. In an efficient time span of twenty minutes, the spectators are flown from the Bolivian highlands to the deserts of Arabia with some stopovers in African villages, Brazilian brothels, and Central American war scenes. "Third World" women's lives are briefly but effectively displayed in a dramatic, fast-paced sequence that exhibits a collection of "barbaric" traditions. Female bodies and souls are shown being subjected to the very thresholds of inhumanity. Blatant macho practices, veiling, infibulation, prostitution, and violence parade hastily before the eyes of an increasingly indignant audience. As an epilogue, the room remains in silent tension loaded with shared undercurrents of rage and pity. The ritual is over.

After going through this experience on several occasions, and realizing that it is not restricted to films but, to the contrary, is also frequently reproduced in books, courses, conferences, and research projects on "Third World" women, I have seriously wondered about the meaning of this feminist practice. Some would say that it is related to feminine masochism, and the discussion moves on to whether masochism is an innate characteristic in women or the result of socialization. Others would argue that such exercises are a painful but necessary step on the road to self-awareness—the awareness of women's universal subordination—or a part of the process of consciousness-raising toward global feminism. Unsatisfied with these overencompassing and seemingly clean-cut explanations, I remain wondering whom this exercise is supposed to benefit, and at what cost.

In the name of consciousness-raising of a shared subordination, feminism has been caught up in the practice of reproducing Third World women's reification as exotic objects. The intentions are different, but Third World women are often represented the same way in women's studies courses as they are in *National Geographic*. The willingness to help Third World women overcome local patriarchies has ended up reinforcing stereotypes of "Third World," uncivilized traditions and of "Third World" women's passivity and ignorance.

Third World women are addressed by Eurocentric or Westernized feminists full of good intentions, offering their sisterly hands to fight universal subordination, but in the same move we see ourselves depicted as victims of backwardness, barbarism, and underdevelopment who need to be enlightened about these very facts so that we can join in global feminist reaction. Thus, we are trapped in a double bind, and our indignation and frustrations become doubled. We become obsessively suspicious—paranoid. We smell betrayal and violence behind misrepresentations and insensitivity. Global feminism starts looking like a new trick of Western imperialism. And we resist. We resist being converted to a faith—feminist consciousness—because to do so would mean risking further alienation.

This does not mean that we do not recognize our subordination as women; we have suffered it and benefited from it for a long time. But why should we join other abused women who use our "exotic," caricatured pain to raise their own consciousness? Why do Western feminists often avoid dwelling on their own victimization and feel the inappropriate urge to stir the wounds of others? We can show our wounds to each other, we can even share healing practices and other tricks, but to use someone else's pain to cover up one's own is sick and abusive; to undermine our complex rebellions by rejecting or attempting to co-opt our efforts is a long way from sisterhood.

Some of us Third World women have started to voice our discontent both with Western feminisms and with native patriarchies, but the necessary ears seem not to be ready to hear us. We are found guilty of treason on both counts. Local patriarchies accuse us of selling out to Western imperialism and Western feminists accuse us of misleadingly representing Third World women. The Western feminists find their own stereotypes about "Third World" women more compelling than the scenarios presented by Third World women themselves. Vocal Third World women are dismissed and marginalized on the grounds of using Western feminist tools to attack local patriarchies, of belonging to privileged elites within the Third World, and of exploiting their exoticism by constituting themselves as scholarly divas who unfairly compete with Western feminists for scarce academic resources. Thus, Third World women, who speak up for a brand of feminism that challenges imperialist practices embedded in Western feminism, are chastised and judged as sleazy exploiters of both the other Third World women, whom they claim to represent, and Western feminists, whose teachings have helped them to confront native patriarchies.

There are no ears ready for Third World women's voices. We continue to be carefully inspected as untrustworthy candidates for feminism and for our own cultures. Is she brown enough? Is she poor enough? Is she thirdworldish enough—usually meaning picturesque and untheoretical enough—for her voice to be legitimate, her words to be taken seriously, her claims to deserve respect? Either too exotic or not exotic enough, too Westernized or not Westernized enough, there seems to be no legitimate place for our conflictive, unfit protests.

SCENE NINE: THE POSTCOLONIAL ENCOUNTER[51]

Tango Parade.

Cast: Choreocritic, Postmodern Academics, Postcolonial Intellectuals, Subalterns, Immigration Officer.

The Choreocritic reads her essay at a conference for an audience of Postmodern Academics. They sit, listen, take notes. The Postcolonials arrive late. The Immigration Officer, sitting in a booth, stops each of them at the entrance and glances at their documents. The Postcolonial Intellectuals leave their suitcases at the edge of the conference setting and find a seat, perturbing the general attention. Subalterns start walking into the scene, some alone, others in small groups, tired and carrying heavy bags, oblivious to the conference. They interfere with the audience's view of the "conference" setting. The Immigration Officer steps nervously out of his booth and attempts to impose order by asking the Subalterns for their documentation, resident status, return tickets, and so on.

Choreocritic's "essay" (spoken text):

Others are pure bodies, nothing but flesh, unspeakable. They are always waiting, out there, in a long line, to be interpreted, represented, and translated.[52] Postcolonial intellectuals are Others who attempt to represent and position themselves in a world constituted as such by a long history of colonialism.[53] As a perspective, postcoloniality emerges in postmodern times: times of reordering the world and of redefining (reorganizing?) imperialism without many philosophical clues but with plenty of experience in exerting power.[54] Postcolonial intellectuals are particularly interested in the possibilities that this crack opens for a reconceptualization of the margins and peripheries of a world globalized by imperialism and transculturation, margins so intensely articulated to the center, so entrenched at its very core, that those very entities (cores/peripheries) become dislocated. These confusions announce changes, and changes entertain promises, again soaked in confusion. Postmodernism performs a confession of exhaustion while claiming control over the confusion through its very consciousness—that is, the confession. Postcolonial cultural workers build up in the cracks exposed by postmodernism as quickly and as surprisingly as possible. Moving theoretically as if postmodernism were a reality, beyond discussions of factual or virtual truth, "postcolonials"—as the Others of postmodernism—confirm the breakdown of modernity. In so doing, postcoloniality embraces postmodernity, positioned from an outside that lies in the middle.

In the postcolonial encounter, postcolonial critics are the internalized Other now impersonated and politicized, pushing postmodernity to take the necessary steps into postimperialism. In order to do so, postcolonial intellectuals must part-take of postmodern myths and realities from an/Other dimension, the one of postcoloniality. Already an Other asserting the historical import of colonialism in the making and collapse of modernity, now displaced into postmodernity, the postcolonial intellectual becomes an excolonial recolonized under postmodernity, struggling for decolonization.

Postcoloniality evokes at once postmodernism and colonialism and conjures the image of the postcolonial space as postmodern colony, bringing in the presence of the resistant and subversive Other so indispensable in these colonial and postmodern matters. Alterity is internalized, assimilated (where it should have always been), saturated by the embodiment of the imagination or the fantasy of total fusion: the postcolonial encounter. An encounter provoked, this time, by the displacement of the excolonized, who are still searching for decolonization. Identity fragmentations proliferate at the dissolution of the radical border of imperialism. Mobility, nomadism, transmutedness. Homelessness, nostalgia. Exile, uprootedness. Diaspora. Migration, invasion of the territories of former invaders. Exploitation turned into cannibalization, reversed, returned against itself since paramount alterity does not acknowledge difference in clusters. Hybridity.

As I think about the postcolonial encounter, these questions prompt my tango parade: If postmodernism were, among other things, a newly situated colonial attitude, how would it subject postcolonials? What do postcolonials come to represent in the postmodern imagination? Are the politics of postcoloniality engulfed by the postmodern logic?

It might be helpful to go back to Kwame Anthony Appiah's (1991) question: "Is the Post- in Postmodernism the Post- in Postcolonial?" The "post" in postcoloniality cannot be severed from that other "post" of the postmodern condition that made it think of itself, simultaneously, in the past and future tenses. Postcolonial intellectuals inhabit postmodernity clinging to a "post" that talks back as a parody of postmodernism in several ways. Postcoloniality performs the pendular gesture of shoving colonialism toward the past and bringing it back into the future implicated in the "post," while not forgetting to sweep by the omitted "modern" that it replaces with "colonial," as a reminder that modern and colonial enterprises have historically gone hand and hand. Postcolonial intellectuals use a variety of modern and postmodern analytical tools, frequently displacing them from the theoretical narratives, intellectual histories, and political contexts in which they were originally elaborated, purposefully combining them in anarchic ways.[55] In so doing, the postcolonial critic mimics postmodern messiness and introduces an ambivalent suspicion regarding abandonment to this condition and ironic control over it: Is the postcolonial colonized into postmodern disorientation or is s/he doubling and subverting the colonizing logic that persists in modern rationality, which is disavowed and continued through postmodernism?

Hybridity, for example, while overtly calling attention to the complexities embedded in the colonizer/colonized plays of identification—often addressed at pinpointing the pitfalls of decolonization projects that rely on the recovery of roots and the authentic—also brings to mind the hybrid position of the postcolonial intellectual vis-à-vis postmodernity.[56] Postcolonials, knowing postmodernism from within, implode the nostalgic side of nihilistic postmodernity and promise some (political) action from the margins of the overall decentered world by retracing the lost memories of colonialism, that is, the memory of power ... the memory of change? The hybrid postcolonial critic juggles the memories of colonialism and the learnings of postmodernism into an expectant, rarified air. The postmodern spectator watches and awaits, ambivalent, the postcolonial performance of unlearning colonial teachings while suspecting or announcing that it is too late. Too late for decolonization. For decolonization already took place in a dramatic although unglamorous way, selffulfilling the prophecies on the colonizer rather than the colonized side.

Perhaps postcolonial intellectuals' decolonization entails unlearning the privilege of representing the unrepresentable, those whose marginality is unimaginable. "The postcolonial intellectuals learn that their privilege is their loss. In this they are a paradigm of the intellectuals" (Spivak 1988a: 287). In looking for clues on how to address the decolonization of our colonized thirdworldean minds, I read in this phrase an invitation to learn that our words cannot take hold of those bodies, purposes, and fates toward which we merely point by naming the subalterns.[57]

> Outside (though not completely) the circuit of the international division of labor, there are people whose consciousness we cannot grasp. [...] Here are subsistence workers, the tribals, and the communities of zero workers on the street or in the countryside. To confront them is not to represent (vertreten) them but to learn to represent (darstellen) ourselves (Spivak 1988a: 288–289).

As we speak, the theoretical carnival parades the avatars of the postcolonial encounter—that is, the encounter between postmodern and postcolonial intellectuals that occurs in a U.S. conference room. Meanwhile, at home the once literally decolonized now long for recolonization. De-linking has now turned from a revolutionary strategy into a nightmarish reality. "Exploit me! Extract my surplus! Give me a chance!" say politely the excolonized as they attempt to move to those still titillating, shifting centers they skillfully detect in a world that pronounces itself as decentered and thoroughly marginalized. The memory of power, in its full ambivalence as exploitative and enabling, repressive and productive, is kept in the bodies of the excolonials and performed through the body politics of migration, exile, self-exile, and diaspora, on the one hand, and on the other, through soliciting foreign investments, international tourism, and the privatization of formerly state-administered industries and services. The once national bodies are thus exposed to transnational fates. Under these conditions, subalterns from the former colony, once decolonized, work and hustle. What else can I say? Unable to represent them, I see ourselves, intellectuals, longing for a recolonization on our own terms. Do we know any other version of freedom?

Chorus (all characters in the scene) recite together with the Choreocritic the last line of her "essay": "Do we know any other version of freedom?" [Pause.]

As the lights go down, the chorus repeats the refrain: "Memory of Power, Memory of Power, Memory of Power," as in conjuring the final scene.

Blackout

Female Intellectual Invaders

> We [latinoamericano intellectuals] have been so thoroughly steeped in colonialism that we read with real respect only those anticolonialist authors disseminated from the metropolis (Fernández Retamar 1989: 18).

Roberto Fernández Retamar, whom I shamefully read in English in a recent edition foreworded by Frederic Jameson, is one of the most powerful contemporary authors addressing issues of decolonization in América Latina. More than a revolutionary writer, Fernández Retamar is writing from within a revolution. He is an intellectual in Cuba. An intellectual engaged in an ongoing decolonizing process among many other revolutionaries working in the many dimensions that such a process entails. He has the strength of the ones who, although in power today, clearly remember that it has not always been so and that their power is fragile—the strength of ambition without arrogance—but perhaps more than that he has the helpful reminder of the U.S. imperial eyes piercing his back.

For an intellectual in Fernández Retamar's position, using the tools of the colonizer and representing the colonized are more a challenge than a dilemma. There are questions to be faced and acted upon on a daily basis in the practice of an intellectual counterhegemony. The question is not whether to use or avoid using the tools of the colonizer, whether to represent the colonized or leave them alone. The colonized have been and are continuously being represented, homogenized, stereotyped, and appropriated by the colonizers. The tools of the colonizer are already our tools. Both colonizer and colonized know about the significance of these facts. "The white man had the anguished feeling that I was escaping from him, and that I was taking something with me" (Fanon 1967: 128). The colonized take the tools of the colonizer, break them into pieces, inquisitive to find the source of his power. The colonized discard some parts, overlook others, put something else together—not a tool but an attitude. The question is how to develop an anticolonialist attitude, a subversive questioning of these very questions, a "complicitous criticism" (Mario Benedetti's terms, 1971).

A Third World intellectual is a colonized intellectual. Third World, colonized intellectuals are not necessarily anticolonial. An anticolonialist intellectual is an already colonized intellectual struggling for decolonization. Colonized but stubbornly anticolonial, these intellectuals shake up their own colonialism in order to constantly reshape a decolonizing practice. Sometimes anticolonialism takes the shape of searching for the roots, the origins, the precolonial, but history has been already colonized and the roots have been fixed, crystallized, exoticized in the colonial memory (Fanon 1968). Other times, the anticolonial search leads to the shaping of an ideal future and becomes contaminated by either the "development" or the "proletarian community" colonial dreams. In the search for decolonization, the anticolonial, colonized intellectual cannot ignore the borders of the colonial discourse; she bounces against them, attempts to devour them, falls back frequently, bruised and intoxicated. She encounters not only the problem of both "using the tools of the colonizer" and "claiming to represent the colonized" but also the problem of using the tools of the colonizer that represent the colonized. It is not a dilemma but a fact.

Colonialist tools already represent the colonized; colonialism goes hand in hand with the practice of representation; representation is a tool of colonialism in itself. A conquest for the benefit of the natives; civilization for the good of the barbarians; development as aid for the poor; revolution in the name of peasants and workers; global feminism for the awareness of Third World women; post-modernism for the enlightenment of the postcolonial intellectuals, and so on. Colonialism always counts on a vanguard, and in the vanguard, intellectuals find their place. Thus, it could be argued that Edward Said, in his devastating critique of Western anthropologists' representation and appropriation of the colonized, cannot escape assuming the representation of the colonized whose self-determination he so vehemently defends (Said 1989). Roberto Fernández Retamar, Aimé Césaire, Frantz Fanon, Jose Martí, Angela Davis, Eduardo Galeano, Ngũgĩ wa Thiong'o, Haunani Kay Trask, Cherríe Moraga, Ernesto Guevara, and many other anticolonial intellectuals could be found guilty of these same flaws, namely, of representing and hence reproducing colonialism. *Stop.* This finding is in itself a colonialist, totalizing interpretation. An interpretation not capable of recognizing purposes, audiences, locations, specificities. The represented themselves can often tell the difference between a procolonial and an anticolonial representation, and the acceptance or rejection of being represented is based on this fact. I do not mind, and quite to the contrary, am extremely grateful whenever an intellectual succeeds in giving me back some dignity, some control over my life—whenever a claim to power is made in my name. I am all ready for it.

These kinds of representations—anticolonialist representations—are actually strategies of counterrepresentation: They are representations that challenge the colonial representation and appropriation to which I am always already subjected. All kinds of challenges to colonial representations are welcome, including counterrepresentations. I know the rules of the game, in this case the need for a "critical mass" in order to make an argument sound—both in the sense of "heard" and of legitimate. I cannot completely redefine the game, but I cannot avoid playing it either; hence, I aim for a better position from which I can challenge more. And I hope that my language does not convey the impression that I am talking about personal preferences. I am talking about colonialism. Paraphrasing Said, I am talking about the constant reinforcement of "the dreadful secondariness of people, colonized people, fixed in zones of dependency and peripherality, stigmatized in the designation of underdeveloped, less-developed, developing states, ruled by a superior, developed, or metropolitan colonizer. A world divided into betters and lessers, where the category of lesser beings has expanded, where the colonized are a great many different, but inferior things, in many different places, at many different times" (quoted and paraphrased from Said 1989: 207).

For colonized or Third World people, as well as for Western alternative people, the problem is not only that of representation but also that of not having enough anticolonial representatives, strong anticolonial voices, and among these, intellectuals with anticolonial commitments. James Petras, in a much-debated and very depressing article (1990a), addresses the decadence of latinoamericano intellectuals. He describes the impact that the region's worsening economic recession and escalating dependency has had on intellectuals' political engagement. Intellectual work in América Latina is becoming increasingly co-opted by international development funding, and as a consequence, the kind of research—including topics and methodologies—has become more and more alienated from popular movements and alienating for the intellectuals themselves. In order to make his point, Petras offers a simplified typology of the intellectuals' possible roles: "organic intellectuals" versus "institutional" or "research institute–oriented" intellectuals. (The latter is an adaptation of Antonio Gramsci's "traditional intellectual" to current latinoamericana circumstances.) The organic intellectuals of the 1960s, in the midst of self-financing and self-sustaining hardships, managed to integrate their work with the social struggles of their countries. The institutional intellectuals of the 1980s "live and work in an externally dependent world, sheltered by payments in hard currency and income derived independently of local economic circumstances" (Petras 1990a: 106).[58]

Having started my university studies in Argentina at the beginning of the 1970s, I can corroborate Petras's appreciation of this turning point in intellectuals' roles and lives. However, perhaps his disappointment, and certainly his decision to unmask the intellectual entrepreneurs of today, precludes him from carefully analyzing the turning point itself: the military regimes, the slashing and burning repression, the "politics of silence" (term borrowed from Corradi 1979). True, latinoamericano intellectuals have been lured by the development industry and the academic multinationals, but at least some have also been refugees, exiles, and survivors, and all have been victims of military terror.[59]

> The problems and issues that in the course of development in some central countries have been dealt with discursively appear, in the context of peripheral development, as unacceptable challenges to the status quo. [...] The discursive regression here characterized as the "politics of silence" is more extreme in countries where the dismantlement has not been followed by sustained accumulation. Here cultural destruction is but a chapter in a process of national disintegration from which some might never re-emerge (Corradi 1979: 73–74).

Of course, the politics of fear and silence was not directed exclusively toward intellectuals. Everyone was wounded to a greater or lesser degree. As a consequence, the potentially organic intellectuals of the redemocratization period, on top of coping with their own internalized censorship regarding openly anticolonial and revolutionary attitudes, had to face radical self-criticism given their failed performance as vanguards. As a result, in Argentina, for example, some intellectuals have adopted a healthy distance from political pragmatism to enable the emergence of alternative positions; they teach for fairly low pay at the universities. Others have chosen to engage fully in government posts as technocrats of the new free-market, ideology-free democracies. Many have compromised their intellectual practice and struggle to survive by selling their expertise as consultants to businesses and organizations. In these situations—and all possible combinations of the above—all intellectuals have been facing the fear, mistrust, and apathy of the people and of immobilized "social movements."

Petras is right in pointing out the political exhaustion of the latinoamericano institutional intellectuals and their reconciliation with the prodevelopment, technocratic scientificity demanded by the overseas funding agencies—to which I would add at least all the cases, reasons, and circumstances already mentioned, demanding a more complex categorization than the one suggested by an institutional/organic opposition. Here, however, I am more concerned about the idealization of the popular movements, since it misses the tragic fact of the impact of socioeconomic regression and political repression on the rest of the latinoamericana people. Everyone has been dollarized; everyone has to deal with a cynical, fatalist attitude toward politics. In this sense, intellectuals are always "organic." This is not to say that the current intellectual entrepreneurs should not be held responsible for their financial manipulations, especially when in order to receive funds from overseas they promise enlightenment and relief for "women," "natives," and the "poorest of the poor." Rather, my opinion is that too much has been invested in intellectuals; the magnitude of both hopes and disappointments indicates a belief in a "vanguardism" of which I am suspicious. Intellectuals, in the sense of enlightened vanguards, are a colonial creation, a tool of the colonizer—a tool of the colonizer that has come to represent the colonized.

A Third World intellectual is not necessarily anticolonial, and a vanguard might be thoroughly colonized into "vanguardism." In addition, an anticolonialist vanguard is not necessarily or exclusively or mainly made up of intellectuals. Clear, bright anticolonialist minds might not be the minds of the intellectuals.

If the goal is decolonization and you want to push for it, whether to be a part of the vanguard, the masses, or the stragglers is a question of strategy. Intellectuals could be in any of these positions, but, with few exceptions, they are usually among the stragglers (even though they look at the whole scene from above). Anticolonialist intellectuals must come to understand how "organic" and how institutionally privileged they are. Romanticizing "the people's" power to resist or overcome exploitation and forgetting the protected, legitimate spaces from which intellectuals choose to pursue decolonizing projects (including the decolonization of their own minds) may not have much effect on the world, but what effect they have does not advance decolonization.

The responsibilities of intellectuals and, in particular, of anticolonialist intellectuals, are a debatable matter. Should intellectuals voice the position of particular sectors of their society; analyze the specific conditions under which particular social projects can develop; provide arguments that effectively link specific demands with values and actions; envision alternatives for the problems of injustice; provide new ways of teaching, rethinking, learning, or understanding all these problems and their very problematization?

Specificities would be necessary to advance this discussion. At this point (the dot, the stain of my conclusion) I only wish to add that all of these responsibilities are political, whether undertaken in the "real" world, in the world of texts, or in both. Political positioning is embedded in the role of the intellectual because intellectuals represent, by their own choices or by the uses that others make of them, dominant or subaltern sectors and projects. Intellectuals are privileged pawns of the knowledge/power struggle, but they are not necessarily more enlightened than anyone else; those ghostly lights are the signals of colonialism. And the anticolonial intellectual should constantly question her or his homage to intellectuality and her or his intellectualizing practices. Remember, these are the tools of the colonizer; they shouldn't represent *us* (those whom I am representing, since I know they share my anticolonial concerns).

Us, silenced but not mute, speaking louder and louder, rumor or roar, so thick, so full, so pouring rain and *tormenta*. We don't ask each other anymore, "Can the subaltern speak?"[60] We have learned to stop practicing self-marginalization. Now we wonder with hunger who will listen to us. Deaf world of unscripting writers, not daring to look the hybrid "invaders" in the eye. First World flooded by *mojados* and a few intellectual freaks; existential nightmare of postmodern property holders, their identities under threat by the proliferation of this Otherness, the passionate "exotics" of their own creation; legal and illegal immigrants, loved and hated for doing your work, thinking aloud or silently sweeping streets. Challenging, representing, or ignoring one another, we trespass your borders, your identity at the "core." Installed in you to the point that an Other haunts every self, you can no longer control these Otras. Your desire is to join. Apologizing for your dark thoughts, still attributed to us—women on each side of the male borders of the world. To our hair, threaded in the hair of how many women? How many Third World women, how many women speaking thirdworldish in colors, how many, moving rebelliously, following untamable thoughts? "Between patriarchy and imperialism, subject-constitution and object-formation, the figure of the woman disappears, not into pristine nothingness, but into a violent shuttling which is the displaced figuration of the 'third world women' caught between tradition and modernization" (Spivak 1988a: 306).

Resisting through how many bodies, how many, in one single woman? Stretching her blood through so many lives carried by one body that seems to reproduce itself infinitely, mothering with the same belly that dances for the pleasure of her beloved lover, *Farideh*, of the imperial gaze and of herself. One life and so many bodies, *Salome, Raj*, so many, dragging ourselves from one continent to another, by our own feet, so fast, that we can hardly feel the ocean wetting our toes, *Lehua. Teresia*: How many bodies, can you tell me? Surviving with the same bloody inexplicable violence, layer over layer from the ancestral to the present, only because you know exactly where you are going. *Mary, Nahua.*

Gerry, never lost except when you leave your wise thoughts in pidgin, battered pidgin and still wise, moving with that only body hooked to so many lives by our transgressive bloods, *Adella,* dropping from your fairy-tales into my tango-tales, our bodies almost adrift in the forest where we find our way only when it gets dark. *Soledad.* Chased and still chasing those words, in the dark, to denude them so we can see. *Saba.* Through your gauze scarfs, wild in the air, entangling all these brown bodies, rescued together. *Gudrun.* In those riddles of "yes/no, what else? Tell me more." Female bodies.

How many? *Riselia!* Let's look for them under your ruffled skirts, clinging onto your baiana doll. In color reciprocity, *Dawna,* struggling in a shaded, clear voice to join a mismatching skin, *Susan.* How many women, *Jeanne,* and how many bodies? As plenty as can be fed, *Jamila,* from your generous eyes pouring couscous and wisdom into our mouths. *Beth,* count them for us aloud, in your singing voice; are there as many as the dishes piling up every day in the kitchen sink? *Aixa,* you, glancing at female beauty through your fingertips, remaking how many of us, again, out of clay? How many lives? How many bodies? *Pam,* you must know! Your lips, so readily red, waiting to speak in friendly ears. *Sue-Ellen,* voodoo queen possessed at the queer screen; *Susan,* duende, laughing at it all; *Michelle, taconeando; Alicia, tamaleando; Jennifer,* refusing to pass for divine. *Angela, disfrutando,* and *Clarita, chillando. Analinda,* dusting carefully our dreams with the tips of your endless hair. Entangled in so many mazes, *Turia,* so much wet hair. *Vidhu,* and your sister and all our other sisters, carved in your plays of moaning, screaming women with so many bodies and how many lives? Roughly, *Petra,* take a guess in your rowdy, trustworthy blood. Passionate blood, *Cherríe:* "But what of passion? I hunger to ask. There's got to be something more than hand-to-mouth survival. [...] The *right to passion* expressed in our own cultural tongue and movements" (Moraga 1983: 136). Knowing, as you say, through persistent hunches that there is no betrayal in *la familia.* It's in our memory, kept in our blood through so many lives, in so many bodies, in *la familia. Jean,* demanding of you always more *familia.* The ritual of kissing every time we come and go, finding *familia,* blood ties, with loyal friends in suffering and celebration, *Cindy.* Sharing contagious words, coming out of colonized mouths, confused by our skins. Contagious bodies, *Adriana,* shaken through dances of common blood. *Susanita,* choreograph it for us: salsa, samba, hula, tango. So that in going home, *pueda mostrarle a la Cris, a Moni, a Adri, a Elena, a Analía, a la Nue, a Graciela y a las demás lo que acabo de descubrir y que no nos para nadie. Nadie. Tantas mujeres, peleando, como nosotras, como con cuerpo latino, contagiadas, como en malón.*[61]

Glossary

Abuelo/a: grandfather/grandmother.

Academia: dancing locale of the initiated in the tango. (These places were somewhat underworldish but were not brothels.) Also dance academy.

Aliados: allies.

Argentinidad: the quality of Argentine-ness; Argentinean nature or identity.

Argentino/a: Argentinean.

Arrabalero: from the suburban and urban slums.

Bailaora: flamenco (Spanish) female dancer.

Bailarinas/es: dancers.

Bailetines: slummish dancing locales.

Bandoneón: musical instrument similar to the concertina.

Barrio: neighborhood; city quarter.

Cabecita negra: mestizo person from the interior of the country.

Canfinflero: pimp.

Canyengue: a pronounced movement of the hips considered to be distinctive of the *tango criollo* as danced by the lower classes; often extended to dancing tango with a local flair.

Cariños entrañables: most beloved ones.

Carnaval: carnival.

Carpas: precarious locales (shacks, tents) frequented by marginals and low working-class men where they danced tangos and hired prostitutes.

Carrerita: tango figure that resembles a short run or escapade with small, tight steps.

Casita: house (diminutive).

Chileno/a: Chilean.

Chillando: screaming.

China, chinita: woman from the interior of the country, usually mestiza (mixed Spanish/Amerindian ancestry). The female partner of the gaucho.

Chinitero: womanizer.

Civilización y progreso: civilization and progress.

Compadre: courageous, trustworthy man of the "land." Idealized as a male short in words and large in deeds.

Compadrito: male of the urban slums, arrogant and defiant; ruffian, usually also a pimp.

Compañero/a: comrade.

Comparsas: groups of people who danced and played music together during the Carnival. Traditionally these activities were associated with the *Sociedades de Negros,* but in the late 1800s some young males of the Argentinean elite started imitating them, their faces painted in black, their movements mocking the *tangos de negros.* This entertainment of the young elite often led to fights and violence, which increased the fun for these young men. If someone was to be penalized by the authorities, it was certainly not them.

Cordobes/a: from Córdoba, Argentina.

Cortes y quebradas: the halt or interruption (coupe) of the dancing trajectory (at which the tango figures take place) and a disjointed movement of the hips (cleave).

Costurerita que dió el mal paso: "little seamstress who took a misstep."

Criollo/a: persons born in the South American colonies of European parents (often extended to mixed Spanish/Amerindian ancestry). Also, people of the "land"—that is, the interior and rural areas.

Desaparecidos: disappeared, missing people, particularly those who were killed during the last military dictatorship in Argentina (1976–1983).

Disfrutando: enjoying.

Duende: mischievous genie.

Estadounidense: of the United States.

Familia, la: the family.

Ficciones femeninas: feminine fictions.

Figuras: dance figures; complex dance footwork.

Flor de fango: flower of mud, of the slums.

Foquismo: the theory of revolution that places concentrated military efforts ahead of mass political organizing. Contrasts with approach that envisions armed revolution following from party politics.

Franchutes/as: French.

Gaita: Spanish.

Garçonniers: love-nests; apartments, usually shared by single, wealthy young men, devoted to parties with prostitutes, mistresses, and lovers. (The men did not reside there permanently.)

Gauchos: rural characters associated with the Argentinean *pampas* (plains).

Gracias a las diosas: thanks to the goddesses.

Guapo: defiant, streetwise, courageous male characters of the tango environment.

Lancero/a: thief who specializes in pickpocketing.

Latinoamericano/a: Latin American.

Lunfardo: slang of Buenos Aires.

Machismo: male chauvinism; cult of maleness.

Malevo: ruffian.

Malón blanco: the savage white horde.

Marcar: to "mark," that is, to "lead" a tango dance by signaling the coming figure to the other dancer.

Mestizaje: cross-breeding, hybridity.

Mestizo/a: a person of mixed Amerindian/Spanish ancestry.

Milonga: a musical genre developed by the *gauchos*; extended to an early tango style. Also, the locales where tango is danced.

Milonguero/a: one who frequents the *milongas*; a master of the *milonga* dancing technique.

Milonguita, milonguera, milonguerita: a female dancer of the *milongas* or a woman of the tango environment; usually associated with loose morals.

Mina: broad.

Mojados: "wetbacks"; illegal immigrant workers.

Moreno/a: dark-skinned; dark complexion.

Morocho/a: literally, Moorish-like, meaning a dark complexion.

Musa de la mala pata: bad luck muse.

Niño bien: naughty boys from wealthy families.

No está muerto quien peléa: "s/he who fights back is not dead."

Ojalá: hopefully.

Ombligadas y culeadas: pronounced pelvic movements while walking back and forth in the course of a dance. *Ombligadas* ("navelings") describe the displacement by which the members of the dancing couple approximate each other with their abdomens, and *culeadas* ("rumpings"), with their rears.

Orillero: from the margins, suburbs, or urban slums.

Pampa(s): South American plains.

Papusa: gal.

Parada: in tango choreography, a "standstill" or abrupt interruption of the trajectory.

Pardo/a: dark-skinned, usually descendants of African slaves.

Pasteles: pies.

Pebeta: babe.

Percanta: broad.

Pericón: a genre of music and dance practiced by *gauchos* and *criollos.*

Peringundines: run-down bars where patrons enjoyed drinking, gambling, dancing tangos, and picking fights.

Polaco, polaquito/a: Polish.

Porteño/a: from the port of Buenos Aires.

Quebradas: a figure characteristic of the tango choreography by which, in "breaking" the alignment of the torso and hips at the waist, the hips move back and forth, creating a contorted effect.

Querido/a: dear.

Río de la Plata: River Plate; region that comprises the parts of Argentina and Uruguay that surround this river.

Rioplatense: from the Río de la Plata region (Argentina/Uruguay).

Romerías: marquees set up on holidays for the purpose of dancing.

Rubia/o: blond.

Rusos, rusitos/as: Jewish people.

Sainete: a popular theatrical genre, usually in one act, of a satirical and picturesque nature, where local events and characters were paramount.

Saladeros: meat-packers.

Salas: theater halls and restaurants rented out as dance halls for special occasions.

Salida: escape, exit; also the *promenade* figure in dance.

Sentada: a tango figure in which, after performing a *parada* (standstill), the male dancer (feet flat on the floor and set apart) flexes his knees and the female dancer "sits" (her legs crossed loosely) on one of his thighs.

Sociedades de Negros: Associations of Blacks. In around 1820, the black population of Argentina and Uruguay began to organize into self-help associations by nation or tribe of African origin. These associations were extremely active in the Carnival parades and patriotic feasts. The earliest records of the tango as a dance have been found in documents issued by the Municipal Council of Montevideo forbidding the practice of the *tangos de negros* in public spaces (Novati and Cuello 1980: 3).

Soldaderas y cuarteleras: women who followed soldiers in battle as logistic support. Among other services they acted as prostitutes.

Sudamericano/a: South American.

Taconéo: stomping of the heels.

Tango criollo: creole, or authentic, tango as performed by dancers knowledgeable about the original choreography.

Tango de espectáculo: staged tango.

Tango de negros: tango of blacks; tango choreographic style as performed by the black slaves and their liberated descendants in the Río de la Plata.

Tango de salón: ballroom tango.

Tango liso: simple, bland tango; lacking in sophisticated figures.

Tangueaba: past imperfect of "to tango."

Tanguería: tango club.

Tanguero/a: related to the tango genre and to the tango world (musicians, dancers, poets, fans).

Tano/a: Italian.

Técnica milonguera: tango-*milonga* dance technique.

Tormenta: storm.

Turco/a: Middle Eastern people.

Uruguayo/a: Uruguayan.

Vasco/a: Basque.

Zamba: a genre of music and dance performed by *gauchos* and *criollos* and characterized by the flapping of skirts and the stomping of feet (*zapatéo*).

Zarandéo: flapping of skirts in the course of a dance.

Notes

Preface

1. I have committed the double sin of excerpting fragments of tango lyrics and of translating them. Jeff Tobin has kindly done the editing. Much of the *lunfardo* (slang of Buenos Aires) has been lost and the result is a tamed version of the originals. In addition, all quotations from non-English-language sources are my translation, unless otherwise indicated.

2. *Vuelvo al Sur*, written in the 1980s, is an homage to the young generation of argentinos whose personal and political consciousness, desires, and hopes the military dictatorship (1976–1983) attempted to exterminate.

3. Refer to the Glossary for all Spanish terms and phrases.

4. I use the term "exile" to designate the uprootedness experienced by more than 2.5 million argentinos (of a total population of 32 million) for political and economic reasons. I acknowledge with respect the important differences between cases of voluntary migration and those by implicit or explicit imposition under life threat. However, I claim (with due clarification) the importance of extending the meaning of "exile" to encompass those displaced from their land and culture due to the playings of the global political economy, those for whom marginality, deterritorialization, and be/longing turned into an unsolvable questioning—and this can occur whether one is at home or abroad (see Parcero et al. 1985).

5. "El tango es us pensamiento triste que se puede bailar" (attributed to Enrique Santos Discépolo). In this description of tango I have not taken into account the different stages of its historical evolution, according to which in a first period, the tango was gay like the *milonga*, and only became saddened after the introduction of the *bandoneón* and its sounds of lament. The *tango-canción* genre, where the focus on the lyrics displaced the emphasis previously given to the dance, might have also contributed to this effect. For a careful analysis of these and other distinctions, see Assunção (1984) and Salas (1986).

Chapter One

1. For example, Bernardo Bertolucci's *Last Tango in Paris* (1972); and Fernando Solanas's *Tangos: El Exilio de Gardel* (1985) and *El Sur* (1988).

2. For an interesting discussion of this subject, carried through the analysis of particular tango authors, see Ulla (1973), Romano (1973), Rivera (1973), Ford (1973), and Matamoro (1973).

3. Horacio Ferrer believes that the survival of the tango has to do precisely with this commitment on the part of the artists to maintaining their political militancy separate from the tango poetry. Although many tango artists were well known for their political positions, they seldom let their political positions transpire into their creations (Ferrer, personal communication, January 1991).

4. Ferrer does a magnificent job of clarifying the convergence of four arts in the tango: music, dance, lyrics, and poetry (Ferrer 1980a).

5. Tango has gone through dramatic changes from its emergence in the 1880s to the present, participating—as popular culture does—in major argentino and global developments.

It is nonsensical to speak of one tango or of a consistent tango, free of contradictions. However, there is an ironic, sensual, sentimental, pessimistic, resentful, nostalgic, melodramatic tone to the tango that bounces, rhythmically and aggressively, between defiance and conformism.

6. Feminists have made analogous observations regarding theory and resistance. See, for example, Cixous (1976) and Kristeva (1984).

7. FORJA stands for *Fuerza de Orientación Radical de la Joven Argentina* (The Force of the Radical Orientation of the Young Argentina), a group founded in 1935. Their slogan was, *"Somos una Argentina colonial, queremos ser una Argentina libre"* (We are a colonized Argentina, we want to be a free Argentina). Many FORJA members became Peronists after 1945.

8. Sarmiento was president of Argentina between 1868 and 1874. For a contemporary version of these political positions that calls for "assimilation of the indigenous culture" instead of extermination of the indigenous people, see Vargas Llosa (1990). Vargas Llosa was a recent candidate to the presidency of Perú.

9. For an interpretation of Argentina's political culture and its problem of instability that reverses these terms in order of importance, see Calvert and Calvert (1989).

10. "Through direct investments, credits, legislation and the creation of administrative units in charge of production and services, the State offered security to individuals, goods and transactions, facilitated conditions for the establishment of an internal market, extended the benefits of education and health services, and contributed to the population of the territory and used extra-economic coaction so as to guarantee the employment of the often scarce labor force" (Oscar Oszlak [1982], quoted in Suriano 1988: 2).

Chapter Two

1. For a comprehensive description of the hectic, convulsive times lived in the Río de la Plata when the "birth" of tango occurred, see Assunção (1984).

2. After gaining independence from Spain, Argentineans engaged in more than forty years of inter-provincial wars; the unification of the country was established in 1852. The federal alliance of provinces was brought into the hegemony of Buenos Aires (declared the federal capital) in the 1880s, under pressure from political leaders allied to British economic interests (Justo 1989; Romero 1989).

3. In defining scarcity one is always faced with the problem of how needs are created, conceptualized, and assessed. Horacio Salas reports that during this period (1860s to 1890s), the city of Buenos Aires had 60,000 to 100,000 fewer women than men. This demographic imbalance might have allocated a precious value to women and turned them into a "scarce resource," since these men sensed that they could not hope to hold on to ("embrace") anything other than women (see Salas 1986).

4. For an exhaustive compilation of the debates on "who" (by race and class) introduced "what" into the tango choreography, see Natale (1984) and Guibert (1973).

5. See, for example, Puertas Cruse's *Psicopatología del Tango* (1959); Mafud's *Sociología del Tango* (1966); and Molloy's documented references to homosexuality in Buenos Aires toward the turn of the last century in "Too Wilde for Comfort: Desire and Ideology in Fin-de-Siècle Spanish America" (Molloy 1992). For an example of the reactions on the part of tango historians to such associations between compadritos and the practice of homosexuality or homosociality, see Salas (1986: 38). Salas curiously attempts to save the compadritos' "honor" by stressing that although it had been documented that men danced with each other in the streets and, exceptionally, in some other locales (Bates and Bates 1936: 36), "they did not have a trace of misogynism." His argument is that there were always women around with whom to dance and in whom the compadritos were inter-

ested. He equates misogyny with the lack of interest in women and not with the shape and nature of that interest.

6. For an insightful analysis of the emergence of modern nationalism and fixed notions of manliness in Europe (Germany and Great Britain, in particular) see Mosse (1985).

7. Tango historians and literary critics establish 1918–1920 as the turning point from openly pornographic verses to ruffianesque and sentimentalized ruffianesque tango lyrics. See, for example, Romano (1983: 90–99) and Ulla (1982: 78–84).

8. Tango lyrics do not deal exclusively with love relationships, and women in tango are not exclusively lovers. I have chosen to deal with passional plots and women as lovers because these tango themes are, in my view, more closely related to the stakes of the dance and its displays of sensuality. For a comprehensive analysis of tango themes, see Villarino (1965); for a very interesting analysis of women's roles in tango pivoting around the figure of the mother, see Ulla (1982, 1973).

9. Jean Franco together with other feminist critics argues that this difference (between being a dead and a living object) is superfluous. In analyzing both male and female Latin American authors and the different shades of mobility or creative existence that they allow their women characters, Franco concludes that in the best of (literary) worlds, women are allowed to make a spectacle or parody of themselves (Franco 1984). According to this approach, the dominant "discourse" on women is so complete and pervasive that all attempts at resistance end up feeding the monster, as in a double-bind or sadomasochistic relationship. Even oversimplified, as I am presenting it here, this account makes a strong and important contribution. I am reluctant, however, to buy into single-tailed endings. The operation of power—both in its imposition and insurgency strategies—permanently reproduces subjection and rebellion—at least as long as the subjected ones are present and alive. To me, this makes the difference between a dead and a living object.

10. Vacarezza, through these lines, attempts to provide a recipe for a successful *sainete* (a popular local theater genre) in which local characters and scenes should be taken into account. Popular theatrical plays included tango choreographies and music before tango lyrics developed on their own account as *tango-canción* (tango songs) (Salas 1986; Ordaz 1977).

11. This same perspective is reproduced by Jorge Luis Borges in his short stories "The Intruder," "Streetcorner Man," and "Rosendo's Tale." Women are speechless, and the reader never gets to know about their thoughts or feelings. In reference to "The Intruder" (La Intrusa), Borges himself remarks in a commentary included in the English edition that the story actually has only two characters, though the plot apparently calls for three (Borges 1970: 278). These are the two brothers who struggle over the possession of Julia's body and murder her in the end. Furthermore, in his *History of the Tango*, Borges refers extensively to the male bonding focus of the tango genre. He chooses the concept of an epic of courage to synthesize the spirit of the tango and tracks down through Western history the roots of "the belief that a fight may be a celebration" (Borges 1984: 104).

12. For a detailed description of these bars, dancing "academies," "cafes," and so on, see Assunção (1984), Novati and Cuello (1980), Salas (1986), Puccia (1990), and Rivera (1976). See Carretero (1964) for his discussion aimed at disturbing the stereotypical depiction of tango scenarios and characters that usually enhance a delictive environment.

13. For an extensive list and treatment of these early lyrics, see Assunção (1984) and Gobello (1976b).

14. On the complex organization of the international prostitution network, its relations with the emerging public health policies, and the tango culture, see Guy (1991).

15. For historical references regarding a few women immortalized in tango lyrics, see Bra (1984).

16. *La Morocha* (1905), music by Enrique Saborido and lyrics by Angel G. Villoldo, was one of the first tangos to achieve great popularity both in Argentina and abroad (more than 390,000 copies of the sheet music were sold over several editions). The lyrics of *La Morocha* evoke an image of an Argentinean woman who is very different from La Moreira. The refrain of *La Morocha* reads: *"Soy la morocha argentina / la que no siente pesares. [...] / Soy la gentil compañera / del noble gaucho porteño, / la que conserva el cariño / para su dueño"* (I am the argentina morocha / the one who feels no sadness. [...] / I am the gentle companion / of the noble *gaucho porteño*, / the one who keeps her love / for her owner). Both popular images of Argentinean femininity coexisted conflictively at the time.

17. These thoughts on the performance of masquerade as opposed to the spectacle of masquerade have been triggered by my reading of Case (1993).

18. References to racial differences faded in tango lyrics at some point. Racial tensions did not disappear, however; they were displaced onto ethnic tensions. Milonguitas are shown working hard to acquire French looks and manners and to become more refined and "whiter" than the women of their own mixed (darkened) ethnicities. There are more references in ruffianesque tango lyrics to French women dancers/prostitutes than to women of any other ethnicity and culture. The sexual/sensual stigma of "dark" women was being contested by this equally prejudiced attribute attached to the French, but it was a contest (a new tension) and not a replacement. French, that is, whiter, sensual women were more distinguished and more expensive ("white slaves") than other milongueras. The high valuation placed on female Frenchness in the sexual market generated imitation on the part of the darker, non-French women.

19. See Borges (1984) on Evaristo Carriego.

20. This is an extremely rough calculation I have made on reviewing more than 500 tango lyrics. It is by necessity inexact; no exhaustive compilation has yet been made. The recently opened (July 1990) Academia Nacional del Tango has collected 35,000 titles of tangos written exclusively in Argentina and Uruguay. This list would increase considerably if tangos composed elsewhere were taken into account (Horacio Ferrer, personal communication, January 1991).

21. My reconstructions of these choreographic ways of creating trouble for male partners are based on published interviews with the Argentinean dancers Carmencita Calderón (Pereyra 1992: 59–75) and María Nieves (Azzi 1991) and on my own conversations and tango practices with Carlos Rivarola, Carlos Gómez, Natalia Hill, Eduardo Arquimbau, and Celia Blanco.

22. See "First Steps in Tango," Chapter Six in this book.

23. See the reference in the cabaret scene of *Los Dientes del Perro* in Ferrer (1980a).

24. The choreography of the tango dance and tango "fashions" (low-cut black dresses, tight skirts with deep slits, and the like) create this atmosphere. In order to make this idea more striking, some contemporary tango choreographers have included scenes suggestive of rape (see, for example, Graciela Daniele and Jim Lewis's stage notes for *Dangerous Games: Two Tango Pieces*, in Bilderback 1989). The motives, experiences, and feelings of the male rapist are pushed aside by focusing on the woman's provocative attitudes or, in the best of cases, on what happened to the woman's body. Women's intimacy is more "powerful" than that of men because it is displayed on the surface, on their bodies. Women in tango display their bodies and their intimacy; men talk about their feelings. Women's intimacy is more appealing and compelling. Pornography is another good example: Women's eroticism is more erotic; female nudity is more arousing. This is not an essentialist statement but a description of how a macho culture operates.

25. For an analysis of the role of the prostitute as a class "broker" see Peter Brooks's (1980) article in which he establishes interesting connections between sexuality, money, and storytelling.

26. This traditional theme, however, continued with variations over time. Tango historians' chronologies for the evolution of this genre differ according to the emphasis they choose to place on the music and the different formations of tango orchestras; the lyrics and Carlos Gardel's fostering of the *tango-canción*; the places in which tango was performed and practiced; and the dance technique, which is usually considered to be less important than the other factors. As a result it is highly problematic to establish definite and generalizable "stages" for the history of the tango. I propose the following periodization as a rough guide.

Between the late 1870s and 1918 the tango was characterized by jumpy, playful, catchy music improvised by small, usually "nonprofessional" bands (using violins, flutes, guitars, and, beginning in 1900, after some experimentation, bandoneones). In those years, the music closely followed the dancers and their own improvisations. The lyrics were scarce and unimportant; the dance was energetic and central. The golden era (*época de oro*) of the tango developed roughly between 1918 and 1935: These were the times of Carlos Gardel and other remarkable poets and singers, the era of the cabaret and of the popular theater. During these years, the verses, in a way, shared centerstage with the music, and dancing, in Argentina, became more bland, adopting a simplified technique. Before 1920, the early bands were turned into orchestras, incorporating piano, stand-up bass, and more violins and bandoneones (flutes and guitars started to disappear from the formations). From 1929 to the late 1930s, economic and political crisis, the "swing era," and the talkies dealt a blow to tango's popularity. The 1940s, however, are known for the strong revival of impressive and innovative orchestras and superb lyricists. The general effect was more grave, paused, "embellished," and emotional. These times coincided with Argentina's isolationist policy during the World War II, which brought prosperity. Dancing tango, though, wound down noticeably (and was replaced by Big Band jazz style and "tropical" rhythms). Tango audiences congregated to listen to musical and vocal experimentations. Dancing to this music was often considered an insult to the musicians' art, which was just as well since the music was difficult to follow on the dance floor. Between the 1950s and the 1960s, tango collapsed. Tango historians and fans debate whether the reasons were internal (the revival of folklore as new laborers arrived from the provinces, Perón's national policies of radio broadcasting, the lack of an esprit de corps and innovative techniques on the part of the most famous tango performers, and so on), external (Americanization, TV, media globalization, transnational culturalism), or both. The past forty years have not been subject to periodization and the ups and downs of the tango are referred to by isolated composers and musicians (such as Aníbal Troilo, Osvaldo Pugliese, and Astor Piazzolla) or by particular events that had international repercussions (such as the *Tango Argentino* show, created by Héctor Orezzolli and Claudio Segovia in 1983). (See Lara and Roncetti de Panti 1969; Assunção 1984; Scenna 1974a and 1974b; Gobello 1980; Salas 1986.)

27. Most authors attribute this fact to the introduction of the bandoneón.

28. *Mi Noche Triste* (My Sad Night), lyrics by Pascual Contursi and music by Samuel Castriota, had been sung, recorded, and presented in public by Carlos Gardel in 1917, the same year it was composed. It was the first tango he recorded. The theme was relaunched a year later by Manolita Poli with great success.

29. For an excellent account of the evolution of tango music, see Scenna (1974a, 1974b).

30. In "Tango, Rebelión y Nostalgia" (1982), Noemí Ulla also devotes a couple of pages to the topic of machismo in tango lyrics. However, she seems to be concerned with comforting and calming those male critics worried about the belittling of the male image in view of the proliferation of the "abandoned ruffian" plots (Ulla 1982: 75–76).

31. Estela dos Santos (1978) establishes a rough figure of 80 percent women, taking into account the audiences of the tango shows at the theaters and radio studios of Buenos Aires, before the popularization of the TV (early 1960s). Julie Taylor, on the basis of her field-

work in Argentina, states a contrasting opinion: "Active interest in the [tango] dance complex appears to be entirely male; women develop an interest in tango only if they develop interest in an *hombre tanguero*" (Taylor 1976: 289). I do not wish to discuss her ethnographic authority. Her observations may have been accurate when she carried out her research in tango clubs in the 1970s.

32. I "resist" those interpretations that claim the universal truth of a feminine sadomasochistic complex in order to explain the violence inflicted on our bodies. Such interpretations are, in themselves, one more violence to be resisted.

33. See Mazziotti (1989) and Sarlo (1985) on women viewers of latino-style soap operas and readers of latinoamericano versions of harlequin romances.

34. Perhaps "power" is the wrong metaphor altogether to address the kind of struggle that I am talking about. "Power," as a concept-metaphor derived from the field of physics, might contribute to covering up the political economy of violence.

35. Consider Raymond Williams's troubling observation: "It can be persuasively argued that all or nearly all initiatives and contributions, even when they take on manifestly alternative or oppositional forms, are in practice tied to the hegemonic: that the dominant culture, so to say, at once produces and limits its own forms of counter-culture" (Williams [1977], excerpted in Marcus 1990: 393). I would add that "it can be persuasively argued," but that does not make it true.

Chapter Three

1. In this analysis I have been loosely following and unorthodoxically confronting the Lacanian findings of Mulvey (1988a, 1988b), Doane (1987, 1988), Silverman (1986, 1989), Owens (1983), and others.

2. For a similar understanding of the "exotic," see Rousseau and Porter (1990). Michael Taussig (1986) has followed a so-called "surrealist" path in analyzing the constitution of "wildness" with a complexity and fluidity I have been incapable of developing in this description of the "exotic" tango. I thank Peggy Phelan for calling my attention to Taussig's text.

3. For an analysis of "Le Turc Généreux," the first act of the opera *Les Indes Galantes* (1735), as well as of the last scene (through an engraving of the 1758 version choreographed in Vienna), see Foster (1986: 138–140). Foster calls attention to the different modes of representation inaugurated by the neoclassical, proscenium ballets of the eighteenth century. Having moved from the courtly dance hall to the stage, dance was now set to represent "the world." Jean George Noverre, a dance theoretician and choreographer of the time, established the intentions of the proscenium ballets in his *Letters on Dancing and Ballet* (1760): "The well composed ballet is a living picture of the passions, manners, customs and ceremonies of *all nations of the globe*. [...] It is dependent on the faithful imitation of nature" (Noverre [1760], quoted in Foster 1986: 126).

4. For a similar, although more cautious analysis of the capitalist, consumerist appropriation of Third World rhythms, see Wallis and Malm (1984).

5. On gender and sexuality in the Romantic ballet, with regard to the performers' techniques, audience responses, and the overall spectacularization and feminization of the genre, see Foster's forthcoming article "The Ballerina's Phallic Pointe" (Foster n.d.).

6. On the fetishization of the female body through the early structuring of the cinematic apparatus, see Williams (1981). She argues that both narrativity and the multiple reduplication of the female nude were strategies devised to contain the threatening powers attributed to the feminine.

7. The minuet had been developed in the Imperial Court of Louis XIV and, as such, was regarded as a reactionary, antibourgeois practice after the French Revolution. For the political implications of the minuet, see Leppert (1988).

8. For a brilliant analysis of the different factions/interests playing in the antibourgeois reactions at this time in European history, see Williams (1989).

9. For a detailed description of these events from the point of view of social history, see Laver (1966).

10. For a description of national consolidation in Europe from the point of view of the mastery of technological progress and mastery over the Rest of the world, see Burchell (1966).

11. The British published a variety of travel guides to Paris that focused on its luxurious and lustful dissipations. For a detailed account of their contents, see Rearick (1985). The French themselves provided such enticing guides to the Paris of pleasures: *Guide de Plaisirs à Paris* (1899); *Guide Complet des Plaisirs Mondains et des Plaisirs Secret à Paris* (n.d.); J. Ciccerone's *A Travers les Plaisirs Parisiens: Guide Intime* (1900), for example (see Rearick 1985; Siegel 1986).

12. For an analysis that connects the spectacles of nineteenth-century Europe (from the point of view of the entertainers) to the process of urbanization and the constitution of crowds and explains how purely visual relations started to take precedence over the other senses, see Ritter (1989).

13. As defined by Braudel (1981).

14. On the close relationship between bodily movements and costumes in dance, see Keali'inohomoku (1979).

15. Silverman (1986), Steele (1985, 1989), and others have suggested strong relationships between clothing and the constitution of gender identity. They also identify a major turning point in Europe in the mid-eighteenth century when attention shifted radically from male to female fashion. I wish to add that dance followed the same trends at a slightly later time. Performers and spectators split along gender lines: Women were primarily on the stage, whereas audiences were heavily masculine. Since then, female bodies, clothing, and movement seem to be the locus of female identity, dependent on the male gaze, whereas the male identity has been detached from male bodies and has become more dependent on the capacity to produce wealth and to exhibit women partners before the eyes of other men.

16. For a brilliant description/interpretation of the techniques ruling over bodies in Europe from the Renaissance to court society, see Vigarello: "In court society in the end, it is dance that sets up models aimed at excellence and distinction. It was to be the foundation for an art of controlled, developed and privileged performance. [...] Dancing was to be practiced with a great deal of caution, as it threatened to become 'dirty and immodest', and to go beyond all degrees of propriety. Dancing must be [...] the restrainer of passions [fear, melancholia, rage and joy]. [...] From that point on, dance inevitably appeared full of contradictions" (1989: 179–181). See also Foster (1986) on dance theoreticians' training strategies, from courtly to neoclassical ballet, as well as on modern dance techniques and approaches to body politics.

17. I use the term "cultural capital" following Bourdieu (1984).

18. For a description of the transformations of erotic imagery in France since the 1860s, and the emergence of seduction and flirtation within a new amorous code parallel to the elaboration of a new *sciencia sexualis*, see Perrot (1990).

19. Sorell (1981) and Laver (1966) mention that the dance halls, and, later on, the music halls, offered an opportunity for intermingling between the higher and lower strata of so-

ciety. More precisely—as shown by the characters they describe—it was the elite young men and the working-class women of "loose moral standards" who got together. The female dancers who performed for and with the audience were usually nonprofessionals who worked in low-paying jobs during the day. The more famous these dancers got, the more they could charge for "sexual favors." Although Paris was the center of these happenings, both authors comment on the existence of such places and practices in every great capital of Europe at the time. For an extremely interesting interpretation of the connection between this new type of prostitution and the changing practices surrounding sex and love among bourgeois families in France, see Perrot (1990).

20. For a detailed description of the locales, artists, and publications issued by the cafés and cabarets of Montmartre, see Oberthur (1984).

21. Fin-de-siècle Montmartre has usually been rendered as the epicenter of bohemian, transgressive behaviors, that is, a site for the violation of social and artistic norms prevailing among the bourgeois. See Siegel (1986) and Wilson (1991), for example, for interpretive attempts to unsettle this familiar opposition in terms of more complex relations of mutual affirmation and undermining.

22. Paul Lafargue was one of the main promoters of "the right to be lazy" (1883). His teachings were followed by other revolutionary intellectuals, such as Georges Chevrier, who demanded "the right to integral passion" and "the liberty of the body" (1885) (Siegel 1986). These belle époque intellectuals were reacting—using the same rhetoric of rights as the French revolutionaries of 1789—against those rights of man that had actually ensured "capitalist domination." The rights to work, to property, and to freedom of commerce meant, in their opinion, the workers' "rights to misery." Lafargue (Karl Marx's son-in-law) fostered a revolutionary idea of freedom by which the workers could achieve liberation by leisurely releasing their "joys and passions" (Rearick 1985: 34; Galeano 1987: 219). Happy and sensual "natives," "primitives" whose natural instincts had not yet been corrupted by capitalism and "its prudery and hypocritical moral standards," were his major examples for liberation.

23. Naomi Schor claims that in French literature, "representation in its paradigmatic nineteenth century form depends on the bondage of woman" (Schor [1985], quoted in Bernheimer 1986: 373). Linda Nochlin shows graphically that "since the nineteenth century, the woman's body has been presented for the man's erotic pleasure, rarely the man's body for the woman's" (Nochlin [1973], quoted in Caws 1986: 268). Both in literature and in visual representations, Ritter states, "the latter half of the nineteenth century [could be labeled] as the heyday of the fatal woman. [...] The *femme fatale* dominates the imagery of the Symbolists and others of the *fin de siècle* [... and] the *femme fatale*, expressed in literature written mainly by men, characterizes a male view of women [where] woman as a product [is] designed to meet the needs of male sexuality" (Ritter 1989: 108–109). Steele emphasizes the fact that since the mid-eighteenth century, and especially in the nineteenth century, "men seem to have renounced fashion in favor of a drab uniform, while women's fashion seemed to change more rapidly and dramatically, and to be adopted by increasing numbers of women of all classes" (Steele 1985: 9). Steele analyzes the relationship between fashion and female ideals of beauty. Silverman (1986), departing from the same historically situated premises, focuses on fashion's implications in the constitution of gender identity. In dance, Foster (n.d.), Sorell (1981), Anderson (1974), and others mention the displacement of men from the stage and the choreographic undertakings pivoting around female dancers since the mid-eighteenth century. Ritter establishes important connections between the modern version of the femme fatale and the fin-de-siècle dancer as portrayed in German, French, and English literature (1989).

It is important to note that the generic feminist literature (with the exception of Sorell and Anderson) cited in this note deals in a sophisticated manner with the ambivalent consequences for women of the male attention and devotion exhibited since (roughly) the mid-eighteenth century. The ongoing debate is centered on the question of women as objects and/or subjects and women's consequent strategies of resistance through subservience as well as rebellion. Are women suffering male manipulations? Are they enjoying them? Are they participating in them? Are they remanipulating male manipulations? Are women empowering themselves despite and/or because of their objectification (which never reaches a complete subjectification)? These are the major questions.

24. Michelle Perrot (1990) writes about this mutation of the erotic imagination in which, contrary to the sighs and diaphanous gowns of the Romantics, women deliberately arouse desire. She relates these changes to the bourgeois expansion of private life.

25. La Goulue and Valentin's performance has been reconstructed cinematographically in John Huston's *Moulin Rouge* (1953) and Jean Renoir's *French Can Can* (1955).

26. For an interesting analysis of literary portraits of femme fatale dancers in European literature at the end of the nineteenth century, see Meltzer (1987).

27. On the changing nature of erotogenic female zones (bosom, rear, neck, legs, and so on) and the telling contrast with respect to the stability of males' erotogenic zones as seen through the evolution of fashion since the eighteenth century, see Flugel (1950). See also Steele (1985) and Silverman (1986) for insightful and critical follow-ups on the same theme.

28. For a detailed description of the ways in which these "clandestine" dance locales operated in Paris, see Humbert (1988).

29. In this analysis, specifically in "making" messages embodied in leg and foot movements, I have been inspired by the polemics between Birdwhistle (1974) (on "multi-channel redundancy") and Ekman and Friesen (1974) (on "non-verbal leakages and clues to deception"). Briefly, the debate is about the possibility of reiterating or contradicting verbal expressions through nonverbal behavior.

30. Tango historians have drawn on a variety of sources (anecdotes, memoirs, journalistic accounts, interviews) to determine the precise date of tango's introduction in Paris. The matter has not been settled. In 1906, sheet music for the early tangos *La Morocha* and *El Choclo* were distributed at several European harbors by Argentinean navy cadets on board the frigate *Sarmiento*. In 1907, Angel Villoldo, Alfredo Gobbi, and Flora Rodríguez—tango composers and performers—moved to Paris where they spent more than seven years working in music halls. From then on, numerous argentino dancers, musicians, and singers toured through Europe (Carella 1956; Assunção 1984; Bates and Bates 1936; Gobello 1980; Salas 1986). The war and the prohibition on dancing tango between 1914 and 1918 interrupted the flow, which was resumed after 1918 (Humbert 1988: 50). Casimiro Aín, in an interview published in 1923 in the magazine *El Suplemento*, reported having been in London and Paris working as a tango dancer in 1903 (Del Greco 1993: 5).

31. Several diaries and letters of these distinguished argentino travelers that relate their leisurely and morally dissipated lives in Paris during la belle époque have been collected in Jitrik (1969). See also Lara and Roncetti de Panti (1969) for excerpts of chronicles and essays by illustrious argentinos participating in the first steps of the tango in Paris. Regarding the first tango musicians in Europe, see Humbert (1988), Assunção (1984), Gobello (1980), Cadícamo (1975), and Salas (1986). On the first tango dancers in Europe see Salas (1986), Lara and Roncetti de Panti (1969), and Del Greco (1993).

32. Buenos Aires was one of the main "consumers" of European prostitutes at that time. See Labraña and Sebastián (1988), Londres (1928), and Guy (1991).

33. See Perniola (1989) on the concept of eroticism as transit.

34. For an extensive treatment of these events, see Humbert (1988) and Lara and Roncetti de Panti (1969).

35. Gauchos are the rural characters associated with the Argentinean plains (*pampas*). It would be somewhat similar to impose a cowboy costume on a Charleston dancer. Yet both

gauchos and tango were identified as Argentinean, abroad as well as at home. Some authors point out that the "native" or "folkloric" costume was imposed by the French Association of Actors and not by the owners of the locales (Lara and Roncetti de Panti 1969: 87).

36. L'Académie des Professeurs de Danse de Paris published a declaration in 1921 deploring "those erotic fantasies performed at the sound of a music of savages or any other dance of such sort." The following reasons were given, quoting diverse personalities: "The tango reduces intellectual performance, incites youngsters to sexuality, provokes cystitis and other gynecological anomalies in women, draws youngsters to places where Germans traffic in cocaine, and encourages the multiplication of gigolós" (Humbert 1988: 75–76).

37. See, for example, Hervé Lauwick's "Le Vrai Tango," published in *La Vie Parisienne*, May 10, 1913, pp. 337–338; Flossie's "Quelques Figure de Danses Excentriques," published in *Fémina* 287 (January 1, 1913), p. 21; and M. Letellier's "Danse, Dance, Tanz," published in *La Vie Parisienne*, January 24, 1914.

38. For a thorough archival work on exhibition ballroom dancing in the United States, see Malnig (1992). References to the tango and the efforts devoted by these professionals to moralizing and promoting its steps are endless.

39. For a full description of "Around the Hall in Texas and Gringo Tango," see Sherman (1979).

Chapter Four

1. Leopoldo Lugones expressed these opinions in Paris in 1913. In 1916 he included similar remarks in *El Payador*, this time stressing the differences between the noble dances of the gaucho argentino and the degraded tango: "It [Argentine-ness] is not to be found in the contortions of the tango, that reptile of the slums, so unjustly called *argentino* during the days of its unshameful fad" (Lugones [1916] 1961: 174).

2. As an old Jewish joke goes: "The food in this place is terrible." "Yea. And the portions are so small."

3. Reported by Cadícamo who, like many other tango musicians before the "legitimation" of tango, played the piano at the brothels (Cadícamo 1975).

4. These gangs of young elite intruders had, interestingly, adopted for themselves the name "*indiada*" (Amerindian savage horde).

5. This analysis has been based on the descriptions of various local elite responses to the tango rendered by Ferrer (1980a), Cadícamo (1975), Matamoro (1969, 1971), Novati and Cuello (1980), Ulla (1982), Romano (1983), Salas (1986), and Gobello (1980).

6. Lines from an interview with Aníbal Troilo, a famous Argentinean tango composer and bandoneonista, by María Esther Gilio (1986).

7. Lines from an interview with Silvina Ocampo, a contemporary Argentinean fiction writer, by María Esther Gilio (1986).

8. The first choreographic tango manual published in the Río de la Plata was written by Nicanor M. Lima circa 1916 and entitled *El Tango Argentino de Salón. Método de Baile Teórico y Práctico*. Among the first European tango "methods" to arrive in Buenos Aires was Giovanni Franceschini's (1914) *Balli d'Oggi—Con 70 Figure Demonstrative, Grafici e Brani Musicali, E Uno Studio Critico sulle Danza Nouvissime*. This manual was published under the pseudonym F. Giovannini.

9. This classification of tango styles as developed in Argentina after the Parisian rage has been based on Ferrer (1980a), Novati and Cuello (1980), Assunção (1984), Bates and Bates (1936), and Benarós (1977), but I have modified some of their interpretations in an important way. My reconstruction of specific movements, postures, and techniques corresponding to the different local tango styles, especially the *tango de espectáculo*'s contrasting features as compared to the French stage version, is based on the choreographed

tango histories performed by Juan Carlos Copes and María Nieves in *La Pesada del Tango* (Teatro Astral, Buenos Aires, 1991) and *Tango x 2*, by Milena Plebs and Miguel Angel Zotto (Teatro Municipal General San Martín, Buenos Aires, 1991). In reconstructing the tango criollo I have benefited greatly from conversations and dance instruction with Carlos Rivarola.

10. Alicia Dujovne Ortiz, in *Buenos Aires*, borrows the concept of *horizontal vertigo* from Drieu La Rochelle and applies it to describe the pampas' "ideal metaphysical space": a baroque space of too much emptiness. See Dujovne Ortiz (1991).

11. A popular saying usually attributed to Enrique Santos Discépolo (see Preface, note 5).

12. This textual polemic has been reconstructed on the basis of publications by Matamoro (1969, 1971, 1976), Borges (1984), Ferrer (1980a), Rossi ([1926] 1958), Ulla (1982), Sábato (1963, 1964), Martini Real (1980), Gobello (1976b, 1980), Vega (1936), Assunção (1984), Salas (1986), Labraña and Sebastián (1988), Bates and Bates (1936), Tallón ([1959] 1964), Carella (1956), Carretero (1964), Guibert (1973), García Jiménez (1965a), and Rivera (1976).

13. Oscar Bozzarelli has recently published a succinct article in which he claims "to have put together the puzzle" after endless polemics. The rhythm and the melody of tango have different origins. The former is African and the latter, European. The European melodic roots followed two different routes. "The melodic roots of tango are Latin: the one comes from the Spanish counterdance, through the Europe-Montevideo-Buenos Aires route, originating the *candombe* or tango of the Río de la Plata blacks; the other is French and Spanish and arrives through the Europe-Cuba-Montevideo-Buenos Aires route, and constitutes the remote origin of the milonga and tango melody" (Bozzarelli 1989: 22). He does not provide a clear itinerary for the African rhythmic roots of the tango.

14. An exception to this rule can be found in Vicente Rossi's *Cosas de Negros* ([1926] 1958), in which he first claimed tango-originating rights for the rioplatense blacks and for the Amerindian population of the area, by then long "disappeared."

15. In twenty-six years (1869–1895), the population of Buenos Aires grew from 187,000 to 664,000 inhabitants, 345,000 (over 50 percent) of whom were foreign immigrants (Assunção 1984). Between 1850 and 1890 Argentina's demographic growth was proportionally superior to that of the United States (Rodríguez Molas 1988).

16. Although the participation of Italian and Spanish immigrants in composing and performing tango music has been widely recognized, the input of immigrants (with the exception, perhaps, of French prostitutes) in tango choreography has been vastly ignored. Some important exceptions to this xenophobic trend of forgetfulness are Assunção (1984), Pujol (1989), Salas (1986), and Labraña and Sebastián (1988).

17. José Hernández wrote the adventures of the gaucho Martín Fierro in two volumes, published in 1872 and 1879, respectively. This nativist literature inaugurated the reification of the criollo argentino male.

18. My analysis of the "criollo" identity has been inspired by Fernández Retamar's (1989) examination of "Our Mestizo America"—a concept developed by José Martí.

19. For a very different interpretation of Argentinean nationalism and political culture, see Calvert and Calvert (1989). These authors argue that Argentina's pride (born of Iberian individualism, egotism, racism, and lack of self-criticism) and "the view that Argentina's potential greatness has been blocked by external factors have made dependency easy to accept as an explanation of national failure" (Calvert and Calvert 1989: 240). They continue: "Pessimism was not the result of a simple transfer of Hispanic values. [...] Rather those values were reinforced by national history. [...] The harsh isolated frontier experience [in Argentina's case, a geophysical and psychological frontier] could offer reinforcement to such beliefs, just as in North America it served to reinforce the opposite. [...] The Northamerican example is a slap in the face for Argentine pride. [...] Blaming those external forces which gave once, but failed to maintain, the perception of national economic

greatness is understandable, if unconstructive" (Calvert and Calvert 1989: 246). And lastly: "Fatalism may not be entirely negative in its effects. [...] It has been suggested that the positive, optimistic appeal of gambling makes revolutions, which are tantamount to political lotteries, attractive to Latin Americans. This emphasizes the wrong aspect of fatalism as a contributory factor to political instability. It is rather the negative aspect, '*la pereza criolla*' (the creole laziness) in Bunge's terminology, which is important" (Calvert and Calvert 1989: 247).

20. For a different interpretation of the gaucho and tango as symbols of national integration in Argentina, see Taylor (1976).

21. In this discussion I have been following Fanon's (1967) critique of Mannoni (1956), Bhabha's (1990a) critique of Fanon, my own critique of Bhabha, and Ngũgĩ (1986). In general, it is a contra-Lacanian analysis.

22. On Latin America's production of alternative Western cultures, as opposed to West/non-West paradigms, see Yúdice (1992a).

Chapter Five

1. An earlier and shorter version of this chapter was published in Joseph J. Tobin, ed., *Re-Made in Japan: Everyday Life and Consumer Taste in a Changing Society* (New Haven: Yale University Press, 1992), pp. 235–252.

2. Two events are usually mentioned as highlights in Japanese-Argentinean diplomatic life. The first one was in 1905, when the Argentinean Navy ceded to Japan two war vessels that were being built at an Italian shipyard, recognizing the emergency that Japan was undergoing on the occasion of the Russian-Japanese conflict. The second one was Argentina's shipment of two cargos of wheat toward the end of World War II to alleviate the food crisis that the Japanese people were suffering.

3. This account is based on Ferrer (1980a, 1980b), Alposta (1987), and Cadícamo (1975).

4. For an interesting account of the influence of tango rhythms in early American jazz, see Roberts (1979).

5. Some of Megata's students believe that he never had a chance to see argentinos dance tango in the true *canyengue* style, but others avow that, having had this opportunity, he confirmed the dance's improvement in the French capital.

6. On the active Japanese pursuit of Western learning, see Wakabayashi (1986), Yunesuku (1964), Shively (1971), and Joseph Tobin (1992).

7. Argentina remained neutral for almost the entire World War II period.

8. On the avatars undergone by Argentina in remaining neutral during World War II, see Escudé (1988).

9. I appreciate Yoshihiro and Chizuko Oiwa's comments on the Japanese performers of tango argentino, which helped me to figure this out.

10. The following dialogue consists of excerpts from "Pasión por el Tango," *Asahi Graph* (June 1, 1987): 52–55. Freely translated by Raj Pandey.

11. Some Japanese tango argentino fans travel regularly to Argentina to keep up with the latest "authentic" tango developments, and some own some of the world's most complete collections of tango records and tango publications. In addition, the importation of AA bandoneónes (concertinas of an old German make that are no longer produced) from Argentina to Japan has affected argentino musicians' access to this precious tango musical instrument (Dragone 1990; Nishimura 1990).

12. Some postmodernists believe that this is a simple task that can be engaged playfully and that the Japanese have precisely that postmodern "nature" that will allow them to do so. ... But isn't this interpretation an exoticizing practice in itself? (I am grateful to Jeff Tobin for this suggestion.)

13. As early as 1936, Héctor and Luis Bates included in their *Historia del Tango* a brief section on "Tango in the Orient" in which they asked themselves, in awe, about the "powers" of the tango, given its capacity to "penetrate" such foreign and secluded cultures as the ones of Japan and Turkey (Bates and Bates 1936: 73–74). Finland and Colombia (Medellín) have also been reported as tango-sites by tango performers and historians. The appropriation of "exotic" and "authentic" tangos has taken different paths in each setting, following local and global adaptations. For example, in Medellín, Colombian tangueros cultivate tango musical and lyrical forms, whereas in Finland, tango choreographies are also central. These and other issues of Western mediation and local restylization deserve more attention than I have been able to provide.

14. As used by Attali (1985).

15. For vehement calls to incorporate political dimensions into the analysis of music, see McClary (1987), Frith (1987), and Wolff (1987). For the need to contemplate the dimension of pleasure in the analysis of popular music, see McClary and Walser (1990) and Shepherd (1987). For the importance of connecting sounds and dance in the understanding of popular music, see Frith and McRobbie (1990) and Dyer (1990).

16. As used by Lyotard (1990), from whom I borrow the term and with whom I share the purpose of "tracing passion in economics and economics in passion," but not his understanding of the dynamics of power that intervene in the economy of the libidinal. See also Smith (1989).

17. See Debord (1967: 138): "This society [capitalist] that suppresses geographical distances recovers internal distance, by way of the spectacular separation."

Chapter Six

1. I borrow the term "phallologocentric" from Cixous (1976).

2. This story was published in *Voices: The Hawai'i Women's Newsjournal* 4, no. 1 (Spring/Fall 1990): 19–22.

3. Horacio Ferrer, Blas Matamoro, Noemí Ulla, Ernesto Sábato, and practically every other author who has written on tango has established, sooner or later, the connection between the origins of the tango and the brothels and cabarets of the Río de la Plata region.

4. In reference to this point, Blas Matamoro writes: "The social world of the tango was static: there are rich and poor, but nobody knows why" (Matamoro 1971: 89).

5. I borrow these images from Jean Franco's (1984) insightful discussion of women's confinement and the uses of women by male authors in *hispanoamericana* literature. I have benefited much from her contribution.

6. Tango choreographies are improvised on a combination of traditionally set figures. This description is based on the dance style of Gloria and Eduardo, one of the few professional tango dance couples who have been recorded on video. I appreciate the crucial help of Judy Van Zile in the analysis of their dance movements.

7. As a rule, tangos are either sung or they are danced to, not both at the same time. However, this "rule" is sometimes broken in informal tango clubs and does not apply at all to dancing in the home, with members of the family.

8. In Jean Franco's words, I am talking here about the sexual politics of sadomasochism (1984).

9. At this point my interpretation of sexual politics in tango departs from the Foucauldian account of "docile bodies" (1984a) (although I borrow this term), as well as from Franco's (1984) conclusions, which are influenced by Lacan. For further discussion, refer to Chapter Two.

10. Julie Taylor synthesized the question of the isolation of the tango dancers in the following sentence: "They dance together in order to relive their disillusion alone" (1976: 290).

11. On the uses of plagiarism in tango see Arnold Hauser's poem in Ulla (1982: 15).

12. For an apotheosical depiction of the embrace in tango and its original impact in ballroom dancing all over the world, see Ferrer (1980a: 46–55).

13. Here I am playing with the opening words of Foucault's Inaugural Lecture at the College of France, December 2, 1970 (Foucault 1971).

14. Excerpts from *La Ultima Curda* (The Last Bender), a tango written by Cátulo Castillo in 1956.

15. "The South also exists."

16. When I first drafted this essay in 1989, the polemic over "postmodernism" and "postmodern" positions was already well under way. Since then much more has been written from the Left and from the Right. I refer readers only to a few now-classic texts that I have found especially helpful: Jameson (1984), Lyotard (1988), and the collections of essays edited by Arac (1986) and Ross (1989).

17. For a more equitable analysis of postmodernism that proposes a distinction in contemporary cultural politics between a "postmodernism of resistance" and a "postmodernism of reaction," see, for example, Hal Foster's preface to *The Anti-Aesthetic: Essays on Postmodern Culture* (Foster 1983).

18. I thank Farideh Farhi for encouraging me to engage in melodramatic politics of exaggeration.

19. I thank Randy Martin for his comments on the generation of surplus in the context of the political economy of passion.

20. I thank Sue-Ellen Case for urging me to explain my obstinate use of the first person.

21. I am paraphrasing the opening question in Spivak (1989).

22. See Bataille (1988, 1979, 1954).

23. See Baudrillard (1984, 1981).

24. See Derrida (1976, 1986, 1982).

25. See Foucault (1977a, 1984a, 1987).

26. See Lacan (1977a, 1977b, 1981, 1982); see also Butler (1987: 186–204).

27. See Lyotard 1990.

28. For a sophisticated, methodical proposal aimed at analyzing the passional universe as it appears in discourse, see Greimas and Fontanille (1993).

29. While passional taxonomies were disappearing, a concept of passion akin to a life principle, indivisible and unclassifiable, was developing, although it would not become important until the so-called age of Romanticism. Nietzsche (1968, 1974) and Freud (1955, 1961), for example, reinstalled passion at the center of all things human and at the origin of culture, as the moving force of both collective and individual history (Greimas and Fontanille 1983; Lebrun 1987; Rouanet 1987; Kehl 1987).

30. See Sartre (1966) and Lacan (1977a and 1977b). For an outstanding alternative view, see Deleuze and Guattari's emancipatory interpretation of desire in *Anti-Oedipus: Capitalism and Schizophrenia* (1983).

31. For a comprehensive analysis of contemporary interpretations of desire, see Butler (1987: 175–238). On the triangulation of desire and mimetic desire, see Girard (1978).

32. For a contemporary philosophical elaboration on the ontological differences between passion and desire, see Trías (1991: 135ff).

33. The term "sentimental education" is borrowed from the title of Gustave Flaubert's famous volume.

34. Gitlin (1989) mentions anxiety as a feature of postmodernism.

35. The death of God and Man has been repeatedly addressed by Nietzsche, Heidegger, Foucault, and others. My point here is that the Devil has been resurrected by postmodern thinkers, although rather than in supernatural proportions—like in premodernism—this time on a human scale.

36. On the interjection of the Other in the self as part of identity constitution, see Lacan (1977a, 1977b, 1981).

37. In "What Is Enlightenment?" Foucault suggests analyzing "modernism" as an attitude rather than as an epoch (1984c: 39). I play with his words.

38. Heller repeatedly uses this definition of feeling in *A Theory of Feelings* (1979).

39. Foucault (1971). I thank Jeff Tobin for calling my attention to the parallel between Discépolo's *Yira ... Yira* and Foucault's repeatedly cited phrase from "Orders of Discourse."

40. That is, Lacan's (and his followers') understanding of desire as an outcome of the impossible quest for refurbishing the stubborn and abstract "lack"; or the need to suture the "split" by which identity is constituted, threatened, and, in the same move, enabled to develop (Lacan 1977a, 1981).

41. To this effect Frederic Jameson writes: "In faithful conformity to poststructuralist linguistic theory, the past as 'referent' finds itself gradually bracketed, and then effaced altogether, leaving us with nothing but texts" (1984: 66). See also Said (1983). I understand that writing and textuality are imperfect allegories that allude to the violence inherent in the pursuit of knowledge. It is precisely to this imperfection that I wish to call attention since the frequent misunderstanding of these concepts points to their political connotations. For a careful discussion of these issues, see Spivak 1988a.

42. See Foucault 1977e and Gayatri Spivak's discussion of the Foucault-Deleuze dialogue in Spivak 1988a.

43. "If the postmodernist emphasis on multivocality leads to a denial of the continued existence of a hierarchy of discourse, the material and historical links between cultures can be ignored, with all voices becoming equal, each telling only an individualized story. Then the history of the colonial, for example, can be read as independent of that of the colonizer. Such readings ignore or obscure exploitation and power differentials and, therefore, offer no grounds to fight oppression and effect change" (Mascia-Lees et al. 1989: 29).

44. See, for example, Sandra Lee Bartky's comments: "Foucault often writes as if power constitutes the very individuals upon whom it operates. [...] If individuals were wholly constituted by the power-knowledge regime Foucault describes, it would make no sense to speak of resistance to discipline at all. Foucault seems on the verge of depriving us of a vocabulary in which to conceptualize the nature and meaning of those periodic refusals of control that, just as much as the imposition of control, mark the course of human history" (Bartky 1988: 82).

45. Doane (1988) points out a similar problem with Lacanian analysis.

46. On the risks of subjecting intellectual analysis to party politics, see Sarlo (1989).

47. See P. Steven Sangren's (1988) ironic remarks on the lack of reflexivity among postmodernists regarding their own institutional advantages.

48. Paraphrasing Nancy Harstock, Mascia-Lees et al. suggest that: "The postmodern view that truth and knowledge are contingent and multiple may be seen to act as a truth claim itself, a claim that undermines the ontological status of the subject at the very time when women and non-Western peoples have begun to claim themselves as subjects" (1990: 15).

49. "The space I occupy might be explained by my history. It is a position into which I have been written. I am not privileging it, but I do want to use it. I can't fully construct a position that is different from the one I am in" (Spivak 1990a: 68).

50. This section was first published in *Voices: The Hawai'i Women's Newsjournal* 4, no. 2 (Winter 1990–1991): 37–38, along with other opinionated contributions to a debate titled "Challenging Feminism." All the central concepts on which I develop this argument ("Third World"; "Western"; "feminism"; and "women") are problematic in that they carry heavy essentialist connotations and have been used throughout the entire ideological spectrum for a variety of political purposes. For a lack of better and still compelling words,

I use them in this protest emphasizing political rather than biological or cultural bases for alliance (see Mohanty 1991a, 1991b).

51. I thank Gayatri Spivak and Parama Roy for reading and commenting on this "scene" in the context of a seminar held at the Center for Ideas and Society at the University of California–Riverside in the spring of 1994. I cannot, however, implicate them in the results. Their criticisms have been incorporated imperfectly and are still haunting the choreocritic's text and my desire for decolonization.

52. See, for example, Spivak (1985, 1988a).

53. See Spivak (1990a, 1990b).

54. See Shohat (1992) and Young (1990).

55. See Bhabha (1985) on "theoreticist anarchism."

56. See Bhabha (1986, 1985).

57. I am tentatively following here Gayatri Spivak's elaborations on postcolonial intellectuals and their attempts to represent the subaltern (Spivak 1988a: 287–289). I have appropriated, stretched, and run away with her concepts. I assume that postcolonial intellectuals are scholars like her who have made the field of colonial studies known in the U.S. academy from a postcolonial perspective. I also recognize a common ground between these "postcolonial" intellectuals originally from India and other Third World intellectuals who were raised in settler colonies like Argentina and are now teaching at U.S. universities. Thus, I picture the Choreocritic (and myself) as "postcolonial" intellectuals. Through the character of the Choreocritic I attempt to represent the conflations and misrepresentations that are present and vibrant in the U.S. academic vulgarizations of postmodern and postcolonial intellectual positions. The theatricalization of a postcolonial encounter is thus a parody of the colonial encounter—an encounter between so-called postmodern intellectuals and so-called postcolonial intellectuals in the U.S. academic conference setting. My intention is to represent this encounter broadly and to learn from it rather than to pursue a careful textual analysis for which other scholars are better qualified.

58. For a powerful critique of Petras's homogenization of latinoamericano intellectuals, see Vilas (1990).

59. A Symposium on Fear and its politico-socio-psychological consequences was held in São Paulo in the mid-1980s to analyze the devastating effects of what is considered one of the indisputable victories of the latest military rules in América Latina.

60. I borrow this phrase from Spivak (1988a).

61. "To show Cris, Moni, Adri, Elena, Analía, Nue, Graciela and the rest what I have just discovered and that nobody can stop us. Nobody. So many women, fighting, as we fight, with a *latino* body, contagious, as in a savage horde."

Sources Consulted

Abo Ikuo. 1990. Interview. Tokyo, November.

Acosta, Leonardo. 1982. *Música y Descolonización*. La Habana: Editorial Arte y Literatura.

Adam, Paul. 1896. "Les energies." *Revue Blanche* 71(10): 433–441.

Adellach, Alberto, Mariano Aguirre, and Ignacio Colombres. 1981. *Argentina: Cómo Matar la Cultura. Testimonios 1976–1981*. Madrid: Editorial Revolución.

Alberdi, Juan B. 1969. *Las "Bases" de Alberdi*. Edited by Jorge M. Mayer. Buenos Aires: Sudamericana. (First published in 1852.)

Allen, Virginia M. 1983. *The Femme Fatale: Erotic Icon*. Troy, N.Y.: The Whitston Publishing Company.

Alposta, Luis A. 1987. *El Tango en Japón*. Buenos Aires: Corregidor.

Anderson, Benedict. 1983. *Imagined Communities: Reflections on the Origin and Spread of Nationalism*. London: Verso.

Anderson, Jack. 1974. *Dance*. New York: Newsweek Books.

Andrews, George R. 1980. *The Afro-Argentines of Buenos Aires, 1800–1900*. Madison: University of Wisconsin Press.

Anzaldúa, Gloria, ed. 1990. *Making Face, Making Soul. Haciendo Caras: Creative and Critical Perspectives by Feminists of Color*. San Francisco: Aunt Lute Foundation Book.

———. 1992. "How to tame a wild tongue." In R. Ferguson, M. Gever, Trinh T.M., and C. West, eds., *Out There: Marginalization and Contemporary Cultures*. New York: The MIT Press, pp. 203–213.

Appiah, Kwame Anthony. 1991. "Is the post- in postmodernism the post- in postcolonial?" *Critical Inquiry* 17 (Winter): 336–357.

Arac, Jonathan, ed. 1986. *Postmodernism and Politics*. Minneapolis: University of Minnesota Press.

Asada Akira. 1988. "Infantile capitalism and Japan's postmodernism: a fairy tale." Translated by Kyoto Salden. *South Atlantic Quarterly* 87(3): 629–634.

Aschengreen, Erik. 1974. " 'The beautiful danger:' facets of the romantic ballet." Translated by P. M. McAndrew. *Dance Perspectives* 58.

Assunção, Fernando O. 1984. *El Tango y Sus Circunstancias (1880–1920)*. Buenos Aires: Librería El Ateneo Editorial.

Attali, Jacques. 1985. *Noise: The Political Economy of Music*. Translated by Brian Massumi. Theory and History of Literature, Volume 16. Minneapolis: University of Minnesota Press.

Azzi, María Susana. 1991. *Antropología del Tango: Los Protagonistas*. Buenos Aires: Ediciones de Olavarría.

Bade, Patrick. 1979. *Femme Fatale. Images of Evil and Fascinating Women*. London: Ash and Grant.

———. 1985. "Art and degeneration: visual icons of corruption." In J. E. Chamberlin and S. L. Gilman, eds., *Degeneration: The Dark Side of Progress*. New York: Columbia University Press, pp. 220–238.

Baez, Martha. 1990. *Los Herederos del Exilio*. Buenos Aires: Corregidor.

Balibar, Etienne. 1990. "Paradoxes of universality." In D. T. Goldberg, ed., *Anatomy of Racism*. Minneapolis: University of Minnesota Press, pp. 283–294.

Barbero, María I., and Fernando Devoto. 1983. *Los Nacionalistas (1910–1932)*. Buenos Aires: Centro Editor de América Latina.

Barthes, Roland. 1977. *Image, Music, Text*. New York: Hill and Wang.

Bartky, Sandra Lee. 1988. "Foucault, femininity, and the modernization of patriarchal power." In I. Diamond and L. Quinby, eds., *Feminism and Foucault: Reflections on Resistance*. Boston: Northeastern University Press, pp. 61–86.

Bataille, Georges. 1954. *L'Expérience Intérieure*. Paris: Gallimard.

————. 1979. *El Erotismo*. Translated by Toni Vicens. Barcelona: Tusquets Editores.

————. 1988. *The Accursed Share: An Essay on General Economy: Volume 1, Consumption*. Translated by Robert Hurley. New York: Zone Books.

Bates, Héctor, and Luis J. Bates. 1936. *La Historia del Tango*. Buenos Aires: Taller Gráfico de la Compañía. General Fabril Financiera.

Baudrillard, Jean. 1981. *For a Critique of the Political Economy of the Sign*. St. Louis: Telos Press.

————. 1984. *Las Estrategias Fatales*. Translated by Joaquín Jorda. Barcelona: Editorial Anagrama.

Beauroy, Jacques, Marc Bertrand, and Edward T. Gargan, eds. 1976. *The Wolf and the Lamb: Popular Culture in France*. Saratoga, Calif.: Anma Libri.

Beck, Jill. 1986. "Systems of dance/movement notation." In B. Fleshman, ed., *Theatrical Movement: A Bibliographical Anthology*. Metuchen, N.J.: Scarecrow Press, pp. 89–100.

Benarós, León. 1977. "El tango y los lugares y casas de baile." In *La Historia del Tango: Primera Epoca 2*. Buenos Aires: Corregidor, pp. 205–285.

Benedetti, Mario. 1971. *Crítica Cómplice*. La Habana: Instituto Cubano del Libro.

Bennett, Tony, Colin Mercer, and Janet Woollacott, eds. 1986. *Popular Culture and Social Relations*. Milton Keynes, England: Open University Press.

Bergstrom, Janet, and Mary Ann Doane. 1989. "The female spectator: contexts and directions." *Camera Obscura* 20/21: 5–27.

Bernheimer, Charles. 1986. "Huysmans: writing against (female) nature." In S. Rubin Suleiman, ed., *The Female Body in Western Culture: Contemporary Perspectives*. Cambridge: Harvard University Press, pp. 373–386.

Bhabha, Homi K. 1984. "Of mimicry and man: the ambivalence of colonial discourse." *October* 28: 125–133.

————. 1985. "Signs taken for wonders: questions of ambivalence and authority under a tree outside Delhi, May 1817." *Critical Inquiry* 12(1): 144–165.

————. 1986. "The Other question: difference, discrimination and the discourse of colonialism." In F. Backer et al., *Literary Politics and Theory: Papers from the Essex Conference, 1976–1984*. London: Methuen, pp. 148–172.

————. 1990a. "DissemiNation: time, narrative, and the margins of the modern nation." In H. K. Bhabha, ed., *Nation and Narration*. London: Routledge, pp. 291–322.

————. 1990b. "Interrogating identity: the postcolonial prerogative." In D. T. Goldberg, ed., *Anatomy of Racism*. Minneapolis: University of Minnesota Press, pp. 183–209.

Bifani, Patricia. 1988. "Ursula Iguarán: mujer y mito: ensayo sobre la personalidad creadora." *Nueva Sociedad* 93: 94–104.

Bilderback, Walter. 1989. *Stage Notes for "Dangerous Games: Two Tango Pieces."* La Jolla, Calif.: La Jolla Playhouse.

Birdwhistle, Ray L. 1974a. "Masculinity and femininity as display." In S. Weitz, ed., *Non-verbal Communication*. New York: Oxford University Press, pp. 144–150.

————. 1974b. "Toward analyzing American movement." In S. Weitz, ed., *Non-verbal Communication*. New York: Oxford University Press, pp. 134–143.

Birken, Lawrence. 1988. *Consuming Desire: Sexual Science and the Emergence of a Culture of Abundance (1871–1914)*. Ithaca: Cornell University Press.

Blanco, Celia. 1993. Interview. Buenos Aires, July.

Bonafoux, Luis. 1992. "Testimonios: pláticas parisienses con 'Fray Mocho.'" *Club de Tango* 2: 16–19. (First published in 1913.)

Bonfil Batalla, Guillermo. 1966. "Conservative thought in applied anthropology: a critique." *Human Organization* 25(2): 89–92.

Borges, Jorge Luis. 1963. "El idioma de los argentinos." In J. L. Borges and J. E. Clemente, *El Lenguaje de Buenos Aires*. Buenos Aires: Emecé, pp. 13–36. (First published in 1928.)

———. 1970. *The Aleph and Other Stories: 1933–1969*. Edited and translated by Norman Thomas Di Giovanni. New York: E. P. Dutton.

———. 1984. "A history of the tango." In *Evaristo Carriego: A Book About Old-time Buenos Aires*. Translated by Norman Thomas di Giovanni. New York: E. P. Dutton, pp. 131–148.

Borges, Jorge Luis, and Silvina Bullrich Palenque, eds. 1968. *El Compadrito*. Buenos Aires: Compañía General Fabril Editora.

Bourdieu, Pierre. 1984. *Distinction: A Social Critique of the Judgement of Taste*. Translated by Richard Nice. Cambridge: Harvard University Press.

Bozzarelli, Oscar. 1989. *El Africa, El Tango y El Jazz*. Buenos Aires: Academia Porteña del Lunfardo.

Bra, Gerardo. 1984. "Las heroínas del tango." *Todo es Historia* 17(204): 28–38.

Brathwaite, Edward. 1969. *Islands*. London: Oxford University Press.

Braudel, Fernand. 1981. *Civilization and Capitalism, 15th–18th Century: Volume 1, The Structures of Everyday Life: The Limits of the Possible*. Translated by Siam Reynolds. New York: Harper and Row.

Brillat-Savarin, Jean Anthelme. 1972. *The Physiology of Taste, or Meditations on Transcendental Gastronomy*. Translated by M.F.K. Fisher. New York: Alfred A. Knopf. (First published in 1825.)

Bronner, Stephen E., and Douglas Kellner, eds. 1983. *Passion and Rebellion: The Expressionist Heritage*. South Hadley, Mass.: J. F. Bergin.

Brooks, Peter. 1980. "The mark of the beast: prostitution, melodrama, and narrative." In D. Gerould, ed., *Melodrama*. New York: New York Literary Forum, pp. 125–140.

Bryson, Norman. 1988. "Introduction." In N. Bryson, ed., *Calligram: Essays in New Art History from France*. New York: Cambridge University Press, pp. xiii–xxix.

Buckman, Peter. 1978. *Let's Dance: Social, Ballroom and Folk Dancing*. New York: Paddington Press.

Bunch, Charlotte, and Roxanna Carrillo. 1990. "Feminist perspectives on women in development." In I. Tinker, ed., *Persistent Inequalities: Women and World Development*. New York, Oxford: Oxford University Press, pp. 70–83.

Burchell, Samuel C. 1966. *Age of Progress*. New York: Time, Inc.

Burke, Peter. 1981. "The 'discovery' of popular culture." In R. Samuel, ed., *People's History and Socialist Theory*. London: Routledge and Kegan Paul, pp. 216–226.

Buruma, Ian. 1984. *Behind the Mask: On Sexual Demons, Sacred Mothers, Transvestites, Gangsters, Drifters and Other Japanese Cultural Heroes*. New York: Pantheon Books.

Butler, Judith P. 1987. *Subjects of Desire: Hegelian Reflections in Twentieth-Century France*. New York: Columbia University Press.

Byrón, Silvestre. 1977. "Los años veinte." In *La Historia del Tango: Volume 6, Los Años Veinte*. Buenos Aires: Corregidor, pp. 815–836.

Cabrera Alvarez, Guillermo, ed. 1987. *Memories of Che*. Translated by J. Fried. Secaucus, N.J.: Lyle Stuart.

Cadícamo, Enrique. 1975. *La Historia del Tango en París*. Buenos Aires: Corregidor.

———. 1987. *Bajo el Signo de Tango (Memorias)*. Buenos Aires: Corregidor.

Calvert, Susan, and Peter Calvert. 1989. *Argentina: Political Culture and Instability.* Pittsburgh: University of Pittsburgh Press.

Carella, Tulio. 1956. *El Tango, Mito y Esencia.* Buenos Aires: Ediciones Doble P.

Carpentier, Alejo. 1981. "América Latina en la confluencia de coordenadas históricas y su repercusión en la música." In *La Novela Latinoamericana en Vísperas de un Nuevo Siglo, y Otros Ensayos.* Madrid: Siglo XXI de España Editores, pp. 159–176.

Carretero, Andrés. 1964. *El Compadrito y el Tango. (El Hombre de la Argentina Comercial).* Buenos Aires: Ediciones Pampa y Cielo.

Carriego, Evaristo. 1977. *La Costurerita Que Dió Aquel Mal Paso y Otros Poemas.* Buenos Aires: Torres Aguero Editores.

Carter, Ernestine. 1975. *20th Century Fashion: A Scrapbook, 1900 to Today.* London: Eyre Methuen.

Case, Sue-Ellen. 1993. "Toward a butch-femme aesthetic." In H. Abelove, M. A. Barale, and D. M. Halperin, eds., *The Lesbian and Gay Studies Reader.* New York: Routledge, pp. 294–306.

Castellanos, Pintín. 1948. *Entre Cortes y Quebradas: Candombes, Milongas y Tangos, su Historia y Comentario.* Montevideo.

Castro, Donald. 1991. *The Argentine Tango as Social History, 1880–1955: The Soul of the People.* Lewiston, N.Y.: The Edwin Mellen Press.

Caws, Mary Ann. 1986. "Ladies shot and painted: female embodiments in surrealist art." In S. Rubin Suleiman, ed., *The Female Body in Western Culture: Contemporary Perspectives.* Cambridge: Harvard University Press, pp. 262–287.

CEPAL (Comisión Económica para América Latina [Economic Commission for Latin America, ECLA]). 1959. *El Desarrollo Económico de la Argentina. Parte 1.* México D.F.: Naciones Unidas, Consejo Económico y Social.

Césaire, Aimé. 1969. *Une Tempête: D'apres "La Tempête" de Shakespeare: Adaptation pour un Théâtre Nègre.* Paris: Editions du Sevil.

Chaui, Marilena. 1987. "Sobre o medo." In *Os Sentidos de Paixão.* São Paulo: Funarte, Editora Schwarcz, pp. 35–76.

Cixous, Hélène. 1976. "The laugh of the Medusa." Translated by K. Cohen and P. Cohen. *Signs* 1: 875–893.

Cocks, Joan. 1989. *The Oppositional Imagination: Feminism, Critique, and Political Theory.* London: Routledge.

Collier, Simon. 1988. *Carlos Gardel. Su vida, su música, su época.* Buenos Aires: Editorial Sudamericana.

————. 1992. "The popular roots of the Argentine tango." *History Workshop Journal* 34: 92–100.

Comolli, Jean-Louis. 1980. "Machines of the visible." In T. de Lauretis and S. Heath, eds., *The Cinematic Apparatus.* New York: St. Martin's Press, pp. 121–142.

Connolly, William E. 1985. "Taylor, Foucault, and Otherness." *Political Theory* 13(3): 365–376.

Connor, Steven. 1989. *Postmodernist Culture: An Introduction to Theories of the Contemporary.* Oxford: Basil Blackwell.

Copes, Juan Carlos. 1989. *Let's Dance: Bailemos Tango.* Buenos Aires: La Canción.

————. 1992. Interviews and tango instruction. Buenos Aires, July.

Cornell, Drucilla, and Adam Thurschwell. 1987. "Feminism, negativity, intersubjectivity." In S. Benhabib and D. Cornell, eds., *Feminism as Critique: On the Politics of Gender.* Minneapolis: University of Minnesota Press, pp. 143–162.

Corradi, Juan E. 1979. "The avatars of socio-political discourse in Latin America." *Social Science Information* 18(1): 59–77.

Cortés Conde, Roberto, and Ezequiel Gallo. 1967. *La Formación de la Argentina Moderna*. Buenos Aires: Paidos.

Couselo, Jorge M. 1977. "El Tango en el cine." In *Historia del Tango: Volume 8, El Tango en el Espectáculo*. Buenos Aires: Corregidor, pp. 1289–1328.

Cunninghame Graham, Roberto. 1938. *El Río de la Plata*. Buenos Aires: Joaquín Gil. (First published in 1914.)

Curubeto, Diego. 1993. *Babilonia Gaucha: Hollywood en la Argentina, la Argentina en Hollywood*. Buenos Aires: Planeta.

D'Alessandro, Antonio. 1991. *Yo Fui al Japón con Canaro. Memorias de un viaje inolvidable*. Buenos Aires: EP.

Davis, Flora. 1973. *Inside Intuition: What We Know About Non-Verbal Communications*. New York: McGraw Hill.

Debord, Guy. 1967. *La Societe du Spectacle*. Paris: Buchet/Chastel.

de Certeau, Michel. 1986. *Heterologies: Discourse on the Other*. Translated by B. Massumi. Minneapolis: University of Minnesota Press.

Deleuze, Gilles, and Felix Guattari. 1983. *Anti-Oedipus: Capitalism and Schizophrenia*. Translated by Robert Hurley, Mark Seem, and Helen R. Lane. Minneapolis: University of Minnesota Press.

Del Greco, Orlando. 1990. *Carlos Gardel y los Autores de sus Canciones*. Buenos Aires: Ediciones Akian.

———. 1993. "Cuando Casimiro Aín, El Vasco, bailó el tango ante el Papa." *Club de Tango* 5: 13–14.

Dellepiane, Antonio. 1967. *El Idioma del Delito y Diccionario Lunfardo*. Buenos Aires: Compañía General Fabril Editora.

Derrida, Jacques. 1976. *Of Grammatology*. Translated by G. Spivak. Baltimore: Johns Hopkins University Press.

———. 1982. "Différance." Translated by A. Bass. In *Margins of Philosophy*. Chicago: University of Chicago Press, pp. 1–27.

———. 1986. *Glas*. Translated by J. P. Leavey and R. A. Rand. Lincoln: University of Nebraska Press.

Díaz Alejandro, Carlos F. 1975. *Ensayos sobre la Historia Económica Argentina*. Buenos Aires: Amorrortu.

Diijkstra, Bram. 1986. *Idols of Perversity: Fantasies of Female Evil in Fin de Siècle Culture*. New York: Oxford University Press.

Discépolo, Enrique Santos. 1977. *Cancionero*. Buenos Aires: Torres Aguero Editor.

Di Tella, Guido, and Manuel Zymelman. 1967. *Las Etapas del Desarrollo Económico Argentino*. Buenos Aires: Editional Universitaria de Buenos Aires.

Doane, Mary Ann. 1987. *The Desire to Desire: The Woman's Film of the 1940s*. Bloomington: Indiana University Press.

———. 1988. "Woman's stake: filming the female body." In C. Penley, ed., *Feminism and Film Theory*. New York: Routledge, Chapman and Hall, pp. 196–215.

———. 1991. *Femmes Fatales. Feminism, Film Theory, Psychoanalysis*. New York: Routledge.

Dragone, Jorge. 1990. Interview. Tokyo, November.

Dujovne Ortiz, Alicia. 1991. "Buenos Aires." In P. Mariani, ed., *Critical Fictions: The Politics of Imaginative Writing*. Seattle: Bay Press, pp. 115–130.

Dyer, Richard. 1990. "In defense of Disco." In S. Frith and A. Goodwin, eds., *On Record: Rock, Pop, and the Written Word*. New York: Pantheon Books, pp. 410–418.

Eguchi Yuko. 1990. Interview. Tokyo, November.

Eibl-Eibesfeldt, I. 1974. "Similarities and differences between cultures in expressive movements." In S. Weitz, ed., *Non-verbal Communication*. New York: Oxford University Press, pp. 20–34.

Ekman, Paul, and Friesen, W. V. 1974. "Nonverbal leakage and clues to deception." In S. Weitz, ed., *Non-verbal Communication*. New York: Oxford University Press, pp. 269–291.

Eksteins, Modris. 1990. *Rites of Spring: The Great War and the Birth of the Modern Age*. New York: Anchor Books–Doubleday.

Elshtain, Jean B. 1993. "Politics without cliché." *Social Research* 60(3): 433–444.

Emberley, Julia. 1987. "The fashion apparatus and the deconstruction of postmodern subjectivity." In A. and M. Kroker, eds., *Body Invaders: Panic Sex in America*. New York: St. Martin's Press, pp. 47–60.

Escobar, Elizam. 1988. "The fear and tremor of being understood." *Third Text* 3/4: 119–141.

Escudé, Carlos. 1988. "El boicot norteamericano a la Argentina en la década del 40." In *Conflictos y Procesos de la Historia Argentina Contemporánea*, Volume 1. Buenos Aires: Centro Editor de América Latina.

Estrázulas, Enrique. 1990. *Tango para Intelectuales*. Buenos Aires: Sudamericana.

Etchebarne, Miguel D. 1955. *La Influencia del Arrabal en la Poesía Argentina Culta*. Buenos Aires: G. Kraft.

Ewen, Stuart. 1988. *All Consuming Images: The Politics of Style in Contemporary Culture*. New York: Basic Books.

Fabian, Johannes. 1983. *Time and the Other: How Anthropology Makes Its Object*. New York: Columbia University Press.

Fals Borda, Orlando. 1990. "El Tercer Mundo y la reorientación de las ciencias contemporáneas." *Nueva Sociedad* 107: 83–91.

Fanon, Frantz. 1967. *Black Skin, White Masks*. Translated by Charles Lam Markmann. New York: Grove Weidenfeld.

————. 1968. *The Wretched of the Earth*. Translated by Constance Farrington. New York: Grove Weidenfeld.

————. 1988. *Toward the African Revolution: Political Essays*. Translated by Haakon Chevalier. New York: Grove Press.

Fernández Retamar, Roberto. 1989. *Caliban and Other Essays*. Translated by E. Baker. Minneapolis: University of Minnesota Press.

Ferrer, Aldo. 1968. *La Economía Argentina: Las Etapas de su Desarrollo y Problemes Actuales*. México D.F.: Fondo de Cultura Económica.

Ferrer, Horacio. 1980a. *El Libro del Tango: Arte Popular de Buenos Aires: Tomo 1, Crónica del Tango*. Barcelona: Antonio Tersol.

————. 1980b. *El Libro del Tango: Arte Popular de Buenos Aires: Tomo 2, Diccionario A-J*. Barcelona: Antonio Tersol.

————. 1980c. *El Libro del Tango: Arte Popular de Buenos Aires: Tomo 3, Diccionario K-Z*. Barcelona: Antonio Tersol.

————. 1991. *Moriré en Buenos Aires: Vida y Obra de Horacio Ferrer. Antología de su Teatro Lírico, su Poesía, su Prosa, 1951–1991*, 3 vols. Buenos Aires: Manrique Zago Ediciones.

Figari, Pedro, and Fernando Guibert. 1979. *Tango y Candombe en el Río de la Plata*. Río de la Plata: Librería Colonial.

Fiske, John. 1989. *Understanding Popular Culture*. Boston: Unwin Hyman.

Flores, Celedonio Esteban. 1977. *Cancionero*. Buenos Aires: Torres Aguero Editor.

Flugel, J. C. 1950. *The Psychology of Clothes*. London: Hogarth Press/Institute of Psychoanalysis.

Fonteyn, Margot. 1979. *The Magic of Dance*. New York: Alfred A. Knopf.

Ford, Aníbal. 1973. "Manzi en el sótano de FORJA." *Crisis* 67: 14–19.

Foster, Hal. 1983. "Postmodernism: a preface." In H. Foster, ed., *The Anti-Aesthetic: Essays on Postmodern Culture*. Seattle: Bay Press, pp. 3–15.

_____. 1985. *Recodings: Art, Spectacle, Cultural Politics*. Seattle: Bay Press.

Foster, Susan L. 1986. *Reading Dancing. Bodies and Subjects in Contemporary American Dance*. Berkeley: University of California Press.

_____. n.d. "The ballerina's phallic pointe." Forthcoming in S. Foster, ed., *CorpoRealities*. New York: Routledge.

Foucault, Michel. 1970. *The Order of Things: An Archaeology of the Human Sciences*. New York: Vintage Books.

_____. 1971. "Orders of discourse." Translated by Rupert Swyer. *Social Science Information* 10(2): 7–30.

_____. 1977a. "Fantasia of the library." In D. F. Bouchard and S. Simon, ed. and trans., *Language, Counter-Memory, Practice: Selected Essays and Interviews*. Ithaca: Cornell University Press, pp. 87–111.

_____. 1977b. "A preface to transgression." In D. F. Bouchard and S. Simon, ed. and trans., *Language, Counter-Memory, Practice: Selected Essays and Interviews*. Ithaca: Cornell University Press, pp. 29–52.

_____. 1977c. "Theatrum philosophicum." In D. F. Bouchard and S. Simon, ed. and trans., *Language, Counter-Memory, Practice: Selected Essays and Interviews*. Ithaca: Cornell University Press, pp. 165–197.

_____. 1977d. *Historia de la Sexualidad: Volume 1, La Voluntad de Saber*. Translated by Ulises Guiñazu. México D.F.: Siglo Veintiuno.

_____. 1977e. "Intellectuals and power: a conversation between Michel Foucault and Gilles Deleuze." In D. F. Bouchard and S. Simon, ed. and trans., *Language, Counter-Memory, Practice: Selected Essays and Interviews*. Ithaca: Cornell University Press, pp. 205–217.

_____. 1984a. "Docile bodies." In P. Rabinow, ed., *The Foucault Reader*. New York: Pantheon Books, pp. 179–187.

_____. 1984b. "What is an author?" In P. Rabinow, ed., *The Foucault Reader*. New York: Pantheon Books, pp. 101–120.

_____. 1984c. "What is enlightenment?" In P. Rabinow, ed., *The Foucault Reader*. New York: Pantheon Books, pp. 32–50.

_____. 1985. *The History of Sexuality: Volume 2, The Use of Pleasure*. Translated by R. Hurley. New York: Vintage Books.

_____. 1987. "Nietzsche, genealogy, history." In D. F. Bouchard and S. Simon, eds., *Interpreting Politics*. New York: New York University Press, pp. 221–240.

Fouquiéres, André de. 1913. "Les danses nouvelles: le tango." *Fémina* 284: 58–61.

Franco, Jean. 1984. "Self-destructing heroines." *The Minnesota Review* 22: 105–115.

_____. 1986. "The incorporation of women: a comparison of North American and Mexican popular narrative." In T. Modleski, ed., *Studies in Entertainment: Critical Approaches to Mass Culture*. Bloomington: Indiana University Press, pp. 119–138.

Frank, Waldo. 1969. "América Hispana." In T. de Lara and I. L. Roncetti de Panti, eds., *El Tema del Tango en la Literatura Argentina*. Buenos Aires: Ediciones Culturales Argentinas, Ministerio de Educación y Justicia, Dirección General de Cultura, pp. 349–350. (First published in 1931.)

Franks, Arthur H. 1963. *Social Dance: A Short History*. London: Routledge and Kegan Paul.

Fraser, Nancy. 1989. *Unruly Practices: Power, Discourse and Gender in Contemporary Social Theory*. Minneapolis: University of Minnesota Press.

Freud, Sigmund. 1955. "Beyond the pleasure principle." In *Standard Edition of Complete Psychological Works*, Volume 18. Translated by James Strachey. London: Hogarth Press, pp. 1–64.

————. 1961. "Civilization and its discontents." In *Standard Edition of Complete Psychological Works*, Volume 21. Translated by James Strachey. London: Hogarth Press, pp. 57–145.

Frith, Simon. 1987. "Towards an aesthetic of popular music." In R. Leppert and S. McClary, eds., *Music and Society: The Politics of Composition, Performance and Reception*. New York: Cambridge University Press, pp. 133–149.

Frith, Simon, ed. 1989. *World Music, Politics and Social Change: Papers from the International Association for the Study of Popular Music*. Manchester, England: Manchester University Press.

Frith, Simon, and Angela McRobbie. 1990. "Rock and sexuality." In S. Frith and A. Goodwin, eds., *On Record: Rock, Pop, and the Written Word*. New York: Pantheon Books, pp. 371–389.

Galeano, Eduardo. 1986. *El Descubrimiento De América Que Todavía No Fue y Otros Escritos*. Barcelona: Editorial Laia.

————. 1987. *Memory of Fire: Volume 2, Faces and Masks*. Translated by Cedric Belfrage. New York: Pantheon Books.

————. 1988. *Memory of Fire: Volume 3, Century of the Wind*. Translated by Cedric Belfrage. New York: Pantheon Books.

Gallo, Blas R. 1970. *Historia del Sainete Nacional*. Buenos Aires: Editorial Buenos Aires Leyendo.

García, Germán L. 1990. "El tango, ese murmullo." *Dossier: Tango, el Himno Pasional Argentino, Babel* 3(21): 23–24.

García Canclini, Néstor. 1989. *Las Culturas Populares en el Capitalismo*. México D.F.: Nueva Imagen.

García Jiménez, Francisco. 1965a. *El Tango: Historia de Medio Siglo (1880–1930)*. Buenos Aires: Editorial Universitaria de Buenos Aires.

————. 1965b. *Así Nacieron los Tangos*. Buenos Aires: Losada.

Gasché, Rodolphe. 1985. "Ecce Homo or the written body." *The Oxford Literary Review* 7: 3–24.

Gates, Henry Louis, Jr. 1984. "Criticism in the jungle." In H. L. Gates, Jr., ed., *Black Literature and Literary Theory*. New York: Methuen, pp. 1–26.

Giardinelli, Mempo, ed. 1989. *Mujeres y Escritura: Las 56 Ponencias Leídas Durante las Primeras Jornadas sobre Mujeres y Escritura*. Buenos Aires: Editorial Puro Cuento.

Gilio, María Esther. 1986. *EmerGentes*. Buenos Aires: Ediciones de la Flor.

Giovannini, Francesco. 1914. *Balli d'Oggi. Con 70 Figure Demostrative, Grafici e Brani Musicali. E Uno Studio Critico Sulle Danza Nuovissime de Giovanni Franceschini*. Milan: Ulrico Hoelpi.

Girard, René. 1978. *Des Choses Cachées depuis la Foundation du Monde*. Paris: Bernard Grasset.

Gitlin, Todd. 1989. "Postmodernism: roots and politics." In I. Angus and S. Jhally, eds., *Cultural Politics in Contemporary America*. New York: Routledge, pp. 347–360.

Gloria y Eduardo. n.d. *El Tango Argentino: Exclusive System*. Volumes 1 and 2. Video.

Gobello, José. 1976a. *Conversando Tangos*. Buenos Aires: A. Pena Lillo Editor.

————. 1976b. "Orígenes de la letra de tango." In *La Historia del Tango: Volume 1, Sus Orígenes*. Buenos Aires: Corregidor, pp. 100–129.

————. 1980. *Crónica General del Tango*. Buenos Aires: Editorial Fraterna.

————. 1990. *Nuevo Diccionario Lunfardo*. Buenos Aires: Corregidor.

Gobello, José, and Eduardo Stillman. 1966. *Las Letras del Tango de Villoldo a Borges*. Buenos Aires: Brújula.

Gómez, Carlos. 1993. Interviews and tango instruction. Buenos Aires, July.

Gómez Peña, Guillermo. 1990. " 'Despiertos' o el deseo de descolonizar." *David y Goliath* 19(57): 21.

Goncourt, Edmond de. 1956. *Journal: Mémoires de la Vie Litteraire, 1879–1890*, Volume 3. Paris: Fasquelle-Flammarion.

Goodwin, Andrew, and Joe Gore. 1990. "World beat and the cultural imperialism debate." *Socialist Review* 20(3): 63–80.

Gramsci, Antonio. 1992. *Selections from the Prison Notebooks of Antonio Gramsci*. Edited and translated by Quintin Hoare and Geoffrey Nowell Smith. New York: International Publishers. (First published in 1971.)

Greimas, Algirdas J., and Fontanille, Jacques. 1993. *The Semiotics of Passions: From States of Affairs to States of Feelings*. Translated by Paul Perron and Frank Collins. Minneapolis: University of Minnesota Press.

Grenier, Line, and Jocelyne Guilbault. 1990. " 'Authority' revisited: the 'Other' in anthropology and popular music studies." *Ethnomusicology* 34(3): 381–397.

Guevara, Ernesto "Che." 1969. "Political sovereignty and economic independence." In R. E. Bonachea and N. P. Valdes, eds., *Che: Selected Works of Ernesto Guevara*. Cambridge: The MIT Press.

_____. 1985. *Guerrilla Warfare*. Edited by Brian Loveman and Thomas M. Davies, Jr. Lincoln: University of Nebraska Press.

Guibert, Fernando. 1968. *The Argentine Compadrito*. Translated by E. Gibson. Buenos Aires: Ediciones Promoción Nacional.

_____. 1973. *Los Argentinos y el Tango*. Buenos Aires: Ediciones Culturales Argentinas.

Gunder Frank, Andre. 1968. "Reply. In Social Responsibilities Symposium." *Current Anthropology* 9(5): 412–414.

Guttierrez-Jones, Carl. 1990. "Legal rhetoric and cultural critique: notes towards guerrilla writing." *Diacritics* 20(4): 57–73.

Guy, Donna J. 1991. *Sex and Danger in Buenos Aires: Prostitution, Family and Nation in Argentina*. Lincoln: University of Nebraska Press.

Hall, Edward T. 1974. "Proxemics." In S. Weitz, ed., *Non-verbal Communication*. New York: Oxford University Press, pp. 205–230.

Hall, Stuart. 1980. "Introduction." In S. Hall, ed., *Culture, Media, Language: Working Papers in Cultural Studies, 1972–1979*. Centre for Contemporary Cultural Studies, University of Birmingham. London: Hutchinson.

_____. 1981. "Notes on deconstructing 'the popular.' " In R. Samuel, ed., *People's History and Socialist Theory*. London: Routledge and Kegan Paul, pp. 227–240.

Hanna, Judith L. 1983. *The Performer-Audience Connection: Emotion to Metaphor in Dance and Society*. Austin: University of Texas Press.

_____. 1988. *Dance, Sex and Gender: Signs of Identity, Dominance, Defiance, and Desire*. Chicago: University of Chicago Press.

Hannerz, Ulf. 1989. "Culture between center and periphery: toward a macroanthropology." *Ethnos* 54(3/4): 200–216.

Harrison, Randall. 1986. "Body language and nonverbal communication." In B. Fleshman, ed., *Theatrical Movement: A Bibliographical Anthology*. Metuchen, N.J.: The Scarecrow Press, pp. 79–89.

Hartsock, Nancy. 1990. "Foucault on power: a theory for women?" In L. Nicholson, ed., *Feminism/ Postmodernism*. New York: Routledge, pp. 157–175.

Hastings, Baird. 1978. "The Denishawn era (1914–1931)." In P. Magriel, ed., *Chronicles of the American Dance*. New York: Da Capo Press, pp. 225–238.

Hegel, Georg W.F. 1953. *Vorleβungen über die Aesthetik I*. In H. Glökner, ed., Hegel Sämtliche Werke, Volume 12. Stuttgart: Fr. Fromanns Verlag.

Heller, Agnes. 1979. *A Theory of Feelings*. Assen, The Netherlands: Van Gorcum.

Henley, Nancy M. 1977. *Body Politics: Power, Sex and Non-Verbal Communication*. Englewood Cliffs, N.J.: Prentice Hall.

Henríquez, Fernando. 1974. *Children of Caliban: Miscegenation*. London: Secker and Warburg.

Hernández, José. 1992. *Martín Fierro*. Buenos Aires: Editorial Altemira. (First published as Volume 1, 1872, and Volume 2, 1879.)

Hernández Arregui, J. J. 1988. *Qué Es el Ser Nacional?* Buenos Aires: Editorial Nueva América.

Hicks, D. Emily. 1991. *Border Writing: The Multidimensional Text*. Minneapolis: University of Minnesota Press.

Hinkelammert, Franz J. 1990. "La libertad académica bajo control en América Latina." *Nueva Sociedad* 107: 131–137.

Hodges, Donald C., comp. 1977. *The Legacy of Che Guevara: A Documentary Study*. Translated by Ernest C. Rehder and Donald C. Hodges. London: Thames and Hudson.

hooks, bell. 1989. *Feminist Theory: From Margin to Center.* Boston: South End Press.

hooks, bell, and Cornel West. 1991. *Breaking Bread: Insurgent Black Intellectual Life*. Boston: South End Press.

Humbert, Béatrice. 1988. *Le tango a Paris de 1905 a 1920*. Mémoire présenté et soutenu pour la Maitrisse de Musicologie. Universite de Saint Denis, Paris VIII.

Hutchinson Guest, Ann. 1970. *Labanotation or Kinetography Laban: The System of Analyzing and Recording Movement*. New York: Theatre Arts Books.

La Ilustración Argentina. 1882. Volume 33 (November 30): 395.

Ipola, Emilio de. 1989. "El tango en sus márgenes." In *Investigaciones Políticas*. Buenos Aires: Ediciones Nueva Vision, pp. 149–156.

Irani, K. D., and G. E. Myers, eds. 1983. *Emotion: Philosophical Studies*. New York: Haven Publications.

Irigaray, Luce. 1985. *This Sex Which Is Not One*. Translated by Catherine Porter with Carolyn Burke. Ithaca: Cornell University Press.

Ivy, Marilyn. 1988a. "Critical texts, mass artifacts: the consumption of knowledge in postmodern Japan." *South Atlantic Quarterly* 87(3): 419–444.

———. 1988b. "Tradition and difference in the Japanese mass media." *Public Culture* 1(1): 21–28.

Izutsu Toshihiko and Izutsu Toyo. 1981. *The Theory of Beauty in the Classical Aesthetics of Japan*. The Hague: Martinus Nijhoff Publishers.

Jakubs, Deborah L. 1984. "From bawdyhouse to cabaret: the evolution of the tango as an expression of Argentine popular culture." *Journal of Popular Culture* 18(1): 133–145.

Jameson, Frederic. 1984. "Postmodernism, or the cultural logic of late capitalism." *New Left Review* 146: 53–92.

Jitrik, Noé. 1969. *Los Viajeros*. Buenos Aires: Editorial Jorge Alvarez S.A.

Justo, Liborio. 1989. *Nuestra Patria Vasalla: Historia del Coloniaje Argentino: Tomo 4, Grandeza y Colapso de la República Argentina como "Dominio" del Imperialismo Británico en la América del Sur (1890–1930)*. Buenos Aires: Editorial Grito Sagrado.

Kagan, Elizabeth. 1978. "Towards the analysis of a score." In *Essays in Dance Research from the Fifth CORD Conference, Philadelphia, Nov. 11–14, 1976*. New York: CORD, pp. 75–94.

Kamenszain, Tamara. 1990. "Personas del tango." In *Dossier: Tango, el Himno Pasional Argentino, Babel* 3(21): 23.

Kaneko Kaoru. 1990. *Shakō Dansu*. Tokyo: Nihon Bungeisha.

Kaplan, E. Ann. 1983. "Is the gaze male?" In A. Snitow, C. Stansell, and S. Thompson, eds., *Powers of Desire: The Politics of Sexuality*. New York: Monthly Review Press, pp. 309–327.

Keali'inohomoku, Joann. 1979. "You dance what you wear, and you wear your cultural values." In J. M. Cordwell and R. A. Schwarz, eds., *The Fabrics of Culture. The Anthropology of Clothing and Adornment*. The Hague: Mouton Publishers, pp. 77–83.

––––––. 1983. "An anthropologist looks at ballet as a form of ethnic dance." In R. Copeland and M. Cohen, eds., *What Is Dance? Readings in Theory and Criticism*. New York: Oxford University Press, pp. 533–550.

Kehl, Maria Rita. 1987. "A Psicoanálise eo domínio das paixões." In *Os Sentidos de Paixão*. São Paulo: Funarte, Editora Schwarcz, pp. 469–496.

Kida Hisashi. 1987. *Tango!* Tokyo: Mainichi Shimbunsha.

Kipling Brown, Ann. 1984. "Labanotation." In *Dance Notation for Beginners*. London: Dance Books Ltd., pp. 533–550.

Klein, Jean-Claude. 1985. "Borrowing, syncretism, hybridization: the Parisian revue of the 1920s." Translated by J. B. Jones. In R. Middleton and D. Horn, eds., *Popular Music: Volume 5, Continuity and Change*. New York: Cambridge University Press, pp. 175–187.

Kleist, Heinrich von. 1989. "On the marionette theatre." In M. Feher, ed., *Fragments for a History of the Human Body: Volume 1*. New York: Zone, pp. 415–430.

Kobayashi Taihei. 1990. Interview. Tokyo, November.

Kondo, Dorinne. 1992. "The aesthetics and politics of Japanese identity in the fashion industry." In Joseph J. Tobin, ed., *Re-made in Japan: Everyday Life and Consumer Taste in a Changing Society*. New Haven: Yale University Press, pp. 176–203.

Kristeva, Julia. 1982. *Powers of Horror: An Essay on Abjection*. Translated by Leon S. Roudiez. New York: Columbia University Press.

––––––. 1984. *Revolution in Poetic Language*. Translated by Margaret Waller. New York: Columbia University Press.

Kyotani Kohji. 1990. Interview. Tokyo, November.

Laban, Rudolf von. 1974. *The Language of Movement. A Guidebook to Choreutics*. Annotated and edited by Lisa Ullmann. Boston: Plays Inc.

LaBarre, Weston. 1947. "The cultural basis of emotions and gestures." *Journal of Personality* 16: 12–19.

Labraña, Luis, and Ana Sebastián. 1988. *Tango: Introducción a la Historia del Tango*. Buenos Aires: Libros de Tierra Firme.

Lacan, Jacques. 1977a. "The subversion of the subject and the dialectic of desire in the Freudian unconscious." In *Ecrits: A Selection*. Translated by A. Sheridan. New York: W. W. Norton, pp. 292–325.

––––––. 1977b. "The mirror stage as formative of the function of the I as revealed in psychoanalytic experience." In *Ecrits: A Selection*. Translated by A. Sheridan. New York: W. W. Norton, pp. 1–17.

––––––. 1981. *The Four Fundamental Concepts of Psycho-Analysis*. Edited by J. A. Miller and translated by A. Sheridan. New York: W. W. Norton.

––––––. 1982. "A love letter." In J. Mitchell and J. Rose, eds., *Feminine Sexuality: Jacques Lacan and the Ecole Freudienne*. Translated by J. Rose. New York: W. W. Norton, pp. 149–161.

Laclau, Ernesto, and Chantal Mouffe. 1989. *Hegemony and Socialist Strategy: Towards a Radical Democratic Politics*. London: Verso.

Lamming, George. 1984. *The Pleasures of Exile*. London: Allison and Busby.

Lara, Tómas de, and Inés L. Roncetti de Panti. 1969. *El Tema del Tango en la Literatura Argentina*. Buenos Aires: Ediciones Culturales Argentinas, Ministerio de Educación y Justicia, Dirección General de Cultura. (First published in 1931.)

Larrain, Jorge. 1989. *Theories of Development: Capitalism, Colonialism and Dependency*. Cambridge, England: Polity Press.

Larsen, Neil. 1990. *Modernism and Hegemony: A Materialist Critique of Aesthetic Agencies.* Minneapolis: University of Minnesota Press.

Lascano, Luis C. 1974. *Homero Manzi. Poesía y Política.* Buenos Aires: Editorial Nativa.

Laver, James. 1966. *Manners and Morals in the Age of Optimism (1848–1914).* New York: Harper and Row.

Lebrun, Gerard. 1987. "O conceito de paixão." In *Os Sentidos da Paixão.* São Paulo: Funarte, Editora Schwarcz, pp. 17–34.

Leclercq, Gerard. 1972. *Antropología y Colonialismo.* Medellín: Editorial THE

Lemert, Charles C., ed. 1991. *Intellectuals and Politics: Social Theory in a Changing World.* Newbury Park, Calif.: Sage.

Leppert, Richard. 1988. *Music and Image: Domesticity, Ideology and Socio-Cultural Formation in Eighteenth-Century England.* New York: Cambridge University Press.

Leppert, Richard, and Susan McClary, eds. 1987. *Music and Society: The Politics of Composition, Performance and Reception.* New York: Cambridge University Press.

Lewis, George H. 1987. "Patterns of meaning and choice: taste cultures in popular music." In J. Lull, ed., *Popular Music and Communication.* Newbury Park, Calif.: Sage, pp. 198–211.

Lima, Nicanor. [1916?] *El Tango Argentino de Salón: Método de Baile Teórico y Práctico.* Buenos Aires.

Limón, José. 1983. "Texas-Mexican popular music and dancing: some notes on history and symbolic process." *Revista de Música Latinoamericana* 4(2): 229–246.

Lipschütz, Alejandro. 1963. *El Problema Racial en la Conquista de América y el Mestizaje.* Santiago: Austral.

Londres, Albert. 1928. *The Road to Buenos Ayres.* London: Constable & Co.

Lorde, Audre. 1984. *Sister Outsider: Essays and Speeches.* Trumansburg, N.Y.: The Crossing Press.

Lugones, Leopoldo. 1961. *El Payador.* Buenos Aires: Centurión. (First published in 1916.)

———. 1968. "Las Orillas hacia 1870." In J. L. Borges and S. Bullrich Palenque, eds., *El Compadrito.* Buenos Aires: Compañia General Fabril Editora, pp. 96–57. (First published in 1911.)

Luhmann, Niklas. 1985. *El Amor Como Pasión: La Codificación de la Intimidad.* Translated by Joaquin Adsuar Ortega. Barcelona: Ediciones Península.

Lull, James, ed. 1987. *Popular Music and Communication.* Newbury Park, Calif.: Sage.

Lyotard, Jean-François. 1988. *The Postmodern Condition: A Report on Knowledge.* Translated by Geoff Bennington and Brian Massumi. Minneapolis: University of Minnesota Press.

———. 1990. *Economía Libidinal.* Buenos Aires: Fondo de Cultura Económica.

Mafud, Julio. 1966. *Sociología del Tango.* Buenos Aires: América Lee.

Malinowski, Branislaw. 1945. *The Dynamics of Cultural Change.* New Haven: Yale University Press.

Malnig, Julie. 1992. *Dancing Till Dawn. A Century of Exhibition Ballroom Dancing.* New York: Greenwood Press.

Mannoni, Dominique O. 1956. *Prospero and Caliban: The Psychology of Colonization.* Translated by Pamela Powesland. London: Methuen.

Mantega, Guido. 1979. "Sexo e poder nas sociedades autoritarias: a façe erotica da dominação." In G. Mantega, ed., *Sexo e Poder.* São Paulo: Editora Brasiliense, pp. 9–34.

Marcus, George, comp. 1990. "Some quotes as queries pertaining to Bourdieu's own scholastic point of view." *Cultural Anthropology* 5(4): 392–395.

Margolis, Joseph. 1983. "Art as language." In R. Copeland and M. Cohen, eds., *What Is Dance? Readings in Theory and Criticism.* New York: Oxford University Press, pp. 376–390.

Mariátegui, José C. 1992. "The Latin American socialist revolution." In M. Lowy, ed., *Marxism in Latin America from 1909 to the Present*. New Jersey: Humanities Press, pp. 37–39. (First published in 1929.)

Martin, Biddy. 1988. "Feminism, criticism, and Foucault." In I. Diamond and L. Quinby, eds., *Feminism and Foucault: Reflections on Resistance*. Boston: Northeastern University Press, pp. 3–19.

Martínez Estrada, Ezequiel. 1968a. "El Tango." In J. L. Borges and S. Bullrich Palenque, eds., *El Compadrito*. Buenos Aires: Compañía General Fabril Editora, pp. 127–131. (First published in 1933.)

––––––. 1968b. *Radiografía de la Pampa*. Buenos Aires: Losada. (First published in 1933.)

Martini Real, J. C. 1980. "Sobre una poética de la vida cotidiana." In *La Historia del Tango: Volume 17, Los Poetas (1)*. Buenos Aires: Corregidor, pp. 3109–3120.

Mascia-Lees, Frances E., Patricia Sharpe, and Colleen Ballerino Cohen. 1989. "The postmodernist turn in anthropology: cautions from a feminist perspective." *Signs* 15(1): 7–33.

Matamoro, Blas. 1969. *La Ciudad del Tango (Tango Histórico y Sociedad)*. Buenos Aires: Galerna.

––––––. 1971. *Historia del Tango: Volume 16, La Historia Popular*. Buenos Aires: Centro Editor de América Latina.

––––––. 1973. "Piazzola, la vanguardia y después." *Crisis* 7: 21–22.

––––––. 1976. "Orígenes musicales." In *La Historia del Tango: Volume 1, Sus Orígenes*. Buenos Aires: Corregidor, pp. 55–98.

Mazziotti, Nora. 1989. "Las voces de la emoción." *Crisis* 70: 28–29.

McClary, Susan. 1987. "The blasphemy of talking politics during Bach Year." In R. Leppert and S. McClary, eds., *Music and Society: The Politics of Composition, Performance and Reception*. New York: Cambridge University Press, pp. 13–62.

McClary, Susan, and Robert Walser. 1990. "Start making sense! Musicology wrestles with rock." In S. Frith and A. Goodwin, eds., *On Record: Rock, Pop and the Written Word*. New York: Pantheon Books, pp. 277–292.

McDonagh, Don. 1979. *Dance Fever*. New York: Random House.

Meltzer, Françoise. 1987. *Salome and the Dance of Writing*. Chicago: University of Chicago Press.

Miller, Christopher. 1985. *Blank Darkness: Africanist Discourse in French*. Chicago: University of Chicago Press.

Mistinguett. 1954. *Mistinguett: Queen of the Paris Night*. Translated by Lucienne Hill. London: Elek Books.

Mitsuhiro, Yoshimoto. 1989. "The postmodern and mass images in Japan." *Public Culture* 1(2): 8–25.

Mohanty, Chandra. 1991a. "Introduction. Cartographies of struggle: Third World women and the politics of feminism." In C. Mohanty, A. Russo, and L. Torres, eds., *Third World Women and the Politics of Feminism*. Bloomington: Indiana University Press, pp. 1–47.

––––––. 1991b. "Under western eyes: feminist scholarship and colonial discourses." In C. Mohanty, A. Russo, and L. Torres, eds., *Third World Women and the Politics of Feminism*. Bloomington: Indiana University Press, pp. 51–80.

Molloy, Sylvia. 1992. "Too wilde for comfort: desire and ideology in fin-de-siècle Spanish America." *Social Text* 31/32: 187–201.

Montergous, Gabriel. 1985. *La Generación del 80 y el Proceso Militar*. Buenos Aires: Centro Editor de América Latina.

Montorgueil, Georges. 1898. *Paris Dansant*. Paris: Theophile Belin.

Monzón, Ana S. 1988. "El machismo: mito de la supremacía masculina." *Nueva Sociedad* 93: 148–155.

Moraga, Cherríe. 1983. *Loving in the War Years: Lo Que Nunca Pasó Por Sus Labios.* Boston: South End Press.

Moraga, Cherríe, and Gloria Anzaldúa, eds. 1983. *This Bridge Called My Back: Writings by Radical Women of Color.* New York: Kitchen Table: Women of Color Press.

Morini, Clare de. 1978. "Loie Fuller, the fairy of light." In P. Magriel, ed., *Chronicles of the American Dance: From the Shakers to Martha Graham.* New York: Da Capo Press, pp. 203–220.

Mosse, George L. 1985. *Nationalism and Sexuality: Middle-Class Morality and Sexual Norms in Modern Europe.* Madison: University of Wisconsin Press.

Mulvey, Laura. 1988a. "Visual pleasure and narrative cinema." In C. Penly, ed., *Feminism and Film Theory.* New York: Routledge, Chapman and Hall, pp. 57–68.

———. 1988b. "Afterthoughts on 'Visual Pleasure and Narrative Cinema' inspired by 'Duel in the Sun.'" In C. Penly, ed., *Feminism and Film Theory.* New York: Routledge, Chapman and Hall, pp. 69–79.

Munck, Ronaldo, with Ricardo Falcón and Bernardo Galitelli. 1987. *Argentina from Anarchism to Peronism. Workers: Unions and Politics, 1855–1985.* London: Zed Books.

Myers, Martha. 1986. "Body systems." In B. Fleshman, ed. *Theatrical Movement: A Bibliographical Anthology.* Metuchen, N.J.: The Scarecrow Press, pp. 100–115.

La Nación. 1889. October 30.

Natale, Oscar. 1984. *Buenos Aires, Negros y Tango.* Buenos Aires: Peña Lillo.

Ngũgĩ, wa Thiong'o. 1986. *Decolonising the Mind: The Politics of Language in African Literature.* London: James Currey.

Nichols, Bill. 1981. *Ideology and the Image: Social Representation in the Cinema and Other Media.* Bloomington: Indiana University Press.

Nietzsche, Friedrich. 1968. *The Will to Power.* Translated by W. Kaufmann and R. J. Hollingdale. New York: Vintage Books.

———. 1974. *The Gay Science.* Translated by W. Kaufmann. New York: Vintage Books.

———. 1983. *Untimely Meditations.* Translated by R. J. Hollingdale. New York: Cambridge University Press.

Nishimura Hideto. 1990. Interview. Tokyo, November.

Nohain, Franc. 1913. "Tangomanie." *Fémina 300* (July 15): 375–378.

Novati, Jorge, and Inés Cuello. 1980. "Aspectos histórico-musicales." In *Antología del Tango Rioplatense: Volume 1, Desde sus comienzos hasta 1920.* Buenos Aires: Instituto Nacional de Musicología "Carlos Vega."

Oberthur, Mariel. 1984. *Cafés and Cabarets of Montmartre.* Salt Lake City: Peregrine Smith.

Ogata San. 1990. Interview. Tokyo, November.

Oiwa Yoshihiro and Chizuko. 1990. Interview. Tokyo, November.

Oliven, Ruben George. 1988. "The woman makes (and breaks) the man: the masculine imagery in Brazilian popular music." *Revista de Música Latinoamericana* 9(1): 90–108.

Ordaz, Luis. 1977. "El tango en el teatro nacional." In *La Historia del Tango: Volume 8, El Tango en el Espectáculo.* Buenos Aires: Corregidor, pp. 1213–1289.

Ostrander, Greg. 1987. "Foucault's disappearing body." In A. and M. Kroker, eds., *Body Invaders.* New York: St. Martin's Press, pp. 169–182.

Otterbach, Friedmann. 1980. *Die Geschichte der Europäischen Tanzmusik.* Wihelmshaven: Heinrichshofen's Verlag.

Owens, Craig. 1983. "The discourse of others: feminists and postmodernism." In H. Foster, ed., *The Anti-Aesthetic: Essays on Postmodern Culture.* Port Townsend, Wash.: Bay Press, pp. 57–82.

Pacini Hernández, Deborah. 1990. "Cantando la cama vacía: love, sexuality and gender relationships in Dominican bachata." *Popular Music* 9(3): 351–367.

Panesi, Jorge. 1990. "La garúa de la ausencia." *Dossier: Tango, el Himno Pasional Argentino, Babel* 3(21): 22–23.

Paquot, Marcel. 1933. *Les Etrangers dans les Divertissements de la Cour de Beaujoyeulx a Molière (1581–1673).* Bruxelles: La Renaissance du Livre.

Parcero, Daniel, Marcelo Helfgot, and Diego Dulce. 1985. *La Argentina Exiliada.* Buenos Aires: Centro Editor de América Latina.

Pareles, Jon. 1989. "The embrace of tango." *Elle* 4(10): 68–74.

Pasi, Mario. 1987. "Excelsior." In M. Pasi, ed., *El Ballet, Enciclopedia del Arte Coreográfico.* Madrid: Aguilar, pp. 137–139.

Paso, Leonardo. 1985. *Raíces Históricas de la Dependencia Argentina: Tomos 1/2.* Buenos Aires: Centro Editor de América Latina.

Pelinski, Ramón. 1989. "Estudios recientes sobre el tango." *Revista de Música Latino Americana* 10(2): 306–312.

Pelleteri, Osvaldo, ed. 1987. *Radiografía de Carlos Gardel.* Buenos Aires: Editorial Abril.

Pereyra, Nicandro. 1992. *Del Cachafaz al Tango.* Buenos Aires: Albino y Asociados.

Pérez Martín, Norma. 1976. "El tango: aproximación a un análisis de la porteñidad." In *Mitos Populares y Personajes Literarios: Trabajos Presentados a la VIII Reunión del Centro de Estudios Latinoamericanos.* Buenos Aires: Ediciones Castañeda, pp. 57–82.

Perniola, Mario. 1989. "Between clothing and nudity." In M. Feher, ed., *Fragments for a History of the Human Body: Part Two.* New York: Zone, pp. 236–265.

Perrot, Michelle, ed. 1990. *A History of Private Life: Volume 4, From the Fires of Revolution to the Great War.* Cambridge: Belknap Press.

Petras, James. 1990a. "The metamorphosis of Latin America's intellectuals." *Latin American Perspectives* 17(2): 102–112.

———. 1990b. "Los intelectuales en retirada." *Nueva Sociedad* 107: 92–120.

Pintos, Victor. 1990. "Algo pasa con el tango: ¿moda o resurgimiento?" *Humor* 270: 42–44.

Priore, Oscar del. 1975. *El Tango de Villoldo a Piazzolla.* Buenos Aires: Crisis.

Puccia, Enrique. 1990. *Intimidades de Buenos Aires.* Buenos Aires: Corregidor.

Puertas Cruse, Roberto. 1959. *Psicopatología del Tango.* Buenos Aires: Editorial Sophos.

Pujol, Sergio. 1989. *Las Canciones del Inmigrante. Buenos Aires: Espectáculo Musical y Proceso Inmigratorio. De 1914 a Nuestros Días.* Buenos Aires: Editorial Almagesto.

Quijano, Aníbal. 1990. "Estética de la utopía." *David y Goliath* 19(57): 34–37.

Rearick, Charles. 1985. *Pleasures of the Belle Epoque: Entertainment and Festivity in Turn-of-the-Century France.* New Haven: Yale University Press.

Revel, Jean-Francois. 1982. *Culture and Cuisine: A Journey Through the History of Food.* Translated by Helen R. Lane. Garden City, N.Y.: Doubleday.

Rhys, Hedley H. 1971. "Afterword on Japanese art and influence." In G. J. Becker and E. Philips, eds. and trans., *Paris and the Arts, 1851–1896: From the Goncourt Journal.* Ithaca: Cornell University Press.

Richards, Alfred, Jr. 1992. *The Hispanic Image on the Silver Screen: An Interpretive Filmography from Silents into Sound, 1898–1935.* New York: Greenwood Press.

Ritter, Naomi. 1989. *Art as Spectacle. Images of the Entertainer Since Romanticism.* Columbia: University of Missouri Press.

Rivarola, Carlos. 1993. Interviews and tango instruction. Buenos Aires, June–July.

Rivarola, María, and Carlos Rivarola. 1987. *Así se baila el Tango.* Tokyo.

Rivera, Jorge B. 1973. "10 perfiles de Discépolo en 4x4." *Crisis* 7: 10–13.

———. 1976. "Historias paralelas." In *La Historia del Tango: Volume 1, Sus Orígenes.* Buenos Aires: Corregidor, pp. 13–53.

Rivera, Max. N.d. *Le Tango et les Danses Nouvelles.* Paris: P. Lafitte.

Rizzo, Jorge, ed. N.d. *Album del Tango: Cancionero Coleccionable*, Volumes 2, 3, 4, 5, 6, 8. Buenos Aires.

Roberts, John Storm. 1979. *The Latin Tinge: The Impact of Latin American Music on the United States.* New York: Oxford University Press.

Rodríguez Molas, Ricardo. 1988. "Vida cotidiana de la oligarquía argentina (1880–1890)." In *Conflictos y Procesos de La Historia Argentina Contemporánea,* Volume 2. Buenos Aires: Centro Editor de América Latina.

Romano, Eduardo. 1973. "Celedonio Flores y la poesía popular." *Crisis* 7: 6–9.

———. 1983. *Sobre Poesía Popular Argentina.* Buenos Aires: Centro Editor de América Latina.

———. 1990. *Las Letras del Tango: Antología Cronológica, 1900–1980.* Rosario: Editorial Fundación Ross.

Romero, José Luis. 1946. *Las Ideas Políticas en la Argentina.* México D.F.: Fondo de Cultura Económica.

———. 1989. *La Experiencia Argentina y Otros Ensayos.* Buenos Aires: Fondo de Cultura Económica.

Rorty, Amelie Oksenberg, ed. 1980. *Explaining Emotions.* Berkeley: University of California Press.

Ross, Andrew, ed. 1989. *Universal Abandon? The Politics of Postmodernism.* Minneapolis: University of Minnesota Press.

Rossi, Vicente. 1958. *Cosas de Negros: Estudio Preliminar y Notas de Horacio J. Becco.* Buenos Aires: Hachette. (First published in 1926.)

———. 1968. "La academia." In J. L. Borges and S. Bullrich Palenque, eds., *El Compadrito.* Buenos Aires: Compañía General Fabril Editora, pp. 1109–1121. (First published in 1926.)

Rossler, Osvaldo. 1967. *Buenos Aires Dos Por Cuatro.* Buenos Aires: Losada.

———. 1974. *Protagonistas del Tango.* Buenos Aires: Emecé Editores.

Rouanet, Sergio. 1987. "Razão e paixão." In *Os Sentidos de Paixão.* São Paulo: Funarte, Editora Schwarcz, pp. 437–467.

Rousseau, George S., and Roy Porter, eds. 1990. *Exoticism in the Enlightenment.* Manchester, England: Manchester University Press.

Sábato, Ernesto. 1963. *Tango: Discusión y Clave.* Tercera edición. Buenos Aires: Editorial Losada.

———. 1964. *Tango, Canción de Buenos Aires.* Buenos Aires: Ediciones Centro Arte.

Sábato, Jorge F. 1988. *La Clase Dominante en la Argentina Moderna. Formación y Características.* Buenos Aires: CISEA/Grupo Editor Latinoamericano.

Sábato, Jorge F., and Jorge Schvarzer. 1988. "Funcionamiento de la economía y poder político en la Argentina: trabas para la democracia." In J. Sabato, *La Clase Dominante en la Argentina Moderna. Formación y Características.* Buenos Aires: CISEA/Grupo Editor Latinoamericano, pp. 243–280.

Sachs, Curt. 1963. *World History of the Dance.* Translated by B. Schonberg. New York: W. W. Norton.

Said, Edward. 1979. *Orientalism.* New York: Vintage Books.

———. 1983. *The World, the Text, and the Critic.* Cambridge: Harvard University Press.

———. 1986. "Intellectuals in the postcolonial world." *Salmagundi* 70/71: 44–64.

———. 1989. "Representing the colonized: anthropology's interlocutors." *Critical Inquiry* 15: 205–225.

Sakai Naoki. 1988. "Modernity and its critique: the problem of universalism and particularism." *South Atlantic Quarterly* 87(3): 475–504.

Salas, Horacio. 1986. *El Tango.* Buenos Aires: Planeta.

Sangren, P. Steven. 1988. "Rhetoric and the authority of ethnography: 'postmodernism' and the social reproduction of texts." *Current Anthropology* 29(3): 405–424.

Santos, Estela dos. 1978. *La Historia del Tango: Volume 13, Las Cantantes.* Buenos Aires: Corregidor.

Sarlo, Beatriz. 1985. *El Imperio de los Sentimientos: Narraciones de Circulación Periódica en la Argentina (1917–1927)*. Buenos Aires: Catálogos Editora.

———. 1989. "Intellectuals: escision or mimesis?" In D. Foster, ed., *The Redemocratization of Argentine Culture, 1983 and Beyond*. Tempe, Ariz.: Arizona State University Press, pp. 49–59.

Sarmiento, Domingo F. 1946. *Conflicto y Armonía de las Razas en América*. Buenos Aires: Editorial Intermundo. (First published in 1883.)

———. 1990. *Facundo. Civilización y Barbarie*. Edited by Roberto Yahni. Madrid: Cátedra. (First published in 1845.)

Sartre, Jean-Paul. 1966. *Being and Nothingness: A Phenomenological Essay on Ontology*. Translated by Hazel E. Barnes. New York: Washington Square Press.

Savigliano, Marta E. 1992. "Tango in Japan and the world economy of passion." In Joseph J. Tobin, ed., *Re-made in Japan: Everyday Life and Consumer Taste in a Changing Society*. New Haven: Yale University Press, pp. 235–252.

Scenna, Miguel A. 1974a. "Historia del bandoneón. Parte 1." *Todo es Historia* 8(87): 8–37.

———. 1974b. "Historia del bandoneón. Parte 2." *Todo es Historia* 8(88): 68–96.

Schechner, Richard N. 1977. *Performance Theory*. New York: Routledge.

Scobie, James R. 1977. *Buenos Aires, del Centro a los Barrios*. Buenos Aires: Solar-Hachette.

Seidensticker, Edward. 1983. *Low City, High City: Tokyo from Edo to the Earthquake*. New York: Alfred A. Knopf.

———. 1990. *Tokyo Rising: The City Since the Great Earthquake*. New York: Alfred A. Knopf.

Selles, Roberto. 1980. "Antes y después de Contursi." In *La Historia del Tango: Volume 17, Los Poetas (1)*. Buenos Aires: Corregidor.

Sem. 1913. "Tangoville." *L'Illustration*, August 16, pp. 282–283.

———. 1925. "Les Possédés." In *La Rue de Nuit*. Paris: A Fayard.

Seminario Científico International (Buenos Aires, 8–11 junio, 1988). 1989. *El Pensamiento Revolucionario del Comandante "Che" Guevara: Intervenciones y Debates*. Buenos Aires: Ediciones Dialéctica.

Shepherd, John. 1987. "Music and male hegemony." In R. Leppert and S. McClary, eds., *Music and Society: The Politics of Composition, Performance and Reception*. New York: Cambridge University Press, pp. 151–172.

Sherman, Jane. 1979. *The Drama of Denishawn Dance*. Middletown, Conn.: Wesleyan University Press.

Shinoda Manabu. 1989. *Dansu Insutorakushion*. Tokyo: Kabushiki Gaisha.

Shively, Donald H., ed. 1971. *Tradition and Modernization in Japanese Culture*. Princeton: Princeton University Press.

Shohat, Ella. 1992. "Notes on the 'post-colonial.'" *Social Text* 31/32: 99–113.

Siegel, Jerrold. 1986. *Bohemian Paris: Culture, Politics and the Boundaries of Bourgeois Life, 1830–1930*. New York: Viking.

Silingo, María del Carmen. 1991. *Tango-Danza Tradicional: Método. Curso de 1er. Nivel*. Buenos Aires: Plus Ultra.

———. 1992. *Tango-Danza Tradicional: Método. Curso de 2o. Nivel*. Buenos Aires: Plus Ultra.

Silverman, Kaja. 1986. "Fragments of a fashionable discourse." In T. Modleski, ed., *Studies in Entertainment: Critical Approaches to Mass Culture*. Bloomington: Indiana University Press, pp. 139–152.

———. 1989. "Fassbinder and Lacan: a reconsideration of gaze, look, and image." *Camera Obscura* 19: 54–84.

Simpson, David. 1989. "Going on about the war without mentioning the war: the other histories of the Paul de Man Affair." *Yale Journal of Criticism* 3(1): 163–173.

Smith, Paul Julian. 1989. *The Body Hispanic: Gender and Sexuality in Spanish and Spanish American Literature.* Oxford: Clarendon Press.

Sobrino, Constantino. 1971. *Manual, Guía, Enciclopedia, Crónica y Diccionario del Tango.* Buenos Aires: Las Llaves.

Solomon-Godeau, Abigail. 1986. "The legs of the countess." *October* 39: 65–108.

Sommer, Doris. 1990. "Irresistible romance: the foundational fictions of Latin America." In H. Bhabha, ed., *Nation and Narration.* London: Routledge, pp. 71–98.

Sorell, Walter. 1981. *Dance in Its Time.* Garden City, N.Y.: Anchor Press.

Spencer, Paul, ed. 1985. *Society and the Dance: The Social Anthropology of Process and Performance.* New York: Cambridge University Press.

Spivak, Gayatri Chakravorty. 1985. "Three women's texts and a critique of imperialism." *Critical Inquiry* 12(1): 243–261.

————. 1988a. "Can the subaltern speak?" In C. Nelson and L. Grossberg, eds., *Marxism and the Interpretation of Culture.* Urbana: University of Illinois Press, pp. 271–313.

————. 1988b. *In Other Worlds. Essays in Cultural Politics.* New York: Routledge.

————. 1989. "Who claims alterity?" In B. Kruger and P. Mariani, eds., *Remaking History.* Seattle: Bay Press, pp. 269–292.

————. 1990a. *The Post-Colonial Critic. Interviews, Strategies, Dialogues.* Edited by S. Harasym. New York and London: Routledge.

————. 1990b. "Gayatri Spivak on the politics of the subaltern." Interview by Howard Winant. *Socialist Review* 20(3): 81–97.

Stasio, Marilyn. 1989. "The last step: when the tango turns deadly." *New York Times,* October 15, section 2, pp. 5, 25.

Steele, Valerie. 1985. *Fashion and Eroticism. Ideals of Feminine Beauty from the Victorian Era to the Jazz Age.* New York: Oxford University Press.

————. 1989. "Clothing and sexuality." In C. Kidwell and V. Steele, eds., *Men and Women: Dressing the Part.* Washington, D.C.: Smithsonian Institution, pp. 42–63.

Stephanson, Anders. 1988. "Interview with Cornell West." In A. Ross, ed., *Universal Abandon? The Politics of Postmodernism.* Minneapolis: University of Minnesota Press, pp. 269–286.

Suarez Salazar, Luis, et al. 1989. *Pensar al Che: Desafíos de la Lucha por el Poder Político.* La Habana, Cuba: Centrado Estudios Sobre América.

Sugi San. 1990. Interview. Tokyo, November.

Suriano, Juan. 1988. "Trabajadores, anarquismo y estado represor: de la ley de residencia a la ley de defensa social (1902–1910)." *Conflictos y procesos de la Historia Argentina Contemporánea,* Volume 9. Buenos Aires: Centro Editor de América Latina.

Sypher, Wylie. 1980. "Romeo and Juliet are dead: melodrama of the clinical." In D. Gerould, ed., *Melodrama.* New York: New York Literary Forum, pp. 179–186.

Tagg, John. 1988. *The Burden of Representation: Essays on Photographies and Histories.* Amherst: University of Massachusetts Press.

Takahashi Masayoshi and Teruko. 1990. Interview. Tokyo, November.

Takashima Masako. 1990. Interview. Tokyo, November.

Tallón, José S. 1964. *El Tango en sus Etapas de Música Prohibida.* Buenos Aires: Instituto Amigos del Libro Argentino. (First published in 1959.)

Tango: Un Siglo de Historia (1880–1980): Tomo 1, Bautismo y Personalidad. N.d. Buenos Aires.

Tango: Un Siglo de Historia (1880–1980): Tomo 2, Crecimiento y Auge. N.d. Buenos Aires.

Tango: Un Siglo de Historia (1880–1980): Tomo 3, Consolidación y Ruptura. N.d. Buenos Aires.

Tango: Un Siglo de Historia (1880–1980): Tomo 4, Los Hombres que Hicieron Historia. N.d. Buenos Aires.

"Tangos de ayer, de hoy y de siempre: cariñoso homenaje al que fuera el rey del bandoneon; don Aníbal Troilo." 1987. *Cancionero Popular* (October).

"Tangos de ayer, hoy y siempre: homenaje a Agustín Magaldi." 1966. *Cancionero Popular* (July).

"Tangos inmortales: cariñoso homenaje a don Enrique Santos Discépolo." 1982. *Cancionero Popular* (August).

"Tangos inmortales: hermosa selección de tangos de ayer y de siempre." 1960. *Cancionero Popular* (July).

"Tangos inmortales: tangos del recuerdo al involvidable Homero Manzi." 1983. *Cancionero Popular* (August).

Taussig, Michael. 1986. *Shamanism, Colonialism and the Wild Man: A Study in Terror and Healing.* Chicago: University of Chicago Press.

Taylor, Julie M. 1976. "Tango: theme of class and nation." *Ethnomusicology* 20(2): 273–291.

———. 1992. "Tango." In G. Marcus, ed., *Rereading Cultural Anthropology.* Durham: Duke University Press, pp. 377–389.

Taylor, Mark C. 1987. *Altarity.* Chicago: University of Chicago Press.

Theunissen, Michael. 1984. *The Other: Studies in the Social Ontology of Husserl, Heidegger, Sartre, and Buber.* Translated by Christopher Macann. Cambridge: The MIT Press.

Tinker, Irene. 1990. "The making of a field: advocates, practitioners, scholars." In I. Tinker, ed., *Persistent Inequalities: Women and World Development.* New York and Oxford: Oxford University Press, pp. 27–53.

Tobin, Jeffrey P. 1992. "A Japanese-French restaurant in Hawai'i." In Joseph J. Tobin, ed., *Re-made in Japan: Everyday Life and Consumer Taste in a Changing Society.* New Haven: Yale University Press, pp. 159–175.

Tobin, Joseph J. 1992. "Introduction." In Joseph J. Tobin, ed., *Re-made in Japan. Everyday Life and Consumer Taste in a Changing Society.* New Haven: Yale University Press, pp. 1–41.

Trías, Eugenio. 1991. *Tratado de la Pasión.* México D.F.: Editorial Grijalbo.

Trimillos, Ricardo. 1986. "Aesthetic change in Philippine performing arts in cross-cultural contexts." In *Come Mek Me Hol'Yu Han': The Impact of Tourism on Traditional Music.* Jamaica: Memory Bank, pp. 95–119.

Trinh T. Minh-ha. 1989a. *Woman, Native, Other: Writing Postcoloniality and Feminism.* Bloomington: Indiana University Press.

———. 1989b. "Outside in inside out." In J. Pines and P. Willeman, eds., *Questions on Third Cinema.* London: British Film Institute, pp. 133–149.

Tulchin, Joseph S. 1990. *Argentina and the United States: A Conflicted Relationship.* Boston: Twayne Publishers.

Turner, Victor. 1988. *The Anthropology of Performance.* New York: PAJ publications.

Ulla, Noemí. 1973. "Las letras de tango: nuestra historia transhumante." *Crisis* 7: 3–5.

———. 1982. *Tango, Rebelión y Nostalgia.* Buenos Aires: Centro Editor de América Latina.

Vargas Llosa, Mario. 1990. "Questions of conquest." *Harper's* (December): 45–53.

Vega, Carlos. 1936. *Danzas y Canciones Argentinas. Teorías e Investigaciones. Un Ensayo Sobre el Tango.* Buenos Aires: Ricordi.

Vigarello, Georges. 1989. "The upward training of the body from the age of chivalry to courtly civility." In M. Feher, ed., *Fragments for a History of the Human Body: Part Two.* New York: Zone, pp. 148–199.

Vila, Pablo. 1986. "Peronismo y folklore: un requiem para el tango?" *Punto de Vista* 9(25): 45–48.

———. 1989. "Argentina's 'rock nacional': the struggle for meaning." *Revista de Música Latinoamericana* 10(1): 1–28.

Vilas, Carlos M. 1990. "Sobre cierta interPetrasción de la intelectualidad latinoamericana." *Nueva Sociedad* 107: 121–130.

Villarino, Idea. 1965. *Las Letras de Tango: La Forma, Temas y Motivos*. Buenos Aires: Shapire.

Wakabayashi, Bob Tadashi. 1986. *Anti-Foreignism and Western Learning in Early-Modern Japan*. Cambridge: Harvard University Press.

Wakahayashi Masao. 1983. *Modanu Dansu Kyotei*. Tokyo: Kodansha Press.

Wallerstein, Immanuel. 1989. *The Capitalist World-Economy*. New York: Cambridge University Press.

Wallis, Roger, and Krister Malm. 1984. *Big Sounds from Small Peoples: The Music Industry in Small Countries*. New York: Pendragon Press.

Weiss, Allen S. 1989. *The Aesthetics of Excess*. Albany: State University of New York Press.

Williams, Drid. 1986. "(Non)anthropologists, the dance and human movement." In B. Fleshman, ed., *Theatrical Movement: A Bibliographical Anthology*. Metuchen, N.J.: The Scarecrow Press, pp. 158–221.

Williams, Linda. 1981. "Film body: an implantation of perversion." *Ciné-Tracts* 12: 19–35.

Williams, Raymond. 1989. *The Politics of Modernism: Against the New Conformists*. Edited and translated by Tony Pinkney. London: Verso.

Williams, Simon. 1985. "Theater and degeneration: subversion and sexuality." In J. E. Chamberlin and S. L. Gilman, eds., *Degeneration: The Dark Side of Progress*. New York: Columbia University Press, pp. 241–262.

Williamson, Judith. 1986. "Woman is an island: femininity and colonization." In T. Modleski, ed., *Studies in Entertainment: Critical Approaches to Mass Culture*. Bloomington: Indiana University Press, pp. 100–118.

Wilson, Michael. 1991. "'Sans les femme, qu'est-ce qui nous resterait:' gender and transgression in Bohemian Paris." In J. Epstein and K. Straub, eds., *Body Guards: The Cultural Politics of Gender Ambiguity*. New York: Routledge, pp. 195–222.

Wolff, Janet. 1987. "Foreword: the ideology of autonomous art." In R. Leppert and S. McClary, *Music and Society: The Politics of Composition, Performance and Reception*. New York: Cambridge University Press, pp. 1–12.

Yamazaki Mieko. 1990. Interview. Tokyo, November.

Yoneyama Eiko. 1990. Interview. Tokyo, November.

Young, Robert. 1990. *White Mythologies: Writing History and the West*. London: Routledge.

Yúdice, George. 1988. "Marginality and the ethics of survival." In A. Ross, ed., *Universal Abandon? The Politics of Postmodernism*. Minneapolis: University of Minnesota Press, pp. 214–236.

———. 1992a. "We are not the world." *Social Text* 31/32: 202–216.

———. 1992b. "Postmodernity and transnational capitalism in Latin America." In G. Yúdice, J. Franco, and J. Flores, eds., *On Edge: The Crisis of Contemporary Latin American Culture*. Minneapolis: University of Minnesota Press, pp. 1–28.

Yunesuku Aigachi et al. 1964. *Acceptance of Western Cultures in Japan: From the Sixteenth to the Mid-Nineteenth Century: An International Research on the Historical Background of the East Asian Countries*. Translated by John Blewett. Tokyo: The Centre for East Asian Cultural Studies.

About the Book and Author

What is tango? Dance, music, and lyrics of course, but also a philosophy, a strategy, a commodity, even a disease. This book explores the politics of tango, tracing tango's travels from the brothels of Buenos Aires to the cabarets of Paris and the *shakō dansu* clubs of Tokyo. The author is an Argentinean political theorist and a dance professor at the University of California–Riverside. She uses her "tango tongue" to tell interwoven tales of sexuality, gender, race, class, and national identity. Along the way she unravels relations between machismo and colonialism, postmodernism and patriarchy, exoticism and commodification. In the end she arrives at a discourse on decolonization as intellectual "unlearning."

Marta Savigliano's voice is highly personal and political. Her account is at once about the exoticization of tango and about her own fate as a Third World woman intellectual. A few sentences from the preface are indicative: "Tango is my womb and my tongue, a trench where I can shelter and resist the colonial invitations to 'universalism,' ... a stubborn fatalist mood when technocrats and theorists offer optimistic and seriously revised versions of 'alternatives' for the Third World, an opportunistic metaphor to talk about myself and my stories as a 'success' of the civilization-development-colonization of América Latina, and a strategy to figure out through the history of the tango a hooked-up story of people like myself. Tango is my changing, resourceful source of identity. And because I am where I am—outside—tango hurts and comforts me: 'Tango is a sad thought that can be danced. ...' "

Savigliano employs the tools of ethnography, history, body-movement analysis, and political economy. Well illustrated with drawings and photos dating back to the 1880s, this book is highly readable, entertaining, and provocative. It is sure to be recognized as an important contribution in the fields of cultural studies, performance studies, decolonization, Latin American studies, and women-of-color feminism.

Marta E. Savigliano is assistant professor of dance history and theory at the University of California–Riverside.

Index

Abo Ikuo, 176(figure), 188–189

Academias, 40, 42, 146

Acosta, Leonardo, 89

Affects, 1, 85. *See also* Emotion/emotional/ "emotions"; Passion

Aín, Casimiro and Martina, 120, 251(n30)

Alberdi, Juan Bautista, 23–24, 164

Alposta, Luis, 189–190, 202–203

Alterity, 10, 25, 213, 230. *See also* Desire; Other/otherness/Otra(s); Passion

Amadori, Luis C., 64

Ambiguous gender, 53

Anticolonial, 6, 21, 233. *See also* Intellectual(s), anticolonialist

Apache, 110, 112(figure)

Appiah, Kwame Anthony, 231

Argentina, 22
- Amerindian population, 36–37
- British-dependent development, 23
- culturalism, 27
- development, 28, 244(n10). *See also Civilización y Progreso*
- and global capitalism, 47
- history, 27
- independence, 19, 21, 24
- neocolonial identity, 166. *See also* Identity; Tango, national identity
- racial politics, 36. *See also* Racial and class tension
- syndrome of colonialism, 28
- urbanization and industrialization, 31, 58

Argentinean bourgeoisie/elite(s), 23, 25–27, 29, 68, 75, 114, 140–142, 146. *See also* Beef barons

Argentine-ness, 3, 6, 47, 123, 140, 143. *See also* Tango, national identity

Arquimbau, Gloria and Eduardo, 192, 198(figure), 255(n6)

Artaud, Antonin, 212

Assunção, Fernando, 111, 114, 164, 251(n31), 252(n9)

Audience, 4–6. *See also* Tango, audience

"Authentic"/authenticity, 6, 92, 96, 140. *See also* Tango, "authentic"

Autoexoticism, 2, 5–6, 9, 75, 82, 119, 153, 179. *See also* Exotic; Exoticism/ exoticization

Ayestarán, Lauro, 36

Ballet/ballerina, 84–85, 90–92, 96, 219, 248(n3)

Bataille, Georges, 214

Bates, Héctor and Luis, 134, 143, 147, 149, 159, 170–171, 252(n9), 255(n13)

Baudrillard, Jean, 70, 179, 213–214

Beef barons, xiv, 29, 109, 165. *See also* Argentinean bourgeoisie/elite(s)

Belasco, David, 177

Belle époque, 102, 109, 190, 192, 251(n31). *See also* Fin de siècle; Mal de siècle

Belly-dancing, 95–96, 102–103, 106, 116, 205

Body/bodies, 3–4, 43, 78, 90, 128, 191, 194–196, 198–199, 209, 214, 218, 227, 229, 232
- black, 33, 40
- dancing, 96, 149
- female docile, 167, 209, 218, 227, 255(n9)
- female/women's/feminine, 44, 50, 61, 91, 96, 98, 103, 109, 114, 134, 164, 167, 208–209, 218, 226–227, 237–239, 248(n6), 249(n15), 250(n23)
- libidinal, 214
- men's and women's, 32. *See also* Tango, couple
- moving, 5, 98, 191

Printed in the United States
26677LVS00003B/121-129

9 780813 316383